THE PENTAGON AND THE MAKING OF US FOREIGN POLICY

The Pentagon and the Making of US Foreign Policy

A Case Study of Vietnam, 1960-1968

Jaya Krishna Baral

HUMANITIES PRESS
ATLANTIC HIGHLANDS, N.J.

First Published 1978 in the United States of America by
Humanities Press
Atlantic Highlands
N.J. 07716

Printed in India

Library of Congress Cataloging in Publication Data

Baral, Jaya Krishna.
    The Pentagon and the Making of U.S. foreign policy.

    Bibliography: p.
    1. United States—Foreign relations—Vietnam.
    2. Vietnam—Foreign relations—United States.
    3. Civil supremacy over the military—United States.
    4. Vietnamese Conflict, 1961-1975. 5. United States.
    Department of Defence. 6. McNamara, Robert S., 1916-
    I. Title
E183.8.V5B29   1977   327.73'0597   77-13333
ISBN 0-391-00549-9

CONTENTS

PREFACE

The present book proposes to study the role of the Department of Defence—both its civilian and military elements—in policy-making in regard to Vietnam. The role of the Defence Department in defence and foreign policy-making drew increased attention of the American public and scholars after President Eisenhower pointed out, in his farewell address, the dangers emanating from the "military-industrial complex." An effort will be made here to examine the validity of the two conflicting hypotheses: (1) that the military, as the most important component of the "power elite," controls foreign policy-making, and (2) that the military is just an instrument of the civilian elites for ensuring the reflection of their interests in foreign policy. The significance of the period covered in this study stems from the fact that the civilian who headed the Department of Defence was Robert McNamara, a dominant and highly capable individual with an innovative approach whose tenure in office was sometimes characterized as the era of the "McNamara revolution."

To start with, a conceptual scheme of American foreign policy-making will be attempted, to be followed by a discussion of the various hypotheses regarding the role of the military in decision-making on defence and foreign policy. In Chapter I, American involvement in Vietnam from the end of the Second World War to 1960 will be described. In Chapter II, the equation between the civilian and military elements of the Pentagon in policy-making with reference to Vietnam from 1961 to mid-1965 will be discussed. In Chapter III, the interaction between the civilian and military elements of the Defence Department in policy-making on Vietnam from mid-1965 to February 1968 will be dealt with. Because of the importance of the escalation point—mid-1965—in the context of the conflict between the civilian and military components of the Pentagon, mid-1965 will be taken as the dividing line in the history of the interaction between the civilian and military components of the Pentagon on Vietnam. In Chapter IV, the competition of the Pentagon with other federal actors to influence policy-making on Vietnam will be studied. In Chapter V, the interaction between the Defence Department and Congress in regard to Vietnam policy-making will be dealt with. Some concluding observations will be made in the end.

After examining certain alternate models on foreign policy-making, an attempt will be made to suggest a theoretical framework for the purpose of studying the present problem.

The materials for the present study were collected from both primary and secondary sources. Besides the *Pentagon Papers* published by the House Armed Services Committee, its other versions—one, edited by Sen. Mike Gravel and the other published by the *New York Times*—were primarily used. Government documents like *Congressional Record*, *Congressional Hearings* and Committee Reports were made use of. Moreover, memoirs, books and articles by knowledgeable persons having some experience in policy-making in regard to Vietnam were of great help. Interviews and discussions with scholars and ex-government officials in the United States made by the author were of considerable help.

The author is greatly thankful to Prof M. S. Venkataramani, Chairman of the Centre of American Studies, School of International Studies, Jawaharlal Nehru University, New Delhi from whose courses the writer initially developed his interest in the making of US foreign policy. Professor Venkataramani kindly made available to the author for consultation materials from his own research concerning some of the issues dealt with in the present study. The author is deeply grateful to him for his guidance at every stage of the present work. He is grateful to Dr B.K. Shrivastava, Associate Professor of American Studies, and Dr R. Narayanan, Associate Professor and Head of the Division of Latin American Studies, SIS, JNU for their kind help and assistance given from time to time. He owes his gratitude to Mohammed Ayoob, Associate Professor, South Asia, SIS, JNU, Manoranjan Mohanty, Associate Professor, Chinese Studies, University of Delhi, and Mrs. Veena Majumdar, Chief Editor, Indian Council for Social Science Research, for their keen interest in his research.

The author remembers with pleasure the valuable assistance he received from his teachers in the School of International Affairs, Columbia University, New York during the academic session 1973-74, especially Roger Hilsman whose course on the "Politics of Defense and Foreign Policy-Making" was of much help in building the theoretical framework for the present study. The author is grateful to Professors W. T. R. Fox, Warner Schilling, Harold Lasswell, James Young, and Stanley Hegginbotham for their valuable suggestions and guidance. Thanks are due to A. Embree, the Associate Dean of the SIA, Columbia University, who was his friend, philosopher and guide.

The author is thankful to his friends L. N. Mishra, Basant Kumar Behera, Devee Chakravarti, Sivananda Pattanaik, P. S. Ghose, Adil Yasin, Christopher Samraj, Girijesh Pant, T. P. Bhatt, Indira Kaul, Sanjukta Banerjee and others for their help. He is obliged to the members of the Department of Political Science, Berhampur University, Berhampur, Orissa for their kind co-operation during his study leave. He is thankful to the authorities of the Berhampur University for having sanctioned him study leave for doing research on the present topic. He expresses his obligation to the University Grants Commission, New Delhi for having awarded a scholarship and to the United States Educational Foundation in India for having awarded a Fulbright scholarship which enabled the scholar to study for two semesters in the SIA, Columbia University, New York and collect research materials from various libraries there.

Finally, the author expresses his gratitude to the members of the staff of the Sapru House Library, New Delhi, JNU Library, New Delhi, the Library of Congress, Washington, D.C., and the Butler Library, Columbia University, New York, for their kind co-operation.

25 November 1977
Berhampur, Orissa

Jaya Krishna Baral

CHAPTER ONE

INTRODUCTION

A CONCEPTUAL SCHEME OF AMERICAN FOREIGN POLICY-MAKING

An examination of the role of the Department of Defence in policy-making relating to Vietnam necessitates at the outset the formulation of an analytical approach to serve as a frame of reference for the subsequent discussion. The present study is concerned with a situation in which US foreign policy in respect of Vietnam was part of national security policy. Policy-making in such a context is a very complex process. In the United States the issue has attracted many eminent scholars of international politics; some of them had direct experience of decision-making on foreign and national security policy. The present writer has had no direct acquaintance with the policy-making process and is conscious of the limitations in his equipment and experience in undertaking the exercise.

For a long time one of the predominant assumptions in writings on international politics had been that the state was the actor in international politics. In recent years some foreign policy analysts have come forth with new approaches. They maintain that more than the state, the internal variables like the decision-making organization and the governmental players play an important role in foreign policy-making. While the former approach almost completely ignores the internal dynamics, the latter approaches, to a considerable extent, minimize the role of the state in influencing the formulation of foreign policy. The three main models of decision-making on foreign policy may first be briefly discussed before outlining the proposed framework.[1]

---

[1] This classification is primarily inspired by Kenneth N. Waltz's "three images" in *Man, the State and War* (New York, 1959); Graham T. Allison, *Essence of Decision: Explaining the Cuban Missile Crisis*

1. *Rational Actor Model or "Black Box" Model*

The traditional approach to the study of international relation is described by some commentators as Rational Actor Model, or the "Black Box Model." Some others call it systemic level of analysis. This model is exemplified by the works of scholars like Hans Morgenthau, Arnold Wolfers, Thomas Schelling, and Herman Kahn, and in some writings and speeches of Henry Kissinger.

Morgenthau holds, "The First World War had its origins exclusively in the fear of a disturbance of the European balance of power."[2] He explains the behaviour of actors by using a "rational outline."[3] This method, Morgenthau says, "provides for rational discipline in action and creates that astounding continuity in foreign policy which makes American, British, or Russian foreign policy appear as an intelligible, rational continuum regardless of the different motives, preferences, and intellectual and moral qualities of successive statesmen."[4] Kissinger's *Nuclear Weapons and Foreign Policy*, and Kahn's *On Escalation* are two other applications of the Rational Actor Model.[5] Wolfers, in his essay "The Actors in International Politics," while taking note of the two new approaches— "minds of men theory" and the decision-making approach— reverts back to the traditional approach—"states-as-the-sole-actors" approach to international politics. He asserts that the "state-as-the-sole-actor" model would best predict the behaviour of states.[6]

What are the basic ingredients of this model? Who are the units? What is "rationality" about this model? These are some

(Boston, Mass., 1971); and J.D. Singer, "The Level of Analysis Problem in International Relations," *World Politics* (Princeton), vol. 14, no. 1, October 1961, pp. 80-1.

[2] Hans J. Morgenthau, *Politics Among Nations* (New York, 1970), p. 185.

[3] Ibid., p. 5.

[4] Ibid., p. 6.

[5] Henry Kissinger, *Nuclear Weapons and Foreign Policy* (New York, 1957); and Herman Kahn, *On Escalation* (NewYork, 1965).

[6] Arnold Wolfers, "Three Actors in International Politics," in W.T.R. Fox, ed., *Theoretical Aspects of International Relations* (Notre Dame, 1959), p. 98.

of the questions which call for further examination.

This model assumes that the nation-state is the basic unit. (It would, however, be unfair to state that the writers mentioned above treat the state just as an abstract entity and are oblivious of the fact that decisions are actually made by human beings. It would be reasonable to argue that they reckon with the fact that human actors are decision-makers, but they do not attach much significance to the various internal dynamics as influencing the decision-making process.) The state is a sub-system within an international system.[7] There is continuous interaction between the sub-systems, and "balance of power" is the mechanism by which the equilibrium of the system is maintained. As Spykman puts it, "Equilibrium is balanced power, and balanced power is neutralized power."[8] Thus, each action of a state is in response to some action from outside.

This approach does not take notice of the domestic structure of a state. It is not concerned with any internal variance within a state. In other words, it assumes that whatever happens inside the "box" will not affect the behaviour of the actor. This model, therefore, is also known as the "Black Box" Model. To quote McClelland, ". . .The international system is an expanding version of the notion of two-actors-in-interaction . . . . Interaction analysis focuses on the outputs of national systems. The national systems, themselves, are black-boxed."[9]

Thus, the Rational Actor Model assumes the state as the basic unit. The state is conceived to be a rational, unitary decision-maker. It has certain broad goals like national security and national interest. For realizing its objectives, various courses of action which will produce a series of consequences

---

[7] Morton Kaplan, *System and Process in International Politics* (New York, 1967); Charles A. McClelland, *Theory and the International System* (New York, 1966); and Herbert J. Spiro, "An Evaluation of Systems Theory," in James C. Charlesworth, ed., *Contemporary Political Analysis* (New York, 1967), pp. 164-74.

[8] N.J. Spykman, *America's Strategy in World Politics: The United States and Balance of Power* (New York, 1942), pp. 15-26.

The "balance of power" concept may relevantly be compared with "homeostasis" theory in biological sciences and Galbraith's concept of "countervailing power" in economics.

[9] McClelland, n. 7, p. 20.

are considered. The state makes a rational choice which is value-maximizing. So it has to select the alternative whose conse-quence ranks highest in term of realizing the main goal.

2. *Organizational Process Model*

This model is based on the assumption that happenings are the outcome of organizational processes. The way information moves inside an organization and the way it reaches a decision-maker will have some bearing on his decisions. Another assumption of this model is that the rules and habits that grow up within an organization will affect the way the decisions are made within that organization.[10]

Organization means the system of activities and the struc-ture of relationships. The activities and relationships will primarily be the outputs of formal rules governing the alloca-tion of power and responsibility, and the flow of information in the organization. An actor tends to take a decision on the basis of his "definition of the situation," which, in its turn, would be influenced by the nature and amount of information that would reach him.[11] Hence decisions on foreign policy need to be studied in their organizational contexts.

The placement of an issue under the jurisdiction of an actor or a unit is of major significance. This may happen in two ways, namely, automatic assignment and negotiation.[12] Some issues, because of their non-controversial nature, may be con-veniently assigned to the concerned decisional units. But there are some other issues which are of importance for more than one unit. This is especially true of foreign policy matters with implications for national and international security which are neither the exclusive domain of the State Department nor

---

[10] The discussion here on "Organization Model" is mainly drawn from Richard C. Snyder, *et al*, "Decision-making as an Approach to the Study of International Politics," in Snyder *et al*, eds., *Foreign Policy Decision-Making: An Approach to the Study of International Politics* (Glencoe, 1962), pp. 104-37; and Allison, n. 1, pp. 67-100.

[11] Harold and Margaret Sprout, "Environmental Factors in the Study of International Politics," in James N. Rosenau, ed., *International Politics and Foreign Policy* (New York, 1969), pp. 41-56.

[12] Snyder, n. 10, p. 98.

that of the Defence Department. Often other Departments too try to get into the act. It is thus not unusual that several decisional units quarrel amongst themselves regarding the jurisdiction of a foreign policy issue. Even within a unit, the subunits may squabble over the jurisdiction of an issue. In such cases the concerned units or subunits may negotiate with one another and reach some compromise. Snyder and others say:

> ...A quite different method of selection is *negotiation* in cases where no routine procedures exist or where new conditions require a special procedure. Some of the great struggles within the total foreign policy-making structure are over *who will decide*. Negotiation may be simply a matter of "springing loose" the right officials for a particular task, or it may represent basic disagreement over the location of authority and power.[13]

Each organization functions under certain rules. Some rules are statutorily prescribed and others are habitually and traditionally respected. The former are explicit and the latter, implicit. However, both the former and the latter, by and large, tend to evoke the same degree of compliance.

These rules provide, more or less, a fixed pattern. Information moves back and forth according to this pattern. In this sense, the organization is a "communication network" with a relatively fixed pattern of communication flow. This results in considerably limiting the range of choice of actors. In other words, their "rationality" is "bounded."[14] To use game jargon, the location of pieces on the chess-board is fixed and they have to be moved according to certain set rules. Thus, the choice of players is considerably limited in deciding their moves.

It is argued that an organization with more of explicit rules may not well adapt itself to crisis situations because of impediments put by these formalized and nagging procedures.

---

[13] Ibid., p. 99; Emphasis in original.
[14] Herbert Simon, *Models of Man: Social and Rational* (New York, 1957), pp. 196-206.

This difficulty may perhaps be modified by prudent and selective "short-circuits." A more centralized and authoritarian organizational structure finds it possible to attempt "short circuits" with greater ease than a less centralized and authoritarian entity; but the relative advantage may not extend beyond a short-term time span.

The decisional unit or the actor gets back constant messages about the effect of the decision it or he takes. The actor would be knowing about the extent of success or failure of the decision taken in realizing the intended goal. Accordingly he would modify his subsequent decisions. To use the vocabulary of the communication theory, the inputs are subjected to constant modification in accordance with the "feedbacks" received about the outputs—information regarding their performance in term of realizing the goal.[15]

The concept of "comprehensive rationality" as applied in the case of the "economic man" or "administrative man" states that individuals and organizations choose the best alternative, taking into account all the relevant information, and calculating the consequences of all possible alternatives of action, as helping the realization of the stated goal. But there are "practical limits to human rationality." Individual human beings are "limited in knowledge, foresight, skill, and time." Therefore, in general, the actor, instead of looking for the best move, stops, in his search, the moment he finds a "good enough" move. As Simon says, "the key to an effective solution appeared to lie in substituting the goal of satisficing, of finding a good enough move, for the goal of minimaxing, of finding the best move."[16] Thus *"satisficing"* not *maximizing*, is by and large, the criterion for selecting one of several alternatives while taking a decision.

Past experiences are stored in organizations and standard responses are made in routine situations. When crisis or some other situations develop where existing routine procedures prove to be inadequate or insufficient to deal with, a search

---

[15] Karl W. Deutsch, *The Nerves of Government: Models of Political Communication and Control* (New York, 1963), pp. 145-95; and Robert C. North, "The Analytical Prospects of Communications Theory," in Charlesworth, n. 7, pp. 300-16.

[16] Simon, n. 14, p. 205.

for new options starts. But such a search would primarily be moving in the borderland of the existing alternatives because of the ease of calculating their consequences. In other words, "search simply builds incrementally on standard operating procedures" depending upon past cases to provide alternatives that may satisfy organizational goals.[17] Allison observes:

> If a nation performs an action of a certain type today, its organizational components must yesterday have been performing [or have had established routines for performing] an action only marginally different from today's action. . . . The best explanation of an organization's behavior at t [at any specific point in time] is $t - 1$; the best prediction of what will happen at $t + 1$ is t. . . .[18]

Roberta Wohlstetter's study, *Pearl Harbor*, illustrates this point. The US Navy, in spite of having received clear signals that a Japanese attack on Pearl Harbor was imminent, did not behave on 7 December 1941 in a way which was much different from the way it had behaved on 6 December and other preceding days. This was due to the fact that the Navy's behaviour was a standard response based on established routines.[19]

Bureaucracy is criticized as prone to inaction and inertia, and hostile to innovations. President John F. Kennedy reportedly assailed the State Department as a "bowl of jelly."[20] Its failure to implement Kennedy's decision to close the missile bases in Turkey is a typical case in this regard. Several times, the President had ordered the State Department to talk to the Turkish Government to effect the withdrawal of the Jupiters from Turkey. But the State Department, after noticing Ankara's opposition to the proposal, dropped the idea. But it did not

---

[17] Raymond Tanter, "International System and Foreign Policy Approaches: Implications for Conflict Modelling and Management," in Raymond Tanter and Richard H. Ullman, eds., *Theory and Policy in International Relations* (Princeton, New Jersey, 1972), p. 18.

[18] Allison, n. 1, pp. 87-8.

[19] Roberta Wohlstetter, *Pearl Harbor: Warning and Decision* (Stanford, California, 1962).

[20] Arthur Schlesinger, Jr., *A Thousand Days: John F. Kennedy in the White House* (Boston, 1965), p. 406.

keep the President apprised of the latest development. Nor did it explore any other means of achieving the objective. It just slept over the matter.

The Organizational Process Model thus underscores the point that the location of an actor and the flow of information within an organization influence, to a great extent, the policy-making process. Moreover, it further points out that inertia and standard operating procedures are significant features of any decision-making unit or subunit. In contrast to the Rational Actor Model, this model directs attention on the importance of internal dynamics. But it stops half-way. It is a partial explanation in the sense that it emphasizes only a few internal forces and ignores others. This lacuna is filled up by the Governmental Politics Model which will be discussed next.

3. *Governmental Politics Model or Bureaucratic Politics Model*

The "Black Box" Model is criticized on the ground that it does not take into account what happens inside the box. Once the box is opened, we may find that the process (of decision-making on foreign policy) is a very complex one. The output is the resultant of many stresses and strains interacting inside the box.

The proponents of the Governmental Politics Model state that the body charged with the task of making foreign policy is not homogeneous in its composition and nature. It consists of several units and subunits which tend to perceive issues more from the point of view of their parochial interests than that of the national interest. Halperin and Kanter say:

> We believe that membership in the bureaucracy substantially determines the participants' perceptions and goals and directs their attention away from the international arena to intra-national, and especially inter-bureaucratic, concerns. ... The bureaucratic perspective ... implies: (1) that change in the international environment is only one of several stimuli to which participants in the foreign policy process are responding [it is possibly among the weakest and least important]; and (2) that events involving the actions of two or more nations can be best explained and predicted in terms

of the actions of two or more national bureaucracies whose actions affect the domestic interests and objectives of the other bureaucracies involved.[21]

As one of the determinants of foreign policy, "change in the international environment" is accorded the lowest place by Halperin. In other words, he underestimates the role of national interest, as perceived by a state in relation to another state in the formulation of foreign policy. On the other hand, he asserts that the equation between two or more national bureaucracies, that is, bureaucratic politics, would best explain the foreign policy of a country.

Richard E. Neustadt, one of the pioneers of the Bureaucratic Politics Model, says that the President of the United States is not as powerful in making foreign policy as he appears to be. He has to carry with him several agencies which may be fighting amongst themselves over a particular policy. The President and his advisers may often not see things from the same point of view. The President, of course, is constitutionally authorized to take a decision he likes in spite of the opposition of any department. But rarely does he do so. He often persuades his advisers to go with him. Neustadt says, "Presidential power is the power to persuade."[22] He again observes:

Underneath our images of Presidents-in-boots, astride decisions, are the half-observed realities of Presidents-in-sneakers, stirrups in hand, trying to induce particular department heads, or Congressmen or Senators, to climb aboard.[23]

According to Neustadt, the policy of a government is the result of the bargaining that goes on amongst the bureaucratic players and political personalities who collectively comprise its working apparatus.[24]

[21] Morton Halperin and Arnold Kanter, *Readings in American Foreign Policy: A Bureaucratic Perspective* (Boston, 1973), p. 3.

[22] Richard Neustadt, *Presidential Power* (New York, 1960), p. 10.

[23] Neustadt, "White House and White Hall," *The Public Interest* (New York), no. 2, Winter 1966, p. 64.

[24] Neustadt, Testimony, US Senate, Congress 88, session 1, Subcommittee on National Security and International Operations, Committee on

Hilsman, whose works approximate to the Bureaucratic Politics Model, and who, like Neustadt, had served as a US government official, says that the decision-making process of foreign policy involves a series of concentric circles.[25] The innermost or first circle, he says, is the President and the men in the different departments and agencies who must carry out the decision—staff men in the White House, the Secretaries of State and Defence who bear responsibility for whatever the particular problem may be. The middle or second circle includes other departments of the Executive Branch, and other layers within the agencies and departments already involved. The third or outermost circle involves Congress, the press, interest groups, and—inevitably—the "attentive public."[26]

In crisis situations, the decision-making is mostly confined to the innermost circle. But if the decision is somehow delayed, it is then likely to spill over to the next circle. If it prolongs very long and if the issues concerned are deemed vital and controversial, the concerned members of the middle circle manage to sneak into the scene, and the competitive groups in the first circle may seek their allies in the second and third circles. In other types of policy decisions, which Hilsman describes as "program policy" and "anticipatory policy," members of the outermost circle—especially Congress and press— play very useful roles."[27]

Policy-making is a slow, long process. It moves in a zig zag way. A decision is the outcome of a "series of incremental

Government Operations, Hearings, *Conduct of National Security Policy* (Washington, D.C., 1965), p. 126.

[25] Roger Hilsman, *To Move a Nation: The Politics of Foreign Policy in the Administration of John F. Kennedy* (New York, 1967), p. 542.

[26] "Attentive Public," according to Almond, is the segment of the public which is informed and interested in foreign policy problems, and which constitutes the audience for the foreign policy discussions among the elites.

Gabriel A. Almond, *The American People and Foreign Policy* (New York, 1950), p. 138.

[27] Roger Hilsman, "The Foreign-Policy Consensus: An Interim Research Report," in *Journal af Conflict Resolution* (Ann Arbor, Michigan), vol. 3, no. 4, December 1959, p. 376.

steps."[28] It is the resultant of interaction amongst multiple players. Karl W. Deutsch says:

> The making of foreign policy resembles a pinball machine game. Each interest group, each agency, each important official, legislator or national opinion leader, is in the position of a pin, while the emerging decision resembles endpoint of the path of a steel ball bouncing down the board from pin to pin. No one pin will determine the outcome. Only the distribution of all the relevant pins on the board—for some or many pins may be so far out on the periphery as to be negligible—will determine the distribution of outcomes. . . . To ask of a government of a large nation who "really" runs—presumably from behind the scenes—is usually as naive as asking which pin "really" determines the outcome of the pinball game.[29]

Players differ in defining goals, objectives and means. They organize themselves into groups or blocs with more or less similar viewpoints. Each group wants to prevail upon the other. But, in the context of American situation, total victory may not be possible. Each group will be ready to accommodate the views of others without yielding too much. It will try to reduce its sacrifice to the minimum. This leads to negotiation. That means, they bargain for best possible outcome. This is a "strain toward agreement "[30] What finally emerges is a compromise. Thus policy-making involves conflict, alliance-building, bargaining and cooperation. Hilsman aptly observes that policy-making is a process of "conflict and consensus build-

---

[28] See Charles E. Lindblom, "The Science of Muddling Through," in *Public Administration Review* (Washington, D.C.), vol. 19, 1959; Lindblom, *The Policy-Making Process* (Englewood Cliffs, N.J., 1968); and Lindblom and D. Braybrooke, A *Strategy of Decision: Policy Evaluation as a Social Process* (Glencoe, Illinois, 1963).

[29] Karl W. Deutsch, *The Analysis of International Relatians* (New Jersey, 1968), p. 78.

[30] Warner R. Schilling, "The Politics of National Defense: Fiscal 1950," in Schilling *et al, Strategy, Politics and Defense Budgets* (New York, 1962), p. 23.

ing."[31] Huntington is probably right in saying that whereas the "locus" of decision is "executive," the process of decision (even in the Executive) is primarily "legislative."[32]

Why is there conflict among players? Why do they differ in defining their goals and means? The "personality" of an actor and his "motives" get reflected in the decisions he takes. Here we are primarily concerned with a "sociological conception of personality." By that is meant, in the words of Snyder and others, "a social person whose 'personality' is shaped by his interactions with other actors and by his place in the system."[33] This does not mean that the "personality" that a decision-maker may have developed before he joins his present post is irrelevant as a factor influencing his role in decision-making. He is a "culture-bearer." Because of his peculiar rearing pattern and learning process, he has his own set of values. Each person comes to his position "with baggage in tow."[34] His bags include his likes and dislikes, his commitments and values, and his various group loyalties and obligations. To go back to somebody's past experiences in order to ascertain his cultural background is not an easy task. It is therefore advisable to first look into his "personality" which is a product of his position in the organization and his interaction with others in that organization.

Once an actor heads or works in a particular organization, he tends to develop a sense of responsibility towards that organization. He feels inclined to safeguard and defend the interests of his organization *vis-a-vis* other competitive organizations. His advancement may well depend on the success of his organization. He has to take into account the views and interests of his subordinates. Thus he is likely to be influenced by "organizational parochialism." As has been aptly remarked, "Where you stand depends on where you sit," and "the face of the issue

---

[31] Hilsman, n. 25, chapter one; and Roger Hilsman, *The Politics of Policy Making in Defence and Foreign Affairs* (New York, 1971), pp. 117-30.

[32] Samuel P. Huntington, "Strategic Programs and the Political Process," in Wesley W. Posvar, *et al*, *American Defense Policy* (Baltimore, Md., 1965), p. 150.

[33] Snyder, n. 10, p. 161.

[34] Allison, n. 1, p. 166.

differs from seat to seat."[35]

A decision-maker would also take into account the cross-currents of domestic politics. He has to keep in mind the direction in which the wind of public opinion blows. He would be keeping track of the results of various public opinion polls and the discussions in Congressional forums. His action is also likely to be affected by his deference to "shared images" dominant within the government.[36] He would be generally cautious in challenging the perception of dominant participants in the decision-making process. In the beginning phase of the Cuban missile crisis, Robert McNamara argued that "a missile is a missile," and that in the overall content of Soviet missile power the presence of Russian missiles in Cuba hardly made a difference to the security of the United States. But he quickly discovered that this argument went against the widely shared view prevailing amongst the senior players that the installation of Russian missiles in Cuba posed a vital threat to the security of the US. McNamara too changed his tone fairly quickly.[37] James C. Thomson who served both the Kennedy and Johnson Administrations and who was for some time an "insider" in relation to Vietnam, observes that several officials did not oppose the Vietnam policy because of their fear of challenging the widely shared image among dominant players of the "world responsibility" of the US for containing "international communism."[38]

The decision-maker may also have in mind his own interests, both "positional" and "progressive."[39] In other words, if he is already at the top, he will try to stay where he is; if he is at a lower level, he will like to rise higher. Moreover, each player may simultaneously have several obligations. At the same time

[35] Ibid., pp. 176, 178.

[36] Morton H. Halperin, *Bureaucratic Politics and Foreign Policy* (Washington, D.C., 1974), pp. 11, 150-7.

[37] Elie Abel, *The Missile Crisis* (Philadelphia, 1966), p. 51.

[38] James C. Thomson, Jr., "How Could Vietnam Happen?" in Robert Manning and Michael Janeway, eds., *Who We Are*: *Chronicle of the United States and Vietnam* (Boston, 1965), p. 207.

[39] Kenneth Prewitt, "Political Ambitions, Volunteerism, and Electoral Accountability," The *American Political Science Review* (Washington, D.C.), vol. 64, March 1970, pp. 5-17.

he has to serve many constituencies.[40] For example, the Secretary of State, first, is the senior personal adviser to the President on foreign policy and political military issues related to foreign policy. Secondly, he is the colleague of the President's other senior advisers, whose jurisdiction may touch on matters having a bearing on foreign policy. Thirdly, he is the ranking US diplomat in negotiations with foreign powers. Fourthly, he is the chief spokesman of the President on issues relating to foreign policy before Congressional bodies. Next, he is Mr. State Department or Mr. Foreign Office for the community. But he is not one at one time and another at another time. He may have to fulfil many of his obligations simultaneously. When he wears one particular hat, he does not throw out other hats. These obligations may conflict with one another. An actor, because of these "cross-loyalties" may be found in different blocs on separate issues. Thus the process of conflict and consensus-building is a dynamic one. Finally, an actor may develop a stake in the outcome of a particular decision. The more he thinks that his prestige is involved with any decision, the more probably will he resist accommodation. All such variables are likely to influence the attitude of a participant in policy-making.

All phases of policy-making may not necessarily involve conflicts. Players, in their own interests, may find it necessary at some point to reach some sort of consensus. But, at times, they fail to do so. In such cases, conflict occurs. How is a conflict resolved? What is the power a player uses? The power is bargaining power. This power has two facets. One is the skill of the player and the other is the skill of the opponent. The strength of his skill depends upon the quality of his opponent's skill.

Bargaining is an interaction dynamic. Each player, in deciding his move, takes into account the anticipated move of his opponent. Thus he has to predict the behaviour of his competitor. In other words, it is a game of "interdependent decision."[41] Such games are primarily of two types, namely, zero-sum game and non-zero-sum game. In zero-sum game there

---

[40] Neustadt, n. 22, p. 7.
[41] Thomas C. Schelling, *The Strategy of Conflict* (New York, 1963), pp. 15-6.

are only two players whose interests are exactly opposite. In this game one player exactly wins the amount the other player loses and *vice versa*. In other words, their payoffs always would add up to zero. A non-zero-sum game is played by two or more than two players and the gain by one is not necessarily the loss to others. All players may, at the same time, gain or lose. As has been aptly said, they may be "simultaneously advantaged or disadvantaged."[42] Thus in the former game, each player would be trying to score the "absolute score" or all the points, yielding not a single point to the opponent. In the latter game, each player would be aiming at the "maximum score." In other words, he would be prepared to concede a few points to his opponents. Non-zero-sum games are also known as the "mixed-motive" games.[43] Such games involve elements such as communication, promise, threat, and more or less explicit or tacit bargaining.[44]

But while treating decision-making as games, one has to bear in mind some important differences between them. Game theory assumes an actor as a black-box, ignoring psychological and behavioural attributes.[45] Both game theory and Governmental Politics Model assume rationality. But rationality in the former is "comprehensive" whereas in the latter it is "limited." Tanter says that in game theory, goals are ranked, alternative courses of action formulated, consequences thereof calculated, and rational choice consists of selecting the alternative with maximum benefits. But in the Governmental Politics Model, actors are constrained by the lack of explicit ranking of choices, insufficient information regarding alternatives and inadequate computational skills to calculate the consequences of each other.[46]

[42] Thomas Schelling, "Experimental Games and Bargaining Theory," in *World Politics* (Princeton), vol. 14, no. 1, October 1961, p. 56.

[43] Thomas Schelling, "The Strategy of Conflict: Prospects for a Reorientation of Game Theory," in *Journal of Conflict Resolution*, vol. 2, September 1958, pp. 203-64.

[44] Thomas Schelling, "Bargaining, Communication, and Limited War," ibid., vol. 1, March 1957, pp. 19-36.

[45] John C. Harsanyi, "Rational-Choice Models of Political Behavior vs. Functionalist and Conformist Theories," *World Politics*, vol. 21, July 1969, pp. 513-38.

[46] Tanter, n. 17, p. 10.

Bureaucratic players go for consensus for several reasons.[47] They fear that once an issue goes to the President because of the failure on their part to reach an agreement amongst themselves, they will, to a large degree, lose control over that issue. They suspect that it would help increase the influence of the White House staff in decision-making at the expense of departments and other federal agencies. Another motivation of the departments favóuring a consensus is their concern for having a quick decision. One is not sure of his capability to induce the President to take a decision on the lines prepared by one. Moreover, there is the fear of hurting one's reputation with the President. It is true that senior players weigh, not to a small extent, with the President. But such weight is limited in quantity and it has to be spent only selectively. A senior player has got the danger of going for a fight and losing it in which case his reputation with the President will be damaged.

There are mainly two ways of reaching a consensus. One is persuasion; the other is compromise.[48] An actor, without changing the proposal he favours, may persuade another actor to accept it in the latter's own interest. An actor may also bring in necessary changes in the proposal in order to make it acceptable to his competitor or competitors as the case may be. It may be pointed out that a compromise may be reached at the outset, thereby averting a conflict; a compromise may also be accepted after a spell of bureaucratic infighting. Here we are concerned with the first type of compromise. The decision to omit from NSC 68 in 1950 costs and details of the planned increases in the US military capability was made with a view to preventing an inter-service conflict and presenting a document which would be acceptable to all of them.[49]

Bureaucratic players enter into a conflict if they fail to reach a consensus amongst themselves. Each adversary then seeks to win the game and in this respect he will face opposition from others. He may choose one or more than one of several tactics usually used by players in such a situation. He may seek allies

---

[47] Halperin, n. 36. pp. 196-8.

[48] Ibid., pp. 208-9.

[49] Paul Y. Hammond, "NSC-68: Prologue to Rearmament," in Warner Schilling *et al.* eds., *Strategy, Politics and Defense Budgets* (New York, 1962), pp. 319-20.

inside the bureaucracy and/or outside it. He may join hands with some Congressional members who share his view. He may encourage defection from the opposing side. Alliance-building is an important feature of a bureaucratic game of policy-making.

An adversary would tend to broaden the circle of players by helping the entry of new ones who are known to share his view. He may also seek to reduce the circle by eliminating from it those who oppose him.[50] Sometimes an adversary may try to change rules to his advantage. For instance, after he ran into troubles with the Air Force and Navy over the question of TFX, Secretary McNamara changed a number of internal Defence Department decision-making procedures.[51]

One of the ploys used by bureaucratic players is not to try to take a bird at one shot. The tactic is to move step-by-step, or to move by inches. Asking at one time for all that you need might misfire; it may not go well with the final decision-maker. But if you ask for a part of it, it is more likely that he may accept it. And once he swallows the first instalment, it may be less easy for him to refuse the next when you request it. This is what the JCS did in February 1968. From the strategic point of view they thought that the US should send ground troops to Laos and Cambodia to "clear Communist sanctuaries." But instead of saying that, they pushed for sending more troops to South Vietnam which, they thought, could later be deployed to Laos and Cambodia.[52]

One of the tactics of winning acceptance of one's line is to avoid getting oneself directly in a fight among other actors. Secretary Rusk mostly avoided taking sides when issues were argued in the NSC and other forums by opposing protagonists. He preferred giving private advice to the President.[53] The efficacy of this tactic would depend upon the actor's personal

---

[50] Halperin. n. 36, pp. 124ff.

[51] Robert J. Art, *The TFX Decision: McNamara and the Military* (Boston, 1968), pp. 164-5.

[52] Marvin Kalb and Elie Abel, *Roots of Involvement: The US in Asia 1784-1971* (London, 1971), pp. 209-12; and Lyndon Bains Johnson, *Vantage Point: Perspectives of the Presidency, 1963-1969* (New York, 1971), pp. 388-415.

[53] Dean Rusk, "Mr. Secretary on the Eve of Emeritus," *Life* (Chicago), vol. 66, 17 January 1969, p. 62B.

equation with the President and the latter's style of administration. Rusk seemed to have been more influential in the
Johnson Administration than in the Kennedy Administration.

An Acheson or a Rusk may have direct access to the
President; he may have the privilege of meeting with him
alone. But the number of such privileged players is very few
in Washington. Most of the junior and subordinate players, in
their desire to be heard by the President, try hard to establish
some link in the White House and use that link for pushing
their views towards the Presidential desk.

One of the most potent instruments used in bureaucratic
games is to affect information.[54] An adversary may suppress
some facts or distort them if they go against him. He may
convey only a part of the story which goes in his favour and
suppress the other part which will contradict him. He may
manoeuvre reporting to the effect that the senior participants
see only his side of the story and its other side does not
reach them. The reporting from Vietnam was allegedly of this
type.[55] An adversary may request a study from those who will
support him. This may strengthen his stand *vis-a-vis* his opponents. Defence Secretary Clark Clifford's initiative in convening
a meeting of the "Wise Men" in 1968 to advise President
Johnson on Vietnam was apparently meant to bring home to
the latter the necessity of de-escalation.[56] Another ploy used in
Washington games is to "circumvent the channel" or to use
the "back channel." Hilsman says that at an NSC meeting it
was decided to seek some information on South Vietnam from
General Paul D. Harkins, then the US Commander in Vietnam.
The Pentagon immediately sent, in "back channel" a message
to General Harkins advising him on how he should answer
Washington's query.[57] If the manoeuvre is discovered, as
happened in that case, one's position may be weakened.

Leaking is a recurrent feature of the Washington politics.[58]
Leaks are made in a piecemeal fashion to influential newspapers

[54] Halperin, n. 36, pp. 159-72.
[55] John Mecklin, *Mission in Torment: An Intimate Account of the U.S. Role in Vietnam* (New York, 1965), pp. 213-5.
[56] Halperin, n. 36, p. 162.
[57] Hilsman, n. 25, pp. 492-3.
[58] Halperin, n. 36, pp. 174-95.

like the *New York Times* and the *Washington Post* in order to gradually orient the attitude of senior participants towards a particular issue. Since Washington players primarily depend upon these newspapers for information, this tactic works well. It is also used to draw the attention of the President to a particular issue. Junior players find it difficult to make their views reach the President. Their views get stuck up at some points of the "action channel." Either out of desparation and/ or because of their strong conviction in their cause, they may leak a story to the press. Sometimes a leak is made to alert the "attentive public" if an actor is not happy with some policy. Leaking is also meant to undermine rivals. A story may be passed to the press portraying one's opponent as advocating a policy which conflicts with the "shared images" or describing him as one who is not loyal to the President. Leaks may also be directed at exposing the weakness and incompetence of the opponent.

The American policy-making process includes both vertical and lateral units. Among the lateral units, the most conspicuous, apart from various departments, are the National Security Council, the Joint Chiefs of Staff and *ad hoc* inter-agency committees. The inter-agency-coordination bodies at lower levels are not very common. Thus, in so far as lateral units are concerned, a policy matter is likely to be put to more of conflict-bargain-consensus treatment in higher levels of the organization than the lower levels. Even in an hierarchical structure, the will of the superior does not necessarily prevail upon that of his subordinate. The authority of the higher official may be successfully counter-acted by the manipulative and persuasive skill of his subordinate.[59] Again, this formal relationship may be considerably modified by the personal equation between the Chief of the organization (here, the President) and the subordinate concerned. Roger Hilsman, who, at the beginning of the Kennedy Administration, was the Director of the Bureau of Intelligence and Research in the State Department, did not pull on well with Secretary Rusk. But, because of his personal equation with Kennedy, he could sometimes bypass the

[59] Huntington, n. 32, p. 150.

Secretary and go directly to the President.[60] Thus there is a strain in the vertical unit, in the lateral unit and the vertical-lateral axis. These strains may have significant impact on policy-making. Huntington has observed that bargaining proceeds along the intra-vertical, intra-horizontal axes and the diagonal axis cutting across both the vertical and horizontal axes.[61]

The Bureaucratic Politics Model (BPM) has been subjected to severe criticisms. It is criticized for over-estimating the roles of organizational procedures and bureaucratic interests in foreign policy-making. It is argued that organizations are the instruments meant for providing different types of advice to the ultimate decision-maker on any question. The essence of a decisional unit or a subunit lies in its ability to help the chief decision-maker in realizing the goal(s) of the organization, not in developing its own vested interest.[62]

The opponents of the BPM challenge the aphorism, "where you stand depends upon where you sit." They argue that decision-makers often do not stand where they sit. Sometimes they do not sit anywhere. In the Skybolt controversy, Defence Secretary McNamara was more concerned about the budgetary implications than the interest of the Air Force. During the Cuban Missile crisis, Robert Kennedy and Theodore Sorensen, two key members of the Executive Committee (Ex Com) were loyal to the President, not to any bureaucratic organization.[63]

The champions of the Bureaucratic Politics Model undermine their position when they concede that bureaucratic politics is not the sole determinant of foreign policy. One's cultural background and psychological motivations also influence his role, Allison admits. Allison does not assert that a decision-maker would be more influenced by his organizational interests than this "culture-bag." Not to assert so is to negate the pre-

---

[60] I.M. Destler, *Presidents, Bureaucrats, and Foreign Policy: The Politics of Organizational Reform* (Princeton, 1972), p. 113; and Halperin, n. 36, p. 111.

[61] Huntington, n. 59.

[62] Bertel Heurlin, "Notes on Bureaucratic Politics in National Security Policy," *Cooperation and Conflict* (Oslo), no. 4, 1975, p. 254.

[63] Stephen Q. Krasner, "Are Bureaucracies Important? (Or Allison's Wonderland)," in Richard G. Head and Ervin J. Rokke, eds., *American Defence Policy* (Baltimore, Md, 1963), p. 314.

eminence of bureaucratic politics in influencing policy-making.[64]

Critics point out that the BPM fails to realize the importance of the Presidential role in foreign policy-making. The President selects his advisers and determines who will have how much access to him. Krasner asserts that "these individuals must share his values." In order to continue as members of the team, they must play ball with him. Krasner concedes some role for bureaucratic interests. But that is possible only when Presidential interest and attention are absent. He says:

> Neither organizational necessity, nor bureaucratic interests are the fundamental determinants of policy. The limits imposed by standard operating procedures, as well as direction of policy, are a function of the values of decision-makers. The President creates much of the bureaucratic environment which surrounds him through his selection of bureau chiefs, determination of "action channels," and statutory powers.[65]

That the President will try his best to create a propitious bureaucratic environment and that he would not countenance any open or suspected show of disaffection are self-evident. But, perhaps, Krasner over-states the case when he holds that "these individuals must share his values." Some of them may say so and give the appearance that they do so. But the reality may not always correspond to the appearance.

After subjecting Halperin's treatment of the ABM case to a critical examination, Heurlin concludes that it was systemic interaction based on the consideration of national interest, not bureaucratic politics, which determined the outcome. He says that "the organizations are not and cannot conduct themselves as actors in the international system. They can only act in the role as representatives for the central leadership. . . ."[66]

It is important to note that these critics are not total in their rejection of the BPM. They concede that in some cases bureaucratic politics may play a significant role in influencing policy-making. In cases where a number or different interests are

[64] Halperin and Kanter, n. 21.
[65] Krasner, n. 63, p. 315.
[66] Heurlin, n. 62, p. 255.

involved and where many bureaucratic players have to take part in the decision-making, it is said that the bureaucratic game "can play a role, even a major role."[67] The critics further concede that at the time of implementation, organizational procedures and bureaucratic interests would have a big say.[68]

On the basis of the preceding discussion, we may make a few inferences and attempt a theoretical framework for purposes of the present study on the role of the Pentagon in policy-making with reference to Vietnam. The Rational Actor Model would explain a large part of decision-making; in some cases it may explain the whole of policy-making. The behaviour of a state may be studied as a response to the behaviour of another state. But this action-reaction model has its own limitations. States are abstract entities. They themselves do not make rules. It is individuals who take decisions and make policies. Policy-making, therefore, is subject to all stresses and strains, and pressures and counter-pressures that individuals are susceptible to. Moreover, the action-reaction chain, for its operation, needs the help of communication. Hence model 1 is not self-sufficient. It needs to be complemented by Model 2 and Model 3.

Whether it is an interaction between two states or two bureaucratic players, the game is to be based on some information which has to be communicated from one side to the other. Normally things move in fixed routes, according to established procedures. Hence is the importance of Model 2. But it is not decisive. Procedures may be changed; routes may be altered. Information may be suppressed or distorted in the perceived interest of a nation, in the interest of an organization or in the interest of a bureaucratic player. Model 2, therefore, is not the sole determinant of foreign policy.

Model 3 touches the heart of the problem. It starts with individuals. It treats them as decision-makers. Individuals are players with their goals, commitments and values. It is wrong to assume that bureaucratic politics model can be a tool to predict accurately the behaviour of a nation. A player, though concerned over the interest of his organization, would hardly ignore the interest of his nation. But his perception of national interest

---

[67] Ibid., p. 256.
[68] Krasner, n. 63, p. 319.

would largely be based upon the information filtered through organizational routes and personal orientations.

Thus, in a foreign policy-making process, all three models often function simultaneously. Instead of representing different lines on the graph, they represent different points of the same line. The relative importance of these models is not fixed. That will differ from time to time, from situation to situation. However, it appears to the present writer with his very limited background, that the important task for a student of foreign policy analysis is to study the movement of a policy between Model 3 and Model 1, prismed through Model 2. That will constitute the main focus of the present study.

In brief, the proposed model would throw the main emphasis upon the individual as a participant in the decision-making process on foreign policy. He would be influenced by the inputs from the internal as well as external environments. The internal environment, for this study, would include public opinion, especially the views of the "attentive public," the pressures from various pressure groups, the opinions of the press and the mind of Congress as reflected in different Congressional forums. The external environment would comprise of the bilateral relationship between the state to which the individual decision-maker belongs and the state in relation to which the policy is to be made, the regional dynamics—the interaction among the constituents of the region of which the latter state is a member and the broad policy of the former state in the region as a whole—and the global politics which is primarily a function of the equation between the Super Powers.

The inputs from these two environments enter into the mind of the decision-maker normally through the designated routes. As a result, the communication-flow would be affected by organizational inertia and "bureaucratic incrementalism" which are functions of standard operating procedures.

The mind of the decision-maker is not a *tabula rasa*. It is charged with some psychological predispositions which include his cultural values which he may have learned and internalized during the period of rearing and his *"in order to"* motives which would impel him to act in order to achieve or maintain a future state of affairs in the decision-making organization, in the internal environment or in the external environment. The present scheme accepts the dichotomy posed by Snyder and others, between *because of* and *in order to* motives. They say, "*In order to* motives refer to an end state of affairs envisaged by the actor. Such motives thus refer to the future. . . . On the other hand, *because of* motives refer to the actor's *past experience*, to the sum total of factors in his life-history which determine the particular project of action selected to reach a goal. . . ."[69] The present framework would give more weight to *in order to* motives than to *because of* motives. Moreover, the *sociological* personality of each actor—the personality shaped by his inter-relationship with other actors and by his position in the system—would also influence his perception. Thus a decision-maker's reception and interpretation of the information, emanating from the internal and external environments and filtered through the communication-routes, would be affected by his *in order to* and *because of* motives, especially the former, and his sociological personality.

The actor is an "organization man." He has to fight for the interest of his organization. Organizations compete for more powers and a larger share of the budget. The actor has to ensure that his organization comes at the top in this competition. Moreover, he is also driven by his personal goals. As a result, there is rivalry and competition amongst bureaucratic players. Hence the conflict-consensus syndrome. Among the techniques used in this game, as mentioned earlier, are pulling and hauling, alliance-building, affecting the information and leaking.

The actor is the President's man. He is appointed by him and is responsible to him. He continues in office during the President's pleasure. It is, therefore, natural that he would be keeping in mind, while taking a stand on any policy-matter, the interests and goals of the President. But it is not an one-way traffic. It is an exaggeration to assert that he must share the values of the President. People of different values may agree on some compromise policy. The President is not an autocrat or a dictator. He is the ultimate decision-maker, but he is not the sole decision-maker. While taking the decision, he has to take into account the views of his advisers. He is the leader of the team. In order to keep the team going, he has to find out the

[69] Snyder, *et al*, n. 10, p. 144; and James N. Rosenau, *The Scientific Study of Foreign Policy* (New York, 1971), p. 263.

best possible compromise which would give something to all disputants and which would not totally alienate anybody. This may entail some compromise on the part of the President himself. Thus a participant in the decision-making process is not just an instrument to carry out the President's policy. He is a player with some influence. Who will have the President's ear will depend upon the cooperation an actor gets from his associates in his unit, the skill and competence with which he presents his views to the President and his personal equation with the latter.

To postulate a framework is one thing. To apply it in analyzing a specific issue is a much more complex matter. The present writer has made an attempt in the chapters, following an introductory chapter, to examine the role of the Pentagon in policy-making relating to Vietnam during the period 1961-1968.

SOME HYPOTHESES ON THE PLACE OF THE MILITARY IN THE POWER STRUCTURE

So far the discussion has been concerned with the broad issue of foreign policy-making. Since the present work is concerned with the role of the Defence Department, an examination of significant issues relating to the making of decisions in the Defence Department needs to be undertaken. The Defence Department consists of a military component and a civilian component. The military component itself consists of uniformed representatives of the Army, the Navy, the Air Force and the Marine Corps. The Chiefs of Staff of the Services, designated by the President, constitute the highest military advisory group to the President in the Executive branch—the Joint Chiefs of Staff. The President designates one of the four as Chairman of the JCS whose position in the group is that of first among equals. There is a civilian Secretary for each of the three principal Services—Army, Navy and the Air Force. At the apex of the organization stands a civilian appointed by the President, with the advice and consent of the Senate—the Secretary of Defence. The JCS are subordinate to the civilian Secretary of Defence, but they also have the right of access to the President.

Civilian control of the military has for long been regarded

as a significant characteristic of the American system of government. In recent years there has been a growing debate in the US whether civilian control is real and effective or whether the military finds it possible to get its own way. Discussion on the issue took a dramatic turn by President Eisenhower's warning in his farewell speech against possible dangers to a democratic society from a "military-industrial complex." An examination in detail of the ramifications of the problem of the "military-industrial complex" is outside the scope of the present inquiry. However a brief exposition of the historical background and of certain theories concerning the role of the military in policy-making that have been adumbrated in recent years may be apposite.

The problem of the civilian control of the military in the US is as old as her Constitution itself. In a way, it was the product of the American struggle for independence. The implications to the liberty of citizens posed by the standing army maintained by England had a deep impact upon the American revolutionaries and the makers of the US Constitution. They included some provisions in the Constitution which would guarantee civilian control over the military. They made a civilian—the President—the Commander-in-Chief, and vested in Congress—another civilian body—the power to raise and maintain the Army and Navy, and to declare war.

With a few exceptions, the pattern of civilian control of military, as envisaged in the Constitution, continued to function almost intact till the outbreak of the Second World War. Prior to that era the United States did not have a large standing army. In earlier wars that the US had fought, a large part of the military forces specifically raised for meeting the requirements of the time was disbanded and the military assumed its normal, modest size. Demobilization took place after the Second World War too, but soon the situation changed.

Policy-makers in the Truman Administration feared that the Soviet Union, the leader of the Communist World, posed a great danger to the "free world" of which, they believed, their country was the natural leader. They believed that a serious security problem existed and that the United States should have the requisite military capability to deter aggression and to "contain" Communism. In pursuance of that objective the US

committed herself to the defence of several areas in th
either bilaterally or multilaterally. Her military prep
were carried on at an unprecedented level. As the "Col
intensified, military industries flourished, retired military officers
were appointed in high civilian posts, especially in arms
industries, and military voices commanded respect in defence
and foreign policy matters as never before.

The allegedly increased military penetration into the civilian
domains in the post-war period raised, as indicated earlier, a
great deal of concern about the traditional civil-military equation
in defence and foreign policy-making. The garrison state hypothesis which Harold D. Lasswell had propounded before the
end of the war gained fresh momentum in its aftermath.[70] It
had predicted that in both the United States and the Soviet
Union, the garrison state would be the necessary product of the
prolonged continuation of a state of mutual suspicion and
hostility.[71] In such a hypothetical state, dominance would pass
over from the businessman to the soldier; belief-systems would
be militarized; all other purposes and activities would be subordinate to war and the preparation of war, and power would be
centralized. Writing as recently as in 1957, Lasswell maintained
that the garrison state hypothesis was still valid today. He concluded that "the Garrison hypothesis provides a probable image
of the past and future of our epoch. . . ."[72]

Slightly different from the garrison state hypothesis but equally
concerned about the "military ascendancy" was C. Wright Mills'
"power elite" hypothesis. According to Mills, the power elite
consists of the economic, military, and the political elites with
the first two placed at the top of the structure and the third, relegated to the second level. He charges that American capitalism
has become "military capitalism" today. According to him, the
highest beneficiary of the three is the military which provides

---

[70] Harold D. Lasswell, "The Garrison State," *The American Journal of
Sociology* (Chicago, Ill.), vol. 46, 1971, pp. 455-68.

[71] For a critical estimate of Lasswell's Garrison hypothesis, see Samuel
P. Huntington, *The Soldier and the State: The Theory and Politics of
Civil Military Relations* (Cambridge, Mass., 1957), pp. 346-50.

[72] Lasswell, "The Garrison State Hypothesis Today," in Samuel P.
Huntington ed., *Changing Patterns of Military Policy* (New York,
1962), p. 51.

personnel for defence and justify the corporate ideology to the people. He says, "The power elite does, in fact, take its current shape from the decisive entrance into it of the military. Their presence and their ideology are its major legitimations, whenever the power elite feels the need to provide any."[73] According to this hypothesis, the military in post-war America is one of the two most powerful actors, though not the sole master, and it is in a position to significantly influence defence and foreign policy.

Gabriel Kolko and Morris Janowitz view the problem differently. Kolko does not dispute the garrison state hypothesis or power elite hypothesis in so far as they say that powers tend to be exercised by a few hands in their own interest. Beyond this he raises an important question about the alleged threat of the military against the civilian supremacy. He asserts that the military has always been used by the civilian leaders—many with links to corporations—in furthering corporate interests, both at home and abroad. The Military Establishment in the United States, according to him, "is an effect rather than a cause of political policy, an appearance and instrumentality rather than the full nature of reality."[74] Thus Kolko does not feel that a threat emanates from the strengthened military establishment. On the other hand, the real threat, according to him, comes from the civilian elites who represent "corporate capitalism."

Another refutation of the "military ascendancy" concept in the garrison state-power elite hypotheses was made by Janowitz in his work, *The Professional Soldier*.[75] He questions the validity of assuming that the military services act as a monolith. He asserts that the cleavage between the services is so deep as to inhibit collusive action. Often they are not able to achieve a unified position," unless forced to it by their civilian heads. He also points out that the military leaders are different from corporation managers; there is hardly any social cohesion between them and the military is not positively interested in politics. He further

---

[73] C. Wright Mills, *The Power Elite* (New York, 1956), pp. 276-8.
[74] Gabriel Kolko, *The Roots of American Foreign Policy: An Analysis of Power and Purpose* (Boston, Mass., 1969), p. 29.
[75] Morris Janowitz, *The Professional Soldier: A Social and Political Portrait* (Glencoe, Illinois, 1960), pp. 320, 351, 391-2; see also Arnold M. Rose, *The Power Structure: Political Process in American Society* (New York, 1967) pp. 147-52.

states that the military pressure groups, because of their frequent clash of interests, are hardly united against their civilian colleagues. In conclusion he says that there is no fear of the military invasion of the civilian supremacy in the field of defence and foreign policy. He observes:

> . . .The military have accumulated considerable power, and that power protrudes into the political fabric of contemporary society. It could not be otherwise. However, while they have no reluctance to press for larger budgets, they exercise their influence on political matters with considerable restraint and unease. Civilian control of military affairs remains intact and fundamentally acceptable to the military; any imbalance in military contributions to political-military affairs—domestic or international—is, therefore, often the result of default by civilian political leadership.[76]

Two differentiating hypotheses are thus put forward. The first holds that "military ascendancy" in post-war America tends to endanger the traditional civilian supremacy in the field of defence and foreign policy. The second asserts that the military though considerably strengthened in post-war America, is still subject to the civilian control and thus has not in fact a dominant role in decision-making in politico-military affairs.

EVOLUTION OF THE DEPARTMENT OF DEFENCE

The role, powers, and the scope of action of the major actors of the civilian component and of the military component are set out in law. When the law gives a decisive edge to the civilian actor, the military actors are in a subordinate position unless the civilian actor fails to exert the full extent of his authority. The historical experience, conventions, usage, and the immediate past as well as the personality of actors will tend to have a bearing on the manner in which business gets done. To understand the play of forces within the Department of Defence, it is necessary to discuss briefly the historical background, to trace the law relating to the Department, and to touch on the other factors referred

---

[76] Janowitz, n. 75, p. viii.

to that have a bearing on the study.

The "substantive" military input into foreign policy-making in the United States is of recent origin. It came to the fore with the struggle against the Axis Powers.[77] With Pearl Harbor, the country went to war. "Total victory" became the national objective. The civilian sector seemed to resign the business of war to the President and the military. Cordell Hull, the Secretary of State, told Henry L. Stimson, the Secretary of War, "I have washed my hands off it and it is now in the hands of you and [Frank] Knox—the Army and the Navy." Stimson himself said that his war-time duty was "to support, protect, and defend his generals."[78]

According to William Emerson, President Franklin D. Roosevelt assumed the role of "Master Strategist."[79] He ordered the military chiefs to deal with him directly. However, while the President took a keen and continuing interest in the planning and managing the war, he did not seek to interfere in operational decisions as Winston Churchill, the British Prime Minister did. He reposed great confidence in his Chief of Staff General George C. Marshall. In the hands of the Chief of Staff was concentrated "the authority and responsibility for the whole military establishment."[80] Despite the enormous power that Marshall wielded, there was no question during the entire period of war of where the supreme authority lay. It lay securely in the hands of the President and Commander-in-Chief.

The State Department continued to believe that its function was diplomacy and that its domain was different from that of the military. But, in its own domain, the State Department was often

---

[77] The following discussion on inter-war foreign policy-making is mainly based on Huntington, *The Soldier and the State* (Cambridge, Mass., 1957), chapter 12; John C. Ries, *The Management of Defence: Organization and Control of the US Armed Services* (Baltimore Md., 1964), chapters 2 and 4; Jack Raymond, *Power at the Pentagon* (New York, 1964), chapters 3 and 4; and Paul Y. Hammond, *Organizing for Defence: The American Military Establishment in the Twentieth Century* (Princeton, 1961), chapters 7 and 8.

[78] Cited in Huntington, ibid., p. 317.

[79] William R. Emerson, "F.D.R.," in Earnest R. May, ed., *The Ultimate Decision: The President as Commander-in Chief* (New York, 1960), pp. 135-77.

[80] Paul Y. Hammond, n. 77, p. 123.

denied its perceived role while the war lasted. Hull was not invited by the President to attend the Atlantic Ocean meeting or the war-time summit conferences. He was also not associated with major war decisions. "I was not told about the atomic bomb," Hull writes plaintively in his memoirs.[81] The "mood" of the country, the Presidential predilection for working with the military, and the "civilian abdication" represented by Hull's willingness to put up with a greatly reduced role for his Department, coupled with the growing appetite of the military leadership, contributed the enormous growth of the military's power in foreign policy-making. Secretary of War Stimson had more intimate access to the President on matters having foreign policy implications than Hull himself. Both Roosevelt and Stimson held the reins fairly tightly on the military in respect of overall controls and decisions but otherwise gave a fairly free hand to the Service Chiefs. By the very nature of situation—the country at total war, the cult of military heroes, and the latitude that the military leadership received from the President—the military leadership found itself in a position to make its impact felt significantly. Admiral William Leahy was reported to have said in 1945, "The Joint Chiefs of Staff at the present time are under no civilian control whatever."[82] While the statement was somewhat of an exaggeration, it did contain an element of truth. Nonetheless, there was no occasion when the military leadership sought to challenge or defy the President.

When the war ended and it became evident that the country would have to maintain a large military establishment to cope with the situation posed by the onset of the Cold War with the Soviet Union, the new President, Harry S. Truman, sought to move in the direction of a reorganization of a national security establishment. The problem was studied by the Commission on Government Reorganization headed by former President Herbert Hoover. The period also witnessed the emergence of the conflicting approaches among the services themselves. Publication of the recommendation of the Hoover Commission was followed by the enactment of the National Security Act, 1947.

---

[81] Cordell Hull, *Memoirs* (New York, 1948), part 2, pp. 1109-10.
[82] Cited in US Senate, Cong. 79, sess. 1, Committee on Military Affairs, *Hearings on S. 84*, p. 521.

The Act was a compromise between the Army which was for "centralization" and the Navy which advocated "confederation."[83] It created the Office of the Secretary of Defence, but with ambiguous powers.[84] It provided for the Joint Chiefs of Staff, and a joint staff, both organized on the basis of equal representation of the Army, Air Force and Navy (including the Marines). The object of the legislation was to create a single, strong, civilian authority functioning under the President, ostensibly capable of rising above inter-service rivalries. Such an authority, through the exercise of powers bestowed on it, was hoped to overcome the weakness that had been brought out during the war-time experiences, provide adequate scope for the different services, and, at the same time promote sounder decision-making. In the years that followed, amendments to the Act gave further powers to the Secretary of Defence. Each service chief wears two "hats"—as head of his service and as a JCS member. The 1949 amendment of the Act increased the powers of the Defence Secretary. The Army-Navy-Air Force Departments lost their cabinet rank and became "military" departments with the Defence Secretary speaking for all these three departments in the National Security Council. The 1953 amendment of the National Security Act was another step in the direction of centralizing authority in the Office of the Defence Secretary. It created Assistant Secretaries of Defence with responsibility in functional areas, such as supply and logistics, and manpower and personnel. The 1958 amendment seemed to tilt the balance even more in favour of the Defence Secretary *vis-a-vis* the JCS. Under this legislation, the JCS, as a corporate body, became "directly responsible" to the Secretary of Defence. Lines of command were clarified. They were to run from the Commander-in-Chief through the Secretary of Defence and from the latter *via* the JCS to the "unified" or "specified"

---

[83] For the evolution of the Department of Defence from 1947 to 1958, see Hammond, n. 77, pp. 227-370; Harry H. Ransom, "Department of Defence: Unity or Confederation," in Mark E. Smith and Claude J. Johns, eds., *American Defence Policy* (Baltimore, Md., 1968), pp. 361-76; and Charles J. Hitch, "Evolution of the Department of Defence," in Richard G. Head and Ervin J. Rooke, eds., *American Defence Policy* (Baltimore, Maryland, 1973), pp. 345-8.

[84] Ransom, ibid., p. 364.

commanders. The Service Secretaries and Service Chiefs were removed from the chain of command. Equally important was the role assigned to the Secretary of Defence in respect of the disposition of weapon systems. He was empowered to assign a new weapons system, regardless of which service might have developed it, to any of the three armed services for production, procurement, and operational control. Thus, successive legislations strengthened the Office of the Secretary of Defence at the cost of the Service Secretaries and the JCS. However, the civil-military equation is not "fixed." It may be affected by the personality factor, the interaction of the Secretary and the JCS with the President, their inter-relationship with Congress and other contextual variables. When a Secretary of Defence enjoyed the full confidence of the President and was able and willing to exercise the powers that were available to him, his role could be truly formidable. This was brought out during the "reign" of Robert S. McNamara.

The one major confrontation involving a very prestigious and popular military figure and civilian authority represented by the President was that between General Douglas MacArthur and Harry Truman. The President's decision to recall MacArthur was unanimously supported by the JCS. The JCS also extended solid support to the President on the issue of sending American troops to Europe. As Huntington points out, the Truman Administration needed the support of the military leaders with prestige and popularity to cooperate with it and carry out its policies.[85] By and large, with the exception of MacArthur, the Administration succeeded in obtaining such co-operation. As Truman's successor, Eisenhower, the hero of the Second World War, did not stand in the same need as Truman of prestigious generals for carrying out his policies. The Administration, as Huntington says, wanted agreement, not advocacy from its military chiefs.[86] Senior military officers like General Matthew Ridgway and Lt. Gen. James Gavin who had reservations concerning the doctrine of massive retaliation, espoused by the Administration, left the service. The President had no difficulty in turning down the recommendation of Adm. Radford for

[85] Huntington, n. 77, pp. 374-99.
[86] Ibid.

American military operations in Vietnam at the time of Dien Bien Phu. And the dominating figure of the Administration was neither the Secretary of Defence nor any military figure but the Secretary of State, John Foster Dulles.

The reorganization brought about by the National Security Act and its amendments could not succeed in ending or mitigating inter-service competitions. With a unified defence organization and unified budgeting, there ensued a bitter struggle among the different services for more funds and more organizational powers. Each service tried to sell its own superiority over others in terms of meeting future military contingencies. Each one stressed its own unique qualifications and credentials to be entrusted with the development of costly weapons. Each knew that acceptance of its plea would mean greatly expanded resources for itself and reduced resources for the other services.[87] Each knew what was in store for it if its plea failed and another service got the green signal. The issue of Universal Military Training (UMT) which the Army tried to sell to the country received no enthusiastic welcome from the Air Force. The Air Force pushed its own 70-group programme against which the Army waged a losing battle. The B-36 programme of the Air Force was opposed by both the Army and Navy who contended that air power would not be decisive in a future war. They argued that all the forces—air, navy and land—would play important roles in the future total war. Therefore, they urged a balanced development rather than over-emphasis on air power.[88] Some middle level naval officers almost succeeded in manipulating opinion within the Administration to develop a carrier-based aircraft which would deliver nuclear weapons. This was a direct challenge to the Air Force which did not believe that the Navy could successfully deliver nuclear weapons.[89]

The Eisenhower Administration too was not free of inter-

---

[87] Samuel P. Huntington, *The Common Defence: The Strategic Programs in National Politics* (New York, 1961), p. 371.

[88] Paul Y. Hammond, "Super-Carriers and B-36 Bombers," in Harold Stein, ed., *American Civil-Military Decisions* (Birmingham, Alabama, 1963).

[89] Vincent Davis, "The Development of a Capability to Deliver Nuclear Weapons by Carrier-Based Aircraft," in Morton H. Halperin, n. 21, pp. 262-75.

service fights. The "massive retaliation" doctrine seemed to tilt the balance decisively in favour of the Air Force. The worst loser was the Army. Some top Army Officers who did not buy the official policy had to leave. Many other dissidents, who did not leave their jobs, continued to fight inside as much as they could.[90] In the field of anti-ballistic missiles, the Army Nike and the Air Force Bomarc sharply collided. So also did the Army Jupiter and the Air Force Thor.[91] Thus, by the time Kennedy occupied the White House, the spotlight was focussed not on the issue of civil-military conflict but on inter-service fights.[92] The civilian leaders had the advantage of playing one service against another or others. Within the Pentagon the Defence Secretary, instead of being an opponent in the game as far as the service chiefs were concerned, emerged, many times, as the referee.

A unified position on the part of the Secretary of Defence and the JCS for a course of action favoured by the President can greatly strengthen the President's hands. Truman's ouster of General of the Army, Douglas MacArthur, is an instance in point. A unified position on the part of the JCS in support of a course favoured by the Secretary of Defence can significantly strengthen the hands of the Secretary as he bargains with the President or other Executive actors. By the same token factionalism and rivalries among the JCS, and the Services they represent, may pose severe complications for a Secretary. The allocation of resources among the fiercely competing services, and especially far-reaching decisions relating to weapons development and procurement with implications for one service or another confront the Secretary with serious problems and pitfalls in maintaining harmony and unity in his domain.

When the Secretary and the JCS are able to achieve a unified position, they can bring into play a significant volume of support

---

[90] For the Army "revolt" against the New Look of the Eisenhower Administration, see General Matthew B. Ridgway, *Soldier* (New York, 1956); Maxwell D. Taylor, *The Uncertain Trumpet* (New York, 1959); and James M. Gavin, *War and Peace in the Space Age* (New York, 1958).

[91] Michael H. Armacost, *The Politics of Weapons Innovation: The Thor-Jupiter Controversy* (New York, 1969).

[92] Huntington, n. 87, p. 371.

from veterans organizations, and "Service Associations." These organizations and associations can, in such circumstances, make a fairly significant impact upon public opinion and also influence Congressional opinion.[93] When the Service Chiefs are more or less placed in a situation of disagreement with the civilian element in the Pentagon, the veterans organizations and service associations tend, most often, to reflect the point of view of the military. When, however, there is disagreement among the services themselves, the service associations work at cross-purposes and the veterans organizations find themselves in somewhat confused position. Inter-service bickerings most often arise in respect of assignment of weapons systems. A particular service may oppose the claims of another service for a weapon system if it perceives the move as a threat to its own role and mission. The differences may be carried into debates on overall strategy in which each service will favour that approach which ensures a significant role for itself.

Another extra-Pentagon variable that sometimes plays a part is represented by the armament industries.[94] The Pentagon is the sole or at least the most important customer of many major corporations. In general, the armament industry deploys its lobbying resources in activities supportive of the Defence Department's course. However, when differences develop among the services, or between a service and the Secretary, the lobbying resorurces of a corporation tend to be mobilized in support of that entity whose stand promotes its own interest.

A very significant extra-Pentagon variable is, of course, Congress in general, and important committees of the two Houses dealing with appropriations, armed services and foreign relations. As indicated in the preceding analysis, the greater the unity among the components of the Pentagon, the greater the likelihood of substantial Congressional support. The armament industry with its potential campaign contributions, and the veterans organizations and service associations with their potential for votes will have significant impact on Congress. But when differences develop among the services or between the services

---

[93] Jack Raymond, n. 77, pp. 189-204; Armacost, n. 91, pp. 10-4; and Rose, n. 75, pp. 134-52.
[94] Fred J. Cook, *The Warfare State* (London, 1963), pp. 162-201.

and the Secretary, the Congressional situation gets complicated. Often a member of Congress—especially one who has a place on the Armed Services Committee—whose constituency has substantial defence installations and industries, tends to view an issue on the basis of its impact on his constituents.

The manner in which decisions are to be made is exceedingly complex and involves far too many variables that only those who are rash and unwise may be able to claim definitiveness for their analyses. The involvement of the US in Vietnam is a very tangled issue. In the present work, after a background survey of the developments from the end of the Second World War to the induction of Kennedy as the President, an attempt will be made to examine the role of the Pentagon in regard to policy-making on Vietnam in the broad context of the framework outlined in this chapter.

CHAPTER TWO

THE AMERICAN INVOLVEMENT IN VIETNAM FROM THE END OF THE SECOND WORLD WAR TO 1961

The evolution of American policy regarding Indochina in general and Vietnam in particular has to be reviewed in the context of the overall objectives of American foreign policy, the priorities that were accorded to different regions of the world, perception of the nature and magnitude of "threats" in the different regions, allocation of resources to respond to "threats," and the adoption of appropriate modalities for actions in various regions geared for the attainment of objectives sought. In the immediate post-war period, American policy-makers identified the Soviet Union as the principal adversary and Communist parties in various parts of the world as accessories of the Soviet Union whose activities were inimical to the interests of the United States. Western Europe was regarded as the area of crucial importance, and collaboration, not only with Britain but with France as well, were regarded as vitally important in bringing about a state of affairs in Western Europe that could deter a possible Soviet attack. The emergence of Communist regimes in Eastern Europe and the subsquent Communist takeover in Czechoslovakia served to deepen the anxiety of American policy-makers to formulate measures for the "containment" of Soviet expansion.[1] The

---

[1] The revisionists in the US do not accept the account of the origin of the cold war as given by the American Government. For their view-point, see William Appleman Williams, *The Tragedy of American Diplomacy* (New York, 1959); Gar Alperovitz, *Atomic Diplomacy* (London, 1966); D.F. Fleming, *The Cold War and Its Origins, 1917-1960*, vols. 1 and 2 (London, 1961); Lloyd C. Gardner, *Architects of Illusion: Men and Ideas in American Foreign Policy, 1941-1949* (Chicago, Illinois, 1970); and Joyce and Gabriel Kolko, *The Limits of Power: The World and United States Foreign Policy 1945-1954* (New York, 1972).

prospect that the Soviet Union might sooner or later attain a nuclear capability was a further stimulus for early implementation of counter-measures. The enunciation of the Truman Doctrine, the initiation of the Marshall Plan, and the establishment of the North Atlantic Treaty Organization, were among the significant steps taken by the United States to respond to what was described as the challenge of "Communist expansionism." The Truman Doctrine was based on a concept to which subsequently the name "domino theory" was given. President Truman argued that unless Greece was promptly aided to frustrate attempted subversion by an armed minority of Communists, Turkey would be endangered and the Middle East would be in jeopardy. The concept was accompanied by a suggested course of action which appeared to be global in scope. The President said, "The free peoples of the world look to us for support in maintaining their freedoms." He voiced confidence that Congress would face these "great responsibilities...squarely."[2] The "threat" that the United States and the "free world" confronted was described by Under Secretary of State Dean Acheson, the person who was mainly responsible for drafting Truman's Message, in briefing Congressional members in the White House on 26 February as:

> In the past eighteen months... Soviet pressure on the Straits, on Iran, and on northern Greece had brought the Balkans to the point where a highly possible Soviet breakthrough might open three continents to Soviet penetration. Like apples in a barrel infected by one rotten one, the corruption of Greece would infect Iran and all to the east. It would also carry infection to Africa through Asia Minor and Egypt, and to Europe through Italy and France, already threatened by the strongest domestic Communist parties in Western Europe....These were the stakes that British withdrawal from the eastern Mediterranean offered to an eager and ruthless opponent.[3]

NATO, the North Atlantic Treaty Organization, came into

[2] For the text of Truman's message, see Richard D. Challener, ed., *From Isolation to Containment, 1·21-1952: Three Decades of American Modern History* (London, 1970), pp. 147-51.

[3] Dean Acheson, *Present at the Creation: My Years in the State Department* (New York, 1969), p. 219.

existence in 1949. The US and France were partners in an alliance that American policy-makers regarded as of utmost importance in responding to the principal identified adversary. The partnership with France and the Europe-centred approach of the principal American policy-makers were factors that were to colour the thinking of the latter in regard to the struggle of the Vietnamese people for emancipation from French imperial rule. The explosion by the Soviet Union of a nuclear device in 1949 served to increase the importance that American policy-makers attached to NATO as well as to France. The establishment of the Peoples' Republic of China in October 1949 raised the spectre of a vast Sino-Soviet bloc which was regarded as having serious implications for American security not only in Europe but in Asia as well. Even though Europe still remained as the area of highest priority, American policy-makers devoted attention to evolving a course of action to respond to contingencies that may arise in Asia as a result of Communist moves. This was to have implications for American policy towards Indochina.

As early as 13 May 1947, the State Department, cabled certain guidelines to the American diplomats in Paris, Saigon and Hanoi,

> . . .the key to our position is our awareness that in respect of developments affecting position Western democratic powers in southern Asia, we essentially in same boat as French also as British and Dutch. We cannot conceive setbacks to long-range interests France which would also be setbacks our own. . . .[4]

The anti-French Viet Minh leader Ho Chi Minh was described by Dean Acheson as an agent of "international communism." In the fall of 1948, the Office of Intelligence and Research of the State Department stated that Ho was a Communist but he was not a Moscovite. It said, "If there is Moscow-directed conspiracy in Southeast Asia, Indochina is an anomaly so far."[5] However,

[4] US House of Representatives, Committee on Armed Services, *United States-Vietnam Relations*, *Prepared by the Department of Defence* (Washington, D.C., 1971), Book 1, p. A-46. (Hereafter this major source would be referred to as the *DOD Documents*)
[5] *DOD Documents*, n. 4, Book 1, pp. A-49, A-50; ibid., V.B. 2, p. 127.

with quick political developments in the Far East and Southeast Asia, Washington's appraisal of Ho also changed. On 1 February 1950 Secretary Acheson charged that Ho was not a nationalist; he was subservient to Russian control and he was the "mortal enemy" of native independence of Indochina.[6] The next day the US, in according recognition to the French-controlled governments in Vietnam, Laos and Cambodia, said that it would be an "encouragement to national aspirations" of the peoples of the colonial areas of Southeast Asia. On 8 May 1950 the Secretary of State, while announcing the American decision extend economic and military aid to France and the "Associated States," again charged that Ho's movement was "dominated by Soviet imperialism."[7]

American policy of support to the French military action against the Viet Minh was based on the belief stemming from the "domino concept" that the "fall" of Indochina to Communism would lead to the spread of Communism to the other parts of Southeast Asia. NSC 64, dated 27 March 1950, stated :

> It is important to United States security interests that all practicable measures be taken to prevent further Communist expansion in Southeast Asia. Indochina is a key area of Southeast Asia and is under immediate threat. The neighbouring countries of Thailand and Burma could be expected to fall under Communist domination if Indochina were controlled by a Communist-dominated government. The balance of Southeast Asia would then be in grave hazard.[8]

American policy-makers believed that the valuable raw material resources of Southeast Asia should not come under the control of elements hostile to the United States and the West.[9]

---

[6] Ibid., p. A-7.

[7] Ibid., p. A-61.

[8] Ibid., Book 1, part 2, pp. A-46, A-47.

[9] An NSC staff study of 13 February 1952 stressed the importance of the raw materials of Southeast Asia to the Western Powers. It said, "...Indonesia is a secondary source of petroleum whose importance would be enhanced by the denial to the Western Powers of petroleum sources in the Middle East."

Moreover, American policy-makers might have been interested in the markets of Southeast Asia for American products. However, the American economic interest in the area should not be overstressed. It was not the economic significance of the area as such but its value as an integral part of the international economic system imposing no restrictions on the access to raw materials and markets which might have led the US to support France in Indochina against the "Communists."

In April 1950 the National Security Council prepared a paper known as NSC 68 which summarized Washington's attitude towards "threats" posed by "international Communism." The paper recommended that the US must resist, with force if necessary, "Communist expansion."[10] Six days after the President signed NSC 68, war broke out in Korea and Truman ordered American combat troops into action to resist what the US described as North Korean aggression against South Korea. In another move that was to have far-reaching implications in future, Truman increased economic and military aid to the French in Indochina. In July the first shipments of American military material to Vietnam were air-lifted to Saigon. The next month a Military Assistance Advisory Group (MAAG) was sent to Indochina with the task of transferring this material directly to the French and to avoid direct dealings with the native people. After the entry of China into the war, Washington's anti-China stance substantially intensified even though it continued to label China as "Moscow's puppet."[11]

With the massive involvement of China in the Korean War towards the end of 1950 and with continued fighting by the Viet Minh against France in Indochina, the policy-makers in Washington increasingly tended to believe that the "enemy" operations in both Korea and Indochina were parts of the common

Senator Gravel, ed., *The Pentagon Papers: The Defence Department History of United States Decision-Making on Vietnam* (Boston, 1971), vol. 1, pp. 375-81.

[10] Paul Y. Hammond, "NSC 68: Prologue to Rearmament," Warner R. Schilling, *et al, Strategy, Politics and Defence Budgets* (New York, 1962), pp. 267-378.

[11] For Sino-American military confrontation in Korea, see Allen S. Whiting, *China Crosses the Yalu* (New York, 1960); and Tang Tsou, *America's Failure in China 1941-50* (Chicago, 1963), pp. 555-91.

effort made by the "Communists" for furthering their expansion in the Far East and Southeast Asia. The danger emanating from China to Southeast Asia came to be increasingly stressed. NSC 124/2, June 1952, stated that "the danger of an overt military attack against Southeast Asia is inherent in the existence of a hostile aggressive Communist China."[12] The document carried the implication that the "loss" of any entity in Southeast Asia would be adverse to the security interests of both Western Europe and the United States. It held that the US should use her influence with France not to give up her military effort in Indochina.

Thus, as the Truman Administration drew to a close, the "domino" concept in respect of Southeast Asia virtually became an article of faith. The device of military alliances to meet the Communist challenge in Asia had come to be accepted and a necessity of supporting French military action against the Viet Minh fully acknowledged. While considerable public criticism had developed concerning the administration's handling of the Korean War, the deepening involvement in Indochina did not attract significant attention.

THE EISENHOWER ADMINISTRATION AND VIETNAM

Despite the Truman administration's vigorous anti-Communist posture, it had come under severe attack from political critics, mostly Republicans, who alleged that it had "lost" China and that it was "soft on Communism." Republican Senator Joseph R. McCarthy had begun to loom large and the phenomenon that came to be known as McCarthyism appeared to assume significant dimensions. The State Department became a major target of McCarthy's attack and even General Marshall was not spared. The Presidential election of 1952 resulted in a landslide victory for the Republican candidate Dwight D. Eisenhower. The popular war hero had charged during the campaign that the Democratic Administration had followed a policy of weakness in the face of Communist challenge and had bungled the war in Korea. His running mate, Senator Richard M. Nixon of California who had shot into political prominence as a fighter

---

[12] *DOD Documents*, n. 4, Book 1, V.B. 2, p. 267.

against Communism, was far more denunciatory than the General in his attacks on the Truman Administration's course in Asia. Indochina did not figure significantly during the campaign.

The man whom the new President chose to be his Secretary of State was John Foster Dulles who soon emerged as the strong personality of the Administration. During the campaign, he had criticized the policy of containment and had asserted that the Republican Party would strive for the "liberation" of captive nations.[13] Dulles asserted that the Truman Administration had not acted vigorously in checking the expansion of Communism in Asia. He regarded Western colonialism as having reached a phase when it was geared to preparing native peoples for self-government, and he viewed the French course in Indochina as one of "gradually promoting self-government in Indochina."[14] Dulles believed that the US, having decided to give recognition to the Bao Dai government that France had sponsored in Indo-China, should not hesitate to give adequate backing to that regime, as against the Communists who were opposed to it. Dulles said:

> Since that is so, we must help the government we back. Its defeat, coming after the reverses suffered by the National Government of China, would have further serious repercussions on the whole sitution in Asia and the Pacific. It would make even more people in the East feel that friendship with United States is a liability rather than an asset.[15]

With the US having acquired a thermo-nuclear capability in 1953 and with the likelihood that the Soviet Union would acquire a similar capacity before long, the Eisenhower Administration came out with the so-called "New Look" based on the doctrine of "massive retaliation." Dulles, as the principal spokesman of the Administration, explained the concept in an address to the Council on Foreign Relations on 12 January 1954. He said, "The way to deter aggression is for the free community to be

[13] John Foster Dulles, *War or Peace* (London, 1950), p. 175.
[14] Ibid., p. 231.
[15] Ibid.

willing and able to respond vigorously at places and with means of its own choosing."[16]

In regard to Indochina, the Eisenhower Administration continued the same course as its predecessor. NSC 5405, dated 16 January 1954, contained the usual reference to the raw material resources of Southeast Asia and reiterated that the loss of Southeast Asia to the Communists would have "serious economic consequences for many nations of the free world and conversely would add significant resources to the Soviet bloc. . . ."[17]

The heavy toll of war in Indochina and the economic and political difficulties it led to domestically led France to seek a deeper commitment on her behalf by the United States. The Eisenhower Administration was committed to the promotion of an European Defence Community (EDC) which was to consist of France, Italy, Belgium, the Netherlands, Luxembourg, and West Germany. The US attached a great deal of importance to the formation of EDC. Secretary Dulles said:

> President Eisenhower is deeply convinced that there can be no long-term assurance of security and vitality for Europe, and therefore for the Western World including the United States, unless there is a unity which will include France and Germany. . . . Until the goals of EDC are achieved, NATO, and indeed future peace, are in jeopardy.[18]

The Administration was concerned when France showed some luke-warmness towards the move. Misgivings over what West Germany might do in the future continued to influence French thinking. It became necessary for the United States to provide appropriate "sweeteners" to keep the French in line: France was finding the ongoing war in Indochina a serious economic drain. The US extended economic assistance to France and the objective probably was both to help France in her effort in Indochina and to induce France to ratify EDC.

The continued deterioration of the French military position

---

[16] *Department of State Bulletin* (Washington, D.C.), 25 January 1954, p. 108.

[17] *DOD Documents*, n. 4, Book 1, p. A-51.

[18] *Department of State Bulletin*, n. 16, p. 109.

in Indochina brought Washington face to face with the issue of possible direct US military involvement in Indochina. There was consensus in Washington about the serious repercussion that a "Communist" victory in Vietnam would have, but major agencies in Washington differed amongst themselves on how to meet this contingency. The State Department was for American intervention with ground forces, if necessary, to avert a French collapse but some elements in the Defence Department were not prepared to accept this view. At an inter-agency meeting of 29 January 1954 General Walter Bedell Smith, the Under Secretary of State, said that the importance of winning in Indochina was so great that if the worst came to the worst he personally would favour intervention with US air and naval forces—not ground forces. Admiral Radford, the JCS Chairman, concurred with him. But Roger Keys, Deputy Secretary of Defence, expressed his reservations about the step advocated by Smith and Radford.[19]

Chairman Radford could not carry the JCS with him. The JCS' hesitation to endorse the proposal of employing US forces in support to France in Indochina might have been due to two factors. One of them was the recent experience of American troops in Korea. The Korean experience showed that even with monopoly of the air and of the sea by the US, a substantial induction of American ground troops was necessary in Korea. In spite of all these, however, the US failed to "win" the war. The JCS said that the prospects in Vietnam might be worse. The adversary was far more formidable and tested. It had shown its fighting prowess against the Japanese and French forces. Moreover, unlike Korea, Vietnam was full of jungles. In view of this, the JCS, apart from the Chairman, could not buy the argument that American air and naval forces would be enough to save the situation at Dien Bien Phu. They feared that the US would be forced to send ground troops there. In Korea, the US had suffered heavy casualties. The millitary chafed under the restraints that had been placed on it in regard to operations in the field owing to various political decisions. Since then, "No more Koreas" had become ingrained in the minds of the military. Secondly, Europe was still accorded the first priority *vis-a-vis*

---

[19] *DOD Documents*, n. 4, vols. 9-10, pp. 240-3.

Asia. The JCS feared that the deployment of US troops in Asia would render Europe vulnerable to possible Russian attack.

In January 1954 the JCS disagreed with the idea of sending US troops to Indochina, but they did not foreclose the possibility of sending them in future. At the same time, it is to be emphasized, they were not less hawkish than any other agency in Washington in relation to Indochina. In a memorandum, dated 12 March 1954, they recommended that France be advised not to accept any proposals of coalition, partition or election in Vietnam.[20]

The Dien Bien Phu siege began on 13 March 1954. From that day to 8 May 1954, the decision-making process in Washington underwent hectic movements by its players. The overwhelming concern of Washington seemed to avert a French collapse. The two actors who were very anxious to help France were still Dulles and Admiral Radford, the JCS Chairman. In a memorandum to the President, dated 24 March 1954, Radford said that the fall of Indochina might lead to the loss of the whole of Southeast Asia to the Communists. He, therefore recommended that the US be prepared "to act promptly and in Force possibly to a frantic and belated request by the French for US intervention."[21] This was the personal opinion of the Chairman. He did not have the unanimous support of the JCS for this recommendation.

General Paul Ely, French Chief of Staff, visited Washington on 20 March. Admiral Radford reportedly mentioned to him that the US Air Force and Navy had a plan for a night-time raid against the perimetre of Dien Bien Phu. Its code name was "Operation Vulture." This plan did not involve the use of US ground forces.[22]

Dulles pressed the President hard to send US forces to Dien Bien Phu to the rescue of France. But the President insisted that he would not do so unless and until he had the approval of Congress for it. Dulles and Radford met Congressional leaders

---

[20] Ibid., pp. 266-70.
[21] Ibid., p. 290.
[22] Senator Gravel, n. 9, p. 97; and Melvin Gurtov, *The First Vietnam Crisis: Chinese Communist Strategy and United States Involvement, 1953-54* (New York, 1967), p. 80.

on 3 April 1954, but the latter were not receptive to Dulles' proposal for US intervention if her allies did not support her in this operation.[23] The next day Eisenhower outlined the following three conditions which must be fulfilled before he would consider ordering US troops to Vietnam. They were: (1) formation of a coalition force with America's allies to pursue an "united action;" (2) declaration of French intent to accelerate the independence of Associated States; and (3) Congressional approval of US intervention.[24]

In his desperate attempt to help France at Dien Bien Phu and prevent the Viet Minh from winning a decisive battle, Dulles shuttled between London and Paris from 11 April to 14 April to get their support and cooperation. But, for different reasons, neither of them accepted Dulles' plan. Britain favoured giving the scheduled Geneva Conference a fair trial. Moreover, the personal incompatibility between Dulles and Anthony Eden, the British Foreign Minister might have partly influenced the British decision not to go along with Dulles' plan of intervention in Indochina.[25] France opposed Dulles' plan for two reasons. She had sought American help only as an emergency measure to save Dien Bien Phu. She was not in favour of any "united action" which would internationalize the issue. Secondly, France wanted a quick settlement. She was afraid that any military intervention in a grand scale might prolong the war and, as a result, delay the settlement. No "united action" involving American forces could be undertaken and Dien Bien Phu fell to the "Communists" on 7 May. The Geneva Conference was already underway by that time.

But the US did not refrain from making efforts in the direction of intervening in Vietnam even after the start of the Geneva Conference. On 7 May, the day on which Dien Bien Phu collapsed, Eisenhower and Dulles decided that France should be informed that Washington was willing to ask for Congressional

---

[23] The meeting between Congressional leaders and the representatives of the Administration on 3 April 1954 will be discussed in Chapter V.

[24] Gravel, n. 9, p. 90.

[25] Richard Good-Adams says, "...But it was basically Eden's rooted distrust of Dulles which made him go all the way and thwart the American plan." Richard Good-Adams, *The Time of Power: A Reappraisal of John Foster Dulles* (London, 1962), p. 135.

authority for intervention if the following preconditions were met. France was to proclaim her desire to grant "genuine freedom" to the Indochinese states—Laos, Cambodia and Vietnam. American advisers in Vietnam should "take major responsibility for training indigenous forces" and share "responsibility for military training."[26] It is important to note that the concurrence of London was no longer pressed as a precondition as it was on 4 April. Thus the 7 May decision indicated the increased concern of the US to avert a total victory of "Communists" in Indochina by the deployment of US forces there. It also suggested that Dulles had finally prevailed upon other agencies in Washington to accept some sort of military intervention by the US in Indochina.

In a memorandum to Charles E. Wilson, the Secretary of Defence, dated 20 May 1954, the JCS recommended that the US should limit her military involvement in Indochina only to air and naval actions. They strongly opposed the deployment of American ground forces. Very bluntly they said, "From the point of view of the United States, Indochina is devoid of decisive military objectives and the allocation of more than token US armed forces to that area would be a serious diversion of limited US capabilities.[27]

The above recommendation was apparently a compromise lately reached among the members of the JCS. Sometime between 3 April meeting between Congressional leaders and the Secretary of State and the JCS Chairman, and 7 May, the day on which Dien Bien Phu fell to Viet Minh, the Chief of Staff of the Air Force Nathan F. Twining and Chief of Naval Operations Robert B. Carney appear to have expressed their support for sending US bombers and aircraft carriers to Dien Bien Phu, but they could not take a strong stand on it because of the stiff opposition of General Matthew B. Ridgway, the Chief of Staff of the Army. Ridgway argued that the US could not reap a military victory in Indochina with air and naval forces alone. He further argued that even if the US used atomic weapons in Indochina, she would still need the deployment of US ground

---

[26] Gravel, n. 9, p. 503.
[27] Neil Sheehan, ed., *The Pentagon Papers*, published by the *New York Times*, 1971, p. 14.

troops there which he vehemently opposed.[28] But subsequently he seemed to have toned down his opposition to the sending of American forces to Vietnam because of the continued pressure of interventionists, especially Dulles and Radford. He would support an intervention if it did not involve the dispatch of US ground troops and if the air force and navy, sent to Vietnam, would merely be a "token" contingent.[29] However, while Washington was still grappling with the question of intervention, the French position in Indochina started to deteriorate rapidly. Paris was also determined to reach a quick settlement. On 15 June 1954 Washington informed Paris that the time for intervention was over.

THE GENEVA CONFERENCE

Since the beginning of the Geneva Conference, the US adopted a policy of "disassociation," so that she could have maximum freedom of action in future.[30] She had also tried to prevent the conference itself from taking place. She put pressure upon France during the Berlin Conference of January 1954 to drop the idea of the proposed Geneva Conference, but the latter did not yield. France, on the other hand, threatened to dissociate herself from the EDC if the Geneva Conference were not held.[31] That was enough to win the concurrence of Washington for holding the Geneva Conference.

But Washington's hostile attitude to the conference did not cease even after the conference started. On 7 May Dulles said that the US would be "greatly concerned if an armistice or ceasefire were reached at Geneva that would provide a road to a Communist take-over and further aggression."[32] On the same

---

[28] Matthew B. Ridgway, *Soldier: The Memoirs of Matthew B. Ridgway* (New York, 1956), pp. 275-8.

[29] James Gavin, "Crisis Now," in Stephen E. Ambrose and James A. Barber, Jr., eds., *The Military and American Society* (New York, 1972), pp. 143-8.

[30] See Chester L. Cooper, *The Lost Crusade: The Full Story of US Involvement in Vietnam from Roosevelt to Nixon* (London, 1970), pp. 75-101.

[31] Dwight D. Eisenhower, *The White House Years: Mandate for Change, 1953-56* (New York, 1963), pp. 342-3; and Cooper, ibid., p. 69.

[32] *Department of State Bulletin*, 17 May 1954, p. 744.

day, the JCS in a memorandum to the Defence Secretary for transmittal to the State Department, recommended that the US should not associate herself with any French proposal directed toward a cease-fire in advance of a satisfactory political settlement. In that case, they felt that the US could have "maximum freedom of action" in future to tackle "Communism."[33] The US delegation at Geneva, throughout the conference, maintained a low key posture, indicating a "hands off" policy.

During the Geneva meeting, the United States undertook a few covert activities against the Viet Minh in Indochina. From June 1954 to August 1955, a team led by Colonel Edward G. Lansdale, a CIA operative who had earned a reputation for counter-guerilla warfare in the Philippines, was instructed to undertake paramilitary operations against the enemy and to wage political psychological warfare."[34] Lansdale's operations indicate how the US was predisposed to follow her own course irrespective of whatever the terms of settlement reached later at Geneva might require her to do or not to do.

At the conclusion of the Geneva Conference, neither the United States nor South Vietnam signed the Geneva declaration. General Walter Bedell Smith, the chief US delegate, however, proclaimed an unilateral American declaration that the US would "refrain from the threat or the use of force to disturb" the Geneva accords.[35] The Eisenhower Administration viewed the Geneva accords as a major "diplomatic defeat" for the United States. In meetings on 8 and 12 August, the NSC concluded that the Geneva settlement was a "disaster" that "completed a major forward stride of Communism which may lead to the loss of Southeast Asia."[36] The foremost concern of the US thenceforward was to prevent "Communism" from spreading into other parts of Southeast Asia.

POST-GENEVA AMERICAN POLICY IN VIETNAM

One of the first acts in the post-Geneva American policy in

---

[33] *DOD Documents*, n. 4, vols. 9-10, pp. 431-4.

[34] Sheehan, n. 27, p. 17.

[35] *American Foreign Policy*, *1950-1955. Basic Documents* (Washington, D.C., 1955), vol. 1, p. 788.

[36] Sheehan, n. 27, p. 14.

Vietnam was the establishment of the Southeast Asia Treaty Organization (SEATO). The treaty establishing the alliance was signed on 8 September 1954. It was in a way the brain child of Secretary Dulles. He had earlier tried, while negotiating the Japanese Peace Treaty in 1951, to promote an alliance for common defence against Chinese "expansion." He was continuing his efforts to set up a "collective security" organization for Southeast Asia even when the Geneva Conference was in progress. However, he encountered some opposition from London.[37]

By the time the SEATO came into existence, the "united action," so often urged by Eisenhower and Dulles, had given place to "collective security" which appeared to be more passive than the former. Out of the eight members of this organization, only two—Thailand and the Philippines—belonged to Southeast Asia. All others were outsiders. Another peculiar feature of this pact was that it threw an unilateral blanket of military protection to South Vietnam, Laos and Cambodia who were forbidden by the Geneva accords to join any military pact.

Soon after the Geneva Conference was over, there started a big debate in Washington on whether the US should impart military training to the South Vietnamese. It was mainly a tussle between the State Department and the Defence Department. Dulles very forcefully argued that the US should take over the responsibility of giving military training to the forces of the Saigon regime. The JCS were opposed to it. They argued that political stability in Saigon was a precondition before the US started training her forces. Dulles reported that political stability was not possible without military security.[38] In the end, Dulles had the last word. The JCS, in a memorandum of 19 October 1954, conceded that if "political considerations" were overriding, they would agree to the training of South Vietnamese forces by the Military Assistance Advisory Group (MAAG), Saigon.[39] On 20 August, the President approved an NSC paper which outlined a threefold programme. Militarily, the US would work with France to build up a native force which would be able to provide internal security. Economically, the US would start giving aid directly to the

---

[37] Cooper, n. 30, pp. 103-8.
[38] *DOD Documents*, n. 4, vols. 9-10, pp. 701, 742.
[39] Ibid., p. 701.

Saigon Government, without sending it through France. Politically, she would work with the Ngo Dinh Diem Government in Vietnam.[40] Thus began at a deeper level the American commitment to Saigon which had taken root with the Truman Administration extending economic and military aid to the Bao Dai regime in 1950.

Diem, a Catholic Christian, belonged to one of Vietnam's important families.[41] A bachelor, and a highly educated person, he was an ardent nationalist. He resigned his post as the Minister of Interior in 1933 as an expression of his opposition to the continued French rule. He was equally opposed to Communism. He would not cooperate with the Viet Minh which he considered as a Communist organization. In 1946 he left Vietnam and for a few years travelled abroad. In the US he met with John Foster Dulles and other important political figures. Some commentators have alleged that Diem was handpicked by the CIA to emerge at the right time as the top man in Vietnam. In 1954 Bao Dai appointed Diem as his Prime Minister. Only a few days before the fall of Diem Bien Phu, Bao Dai who was then in Paris, invited Diem to accept the post of Prime Minister. Diem, who was given full civil and military powers, arrived in Saigon on 25 June 1954.

The Lansdale covert mission which had been launched in June 1954 continued to operate for more than a year more. In course of time Colonel Lansdale became a good friend of Diem and a source of considerable encouragement and strength to his regime. General J. Lawton Collins who had been sent to Saigon as a special representative of the President, was not happy with the Diem regime. He recommended to Washington that Diem should be replaced because his regime was weak and inefficient. Dulles first took the position that there was no alternative to Diem. However being persuaded by Collins, Dulles later reluctantly agreed to Diem's replacement. On 27 April, he sent instructions to the Saigon Mission to that effect. However, Lansdale came to the rescue of Diem in time. He helped Diem, on 28 April, in successfully suppressing a rebellion against him.

---

[40] Sheehan, n. 27, p. 16.
[41] For the life history of Diem, see Anthony T. Bouscaren, *The Last of the Mandarins: Diem of Vietnam* (Pittsburgh, Penn., 1965).

Washington seemed to be impressed by it. The US diplomatic mission in Saigon was immediately asked to ignore the 27 April message.[42] From then onwards the US stood with the Diem regime till November 1963 when he was overthrown and killed.

ELECTIONS NOT HELD

According to the Geneva accords, general elections were to be held in July 1956 throughout Vietnam to form a government which would be followed by the rejoining of the two halves of Vietnam. For this, North and South Vietnam were required to begin consultation in July 1955. But, when that time came, Saigon refused to undertake any consultation with Hanoi. She argued that there was no use in holding the proposed election because it would not be free and democratic in North Vietnam. There might have been some elements of truth in this charge but the motivation of the Diem regime for balking at the election seems to have been different. The Pentagon Papers reveal that the US had a hand in it.

Before the Geneva Conference was over, the JCS had pointed out that "Communists" were likely to win if an election were held in Vietnam. In August 1954, the CIA reported that if elections were held in 1956, the Viet Minh would win.[43] In 1954 President Eisenhower himself was reported to have said that Ho Chi Minh would win 80 per cent of the votes if elections were held that year.[44] Thus Washington was almost convinced that the "Communists" were sure to defeat the Diem regime in election. Against this background, Dulles' instructions to the American delegation in Geneva that it should try to delay the elections and demand guarantees that the "Communists" were likely to reject seems to have been a deliberate ploy to prevent the holding of general elections in Vietnam. On 7 July 1954, Dulles wrote to General Walter Bedell Smith, the Chief US delegate at Geneva:

---

[42] *DOD Documents*, n. 4, Book 10, pp. 941-7; and Edward Geary Lansdale, *In the Midst of Wars: An American's Mission to Southeast Asia* (New York, 1972), pp. 260-1.

[43] Ibid., vols. 9-10, pp. 522-3.

[44] Eisenhower, n. 31, p. 373.

Since undoubtedly true that the elections might eventually mean unification [of] Vietnam under Ho Chi Minh, this makes it all more important they should be only held as long after ceasefire agreement as possible and in conditions free from intimidation to give democratic elements best chance.[45]

From January 1955 onwards, Diem went on indicating his firm resistance to the scheduled election on the ground that there did not prevail in North Vietnam an ideal atmosphere for free voting. He emphasized time and again that since South Vietnam had not signed the Geneva accords, she was not bound by them. The US publicly extended her support to the Saigon stand. On 1 June 1956, Walter Robertson, Assistant Secretary of State for Far Eastern Affairs, stated, ". . . We support President Diem fully in his position that if elections are to be held, there must be conditions which preclude intimidation or coercion of the electorate. Unless such conditions exist, there can be no free choice.[46] In October Robertson repeated this argument. He asked, "Is it possible to obtain in North Vietnam the necessary conditions for a free expression of the national will through general elections?"[47] In the face of this, it is difficult to agree with the Pentagon Papers analyst who says that "the US did not connive with Diem to ignore the elections."[48] On the other hand, one may reasonably argue that the US and the Diem regime joined hands in their mutual interest to frustrate the scheduled elections of July 1956.

RISING TIDE OF INSURGENCY

On 3 August 1954 a National Intelligence Estimate (NIE) said that even with the firm US support, the situation in South Vietnam was very likely to continue to deteriorate over the next year.[49] An NIE, dated 26 April 1955, was similarly critical of

---

[45] Sheehan, n. 27, p. 23.
[46] *DOD Documents*, n. 4, Book 2, IV.A.5, p. 6.
[47] *Department of State Bulletin* (Washington, D.C.), 31 October 1955, p. 693.
[48] For a contrary view, one may refer to Russell H. Fifield, *Americans in Southeast Asia: The Roots of Commitment* (New York, 1973), p. 262.
[49] *DOD Documents*, n. 4, Book 2, IV.A.5, p. 32.

the Diem regime for its inability to provide efficient government and to eliminate corruption. In July 1956 an NIE said: "Over a longer period, an accumulation of grievances among various groups and individuals may lead to development of a national opposition movement. . . ."[50] Thus, according to American intelligence sources, the potential for an insurgency already existed in South Vietnam by the middle of 1956 when Saigon did not cooperate with Hanoi for holding a general election in the whole of Vietnam. The negative attitude of Saigon towards holding the scheduled elections seems to have acted as the catalyst for dissident elements in South Vietnam to start the insurgency. The Pentagon Papers analyst divides the insurgency period into three phases: (i) from 1954 to 1956; (ii) from 1956 to 1958; and (iii) 1959 and thereafter.[51] In the first phase, the "stay-behind cadres" who were very critical of the Diem regime, prepared for the scheduled election. They were confident of winning the election if it were then held. Therefore they did not want to take any military risk which might upset the diplomatic applecart of Geneva, thereby denying them an opportunity for proving their greater political support in an election. However, this is not to suggest that there was no infiltration at all from the North to the South. In fact, as American intelligence reports indicated, infiltration from North Vietnam actually started in 1955.[52] But its level was low as not to damage the prospect of holding the scheduled election. The rejection of the election by Saigon provoked these elements to indulge in sporadic agitations against Diem in the second phase. In December 1959, the National Liberation Front (NLF) was formally constituted and Hanoi directly took over charge of directing the insurgency in the South. Thereafter, North Vietnamese began to infiltrate in large numbers into South Vietnam. But by this time the US had already been involved in Vietnam on the side of Saigon. According recognition to Saigon, sending economic and military aid to her, and giving military training to South Vietnamese had long preceded the active North Vietnamese association with the insurgency in South Vietnam.

[50] Gravel, n. 9, p. 266.
[51] Ibid., p. 79.
[52] Ibid., p. 79.

THE IMPACT OF THE SINO-SOVIET
RIFT ON AMERICAN ATTITUDE TOWARDS VIETNAM

The Sino-Soviet rift which began around the period 1956-1957
opened up new inducements and opportunities for the United
States to take a fresh look at her policy in Southeast Asia.[53] The
territorial, ideological and personal elements that contributed to
the rift between the Soviet and Chinese leaderships have been
dealt with by several scholars and do not call for any discussion
in the present context. When in June 1959 it became known that
the Soviet Union was unwilling to share nuclear weapon technology with the Chinese, and that the Chinese were extremely unhappy about the Soviet attitude, American policy-makers were
probably led to conclude that the rift between the two Communist
giants was likely to become more serious. In view of the seemingly greater intransigence of the Chinese attitude, and also in view
of the approaches that the Soviet Union, in her own interest,
had begun to make, the United States began to demonstrate a certain willingness to be responsive to the Soviet approaches. An
accommodation with the Soviet Union, the nuclear adversary,
was also deemed important by American planners in order to
mitigate the threat of nuclear war with its incalculable consequences. Khrushchev's visit to the United States in September 1959
led to considerable talk in both countries of the "spirit of Camp
David."[54] By the end of the year, agreement was reached on holding a summit conference of Big Four—the US, the USSR, the
UK and France—in the second week of May 1960. Even though
the U-2 incident marred the summit meeting, the trend towards
detente continued accompanied by increasingly sharp attacks on
the Soviet Union by China over a number of issues.

Against this backdrop of gradually intensifying strain between
Moscow and Peking, the continued inclination of the former to
lay stress on "peaceful co-existence" and "reduction of tensions"
might have made Washington believe that the Soviet Union was

[53] Donald S. Zagoria, *The Sino-Soviet Conflict, 1956-1961* (Princeton, N.J.,
1962); William E. Griffith, *The Sino-Soviet Rift* (Cambridge, Mass.,
1964); and Walter Laqueur and Leopold Labedz, eds., *Polycentrism;
The New Factor in International Communism* (New York, 1962).
[54] *American Foreign Policy: Basic Documents, 1959* (Washington, D.C.,
1963), p. 931.

not likely to start a serious military crisis in Europe necessitating an American response nor was she likely to risk getting involved directly against the United States on behalf of a distant "client state." The assessment was that the Soviet Union might fear that any such confrontation with the US would only weaken the former in her developing conflict with the China. By the same token, the Chinese also might be unwilling to risk unilateral confrontation with the United States over an external area despite their rhetoric on "armed struggle." The prospect of joint Sino-Soviet action to counter American probing in some soft-spot or the other appeared less likely than ever before to American planners. Cuba and Vietnam appeared to be possible prospects to US planners as the Eisenhower Administration began to draw to a close. The Eisenhower Administration made ready a plan for a possible attack on Cuba by Cuban refugees trained by the United States. The training programme for the refugees was initiated. The Administration decided to launch an "Operations Plan for Vietnam" which was approved by the Operations Coordinating Board of the NSC on 7 January 1959. The plan provided for preparation of contingency plans by the US Army, Navy, and Air Force and their execution "in accordance with U.S. policy" in the event of an actual or imminent Communist attempt to take control of South Vietnam from within. The plan also envisaged a whole range of American operations to prop up the South Vietnamese regime and to defeat the Viet Cong and its helpers. In accordance with the order of the Secretary of Defence, the plan was launched on 26 May 19⁵9.[55] It seems that the implementation of this plan by the US provoked the Viet Cong to intensify their offensives in South Vietnam. It is possible, as Venkataramani has argued, that those were just the kind of developments that the "Operations Plan" was meant to evoke—thereby enabling the United States to proceed to the next stage of escalation.[56]

---

[55] The Acting Assistant Secretary of Defense, International Security Affairs, Robert H. Knight, to the Secretaries of the Army, the Navy, and the Air Force, the Chairman of the JCS, and the Assistant Secretary of Defense (Comptroller), "OCB Operations Plan for Vietnam (U)," 20 May 1959, *DOD Documents* n. 4, vol. 10, pp. 1185-9.

[56] M.S. Venkataramani, "The United States and Thailand: The Anatomy of Super Power Policy-Making, 1948-1963," *International Studies* (New Delhi), vol. 12, no. 1, January-March 1973, p. 84.

The thrust of policy during the latter half of the Ei
Administration was in the direction of intervention but
practice a rather low-level involvement was the course
even though plans were ready for significant escalation as ...en-
hower handed over the reins of office to his youthful successor,
John F. Kennedy. The fateful decisions were to be made by
Kennedy and his band of New Frontiermen. In the present work
the role of the Pentagon, i.e. the Department of Defence consisting of civilian and military components, in policy-making on
Vietnam during the period 1961-1968 will be examined.

THE PENTAGON

Since 1941 the Pentagon has had the largest civilian bureaucracy of any federal agency in the United States. Ever since the
establishment of the Republic, the doctrine of civilian control of
the military establishment and of the pre-eminence of the political
authority, the President, acting in exercise of his constitutional
powers, had never faced any serious challenge. But so vast had
been the growth of the far-flung American military establishment
since the end of the Second World War, so massive the expenditure on research development and production of a succession of
high-technology weapons, and so complex the task of holding on
to an "alert" posture to respond to "threats" globally, that some
commentators wondered whether the Pentagon had tended to
become a state within a state, "acting on the basis of its own
imperatives," and tending to take the political branches of the
government increasingly for granted. Eisenhower himself highlighted the issue when in his farewell speech he cautioned against
the danger to democracy that might arise out of the "military-
industrial complex." With the escalation of American involvement in Vietnam commentators of the type referred to tended to
view with growing alarm the role of the "Pentagon" as the most
decisive element determining US foreign policy. Whether such
indeed was the case calls for deeper examination.

The Pentagon, like any other agency, is not a monolith. The
civilian and military components do not necessarily and always
see eye to eye with each other on all issues. There may occur
differences within the civilian and military elements themselves.
As an agency, it has to reckon with the rivalry of other agencies
of the government. It has to compete with them for the "ear" of

the President. It has to run the gauntlet of Congress. It has to reckon with important interest groups, the media, and the state of public opinion. It can attempt these tasks with relatively less complications if it is able to present a more or less unified and harmonious front. By the same token, if there is internal disharmony within the Pentagon, the game assumes a very different character.

Brief references has been made to the flurry at the time of Dien Bien Phu when there were internal differences within the Pentagon itself. It was also shown that a rival agency, the State Department, under John Foster Dulles, generally succeeded in playing a more dominant role than the Defence Department in shaping US policy in Indochina. It also showed the President making the ultimate decision according to his own light, after weighing various aspects of the situation. The President was Dwight Eisenhower, the immensely popular military hero, the triumphant victor over the Axis forces in Western Europe, and a world-renowed figure. His successor, to whom he bequeathed his contingency plans for Indochina, could not claim similar credentials. The new President spoke stridently of his country's mission as leader of the "free world." To implement his course at home and abroad including Vietnam, he had to operate through the complex machinery of government of which the Pentagon was an important part. Kennedy did not wait long before turning his attention to the issue of American policy in Vietnam.

CHAPTER THREE

CIVILIAN-MILITARY INTERACTION IN THE PENTAGON—I

When the popular President and old war-hero, Dwight D. Eisenhower, handed over the reins of the presidency to a former lieutenant JG of the US Navy, the Senator from Massachusetts, John F. Kennedy, the nation was at peace. In the locked safes of the Pentagon were contingency plans for dealing with situations that might call for US military action in various parts of the world including Southeast Asia. With the outgoing President also departed the civilian Secretary of Defence, Thomas S. Gates, who was in the past a partner of Drexel and Company, and who had earlier served during both Eisenhower Administrations in different capacities including that of the Deputy Secretary of Defence in the Pentagon. The Secretary, a Presidential appointee, left the office along with the man who had appointed him. But the military component of the Pentagon with the Joint Chiefs of Staff at its apex stayed on. These men, veterans of many battles, and with their names widely known to the American public, were General Lyman L. Lemnitzer, Chairman of the Joint Chiefs of Staff, General George H. Decker of the Army, General Thomas D. White of the Air Force, Admiral Arleigh A. Burke, Chief of Naval Operations and General David M. Shoup, Commandant of the Marine Corps. The tradition of civilian control over the military was well-established in the United States. But the effectiveness with which the control would be exercised would depend upon the personality and capabilities of the Secretary, his equation with the President, his capacity to hold the loyalty of his civilian subordinates, his ability to bargain with extra-Pentagon federal actors, his skill in working with Congress, and, importantly, his dexterity in dealing with the Joint Chiefs of Staff. The man whom Kennedy picked to preside over the vast

American military establishment as Secretary of Defence was Robert S. McNamara, President of the Ford Company.

"MCNAMARA REVOLUTION"

Unlike his predecessors, McNamara was hardly known in Washington. But this "unknown man" was destined to create a lot of "stir" not only in the Pentagon, but also in the whole governmental machinery of the United States. It was not long before the Secretary of Defence, skilfully exercising the powers that were available to him under legislative enactments, succeeded in establishing his authority in so decisive a manner as to compel awe and admiration in the Washington Community. A man of enormous industry, McNamara possessed a sharp eye for detail and extraordinary analytical skill. He was ably served by a group of highly skilled civilian specialists whom he brought into the Department. They introduced or improved several tools of analysis that were regarded by the Secretary as useful in the decision-making process. McNamara never once wilted in the course of numerous appearances before Congressional Committees in the course of which he was subjected to intense questioning on numerous points relating to the huge establishment over which he presided. The coolness, dexterity, and assurances that he invariably displayed often drew admiration even from Senators who had reservations concerning the correctness of some of his views.

The Secretary's activities attracted attention and discussion and evoked praise as well as blame. By early 1963 Hanson Baldwin, the vateran military editor of the *New York Times*, was to talk of the "McNamara Monarchy."[1] Eight months after he came into office, the *Army, Navy, Air Force Journal* said that "the professional military leadership to the nation is being short-circuited in the current decision-making process at the Pentagon."[2] The *Washington Post* referred to this mode as "the closed door policy of the Defense Department."[3] Daniel

---

[1] Hanson Baldwin, "The McNamara Monarchy," *Saturday Evening Post* (New York), 9 March 1963, pp. 8, 11.

[2] Cited in Joseph Kraft, "McNamara and his Enemies," *Harper's Magazine* (New York), August 1961, p. 41.

[3] Ibid.

Bell spoke of the military leadership as the "dispossessed" and pointed to the increasingly important role of the so-called "technipols" (the military's decisive term for technicians and political theorists whom McNamara had brought into the Department of Defence).[4]

Mark Watson, a military commentator, spoke of "the Pentagon's trend toward constant further depreciation of the military as essential advisers—not on political issues, but on strictly military issues."[5] Jerry Greene, another military writer, depicted McNamara as a "civilian on horseback," who had mounted the horse from the offside while the Congress had been concerned with preventing the emergence of a General on Horseback.[6] In June 1963 General Thomas D. White who had in the meantime retired as the Air Chief, alleged that *in common with other military men* I am profoundly apprehensive of the pipe-smoking, trees-full-of-owls type of so-called defense intellectuals who have been brought into this nation's capital."[7]

The increase in the influence of the Secretary of Defence during the Kennedy Administration was largely due to the manner in which McNamara chose to respond to certain major issues. The Kennedy Administration, at the outset, had to tackle three problems. The "menace" of "missile gap" was very much in the air. This was one of the topics Kennedy had emphasized during his election campaign. President Eisenhower's warning against the "military-industrial complex" in his farewell speech was another problem that he had to face. The third was the relevance of the Dullesian concept of "massive retaliation." McNamara decided to face them head on. From the very beginning, he took upon the role of an "active" Secretary rather than that of a "passive one."[8] On another occasion, he said,

---

[4] Daniel Bell, "The Dispossessed—1962," *Columbia University Forum* (New York), vol. 5, Fall 1962, p. 6.

[5] Quoted in Jack Raymond, *Power at the Pentagon* (New York, 1964), p. 280.

[6] Jerry Greene, "Civilian on Horseback?," in Andrew M. Scott and Raymond H. Dawson, eds., *Readings in the Making of American Foreign Policy* (London, 1965), pp. 420-30.

[7] Thomas D. White, "Strategy and the Defense Intellectuals," *Saturday Evening Post*, vol. 236, 4 May 1963, pp. 10-2.

[8] Robert S. McNamara, "McNamara Defines His Job," *New York Times Magazine* 26 April 1964, p. 13.

"I see my position here as being that of a leader, not a judge. I'm here to originate and stimulate new ideas and programs, not just to referee arguments and harmonize interests. . . ."[9]

The civil-military equation seems to have been largely influenced by the change in strategic policy and the change in method to implement that policy. The "massive retaliation" doctrine had meant that top priority was to be accorded to the Air Force. The Kennedy Administration set before itself the task of maintaining a "balanced force structure" in line with its concept of "flexible response" to deal with threats of various levels.[10] McNamara chose the method of the planning-programming-budgeting system (PPBS) to help him in making decisions to implement the new policy. McNamara said that the method demanded a proper balancing of all the elements of the defence effort which could be done only at the Department of Defence level. He favoured "centralized planning" and "decentralized operation."[11] To "coordinate long-range military planning with short-range detailed budgeting," the Secretary required all the proposals of programmes and their costs to be projected over a period of five years.[12] Perhaps the most important technique the Secretary relied upon was that of the System Analysis or Operational Research. He emphasized that while considering the military effectiveness of any weapons system, its cost as well as the effectiveness of alternate systems must be considered. As Hitch said, "military effectiveness and cost are simply two sides of the same coin and must be considered jointly in the decision-making process."[13] Thus, according to this analysis, while taking decision, both the cost and comparative effectiveness of

[9] Quoted in Eugene M. Zuckert, "The Service Secretary: Has he a Useful Role?," *Foreign Affairs* (New York), vol. 44, April 1966, p. 464.

[10] US House of Representatives, Congress 88, session 1, Committee on Armed Services, *Hearings on Military Posture* (Washington, D.C., 1963), p. 373.

[11] Ibid., p. 501.

[12] US House of Representatives, Cong. 87, sess. 2, Committee on Armed Services, *Hearings on Military Posture* (Washington, D.C., 1962), p. 3161.

[13] Charles J. Hitch, The Planning-Programming-Budgeting System, 21 June 1963, quoted in W.W. Kaufman, *The McNamara Strategy* (New York, 1964), p. 180.

each alternative must be taken into account.

To centralize the intelligence flow to the Secretary of Defence and to mitigate if not overcome the problem created by rival motivations of the various intelligence groups, McNamara created the Defence Intelligence Agency (DIA). To aid him in the task of analysing in great detail, the various components of issues he brought into the Department a large number of highly competent specialists in Mathematics, Operations Research, and Systems Analysis. These men employed a variety of techniques involving the extensive use of computers.[14] They not only prepared long critiques of proposals emanating from the JCS, but were ready to initiate presentations of alternative approaches in an effort to focus attention on the concept of cost-effectiveness to which the Secretary attached great importance. The "Whiz Kids," as newspaper reporters called them, were a source of growing concern to the bemedalled senior military leaders who were not accustomed to have their judgement questioned by mere civilians in buttoned-down-shirts, just out of their Ivy League class-rooms. It came to surface when Lyman L. Lemnitzer, Chairman of the JCS, complained that military leaders were being ignored.[15] There was a growing concern among the members of the military that the bookish knowledge was being preferred over the large military experience in military matters. They feared, the systems analysis would lead to the substitution of "what is cheapest" for "what is best."[16] Worst of all, they charged that the Secretary of Defence was not

---

[14] In an estimate in August 1965, the *Journal of the Armed Forces* said, "Of the 27 top officials of the Defence Department—old and new—11 including Secretary McNamara, hold either graduate and/or undergraduate degrees from Harvard; six, including Deputy Secretary of Defense Cyrus Vance, hold graduate and/or undergraduate degrees from Yale; two Assistant Secretary of Defense (Public Affairs), Arthur Sylvester, and Under Secretary of Navy Robert Baldwin, are graduates of Princeton . . ." *Journal of the Armed Forces* (Washington, D.C.), 14 August 1965, pp. 1, 21.

[15] *New York Times*, 16 March 1962.

[16] Hanson Baldwin, Slow-Down in the Pentagon," *Foreign Affairs* (New York), vol. 43, January 1965, pp. 262-80; and Commander Ralph M. Tucker, USN, "Cost-Effectiveness—Fact and Fancy," *United States Naval Institute Proceedings* (Annapolis, Maryland), September 1964, pp. 75-81.

"delegating authority" to the JCS—thereby creating mutual distrust.[17] They complained against the "danger of over-control and over-management." General Wheeler, the Chairman of the JCS, in an attacking mood, bluntly said, "The commander is responsible for military success or lack of it and the manager is responsible to provide maximum efficient support to the commander, not to try to manage him."[18]

McNamara, unlike his predecessors, maintained throughout his tenure a "social distance" between the military and himself. His relationship with the members of the JCS was marked by his studied reserve and detachment. He declined to spend much time in participating in the traditional rituals and ceremonies of the military.[19] He did not add to his popularity when he ordered that no member of the Pentagon should receive "any favour, gratuity, or entertainment" from anyone during business with the department.[20] His tendency to pay attention to detail was yet another irritant. The military complained that the Secretary tended to take decisions even on small matters, which should be decided at lower levels. A more serious charge was that he even tried to involve himself in respect of actual military operations. This happened during the missile crisis of 1962. Much to the resentment of Admiral George Anderson, the Chief of Naval Operations, McNamara insisted on staying in the Navy's Flag Plot, or operation centre and directing the action of American warships.[21] This incident seemed to exacerbate the anti-McNamara feeling of the JCS that had been building up since the first Cuban crisis of 1961 when the civilian leaders seemed to put some blame for the fiasco of the Bay of Pigs on the military.[22]

---

[17] For Lemnitzer's address, which was implicitly critical of McNamara, to the graduate class of the Command and General Staff in the fall of 1962, shortly before he was transferred to command the Allied forces in Europe, see Raymond, no. 5, pp. 283-4.

[18] *The Journal of the Armed Forces*, 25 September 1965, vol. 103, no. 4, pp. 6, 32.

[19] Colonel James A. Donovan, *Militarism, USA* (New York, 1970), p. 126.

[20] "Pentagon's New Standard of Conduct," *Journal of the Armed Forces*, 3 October 1964, p. 13.

[21] Raymond, n. 5, 286; and Elie Abel, *The Missile Crisis* (Philadelphia, 1966), p. 155.

[22] Raymond, n. 5, p. 284.

Perhaps the most important cause of their friction was what the military considered as the civilian "invasion" of their long-held domain—that is, the development and procurement of weapons. Each service was infuriated by what it considered as the Secretary's bid to question and challenge the development of weapons system recommended by it and particularly when he went to the extent of ordering the cancellation of an entire project. The Air Force, for instance, was angered by McNamara's cancellation of further work on the Skybolt Missile Programme and Dyna-Soar Space Project.[23] The Navy resented his demand that the naval yards that were shown, on the basis of DOD studies to be uneconomic and inefficient, to be closed.[24] The Secretary's views on the reduced importance of the manned bomber leading to his decisions to phase out the B-52 and to cut down the appropriations for the development of the B-70 evoked indignation in the Air Force and opposition from friends of the Air Force in Congress.[25] The Army was angered when he resisted its pleas about the vital necessity of going ahead with the production of the Nike-Zeus ABM system.[26] In all these cases the Secretary defended his decisions on the basis of cost-effectiveness calculations. As he put it, his decisions were based on "rational, as opposed to emotional foundation of decisions."[27] He felt that B-52, B-70 manned bombers would be ineffective in view of missile developments. So he decided to gradually replace these bombers by more effective missiles. In the case of ABM, he argued for postponing the actual production, because, he felt, if the ongoing talk on disarmament with the Soviet Union would succeed, then ABM would be unnecessary. But all his "rational" arguments failed to convince the military and increased its apprehensions.

[23] For Skybolt crisis, see Henry Brandon, "Skybolt," in Morton H. Halperin, ed., *Readings in American Foreign Policy: A Bureaucratic Perspective* (Boston, 1973), pp. 262-75.
[24] Julius Duscha, *Arms, Money and Politics* (New York, 1965), pp. 96-7.
[25] Kaufman, n. 13, pp. 205-28.
[26] Ibid., pp. 229-32; Donovan, n. 19, pp. 135-8; and Robert L. Rothstein, "The ABM, Proliferation and International Stability," in Burton M. Sapin, ed., *Contemporary American Foreign and Military Policy* (Glenview, Ill., 1970), pp. 140-9.
[27] Cited in Duscha, n. 24, p. 100.

The typical example of the civil-military "confrontation" in the post-war history was the TFX airplane contract.[28] Instead of having two different fighters as sought by the Air Force and Navy, McNamara opted for a "common" fighter plane which would meet the manoeuvrability and range specifications of both of them and achieve substantial economy. Against the unanimous recommendation of the military to award contract to Boeing, the Secretary, supported by his civilian colleagues in the Pentagon, opted for General Dynamics. The Senate Permanent Investigation Subcommittee headed by Sen. John L. McClellan (Dem. Arkansas) held a year-long intensive hearings in 1963. It has been alleged that Admiral Anderson was not given another extension because of his testimony against McNamara in TFX hearings. The stage seemed to be set for more intense civil-military confrontation in other areas of the defence and foreign policy during the rest of McNamara's stay as the head of the Pentagon.

It is important to point out that except the TFX case, there was hardly any unanimity till 1964 among the JCS in their opposition to Secretary McNamara in relation to weapons policies.[29] During fiscal 1963, the Army and Navy did not support the Air Force in its demand for the B-70. Similarly, the Army and Air Force disagreed with the Navy in its claim for eighteen attack carriers. They felt that fifteen attack carriers would be enough. The Air Force did not support the Army in urging the immediate production of ABM.[30] During the fiscal 1964, similar lack of unanimity among the JCS persisted regarding weapons policies. General Maxwell D. Taylor, the JCS Chairman, did not support the Air Force's Rs-70 bomber and Skybolt programmes. Similarly General Curtis

---

[28] For a detailed and critical account of the TFX controversy, see Robert J. Art, *The TFX Decision: McNamara and the Military* (Boston, 1968); and Vincent Davis, "The Development of a Capability to Deliver Nuclear Weapons by Carrier-Based Aircraft," in Halperin, n. 23, pp. 262-75.

[29] The following discussion of civil-military interaction on weapons policy during the McNamara period has been mainly based on Lawrence Joseph Korb, *The Role of the Joint Chiefs of Staff in the Defence Budget Process from 1961 to 1967* (Ph.D. thesis, State University of New York at Albany, 1969).

[30] Ibid., pp. 1-2.

LeMay, the Chief of Staff of the Air Force, did not extend his support for Army's Nike-Zeus and Navy's SSN's (Nuclear Attack Submarines).[31] A similar pattern was repeated in the fiscal 1965. The JCS again failed to reach unanimity regarding most of the weapons programmes. Both General LeMay and Admiral David J. McDonald who had replaced Anderson as the Naval Chief, were alone in their requests for Rs-70, and a new carrier and six SSN's respectively. Neither of them supported Gen. Taylor in his demand for the full scale development of Nike-Zeus.[32] There was a marked change in the attitudes of the JCS towards weapons programmes *vis-a-vis* the Defence Secretary in the fiscal 1966 which will be discussed later. This might have been partly responsible for having given Secretary McNamara a clear edge over his military colleagues regarding the defence policy. He could claim that he had not overruled any unanimous opinion of the JCS regarding weapons.

McNamara irked the JCS by issuing a directive informing military witnesses before Congressional Committees that they were not to disclose their disagreements with him, unless pressed by Congress, and in those cases, they were also to give his side of the case. Secondly, the statements of the JCS to be presented to Congressional Committees in closed sessions, were required to be reviewed in advance by the Office of the Secretary of Defence (OSD). It was also provided that a member of the Secretary's staff would be present in these sessions. This directive was another addition to the row of charges that the Secretary was "downgrading" and "muzzling" the military.

In spite of this rider, Gen. LeMay in 1962 carried his battle with the Secretary over B-70 and B-52 to Congress. He attacked the new strategy of flexible response which apparently underplayed the strategic importance of the Air Force.[33] The next year, LeMay repeated his Congressional performance of hitting the Secretary not only regarding B-52 and B-70, but also with regard to the cancellation of the Skybolt programme.[34]

[31] Ibid., p. 6.
[32] Ibid., pp. 11-2.
[33] US Senate, Cong. 87, sess. 2, Defence Subcommittee of the Committee on Appropriations, Hearings, *Department of Defence Appropriations for 1963* (Washington, D.C., 1962), pp. 185-90.
[34] US Senate, Cong. 88, sess. 1, Defence Subcommittee of the Committee

Adm. Anderson charged that McNamara was intervening too much in the details of military matters.[35] During the fiscal 1965, the last year of his service, Gen. LeMay spoke out strongly on McNamara's bombers vs. missile policy. He warned Congress against the Administration's preference for missiles at the cost of bombers: "You have two choices: you push the button and you are at war, or you hold your finger off the button and you are at peace."[36] In spite of these strong criticisms by top military members, McNamara carried the day till 1964. The President always sided with the Secretary *vis-a-vis* the JCS, much to the chagrin of the latter.

THE DESPATCH OF COMBAT TROOPS

A narration of the details of the Kennedy Administration's policy toward Vietnam does not fall within the scope of the present work. It will concern itself with the two most important events of the period—decision to increase the number of American military "advisers" in South Vietnam and the overthrow of the Diem regime. An attempt will be made to identify the pattern of civil-military interaction in foreign policy making— mainly the role of the Secretary of Defence and that of the JCS. Of course, at relevant points, the role of other important members of the military and the civilian group—may be, outside the Pentagon—that may bear on the inquiry will be dealt with.

The Bay of Pigs fiasco was the major setback that befell the Kennedy Administration very early in its tenure. The image of a vigorous and a decisive President that had been so laboriously built was seriously tarnished. Understandably the President and his entourage attached the highest importance to the speediest possible rehabilitation of his image and to shift the burden for a failure as much as possible to other shoulders. Several

on Appropriations, Hearings, *Department of Defence Appropriations for 1964* (Washington, D.C., 1963) pp. 349, 353.

[35] Cited in Raymond, n. 5, p. 286.

[36] US Senate, Cong. 88. sess. 2, Defence Subcommittee of the Committee on Appropriations, and the Committee on Armed Services, Joint Hearings, *Department of Defence Appropriation for 1965* (Washington, D.C., 1964), p. 741.

stories that came to be published, perhaps without any opposition from the White House, and possibly with some cooperation from elements in it, sought to convey the impression to the American people that the President failed to receive sound information and advice from the CIA and the JCS. The aftermath of the Bay of Pigs episode resulted in certain other individuals like the Under Secretary of State Chester Bowles falling from official favour because of the suspicion that they had sought to communicate to the public their earlier misgivings over the adventure. The Secretary of Defence was not particularly touched by these developments. Indeed, the fiasco probably contributed to improving his leverage *vis-a-vis* the JCS.

The President could not afford a setback in another critical spot where Communist forces were reportedly on the move. In Laos the Pathet Lao forces were advancing steadily towards Vientiane. There were clear signs of troubles against Diem in South Vietnam. The Kennedy Administration sought, to use Rostow's phrase, to "gear up" to avoid another Bay of Pigs in Southeast Asia.

The President wanted a high level appraisal of the situation in South Vietnam. It is noteworthy that in setting up a task force for this purpose, he designated as its head Deputy Secretary of Defence, Roswell Gilpatric. The move is of some significance in indicating the trend of the President's thinking. It was not to the State Department or to the military to which he turned for assigning the responsibility but to the deputy of McNamara. The central issue that the President wanted the task force to clarify for him appeared to be the "possible commitment" of the US troops in South Vietnam. This can be inferred from the fact that Gilpatric, in his letter to the JCS on 8 May 1961, specifically asked their views on that issue.[37] The Deputy Secretary did not seek to spell out what exactly the US objectives in Southeast Asia were. The JCS, at least in Gilpatric communication, were not informed of any "political decision" having already been made. The JCS' reply, sent on 10

[37] US House Committee on Armed Services, *United States-Vietnam Relations 1945-1967: Study Prepared by the Department of Defence* Committee Print (Washington, D.C., 1971), Book 2, IV.B.1, p. 41. (Hereafter this major source will be referred to as *DOD Documents*.)

May, indirectly indicated no responsibility for any political decision that might be made. They wrote: *"Assuming that the political decision is to hold South East Asia outside the Communist sphere,* the Joint Chiefs of Staff are of the opinion that US forces should be deployed *immediately* to South Vietnam." In their view, such deployment would serve several important purposes: indicating the firmness of US intent to all Asian nations, training the South Vietnamese forces, providing a nucleus for support of any additional US or SEATO military operation in Southeast Asia, providing a visible deterrent to potential North Vietnam and/or Chinese action and preventing a Laos-type situation in South Vietnam.[38]

It may be relevant to point out that all the military actors were unanimous on the question of the commitment of US troops in South Vietnam. The most active of them in pursuing the proposal of sending American combat troops to South Vietnam was Brig. General Edward Lansdale. Assistant to the Secretary of Defence for Special Operations, Lansdale was not an unknown name in the world of American counter-insurgency policy. He had earned a name for his performance in suppressing Huk insurgents in the Philippines. He had reportedly played a key role in installing Diem in power in Saigon in 1955-56. He had developed good rapport with the leading figures in the South Vietnamese government. These had probably lead to his coming to the notice of Kennedy's talent scouts. The new Administration, just after it came to office, decided to send Lansdale to South Vietnam for an appraisal of the latest developments in Vietnam. In his memorandum for the Secretary of Defence, dated 17 January 1961, Lansdale urged that Vietnam should be treated as a "combat area of the Cold War." He asserted that Diem was the best available South Vietnamese leader to take up the challenge of dealing with the Communists. He further said, "We must support Ngo Dinh Diem until another strong executive can replace him legally... We have to show him by deeds, not words

---

[38] Ibid., pp. 42-3; see also Mike Gravel, ed., *The Pentagon Papers: The Defence Department History of United States Decision-Making on Vietnam* (Boston, 1971), vol. 2, pp. 48-9.

alone, that we are his friend."[39] Apparently Lansdale's stand
as an "expert" on Vietnam was sufficiently high as to result in
high level attention being paid to his views. It seems that his
memorandum set the ball rolling and soon the President set up
a Task Force on Vietnam. He seems to have had contacts with
other like-minded advisers who probably made a concerted
effort to reach the President's ear. Walt Rostow of the White
House, in his memorandum to the President dated 12 April 1961,
recommended the appointment of a "full time first-rate back-
stop man in Washington."[40] He apparently had Lansdale in
mind to deal with Vietnam. In a memorandum to the Deputy
Secretary of Defence, dated 25 April 1961, Lansdale reiterated
his preference for Diem as the "man of the hour" in Vietnam.
He declared: "Here is our toughest ally. . . a 60-year old
bachelor who gave up romance with his childhood sweetheart. . .
to devote his life to his country."[41]

President Kennedy's decision on 29 April 1961 not to send
immediately US combat troops to South Vietnam might have
been a temporary setback for the military elements in the
Pentagon who were advocating the same. They were perhaps
further disappointed by Diem's refusal, in the course of his talk
with the visiting American Vice President Lyndon Johnson on 12
May, to admit US troops into South Vietnam for the purpose of
fighting the "Communists."[42] These disappointments, however,
could not make the Washington proponents of sending troops
to South Vietnam change their views. On the other hand, they
tried to "sell" their viewpoints with more vigour and energy. In
a memorandum to Deputy Secretary Gilpatric on 18 May 1961,
Lansdale reported that the South Vietnamese President would
accept the deployment of American combat troops in his country
as trainers of South Vietnamese troops, though not fighters
against Communists.[43] It is noteworthy that on the same day—
18 May—strong support for the proposal of sending American
combat troops to South Vietnam came from other quarters of
the Pentagon. The JCS repeated their earlier recommendation

[39] *DOD Documents*, Book II,, V.B.4, pp. 1-11.
[40] Ibid., Book 2, n. 37, p. 23.
[41] Ibid., Book II, n. 39, p. 41.
[42] Ibid., p. 157.
[43] Ibid.

of 10 May. General McGarr, the Chief of MAAG (Military Assistance Advisory Group) in Saigon, recommended that the US should send 16,000 combat troops; if that was not acceptable to Diem, then a 10,000 contingent may be sent there as "trainers."[44] He seems to have partially succeeded in prevailing upon President Diem to accept his proposal.[45] Apparently under his persuasion Diem agreed to send Nguyen Dinh Thuan, "Secretary of Security, Defence, Interior, etc." to Washington to finalize an agreement to this effect.

By the end of September 1961, the situation deteriorated both in Laos and South Vietnam. Communist forces in both these countries were on the offensive. Decision-makers in Washington, in their concern to stem the military progress of the Communists thought over different strategies, There were mainly two proposals under consideration. One was the JCS-favoured plan to intervene on the ground in Laos and to seize and hold major portions of the country, principally to protect the borders of South Vietnam and Thailand. The other was the "Rostow proposal" which advocated deploying a SEATO force of about 25,000 men into South Vietnam to guard the Vietnam Laos border between the demilitarized zone (DMZ) and Cambodia.[46] The JCS, on being asked on 5 October to comment on the Rostow Plan, rejected it and argued for concentrating on Laos which could save all or substantially all of Laos and, at the same time, protect Thailand and the borders of South Vietnam.[47] In view of the ongoing diplomatic efforts on Laos, the JCS went on to say that if the Laos Plan was "politically unacceptable at this time," they would favour "a possible limited interim course of action" in South Vietnam. This plan provided for the deployment of about 20,000 troops to the central highlands near Pleiku to assist South Vietnamese and free certain South Vietnamese forces for offensive action against the Viet Cong.[48]

Apart from the Rostow Plan and the JCS plan, the NSC which met on 11 October 1961 considered also two other papers prepared by Alexis Johnson, the Deputy Under Secretary of

[44] Ibid., Book 2, n. 37, p. 65.
[45] Ibid., pp. 66-7.
[46] Ibid., p. 76.
[47] Ibid., Book II, n. 39, p. 295.
[48] Ibid., Book II, p. 299.

State and William P. Bundy, the acting Assistant Secretary of Defence. Johnson's paper called "Concept of Intervention in Vietnam" was a mix of the Rostow Plan and the JCS plan. It combined the former's border force and the latter's "possible limited interim course of action."[49] More important from the point of view of the present study was Bundy's memorandum. He stated that there was a seventy per cent chance that immediate American military intervention in South Vietnam would succeed in doing the job for Diem—defeating the Communists. However, he added that there was thirty per cent risk that the US would face disaster like France in 1954. "On a 70-30 basis, I would myself favour going in. But if we let, say, a month go by before we move, the odds will slide. . . down to 60-40, 50-50 and so on. . ."[50] he asserted.

It is difficult to say, on the basis of available documents, where McNamara and his deputy, Gilpatric, stood on this question. It is clear that the military actors and the middle level of civilian leadership in the Pentagon were almost one in advocating the American military involvement, in one way or the other, in South Vietnam. The NSC deferred taking a decision to deploy American combat troops to South Vietnam. It decided that a Presidential mission, consisting of General Maxwell Taylor, Rostow, Sterling J. Cotterell from the State Department and General Lansdale representing the JCS should visit South Vietnam to look into the question of the advisability of military intervention in that country, and to consider the proposal of increasing the US assistance and training of South Vietnam units and supplying more US equipment to her.[51]

Gen. Taylor, considered as one of the few "soldier-scholars" in American history, was appointed by President Kennedy as the latter's military adviser in the beginning of the Administration. He was the Army Chief under President Eisenhower and was at the centre of the controversy around the so-called "New Look" which allegedly imparted pre-eminence to the Air Force at the cost of the Army. After his resignation in protest against the defence policy, he engaged himself in writing a book, *The*

---

[49] Ibid., Book 2, n. 39, pp. 78-83.
[50] Ibid., Book II, n. 39, p. 312.
[51] Ibid., p. 328.

Uncertain Trumpet, which attacked the ' massive retaliation" policy and advocated a policy of "flexible response."[52] Gen. Taylor's views formed an integral part of the defence policy adopted by the Kennedy Administration. Against this background, Taylor's return to serve as head of a Presidential mission was of special significance. Because of his reputed expertise in defence matters, his views on Vietnam were expected to carry much weight with Kennedy. The Taylor Mission, therefore, gave rise to a lot of speculations about the American policy in Vietnam.

On his way to Saigon, Gen. Taylor met Admiral Harry D. Felt, the Commander in Chief, Pacific (CINCPAC) in Honolulu. Although the Admiral did not at that time express his views on the question of sending American combat troops to South Vietnam, he wrote a memorandum on it after a few days to Washington. After stating both the pros and cons, he recommended against such deployment at the time until all other means of helping Diem had been exhausted.[53] The CINCPAC's position was thus at variance with that of the JCS.

It was Gen. Taylor, not Diem, who broached the issue of the deployment of American combat troops in South Vietnam.[54] This suggests that the General had either been specifically asked by Washington to take up this issue with President Diem or, that he did it on his own initiative because of his support for the contemplated decision or both. While Diem took an evasive stand on this question, fluctuating in his position from time to time, the American actors, both military and civilian, who took part in meeting with Vietnamese, seemed to be very much concerned about securing an "invitation" from Saigon for sending American combat troops there. It is important to note that while the Americans and South Vietnamese were still continuing their talks, Gen. McGarr, the Chief of MAAG, sent a cable to Washington on 23 October in which he suggested that US forces could be deployed in the Mekong delta on a "flood relief mission." They could be subsequently retained, if necessary, he added.[55]

[52] Maxwell D. Taylor, *The Uncertain Trumpet* (London, 1960).
[53] *DOD Documents*, Book 2, n. 37, pp. 88-90.
[54] Ibid., p. 90.
[55] Ibid., p. 91.

After his return to Washington General Taylor made several recommendations the most important of which was that the US should offer to introduce into South Vietnam a "military Task Force." It could conduct, Taylor said, logistical operations in support of military and "flood relief" operations, conduct combat operations in self-defence, provide an emergency reserve for the South Vietnamese armed forces, and act as an advance party of additional US forces which might be deployed in South Vietnam in future.[56] He also recommended that the MAAG be reorganized and increased in size. The General was aware that American military intervention in South Vietnam, once initiated, involved the risk of escalation. But he believed that any large-scale intervention by North Vietnam and China would be countered by the threats of American bombing. His recommendation for dispatching a Task Force was, of course, not accepted, but the very fact that such a senior adviser to the President categorically recommended in favour of sending American combat troops to South Vietnam, might have set the ball rolling for the subsequent decision in this direction.

The fact that McNamara did not apparently take any active initiatives in relation to Vietnam need not imply that he was not concerned about it. In fact, as early as April 1961, he seems to have made up his mind in regard to Vietnam. At a high-level meeting held in the State Department on 29 April, Robert Kennedy, the Attorney General, posed the question: what should be the place where the United States should stand and fight in Southeast Asia—"where to draw the line." McNamara replied, "We would take a stand in Thailand and South Vietnam." The situation was worsening by the hour and the US should commit herself "sooner rather than later," the Defence Secretary declared.[57] This clearly indicates the direction in which his mind was working. His relative silence on Vietnam till November might have been due to this pre-occupation with the reorganization of his Department, the psychological constraints upon making a new military move in the face of the Bay of Pigs disaster, and his bureaucratic cautiousness in waiting for

[56] "Top Secret: Eyes Only for the President from General Taylor," 1 November 1961, *DOD Documents,* Book II, n. 39, pp. 337-42.
[57] Ibid., p. 63.

moves by competitors to which he could adjust his bargaining tactics.

On 8 November 1961, McNamara sent a memorandum to the President on behalf of himself, Gilpatric and the JCS. They stated that they believed that the fall of South Vietnam to Communism would lead to Communist victory in the rest of the mainland of Southeast Asia and Indochina.[58] However, they were not even at this time forthright in their recommendation that the US commit herself to the objective of preventing the fall of South Vietnam to Communism by "necessary military actions." They simply said that they were "inclined" to recommend that the US should accept the above objective. They asserted that if such a commitment was agreed upon, they would support the recommendations of General Taylor as the first steps toward its fulfilment.[59]

The 8 November memorandum, in one sense, went beyond the earlier position of the JCS on Vietnam; in another sense, it was a little short of it. The JCS had not earlier themselves defined the American objective in Vietnam. They had apparently chosen to leave it to the State Department to take the lead in this direction. They departed from this position in their 8 November memorandum. Now they, along with McNamara and Gilpatric, expressed their inclination to adopt the political objective of preventing South Vietnam from "falling to Communists." On the other hand, they came down a little bit in their recommendation regarding the sending of troops to South Vietnam. They had earlier urged that US forces be deployed immediately in South Vietnam. The 8 November recommendation was for sending a mix of combat and support forces in the name of "flood relief personnel." It may, however, be pointed out that the change of language hardly made any difference in substance. "Flood relief personnel" were in fact the "functional equivalent" of combat troops. The choice of this language might have been made with a view to averting sharp public reaction by providing the public with less than the truth. Although McNamara was not very explicit on 29 April in

---

[58] "Secretary of Defence Memorandum for the President, 8 November 1961," ibid., p. 343.
[59] Ibid., p. 344

advocating that the US should immediately commit herself to "save" South Vietnam from the Communists, he implicitly said so. The memorandum of 8 November also did not contain a categorical recommendation to that effect. This might have been due to two factors, independently or in combination. It was perhaps considered prudent by the Secretary not to go all the way with his military colleagues at this preliminary stage itself and to introduce an element of tentativeness, thereby inducing the military to put forth stronger arguments in support of their position and, in consequence, being constrained to assume a greater share of responsibility for the decision. Moreover, McNamara might have adopted this posture in anticipation of bargaining with his bureaucratic rival, Secretary of State Rusk, who was known to support the commitment of American forces to the defence of South Vietnam.[60]

On 11 November 1961, Rusk and McNamara addressed a joint memorandum to the President.[61] It was slightly different from the memorandum of 8 November. Most of the recommendations contained in the Rusk-McNamara memorandum were accepted by the President after only three day of its submission.[62]

Inferences

The preceding discussion shows that the JCS were willing to support the deployment of American troops in South Vietnam, in the event that a political decision to that effect were taken by the President. They did not raise any objections on military grounds, though initially they were inclined to favour deployment in Laos rather than in South Vietnam. In the beginning the JCS tended to take the view that the "threat" was greater in Laos than in South Vietnam. If, however, the political decision was to send troops first to South Vietnam, they indicated their

[60] This aspect is dealt in Chapter IV.
[61] State/Defence memorandum to the President, 11 November 1961, *DOD Documents*, Book 11, n. 39, pp. 359-67.
[62] The possible reasons for the difference between the memoranda of 8 November and 11 November, and the possible motivations of President Kennedy in taking the 14 November decision to send American millitary "advisers" will be discussed in Chapter IV.

willingness to go along with it.

Some members of the JCS had, of course, individually given expression to their views at the 21 April meeting concerning the desirability of early action in South Vietnam or elsewhere and were ready to endorse the acceptance of a possible widening of the area and scope of the conflict. But there is no evidence that there was any JCS document advocating such a position.

The fact that it was General Maxwell Taylor who recommended the US deploy a contingent of combat troops in the Mekong delta under the cover of flood relief operations probably had some impact on the JCS. Taylor was known to have very good rapport with the President. The possibility of Gen. Taylor's appointment to some high position might have been known at that time to some segments of the Washington community including the military. (Taylor was shortly thereafter appointed as the Chairman of the JCS.) It is possible that the likelihood of his appointment influenced the JCS in categorically committing themselves, along with the Defence Secretary, in their memorandum of 8 November, to the idea of sending US troops to South Vietnam.

Throughout this period McNamara was very circumspect in his position on sending combat troops to South Vietnam. He would hardly let others know where exactly he stood on this question. He seems to have been watching others in the middle of the stage from the wings. He was more of a listener than a pace-setter in relation to the decision to send US combat troops to South Vietnam.

The most enthusiastic of the Pentagon actors—both civil and military—was General Lansdale. An old hand in counter-insurgency operations and an old friend of President Diem, he tried his best to impress upon the President and his key decision-makers the desirability of not only sending US troops to South Vietnam, but also betting on Diem. He was supported in this direction by Gen. McGarr, the MAAG Chief, Saigon. The solitary voice among the military who opposed deploying immediately US combat troops in South Vietnam was Adm. Felt, the CINCPAC—the person who would have overall military responsibility for the operations that might ensue.

THE OVERTHROW OF DIEM

One of the important elements of the Rusk-McNamara memorandum of 11 November 1961 was that Diem should be asked to undertake reforms before the US committed her troops to South Vietnam. On 13 November President Kennedy took some decisions on Vietnam a summary of which was sent to Ambassador Nolting in Saigon. One of the decisions required "concrete demonstration by Diem that he is now prepared to work in an orderly way [with] his subordinates and broaden the political base of his regime."[63] Washington, however, had to soften her tough posture towards Saigon after a lapse of a few days. The US demand for reforms was cold-shouldered by Diem. His anger over Washington's demand was enough to force the latter to change her stance and underplay the concern for reforms in Saigon. Washington thought that it needed Diem. For a quite some time thereafter the US did not reopen the issue of reforms with Diem. In May 1963, when the situation in South Vietnam appeared to be unsatisfactory, Washington began to reconsider whether its interests would be advanced or hindered by Diem's continuance as the Chief of state.

One of the issues that figures in inter-agency and intra-agency disputes relating to the implementation of foreign policy concerns the suitability or otherwise, from the point of view of American objectives, of the local leader at the helm. When the situation in the country concerned does not appear to move along as favourably as had been expected, different views begin to be expressed on whether American efforts should be directed toward enabling the incumbent to remain in power or toward expediting his exit. The previous services that he might have rendered or his potential for future usefulness tend to be interpreted differently by different interests depending upon whether they want him to be in or out. Thus while in public pronouncements American spokesmen spoke in fervent support of Diem, a debate over his "usefulness" began to gather momentum in the inner councils of the Kennedy Administration by the middle of 1963. An important

[63] *DOD Documents*, Book 11, n. 39, p. 403.

segment of the State Department appears by that time to have developed serious reservations concerning Diem's leadership and to have begun to advocate a change in Saigon. The interaction between the State and Defence Departments in this regard will be dealt with in Chapter IV. The present discussion seeks to examine whether there were any differences between the civilian and military elements of the Defence Department regarding the continuance or ouster of Diem.

The internal debate on the issue was triggered by repressive action taken by the Diem regime to deal with the growing manifestations of disaffection in the country, especially among the Buddhists. The repressive measures and more particularly the self-immolations of a number of Buddhist monks attracted considerable adverse notice in public opinion in the United States. Reports in American newspapers became increasingly critical of the authoritarian nature of the Diem regime and the dominant influence over the President of his brother, Ngo Dinh Nhu and Madam Nhu.[64] Intelligence reports also highlighted the increasing unpopularity of Diem and his relatives. It was in this context that the State Department brought to the fore the question whether the existing political leadership in South Vietnam could promote American political and military objectives. The matter was brought to a head after the midnight attack on the Buddhist pagodas by the South Vietnamese Special Forces on 21 August 1963. These Special Forces had been trained by American instructors.

By this time the Secretary of Defence was much more deeply involved in decisions relating to Vietnam than had been the case in 1961 when he was relatively passive. Throughout 1962 he had expressed guarded optimism about the counter-insurgency operations in South Vietnam.[65] While emphasizing the "progress" made in that direction, he took care not to underestimate the Communist opposition. Twice in the year 1962 he

---

[64] For contradictory pictures of South Vietnam under Diem, see David Halberstam, *The Making of a Quagmire* (New York, 1964); Marguerite Higgins, *Our Vietnam Nightmare*: (New York. 1965); and Anthony Trawick Bouscaren, *The Last af the Mandarins: Diem of Vietnam* (Pittsburgh, Penn., 1965).

[65] *New York Times*, 17 January 1962; 20 February 1962; and 25 July 1962.

met at Honolulu with his military advisers to discuss Vietnam. In his testimony before the House Armed Services Committee on 30 January 1963, McNamara stated that the South Vietnamese struggle against the Communist insurgency, which was supported by the US, was going on well and would eventually succeed.[66] But in his press conferences on Vietnam in the months of February and July, he expressed his concern that it might take several years to defeat the Communists.[67] Available documents do not indicate any expression of misgivings on McNamara's part concerning Diem's leadership.

In the last week of August there were many rumours floating in Saigon about an imminent anti-Diem coup. But the anti-Diem Generals reportedly called off the plot for the time being because of the uncertainty about the US attitude toward a change of regime. It was known both in Saigon and Washington that General Harkins, the Chief of the American Military Assistance Command in Saigon was a staunch supporter of Diem. This might have acted as a damper on coup plans till the anti-Diem elements could get some sort of a signal from another equally highly-placed American source that a coup would not be unwelcome. Any indication that the US intended to apply some sort of pressure against Diem would have been a tipoff to a potential coup-group.

On 1 September 1963 the National Security Council met in Washington and the discussion centred around the question: "Where do we go from here?" Neither McNamara nor General Maxwell Taylor who had by this time been appointed Chairman of the JCS, voiced any support for the idea of replacing Diem or giving encouragement to the elements that might lead a coup against him.[68] In another NSC meeting held on 6 September the Defence Secretary continued to resist any immediate coup against the Diem regime. He favoured buying some more time. He suggested that Ambassador Henry Cabot Lodge should be asked to make another attempt to convince Diem to bring about the desired reforms.[69]

---

[66] Ibid., 31 January 1963.
[67] Ibid., 20 July 1963.
[68] *DOD Documents*, Books 3, IV.B.5, p 22.
[69] Ibid., p. 24.

It was probably because of the reluctance of McNamara and Taylor to endorse the idea of immediate change of leadership in South Vietnam that President Kennedy decided to depute them to make a visit to South Vietnam. He directed them to make the "best possible on-the-spot appraisal" of the military and paramilitary effort required to defeat the Viet Cong. They were also instructed to recommend what steps "Saigon *must* and Washington *should* take to make the anti-Communist efforts more effective." The most important objective, in the immediate context of the McNamara-Taylor mission, was to examine with Ambassador Lodge ways of "tailoring" the American aid to achieve her foreign policy objectives.[70] The team left Washington on 23 September and came back on 2 October.

While in Saigon, General Taylor wrote a letter to Diem in response to the latter's request for an appraisal of the South Vietnamese war effort. Expressing his misgivings about the adverse effect of political tensions in Saigon on the war effort, Taylor stressed the importance of the restoration of "political tranquility."[71] The General had consulted the Secretary of Defence before writing his letter. It is not clear whether the reference to the political tensions was his own idea or whether it came from the Secretary who was more exposed than the General to the deep pessimism of some of his colleagues in the State Department concerning the situation in South Vietnam. In any event, the letter was an indication to Diem that the visiting dignitaries were not wholly satisfied with the state of affairs.

The report that McNamara and Taylor submitted to the President was not free of ambiguity and contradictions. The ambiguity was probably deliberate. It was a typical example of bureaucratic compromise that is frequently encountered in decision-making on defence and foreign policy. It was meant to give something to the proponents of rival points of view in Washington and also the American Embassy and the US Military Mission in Saigon. No element was to be left totally disgruntled. The report stated that the military campaign had made good progress and that it was likely to continue to do so.

---

[70] Ibid., pp. 30-1; Emphasis added.
[71] Ibid., pp. 32-3.

This was a sop to General Harkins. The report went on to warn that the continuing political crisis might erode military effectiveness—a concern voiced by State Department elements and shared by Ambassador Lodge. What then about Diem himself? McNamara and Taylor stated that any effort by the US to increase pressure on the Diem regime might lead the latter to harden its own attitude. Nevertheless they added that unless Diem were pressed, he was unlikely to bring about any change in his repressive policies. How much pressure and what sort of pressure were called for? On this critical point the McNamara-Taylor report moved a little toward the point of view of the State Department, but not all the way. They were aware that the service chiefs as well as General Harkins were opposed to the State Department posture. The report recommended that the US should not actively encourage a coup against Diem. It added, however, that the United States should seek "urgently to identify and build contacts with an alternative leadership if and when it appears."[72] The report also identified one instrument of pressure to be applied on Diem— "suspension of aid."[73] At the same time it was not in favour of making such a decision immediately public as some American officials in Washington and Saigon would have liked. Thus, the report was willing to countenance the prospect of a change of leadership in Saigon and the use of suspension of aid as an instrument to prod Saigon to change its ways and, at an appropriate time, stimulate opposition to Diem. McNamara and Taylor could not have been unaware of the fact that the anti-Diem military leaders in Saigon had already indicated in August that they would consider a move in the direction of the aid suspension as a signal that Washington was not opposed to a change of leadership in Saigon.[74]

---

[72] Ibid., p. 34.

[73] Ibid., p. 33.

[74] Ambassador Lodge argues that the aid cut-off was not meant to encourage the generals to stage a coup against Diem, but to force Nhu to flee the country. Henry Cabot Lodge, *The Storm has Many Eyes: A Personal Narrative* (New York, 1973), p. 211. Marguerite Higgins of the *New York Herald Tribune* who was sympathetic towards the Diem regime, says, "At least six of the generals. . .told me and others that the reduction in U.S. assistance was the decisive event that

The McNamara-Taylor report, ambiguous as it was, was a joint report. The question arises as to whether there were some differences of opinion between the two men on any part of the report. Both the Secretary and the General more than once took the same side in discussions on Diem. They opposed encouraging a coup against Diem, certainly they were not for a coup immediately. It is likely that Taylor might not have initiated the recommendation in regard to applying pressure on Diem by means of suspension of aid. It probably originated from the Secretary and Taylor apparently went along with it. The JCS were apparently opposed to such a type of pressure on Diem. McNamara's position on this was not clear. Since the McNamara-Taylor report recommended pressure on Diem in the form of aid suspension, the inference might be made that Taylor went along with McNamara's view on the matter.

On the recommendation that the US should not actively encourage a coup against Diem, it is probable that McNamara deferred to Taylor, if he was not wholly in agreement with him. The Chairman of the JCS must certainly have been aware of the sentiment among his military colleagues against "ditching" Diem. When on 7 April 1962 President Kennedy had invited the JCS to comment on the memorandum from Galbraith, critical of Diem, the JCS had cited the President's letter of 14 December 1961 to Diem as a public affirmation of US support for him in his fight against the Viet Cong. The JCS had argued that US policy toward Saigon, as announced by the President in that letter, should "be pursued vigorously to a successful conclusion."[75] This indicates that the JCS favoured continued American support for Diem and not his ouster. There is no indication that the JCS had changed their attitude. The inference might be made that General Taylor was unlikely to have taken a position sharply at variance with his colleagues on the JCS. McNamara himself was not known to have taken a rigid position one way or the other regarding the early removal of Diem. The joint report was a compromise in that it recom-

persuaded them to proceed with plans and to overthrow the Diem regime." Marguerite Higgins, n. 64, p. 208.

[75] JCS Memorandum for the Secretary of Defence, JCSM 282-62, April 1962. *DOD Documents*, Book 11, p. 464.

mended further approaches to Diem. This meant that it did not support any moves for his immediate removal while not ruling out action in the future if the projected approaches failed to yield results.

It is important to point out that it was not only the top leaders of the military who defended continued support for the Diem regime, lower down the ladder, other military actors also expressed their consistent support for Diem. The most important among them was General Harkins, the "man-on-the-spot" in Saigon. Till the last moment, he discouraged the coup attempts. In the process he picked up a bitter quarrel with Ambassador Lodge who appears to have evinced a disposition to encourage the anti-Diem elements.[76] General Harkins was so much identified with Diem that the anti-Diem generals in Saigon took special care not to divulge their coup plans to him. It thus appears that the military echelon opposed the idea of ousting Diem at this time and urged that the US should continue her support to Diem in furtherance of her objectives. McNamara appears to have gone along with their position. He supported Diem because he still appeared to be the best horse available and no better one was round the corner. But McNamara gave no indication that he would stick with Diem indefinitely.

In the critical weeks that followed, the point of view expounded by the State Department appears to have gained ground in the Administration. The fact that the documents do not indicate the Secretary of Defence taking any firm line against the encouragement of coup and the further fact that the coup was bitterly opposed to the end by General Harkins indicates that there was possible divergence of opinion between the Secretary of Defence and the military toward the end.

THE TONKIN GULF INCIDENT

The next major public development in regard to the American policy in Vietnam was the Tonkin Gulf incident which took place during 31 July-4 August 1964. While the available materials throw some light on the role of civilian and military elements of

---

[76] The Lodge-Harkins rift on Diem will be discussed in Chapter IV.

the Pentagon regarding the evolution of policy culminating in the episode and the aftermath, one important document that is known to exist, the so-called Command and Control report prepared by the Pentagon military officials, is reportedly not yet declassified. This report does not figure in the Pentagon Papers published by the House Committee on Armed Services. However, the *New York Times* which could procure a copy of the study when the Pentagon Papers were leaked to it, made use of the report in its edition of the *Pentagon Papers*.

There were three main elements in decision-making relating to the Tonkin affair. They were: (1) the planning and launching of covert activities against North Vietnam; (2) preparation of contingency plans in respect of an US response to a Tonkin-type scenario; and (3) the passage of a Congressional Resolution empowering the President to take appropriate military steps to attain American objectives in Vietnam. In studying the role of the Secretary of Defence, the JCS, and other civil-military elements of the Pentagon in respect of these issues, it is appropriate to provide a brief narrative of the Tonkin episode and the domestic and Southeast Asian context at the time when the episode took place.[77]

In the midnight of 31 July 1964 two South Vietnamese patrol boats fired on Hon Me and Hon Ngu, two North Vietnamese islands. At this time the *Maddox,* an American patrol boat, was to the south of the Gulf of Tonkin, nearly 100-120 miles away from Hon Me and Hon Ngu. The next night the *Maddox* approached within four miles of Hon Me before it turned back. On 2 August, at 11 a.m., the *Maddox,* when 11 miles away from Hon Me, reportedly was chased by three North Vietnamese patrol boats which were fired upon by it. The South Vietnamese patrol boats repeated their raides on North Vietnam

[77] *DOD Documents*, Book 4, IV.C.2(b), pp. 1-15; Neil Sheehan, "The Covert War and Tonkin Gulf: February-August 1964," in Sheehan, ed., *The Pentagon Papers*, published by the *New York Times* (1971), pp. 241-78; Joseph C. Gouldon, *Truth is the First Casualty: The Gulf of Tonkin Affair—Illusion and Reality* (New York, 1969); John Galloway, *The Gulf of Tonkin Resolution* (Associated University Press, N.J., 1970); and Thomas Halper, *Foreign Policy Crisis: Appearance and Reality in Decision-Making* (Columbus, Ohio, 1971), pp. 79-106.

in the night of 3 August. The North Vietnamese were provoked to chase the raiders and it was likely that they would confuse the American boats for South Vietnamese ones. The American commanders abroad the *Maddox* and *C. Turner Joy*, an American destroyer, were aware of this. It may be relevant to point out that Admiral Thomas Moorer, Commander-in-Chief of the Pacific Fleet, recommended to his superior, Adm. U.S. Grant Sharp, Pacific Commander-in-Chief, that the American patrol be moved 90 miles to the North to possibly draw North Vietnamese Navy away from the area of 34A operations.[78] These operations, otherwise known as "destructive undertakings" included, besides others, commado raids from the sea to destroy North Vietnamese rail and highway bridges and the bombardment of her coastal installations by patrol boats. This gives rise to the suspicion whether the US patrol was first not serving as a "decoy" for South Vietnamese raids and whether she was not enticing North Vietnam into military exchange which the US could use as cover for her pre-planned retaliation.

The second incident in the Tonkin Gulf took place on August 4. It was immediately followed by 64 American air strikes at four patrol boat bases and a major oil storage depot of North Vietnam. The next day the President sent a message to Congress, requesting the passage of a Congressional resolution expressing the support of the Congress for all necessary action to "protect our Armed Forces and to assist nations covered by the SEATO Treaty."[79] The Tonkin Resolution was overwhelmingly passed by both Houses on August 7. The Senate approved it by a vote of 88 to 2, and the House by a margin of 416 to 0.

To study the role played by civilian and military elements of the Pentagon in the Tonkin episode, we should know the context in which the episode took place. In between November 1963 when Diem and his brother Nhu were killed and August 1964, there occurred significant changes both in South Vietnam and the United States. Diem was replaced by Big Minh who was subsequently ousted by General Nguyen Khanh. After a few days of the coup against Diem, President Kennedy was assassinated and

---

[78] Sheehan, ibid., p. 246.
[79] *Department of State Bulletin* (Washington, D.C.), 24 August 1964, pp. 261-3.

was succeeded by his Vice President, Lyndon B. Johnson.

Nineteen hundred and sixty four was the year of Presidential election and Johnson was seeking re-election. His opponent, Senator Barry Goldwater (Rep., Arizona), was for stronger American action in Vietnam. Both Goldwater and ex-Vice-President Richard M. Nixon continued to urge bombing North Vietnam and "taking the war to the North."[80] Probably, as an election tactic, Lyndon Johnson tried to project himself as the "peace candidate."

However, things were not running well for Johnson in Southeast Asia. Washington was very much concerned over the recurrent political instability in Saigon. The Khanh regime was always in danger of overthrow. In his memorandum of 16 March 1964, McNamara reported, "the situation [in South Vietnam] has unquestionably been growing worse."[81] Equally depressing for the US was the condition in Laos. The Pathet Lao forces were making steady progress. On 17 May 1964, they threatened the collapse of the Souvanna Government. In the context of these internal and external situations, the pre-Tonkin Vietnam policy of the Johnson Administration may be better understood.

The Tonkin scenario involved primarily three elements. They were: covert actions against North Vietnam, the US retaliation, and the Congressional Resolution. In the context of the origin of these elements, the role of the Defence Secretary, the JCS and other civil-military elements of the Pentagon may be studied.

The covert programme dates back to May 1963 when the JCS asked the CINCPAC to prepare for South Vietnam a plan of "hit and run" operations against North Vietnam. The CINCPAC Operation Plan (OPLAN) 34-63, approved by the JCS on 9 September, was discussed at Honolulu conference on 20 November 1963. According to a decision reached there, a combined MACV-CAS (Military Assistance Command, Vietnam-Central Intelligence Agency) plan was forwarded by the CINCPAC on 19 December 1963 to the JCS.[82] McNamara, after a two-day trip

---

[80] *New York Times*, 19 March 1964; 10 April 1964; 17 April 1964; 12 May 1964; and 25 May 1964.

[81] Memorandum "South Vietnam," from Secretary of Defence McNamara to President Johnson, 16 March 1964, in Sheehan, n. 77, pp. 285-91.

[82] *DOD Documents*, Book 3, IV.C.2(a), pp. 1-2.

to South Vietnam, submitted a report to the President. He recommended the above plan of covert actions which, according to him, "present a wide variety of sabotage and psychological operations against North Vietnam from which I belive we should aim to select those that provide maximum pressure with minimum risk."[83] The President approved the Plan in its final form on 16 January 1964 and the first 4-month phase began on 1 February. It may be relevant to point out here that McNamara, throughout his secret testimony before the Foreign Relations Committee on 20 February 1968, tried to "duck," to use Senator Morse's phrase, all the questions on pre-Tonkin plans made by the Pentagon. To a question of Senator Fulbright whether the JCS had argued, before the Tonkin incident took place, for taking the war into the North by bombing or any other means, the Secretary replied, "I can't recall." The reply, supplied later for the record, stated, "We have identified no such recommendations."[84]

"OPLAN 34A" was a three-pronged covert offensive against North Vietnam. First, it included the flying of U-2 spy planes over North Vietnam, kidnapping North Vietnamese citizens for intelligence information, and bombarding North Vietnamese coastal installations by PT boats. The 34A attacks were under the control of General Harkins, Chief, MACV, who was to send regularly an advanced monthly schedule of these raids to Washington for approval. (McNamara continued to maintain, during the 1968 Tonkin hearings of the Foreign Relations Committee, that the 34A operations and the De Soto patrols—the patrolling of the Gulf of Tonkin by destroyers—were completely separate and that the Navy had no knowledge of the 34A operations.)[85]

The second segment of OPLAN 34A consisted of air operations in Laos. Most of these reconnaissance planes were flown by Air America (a pseudo-private airline run by the CIA) and by Thai pilots under the control of US Ambassador to Laos, Leonard Unger. The third element in the American covert war against

---

[83] Memorandum, "Vietnam Situation," from Secretary McNamara to President Johnson, 21 December 1963. Sheehan, n. 77, pp. 279-82.

[84] US Senate, Cong. 90, sess. 2, Committee on Foreign Relations. Hearings, *The Gulf of Tonkin, The 1964 Incidents*, pt. 2 (Washington, D.C., 1968), p. 22.

[85] Ibid., pp. 91-2.

North Vietnam was the De Soto patrolling in the Gulf of Tonkin. The patrols were mainly a psychological mission, as a show of force. Moreover, they also collected the kind of intelligence on North Vietnamese warning radars and coastal defences that would help 34A parties or aircraft pilots in the event of a bombing campaign.[86]

In regard to the covert plans the Secretary and the JCS appear to have been in accord. It was understood that the covert actions might lead to certain contingencies. The JCS had prepared in advance a detailed contingency plan to face Tonkin-type situations. The JCS repeatedly urged the Secretary of Defence in February and March 1964 to take stronger military actions against North Vietnam, because they believed "the root of the problem" lay there.[87] They urged direct strikes against North Vietnam. McNamara, after another visit to South Vietnam, wrote a memorandum to the President on 16 March which the NSC adopted the next day as NSAM 288.[88] The Secretary expressed his opposition to "overt actions" against North Vietnam "at this time" because of military and diplomatic considerations. But he urged that the US should prepare immediately to be in a position on 72 hours' notice to initiate "retaliatory actions" against North Vietnam, and to be in a position on 30 days' notice to initiate the programme of "Graduated Overt Military Pressure" against North Vietnam. He added that the first type would be a reaction on a tit-for-tat basis, whereas the second one would go beyond that. Next day, being instructed by the JCS, the CINCPAC went ahead with planning of 94 North Vietnamese targets. A ready list of targets was thus available at the time of the Tonkin "repraisal." On these matters too McNamara and the JCS were in accord.

There was another difference between the Secretary and the JCS regarding the Laotian aspect of the second element of OPLAN 34A. The members of the JCS proposed in March that the US should undertake low level reconnaissance flights over Laos. The Secretary did not accept this proposal on the ground that it was very risky. On the contrary, he recommended high level reconnaissance flights over Laos which, he thought, were

[86] Sheehan, n. 77, pp. 245-8.
[87] *DOD Documents*, n. 82, pp. 11-2; and Gravel, n. 38, p. 159.
[88] Ibid., Book 3, IV.C.1, pp. 46-54; ibid., IV.C.2(a), pp. 9-10.

less risky.[89]

Over the question of bombing the North, some differences cropped up among the members of the military toward the month of June. Just before the Honolulu Conference on Vietnam met on 1-2 June 1964, the JCS recommended that the US military objective in Vietnam should be to seek, through military actions, to destroy the will and capabilities of North Vietnam. In that case, they argued, North Vietnam would be forced to stop supporting insurgencies in South Vietnam and Laos. As "initial measures," they recommended that target complexes in North Vietnam, directly associated with such support, be destroyed.[90] It is important to note that this recommendation did not have the concurrence of the Chairman of the JCS. He also opposed this view at Honolulu. It is one of the few instances in relation to Vietnam where the Chairman disagreed with the rest of the JCS,[91] the Secretary went along with Taylor.

On 5 June, General Taylor suggested, in order of the intensity of force, three courses of action. They were:

a. A massive air attack on all significant military targets in North Vietnam for the purpose of destroying them and thereby making the enemy incapable of continuing to assist the Viet Cong and the Pathet Lao.

b. A lesser attack on some significant part of the military target system in North Vietnam for the dual purpose of convincing the enemy that it is to his interest to desist from aiding the Viet Cong and the Pathet Lao, and, if possible, of obtaining his cooperation in calling off the insurgents in South Vietnam and Laos.

c. Demonstrative strikes against limited military targets to show U.S. readiness and intent to pass to alternatives *b* or *a* above. These demonstrative strikes would have the same dual purpose as in alternative *b*.[92]

Even though he would personally favour the alternative *b*, he

[89] Ibid., IV.C.2(a), p. 12.
[90] Ibid., p. 29.
[91] Ibid.
[92] Ibid., p. 37.

said, in view of "political considerations" which the civilian officials in Washington would take into account, the JCS might be asked to prepare a strike plan assuming that a decision was made to accept the alternative *c*. It is not clear what were the preferences of McNamara and the JCS. But on the basis of their known views, it may be inferred that while the JCS might have gone for the alternative *a*, the Secretary of Defence might have opted for *c*.

The Congressional resolution, the third element of the Tonkin scenario, had also been planned in advance. The Draft Presidential Memorandum (DPM), prepared by William P. Bundy, John McNaughton, Assistant Secretary of Defence for International Security Affairs and William H. Sullivan, Chairman of the Interagency Vietnam Coordinating Committee, was submitted for the consideration by an executive committee of the NSC on 23 May. Among other things, it had also called for a "Congressional Resolution" supporting US resistance to North Vietnamese aggression in Southeast Asia.[93] The record shows that William Bundy had already drafted a resolution to that effect on 25 May 1964.[94] A Vietnam strategy session of American officials held at Honolulu on 1-2 June 1964 discussed the need of a Congressional resolution at that point. Present in the meeting were Rusk, McNamara, William Bundy, McCone, Sullivan, Ambassador Lodge, General Taylor, Admiral Felt and General William C. Westmoreland who was replacing General Harkins, the head of the American Military Assistance Command in Saigon.

At one stage of the conference, Lodge made a query about the need of a Congressional resolution if the US was to undertake only "tit-for-tat" air attacks against North Vietnam. McNamara, in defence of having such a resolution, stated that such attacks would guarantee South Vietnam's defence against retaliatory actions by Hanoi and Peking. Moreover, he pointed out that "it might be necessary, as the action unfolded. . . to deploy

[93] Ibid., pp. 22-3; and Gravel, n. 38, p. 167.
[94] The testimony of William P. Bundy before the Senate Foreign Relations Committee on 20 September 1966 in which he admitted that he had prepared a draft of the Tonkin type resolution. Cited in Galloway, n. 77, pp. 101-2.

as many as seven divisions."[95] It is not clear if the JCS recognized such a need. By 10 June most agencies had expressed their support for a Congressional resolution and except McGeorge Bundy, who sought to defer this question for the time being, no other agency is known to have opposed it. It seems that the JCS went along with the idea of having an advance Congressional resolution on Vietnam.

Inferences

During the period culminating in the Tonkin episode, the Secretary of Defence and the JCS appear to have been quite close in their positions. Both of them were for application of force against North Vietnam. The more the Secretary felt that the situation in South Vietnam was deteriorating, the more he was prepared to endorse military pressure against North Vietnam. The difference between the Secretary and the JCS seems to have been one of degree—the JCS were in favour of even more forceful and direct action against North Vietnam than the Secretary. The Secretary appears to have moved carefully probably in order to give the impression that while favouring well-planned action he was somewhat less of a hawk than the JCS. While recommending covert military pressure against North Vietnam, he also emphasized "Pacific action" programmes in the South. While, in principle, seemingly not opposed to the use of force, he projected himself as the advocate of a gradual increase in application of force. One factor that might have restrained him to a greater extent than the JCS was taking into account the fact that the Presidential election was to be held that year. He might have calculated that the President, as the "peace candidate" of that year, might be inhibited from going too far in the direction of a military solution in Vietnam at least till the elections were over. In a decision-making process, any player, while making a move, probably calculates its chance of being accepted by other players —especially the head of the organization. It is perhaps more true of the Secretary of Defence than of the JCS because of the differences in the nature of their offices and functions—one, "gene-

[95] *DOD Documents*, Book 3, IV.C.2(a), p. 31; and Gravel, n. 38, p. 174.

ralized" and the other, "specialized." The more generalist an
actor is, the more he is inclined to take into account, while taking
a decision, environmental forces, apart from the interest of the
organization he belongs to. The more specialized is the nature of
his functions, the more he is prone to be influenced by the organizational interest.

BEGINNING OF WAR

In Vietnam-type operations, it is difficult to identify the exact
point of the beginning, but, in the present case, it may be said
with some degree of plausibility that the launching of Operation
Rolling Thunder on 2 March 1965 and President Johnson's
approval for the dispatch of 44 battalions in the middle of July
1965 as requested by General Westmoreland formed two distinct
points in the evolution of the Vietnam war.

It has been discussed earlier that the JCS, in the pre-Tonkin
period, consistently urged the higher authorities to launch air
attacks against North Vietnam. The same pattern continued in
the post-Tonkin period too. On 26 August, the Chiefs made a
similar recommendation. But this proposal was different from
the earlier ones in one respect. Besides recommending the bombing
of the North, it envisaged delibrate attempts to provoke the
Democratic Republic of Vietnam (DRV) into taking actions which
could be countered by systematic American air attacks.[96] The
same sort of thinking seemed to run in the civilian level of the
Pentagon. On 3 September John T. McNaughton, the Assistant
Secretary of Defence (ISA), proposed varieties of "provocative"
and escalation measures against the North. These measures were
meant to make possible the postponement, till November or
December, of the initiation of more serious escalation.[97] In spite
of this near unanimity between the military and some civilian
elements of the Pentagon about the provocation strategy, it was
not accepted by the principle advisers of the President. In a White
House strategy meeting of 7 September, they rejected the provocative strategy on the ground that the Saigon regime was very

---

[96] Ibid., Book 4, IV.C.2(b), p. 25.
[97] Ibid., p. 26.

weak.[98] But the more important reason which was not said but must have been understood by these advisers, as in the earlier Tonkin episode period, was that the Presidential election was not yet over and no major escalation should be risked on its eve. The principal advisers, however, agreed that provocative and escalatory measures against the North might be launched in future —(in hindsight, after the election was over). For the present, De Soto patrols and 34A operations were recommended. It was also agreed that the Tonkin-type "tit-for-tat" reprisal bombings might be launched against North Vietnam.[99]

As earlier, the "specialist" group, the JCS, kept up the pressure. On 21 and 27 October, the Chiefs revived again the case for the bombing of North Vietnam. They argued that "the source of supply and direction [in the North] be eliminated or cut off." They reiterated their old, oft-repeated argument that the bombing of North Vietnam would demonstrate American will and capability to escalate if necessary, bolster the morale of allies, and prevent the march of Communism in Southeast Asia.[100] Four days after the JCS made their recommendation and two days before the Presidential election, the Viet Cong forces attacked the Bien Hoa airfield near Saigon resulting in the loss of four American lives and the destruction of five B-57 bombers. The JCS urged the President to take "prompt and strong military actions in reprisal." The destruction of POL (petroleum, oil and lubricants) storages in Hanoi and Haiphong were recommended by them.[101] Secretary McNamara reportedly did not agree with this recommendation.[102] The Secretary might have anticipated that Johnson, just on the eve of the election, would not risk such a widening of the war.

No retaliatory actions were authorized, but the President set up an interagency group headed by William Bundy, Assistant Secretary of State for Far Eastern Affairs and Southeast Asia to recommend various political and military steps that might be taken against North Vietnam. The group held its first meeting

[98] Ibid.
[99] Ibid., p. 27.
[100] Itid., Book 4, IV.C.2(c), pp. 2-3.
[101] Ibid., p. 4.
[102] Lyndon B. Johnson, *The Vantage Point: Perspectives of the Presidency 1963-1969* (Delhi, 1972), p. 121.

on 3 November 1964. The immediate concern of Washington was whether to initiate punitive measures against the North, as consistently demanded by the JCS, while the Saigon regime was still struggling to stand on its feet. McNaughton devised an argument to get over this dilemma. He pleaded that action against North Vietnam was, to some extent, a substitute for strengthening the government in South Vietnam. According to him, the bombing of North Vietnam would reduce her capacity to help the Viet Cong. In that event, he added, a "less effective GVN" could tackle a "less active VC."[103] Vice Admiral Lloyd Mustin, the JCS representative in the Bundy Group, reiterated the prevailing military position that the North should immediately be bombed. For this, he favoured a programme of "progressively increasing squeeze."[104] Thus, with regard to the bombing of North Vietnam, the civilian and military elements of the Pentagon seemed to be approaching a point of convergence. However, at that point, neither McNaughton nor Mustin clearly stated what type of escalation they exactly stood for.

The Bundy group developed three options for air escalation against North Vietnam.[105] Option A required continued emphasis on counter-insurgency efforts in South Vietnam plus intensified 34A operations and reprisals against Bien Hoa-type situations. Option B, described by McNaughton as "a fast/full squeeze" included graduated but steadily escalating air operations against infiltration routes in Laos and North Vietnam. Option C, called by McNaughton "a slow squeeze," consisted of graduated but variably placed military actions against infiltration routes in Laos and North Vietnam. It would also include diplomatic measures for negotiating a settlement. All these options were criticized by the JCS as insufficient. However, if asked to choose among these three, they would prefer B. McNamara and McNaughton went for C. The JCS, in their turn, developed five alternatives out of which option 4 and 5 corresponded to C and B.[106] They seemed to prefer option 5. Later, McNamara opted for a mix of first phases of A and C. Though both the civilian and military ele-

---

[103] *DOD Documents*, n. 100, p. 8.
[104] Ibid., p. 9.
[105] Ibid., pp. 18-23.
[106] Ibid., pp. 33-4.

ments of the Pentagon were moving in the same direction—hawkish—there was some degree of difference between them, principally in respect of the tempo of escalation. The JCS stood for fast escalation of the war against the North while the Secretary and his civilian colleague in the Department of Defence were in favour of slow escalation.

The NSC, after reviewing the recommendations of the Bundy group, agreed on a two-phase programme. In the first phase of 30-days duration, slightly increased pressure would be applied against North Vietnam. Direct air strikes would be initiated in the second phase.[107] The President, in principle, accepted these recommendations. However, for the time being, he authorized only implementation of phase one. This was another disappointment to the JCS who advocated immediate bombing of the North.[108]

The elections ended in a landslide victory for the "peace candidate," Lyndon Johnson. The political constraints that operated during the preceding months of the campaign were no longer decisive. And the push for escalation gathered momentum in the Pentagon. In late January Saigon underwent yet another political crisis with General Khanh taking away all powers from the civilian government. This was embarrassing from the point of view of depicting a projected escalation as an attempt to defend "democracy." At this point McNaughton made a new argument, different from the official one, to justify the increased American involvement in Vietnam. On 27 January, arguing in favour of bombing, McNaughton wrote that the US objective in South Vietnam was not to help a friend, but to "contain China." South Vietnam should be viewed as a buffer between China and Thailand/Malaysia, he said.[109] McNamara had not till this time gone as far as his Assistant Secretary of Defence (ISA). He had apparently extended, in some occasions, his "qualified support" for air strikes against the North. But in late January, there occurred a decisive change in the Secretary. On 27 January, he along with McGeorge Bundy, the National Security Assistant, addressed a joint memorandum to the President. They stated that they had

---

[107] Ibid., pp. 39-41.
[108] Ibid., pp. 55-6.
[109] Ibid., IV.C.3, p. 14; and Sheehan, n. 77, p. 351.

reached a "critical moment in their thinking" and they felt that the US should move from the "centre" towards taking stronger actions against the North.[110] The civilian and military elements of the Pentagon appeared to have reached almost a point of convergence regarding the bombing of the North. From the point of mobilizing public support, some onslaught by the Viet Cong would be helpful. The Viet Cong attack on the US airbase in Pleiku took place on 7 February 1965. The President ordered a reprisal immediately. He approved Operation Rolling Thunder on 13 February.

The air war was soon followed by escalation of the war on the ground. The first batch of American marines landed at Da Nang on 8 March 1965—a fateful step whose ultimate development might hardly have been foreseen or envisaged by either the civilian or the military actors in the Pentagon.

Westy—as Gen. William C. Westmoreland was called by his friends—was not the kind of person to sit for long in the sidelines and watch others in action. When he joined as the Chief of the American Military Assistance Command, Saigon, the military actors in Washington were pushing hard the proposal to bomb North Vietnam. As a ground soldier, he might have had his reservations on whether air power alone could turn the scales in South Vietnam. At that point it was perhaps not prudent on his part to raise questions relating to ground deployment which might have invited the wrath of the Air Force led by the powerful General Curtis LeMay. If air power was shown to be inadequate, his turn would come and then "Westy" was determined to be heard. At such a time he would not hesitate to cross sword even with his old mentor, General Taylor. The first proposal, from the military side, to send ground troops to South Vietnam was made by the JCS on 11 February 1965—only two days before Rolling Thunder was authorized by the President. The Chiefs, while proposing stronger air strikes against the North, recommended deploying a Marine Expeditionary Brigade in Da Nang to counter retaliatory strikes by DRV/China.[111] The CINCPAC and the Commander, U.S. Military Assistance Command, Vietnam (CUMUSMACV) immediately supported the JCS pro-

---

[110] Johnson, n. 102, pp. 122-3.
[111] *DOD Documents*, Book 4, IV.C.4, p. 15.

posal.[112]

By the middle of 1964 there had occurred a big change in the power-complex of the Saigon Mission. Gen. Westmoreland replaced Gen. Harkins as the Chief of MACV on 25 April 1964 and Gen. Taylor was appointed the Ambassador in Saigon on 23 June 1964. Westmoreland was, like his predecessor, a favourite of Gen. Taylor. In 1955 he served as the Secretary of the General Staff under Taylor, the Chief of the Staff of Army. For three years he was the Superintendent of West Point—a prize post that had been held in the past by MacArthur and by Taylor creditably. The fact that he was a Southerner from South Carolina had probably at least a little weight with President Johnson. For the rest of 1964, Westmoreland played second fiddle first to Ambassador Lodge and then to Ambassador Taylor, a military "hero" in civilian clothes. But in course of time he began to prepare his ground to play a more influential role in 1965 and thereafter.

As early as 30 November 1964, a State Department proposal to deploy American group troops in South Vietnam "in support of diplomacy" was discussed by an NSC Working Group, but no recommendation was made by it. That was probably the only instance, before 8 March 1965, according to the available documents, when the question of the introduction of American GIs in South Vietnam was discussed by civilian advisers. It was later taken up by the military actors who went on pressing their superiors to accept this proposal. On 11 February 1965, the JCS, while proposing air attacks against North Vietnam, also recommended the deployment of a Marine Expeditionary Brigade in Da Nang to counter retaliatory strikes by DRV/China.[113] After a few days, the Da Nang deployment was proposed by Gen. Westmoreland. The CINCPAC, in an urgent message to the JCS on 24 February 1965, urged that two marine battalions be immediately sent to Da Nang.[114] One may remember that in October 1961 the CINCPAC had opposed the immediate deployment of US ground troops in South Vietnam. The one possible factor responsible for this changed attitude of the CINCPAC in 1965 was that Adm. Felt had been succeeded by Admiral U.S. Grant

[112] Ibid., p. 4.
[113] Ibid., p. 15.
[114] Ibid., p. 4.

Sharp. On the same day itself, the JCS forwarded this recommendation with their approval. And after two days, the deployment of Marines at Da Nang was authorized by the President.

At the eleventh hour, the Marine deployment at Da Nang faced some difficulty. On 2 March, McNaughton wrote to Taylor stating that the 173rd Airborne Brigade, then stationed on Okinawa, would replace the Marines. It was highly resented by Westmoreland and the decision to send Marines to Da Nang was sustained.[115] It is not clear how exactly the civilian elements of the Pentagon reacted to this decision regarding the Marines. McNaughton's cable did not indicate his opposition to the policy of sending American GIs to South Vietnam. He wanted some change only in the type of GIs to be introduced there. The Marines had a long history of intervention abroad and deploying them at Da Nang might give an impression that something bigger was in the offing. This might have been McNaughton's perception and it might have been shared by McNamara. The President opted for Marines, but he did not approve of two battalions as recommended by the military. Only one battalion was sent to Da Nang. President's strategy was the "middle course"—neither to please all, nor to displease all, but to give some satisfaction to all.

In the beginning, it was mainly the JCS who were advocating increased American ground involvement in South Vietnam. The support for this used to come from the CINCPAC and the Commander, US Military Assistance Command, Vietnam (CUMUSMACV). But, after some time, the equation was reversed. The "big push" began to come from the CUMUSMACV, and the JCS had to keep pace with it. This was due to the difference in their perception of the military need. Once ground troops are deployed for combat, the man-on-the-spot always asks for more while the JCS have to take a larger view, keeping in mind other global commitments. Moreover, the latter would be taking into consideration the domestic reactions while the former often might not. One may refer to a few memoranda of the JCS and Gen. Westmoreland in order to identify the gradual change in their mutual interaction in regard to getting more and more American ground troops deployed in

[115] Ibid., pp. 6-7.

South Vietnam. On 20 March 1965, the JCS proposed sending two American divisions and one South Korean division to South Vietnam with an "offensive" mission. In order to reverse the trend in the military situation of South Vietnam in favour of Saigon, the objective should be, they argued, to destroy the Viet Cong, not merely to keep pace with them or slow down their progress.[116] It is significant to note that Gen. Westmoreland had so far not proposed any offensive strategy, nor had he yet recommended such a big number of American ground troops to be deployed in South Vietnam. Westmoreland, in his "Commander's Estimate of the situation in SVN," dated 26 March 1965, stated that Rolling Thunder was not going to pay dividends within the coming six months. He proposed that the US should send two divisions to South Vietnam by June 1965 and possibly more thereafter in case the bombing failed. He argued that they would help the Saigon force in enjoying favourable ratio *vis-a-vis* the Viet Cong.[117] In the aftermath of the Honolulu Conference on Vietnam, held on 20 April 1965, the JCS recommended that 48,000 US and 5,250 "Free World" troops should be deployed in South Vietnam. These troops were not only to protect American bases and installations, but also to do fighting against the Viet Cong.[118] This again indicates that at this stage the JCS were ahead of CUMUSMACV in taking initiative for sending more American troops to South Vietnam with more offensive m ssions. The next important initiative, however, came from Gen. Westmoreland when he told Adm. Sharp, the CINCPAC, that the US should send "44 battalions" of ground forces to South Vietnam.[119] From that time onwards Gen. Westmoreland emerged to be the most demanding and vigorous advocate of the American ground involvement in South Vietnam.

The gradual change in the American combat role appeared to be directly linked to the change in combat strategies. The initial deployment of ground troops was meant to maintain the security of coastal bases.[120] But the military actors were un-

---

[116] *DOD Documents*, Book 4, IV.C.5, p. 92.
[117] Ibid., pp. 86-8.
[118] Ibid., p. 78.
[119] Ibid., pp. 94-104.
[120] Ibid., p. 113.

happy with it. Gen. Johnson, the Army Chief of Staff, on his return from a trip to South Vietnam, 5-12 March 1965, recommended to the President two alternate strategies. One was to deploy US Marines in secure bases on the coast, and the other was to send Marines into high land provinces. Gen. Johnson and Gen. Earle Wheeler, the Chairman of the JCS, supported the second alternative. But this was not accepted by the President. He, however, replaced the original strategy of "base security" by that of "enclave strategy." This new strategy required that the US troops occupy coastal enclaves, accept full responsibility for enclave security, and be prepared to go to the rescue of the South Vietnamese forces as far as fifty miles outside enclaves. The military resented the 50-mile limit.[121] Gen. Westmoreland, in his 7 June message, requested that this limit be lifted.[122] This request was endorsed both by the CINCPAC and the JCS. On 26 June he was authorized to commit American GIs to combat in any situation he deemed appropriate for helping the GVN forces. This brought to an end the "enclave strategy" and launched the "search and destroy" strategy.[123] There was thus increase in the number of American ground forces in South Vietnam in correspondence to the change in their missions. And the man whose strategy finally prevailed was Gen. Westmoreland.

The combined offensive of the military for the deployment of American GIs in South Vietnam need not preclude the possibility that there were intra-military differences. In fact, the available documents record that there existed some inter-service cleavages. The Joint Chiefs were apparently unanimous regarding the desirability of securing American bases in South Vietnam, but beyond that they differed among themselves. The Chief of the Staff of the Air Force and the Commandant of the Marine Corps supported the "enclave strategy" whereas the Chairman of the JCS—an Army man—and the Chief of the Staff of Army, were strong proponents of the "search and destroy" strategy.[124] It is noteworthy that each one of them

---

[121] Ibid., pp. 113-6.
[122] Ibid., p. 104.
[123] Ibid., pp. 104, 116-20.
[124] Gravel, n. 38. vol. 3, p. 397.

was propounding a view which was apparently in the interest of the organization that he headed. Colonel James A. Donovan points out that with the launching of the "search and destroy" strategy, there developed strains between the Marines and the Army, and then between the Marines and the Air Force over the question of overall command, roles and operations.[125] This suggests that the interest of an organization—here, an agency—, to some extent, defines its attitude toward policy-matters.

The available records say very little about the role of the Secretary of Defence in decision-making with regard to the sending of American ground troops to South Vietnam. He does not seem to have taken a definite stand on it. He simply reacted to the initiatives taken by military elements. He did not oppose any military recommendations for the deployment of American ground troops in South Vietnam. They were in conformity with his own broad design. He did, from time to time, suggest some changes in details. With regard to the JCS' three division-drive in March 1965, for instance, the Secretary indicated that in order to fend off domestic reactions, further American troops should be sent along with South Korean contingents. He expressed his agreement with the military's "adverse force ratios" and the latter's proposal for further deployment of American troops in South Vietnam. But, at the same time, he expressed some caveats. He pointed out that such deployments should be conditioned by "political [psychological] absorption capacity," "logistical absorption capacity," and "operational absorption— that is, operational requirements."[126] The NSC which met on 1-2 April 1965, did not accept the three division-proposal. But this proposal was not buried there. McNamara wanted it to remain alive. He asked the Joint Chiefs to continue planning for the earliest introduction of three divisions.[127]

Some of the statements of the Secretary made during the build-up stage were very hawkish. In a memorandum to all departments on 1 March 1965, he stated, "I want it clearly

---

[125] Colonel James A. Donovan, *Militarism, USA* (New York, 1970), pp. 157-64.
[126] *DOD Documents*, n. 116, pp. 106-7.
[127] Ibid., p. 107.

understood that there is an unlimited appropriation available for the financing of aid to Vietnam. Under no circumstances is lack of money to stand in the way of aid to that nation."[128] On another occasion he wrote to General Johnson, the Army Chief of Staff, "policy is: anything that will strengthen the position of the GVN will be sent."[129] It is not quite clear whether the Secretary's "anything" meant "anything" in terms of money alone or men also. Spending money and sending soldiers to a foreign country to fight are two different things, and one's commitment to the first does not necessarily reflect commitment to the second. The question of more money would arise if more men would be deployed in South Vietnam. McNamara's assurances *albeit* vague, to spend as much money as required on Vietnam were perhaps a calculated concession on his part to give some comfort to the military who were having a rough time with him at that time regarding their overall budgetary demands for weapons production and procurement. He did not approve of the whole of the military's package. He accepted a part of it—neither complete denial, nor complete acceptance. And his tactic was to ask the JCS to prepare plans for the rest without, however, committing himself in advance on whether his approval would be forthcoming. His options were still kept open.

It seems that Secretary McNamara at this point of time, was not prepared to initiate any positive moves in the direction of troop increases in Vietnam. He was willing to let somebody else take the initiative with possibly some tacit encouragement from him. Assistant Secretary McNaughton seems to have had McNamara's blessing when, on 13 July, he recommended to the Secretary that the US should introduce 44-battalions in South Vietnam and be prepared to send more in future.[130] This hypothesis is reinforced by the fact that McNaughton hardly differed from his boss on any major issue. McNamara was thus playing a smart game—probably using McNaughton as a "stalking horse." Ambassador Taylor was at that time opposed to the introduction of American ground troops in South Vietnam and the Secretary probably did dot want to be locked into direct

[128] Ibid.
[129] Ibid., p. 108.
[130] Ibid., p. 120.

conflict with him on the issue at this stage. Both McNamara and Taylor had been very close to President Kennedy and they continued maintaining good relationship with the Kennedy family during the Johnson Administration. The Secretary and Taylor were personally on excellent terms too. Johnson was reportedly suspicious of their friendship with Robert Kennedy. McNamara moved cautiously probably because of his appraisal that President Johnson was going the military's way.

No decision had been taken on the 44-battalion proposal when the Secretary left for South Vietnam in the middle of July. But while he was in Saigon, he was informed by his Deputy Secretary Vance that the President had decided to go ahead with the plan to introduce 44 American battalions.[131] Johnson's account in his memoirs that he took this decision after McNamara returned to Washington seems to be erroneous.[132]

Both the civilian and military elements of the Pentagon were advocates of the deployment of American ground troops in South Vietnam. The only difference between them was with regard to the number and missions of these troops. While the civilian elements seemed to favour a smaller number and less offensive mission, the military pushed for a bigger number and more offensive mission. The military members were also not wholly unanimous. Being seemingly guided by their organizational interests, they differed in regard to the roles and missions of the troops. At the outset, the JCS were in the lead with Gen. Westmoreland expressing his support. After some time, this equation was reversed. The CUMUSMACV began to take the initiative and it was for the JCS to respond to his proposals. Gen. Westmoreland began to emerge increasingly as the most vigorous and assertive of the Pentagon players. Whether there was any equally determined and skilful contender outside the Pentagon will be examined in Chapter IV.

Inferences

There does not seem to have existed a great distance between

---

[131] Ibid., p. 131.
[132] Johnson, n. 102, pp. 144-52.

the civilian and military actors of the Pentagon so far as launching the air offensive was concerned. Both of them were in favour of taking resort to air operations against North Vietnam. The only difference between them was the degree of intensity of actions they favoured. The military actors were for fast, prompt and very strong operations on a continuous basis whereas the civilians of the Pentagon advocated gradual escalation. To use the jargon of McNaughton, while the former urged "fast squeeze," the latter asked for "slow squeeze," but both of them aimed at "squeezing" the enemy.

In the case of beginning the land war, the military input seems to have been larger and more effective than the civilian one. Secretary McNamara does not appear to have played any significant role. There is hardly anything to show that he was against the ground war. On the other hand, the record shows that he had implicitly supported it. So also had the Assistant Secretary McNaughton. There seems to have existed an important difference between the genesis of the air war and that of the ground war. The Rolling Thunder Operation of February 1965 was the result of a series of actions, originated mostly in 1964, the year in which President Johnson was being hailed as the "peace candidate." That was a great constraint upon the President throughout that year. On the other hand, most of the related steps on ground war were taken in the first part of 1965. By that time the election was over and the President had probably freed himself of the spell of the Kennedy Administration. As it seems, he was closer to the military in his attitude than to the Secretary of Defence. As a result, whereas the military recommendations on air offensive were mostly not approved, most of their recommendations regarding ground war were accepted by the President—without delay too. This leads us to believe that President's personal philosophy or beliefs (relating to war), and his concern for maximization of his personal benefits (Presidential election) greatly influenced his decisions regarding military actions in Vietnam in 1964-1965.

CHAPTER FOUR

CIVILIAN-MILITARY INTERACTION IN
THE PENTAGON—II

The period of escalation of the war in Vietnam extends from about the middle of 1965 to the end of March 1968. On 31 March 1968 President Johnson announced that he would not seek the second term. A few days earlier, McNamara had left the Pentagon. It is proposed to carry our discussion up to the exit of McNamara because the time-gap between that date and 31 March is not very big, and there does not appear to have taken place any significant change in the civil-military equation during that period. The period of escalation is also the period of increasing tension between the civilian and military elements of the Pantagon. The prospect of rifts developing becomes greater when success in the attainment of the objective gets delayed or becomes somewhat doubtful in the context of resources that could be committed as well as other variables.

It appears that the civil-military conflict on Vietnam was influenced by the differences between civilian and military elements of the Pentagon on other defence matters. In the beginning of the last chapter, various factors that seemingly led to the rift between the civilian and military elements of the Pentagon have been pointed out. Some of these forces continued to operate throughout McNamara's tenure as the Secretary of Defence, because they happened to be the functions of his basic approach to decision-making. In the TFX case, he had exposed himself to the charge of having ignored the unanimous advice of his experts. In order to prevent such a situation in future, the Secretary further centralized the decision-making process on defence. He made it a rule that it was the function of his military officers to *advise* him on the selection of sources for the development of advanced weapon systems rather than to *recommend* one to him. Another regulation provided that the

Secretary was responsible for selecting the source though he might choose to delegate the authority to one of the Service Secretaries.[1] Much to the chagrin of the JCS, the Secretary of Defence reaffirmed it in January 1965 in an oral directive of 1961. According to this directive, the military witnesses were required not to offer personal opinions opposing any of the Budget decisions of the Administration unless "pressed by Congressmen" and if they did so, they must state the reasons why the Secretary had overruled them.[2] These changes in the direction of further centralization seem to have considerably angered the military. As a protest against "over centralization" and "over-management" of the Defence Secretary, two senior Admirals resigned from their posts on 27 October 1965.[3]

Meanwhile, there had taken place a significant change at the top of the military echelon. The new JCS members were General Harold K. Johnson, Chief of Staff of the Army, General Joseph McConnell, Chief of Staff of the Air Force, Admiral David McDonald, Chief of Naval Operations and General Earle Wheeler, the Chairman. The new chiefs were the members of a relatively new generation of the military. Hardly any one of them had won any war-time laurel as their predecessors. As Korb says, they were primarily "staff men; men more at home behind a desk than in the field, planners and administrators and not heroes and gladiators."[4] This had a significant impact upon the internal equation of the JCS *vis-a-vis* the Secretary. The new chiefs realized that none of them could rely upon his past glory to fight individually with the Secretary of Defence. Their recourse, therefore, could only be to pose a united front both within the Executive and before Congress in case of major differences with the Secretary. From fiscal 1966 to fiscal 1968, they

[1] Air Force Regulation No. 70-15, Proposal Evaluation and Source Selection Procedures, 20 September 1965; and Department of Defence Directive No. 4105.62 Proposal Evaluation and Source Selection 6 April 1965. Cited in Robert J. Art, *The TFX Decision: McNamara and the Military* (Boston, 1968), p. 164.
[2] Lawrence J. Korb, The Role of the Joint Chiefs of Staff in the Defence Budget Process from 1961 to 1967 (Ph. D. Thesis, State University of New York at Albany, 1969), p. 17.
[3] *New York Times*, 28 October 1965.
[4] Korb, n. 2, p. 15.

were unanimous in their opposition to the Secretary on some important weapons programmes (i.e., Nike X, AMSA, RS-71, F-12A, and SSN's). In fiscal 1966, the President upheld McNamara's stand. In fiscal 1967, the Secretary overruled the unanimous JCS opinions on calling up the reserves and the activation of a Navy cruiser from the Mouthball Fleet.[5] During the same year, Admiral McDonald raised a storm in a tea-cup by refusing to endorse the defence budget during the Congressional hearings. The issue at conflict was relatively unimportant, but the episode had a significant impact upon the civil-military relation in the Pentagon. It revealed the strained relationship between the Secretary and the JCS.

The strained civil-military relationship reached its nadir during the Congressional debate on the ABM issue in fiscal 1968 when the Chairman of the JCS publicly voiced disagreement with the Secretary of Defence.[6] Since the creation of the position of the JCS Chairman in 1949, he had been mostly acting as the "party whip."[7] He was the chief military defender of the Government's defence policies. In a way his position was complementary to that of the Secretary of Defence. This tradition was broken when General Wheeler broke with McNamara on the ABM issue during the Congressional hearings. He was followed by the three other chiefs, each of whom contradicted the Secretary's position. By this time the strained equation between the Secretary and the JCS had considerably intensified. In the context of this progressive deterioration in their interrelationship, the civil-military interaction in policy-making on Vietnam may be studied.

Secretary McNamara in 1965 and thereafter, turned out to be the main focus of public as well as internal debates on Vietnam. He frequently rushed to Saigon to exchange views with American officials and the Saigon Government. He conferred several times with his colleagues and advisers at Honolulu on Vietnam. Both in Congressional hearings and press conferences, he emerged to be the main defender of the Vietnam policy.

---

[5] Ibid.

[6] The conflicting testimonies of the Defence Secretary and the JCS on ABM before Congressional Committee in 1967 will be dealt with in Chapter V.

[7] Maxwell D. Taylor, *The Uncetani Trumpet* (London, 1960), p. 110.

More than anybody else, he was identified with the Vietnam policy. Senator Wayne Morse of Oregon charged that the Vietnam war was "McNamara's war."[8] But those who wanted a quick and decisive "victory" criticized his policies as inadequate. He was thus the main target of both pro-war and anti-war elements.

The available documents reveal that the Defence Secretary was not quite what he appeared to be in public. No doubt, he had so far been an ardent advocate of strong American military posture in Vietnam. It is also true that the ongoing Vietnam policy was largely moulded by him. But as time advanced when the results that had been hoped for remained elusive and when the costs appeared to be heavy, the Defence Secretary began to develop doubts about the war. As early as 16 July 1965 McNamara asked General Wheeler to make a study on whether the US could "win" in South Vietnam if "we do everything we can."[9] A study group consisting of civilians and military officers in the Pentagon observed, "Within the bounds of reasonable assumptions, there appears to be no reason we cannot win if such is our will and if that will is manifested in strategy and technical operations."[10] The lurking diffidence and uncertainty on the part of civilians of the Pentagon was betrayed by their negative attitude. Assistant Secretary McNaughton, in a memorandum dated 2 July 1965, defined "win" as success "in demonstrating to the VC that they cannot win. . . ." The victory for the US, from another angle, McNaughton stated, would be "with a high degree of probability, a way station toward a favourable settlement in South Vietnam."[11] This was far from the positive American objectives in Vietnam, contained, from time to time, in public pronouncements. A little more than a year ago, William Bundy had told a Congressional Committee, "We are going to drive the Communist out of South Vietnam," even if that eventually involved a choice of "attacking the countries to the north."[12] The contrast between the tones of these two statements is revealing even making allowance for the fact that

[8] *New York Times*, 25 April 1964; 3 March 1965.
[9] *DOD Documents*, Book 5, IV.C.6(a), p. 1.
[10] Ibid.
[11] Ibid., p. 4.
[12] *New York Times*, 19 June 1964.

Bundy's statement was intended for public consumption.

44 BATTALIONS—200,000 MEN REQUEST

McNamara, who visited Saigon from 16 to 20 July 1965, submitted a memorandum to the President on his return to Washington. His recommendation in favour of 44-battalion concept of Westmoreland was, in effect, of not much consequence because the President had already approved that while the Secretary was in Saigon. This memorandum, however, was significant in another respect. It reflected the Secretary's optimism at its zenith which he was not to reflect—except in public— during the rest of his stay in the Pentagon. With Wheeler's "win"-study report, the Secretary was encouraged to state that there was a good chance of achieving an acceptable outcome within a reasonable time in Vietnam.[13]

The "Forty-four battalions" plea was not the last of General Westmoreland's requests for increase in the strength of American ground troops in South Vietnam. He tended to ask for more and more as Washington continued to accept his proposals, though not always in full. On the ground that heavy infiltration was allegedly going on from the North to the South, the General requested in November 1965, an increase of 154,000 men. On receiving this request, McNamara visited South Vietnam, 28-30 November 1965. In his memorandum to the President, dated 30 November, the Secretary recommended the despatch of an additional 40,000 American personnel to South Vietnam by the end of 1966. He added that an additional 200,000 men might be needed the next year. However, he went on to warn that deployments as recommended by him, would not guarantee success. "US killed-in-action can be expected to reach 1,000 a month, and the odds are even that we will be faced in early 1967 with a 'no decision' at a higher level. . . ."[14] The optimism, contained in his memorandum of 20 July 1965, was missing here. The 30 November memorandum underlined Secretary's own lurking doubts and suspicions about the Vietnam involvement.

General Westmoreland was apparently not the man to remain

---

[13] *DOD Documents*, n. 9, pp. 10-2.
[14] Ibid., p. 25.

content with any "stabilization ceiling." Hardly was the ink on the 30 November memorandum of McNamara dry when a request came from the CUMUSMACV that the total of American ground troops in South Vietnam be raised to 443,000 by the end of 1966. This request was promptly supported by Admiral Sharp, the CINCPAC. The next month General Westmoreland made another request to increase the troop strength to 459,000.[15] Such requests, made from time to time by military actors, became a regular feature of the civil-military interaction in regard to policy-making on the ground war in Vietnam. In response to such a request of the CINCPAC, dated 18 June 1966, which had been recommended by the JCS on 5 August, McNamara stated on the same day, that "it is our policy to provide the troops, weapons, and supplies requested by General Westmoreland at the times he desires them, to the greatest possible degree." However, he added that he desired and expected a detailed, line-by-line analysis of these requirements to determine that each was truly essential to the carrying out of the war plan. "We must send to Vietnam what is needed, *but only what is needed.*"[16] He warned that deployments on a bigger scale might weaken the economic structure of South Vietnam. This memorandum marked an implicit warning to the military that their requests would thenceforward be subjected to thorough examination— impliedly by system analysts who would use cost-effectiveness criteria. McNamara's posture was rather unusual in the sense that a civilian was warning his military advisers while a war was in progress that their recommendations concerning requirements for the conduct of a war would be examined by some "whiz kids." It must have been a bitter pill for the military actors to swallow. It also underscored the growing doubts of the Secretary. To what extent McNamara had been displeased with the military's pressure for increasing the American ground involvement in South Vietnam may be gauged if his memorandum is examined in the perspective of a Presidential directive only about a month earlier. On 28 June 1966 President Johnson, in a memorandum for the Secretary of Defence, had stated that the schedule of moving men to South Vietnam should be accelerated as much as

[15] Ibid., pp. 26-7.
[16] Ibid., pp. 53-4; Emphasis added.

possible so that Westmoreland could feel assured that he had all the men he needed as soon as possible.[17] That the Secretary could send such a note of warning, in spite of the explicit desire of the President, indicates that McNamara's misgivings concerning the appraisals by the JCS had sharply increased. The Secretary's memorandum presaged a period of increasingly bitter competition between civilian and military elements of the Pentagon in relation to Vietnam.

McNamara again expressed his opposition in October 1966 to the policy of escalation which was supported by the military. In September 1966, Admiral Sharp had recommended, on behalf of General Westmoreland, that the projected strength of US forces designated for Vietnam should be raised from 445,000 to 570,000 by the end of 1967. On 7 October the JCS had urged a "fullblown" mobilization of 688,500 reservists which might make it possible to send more men to South Vietnam. That McNamara had very serious reservations concerning the approach is brought out by the recommendations he made to the President after his return from South Vietnam on 14 October 1966. Tactfully he began with an expression of satisfaction about the progress on the military front. "We have done somewhat better militarily than I anticipated. We have by and large blunted the communist military initiative—and military victory in South Vietnam the Viet Cong may have had in mind 18 months ago has heen thwarted by our emergency deployments and actions. . ." The Secretary followed it up with a more sombre appraisal of the prospect in Vietnam. He stated that he saw no hope of bringing the war to an early end. He saw "no sign of an impending break in enemy morale." He expressed his great disappointment with the results achieved in respect of "pacification"—thereby tacitly acknowledging the lack of noteworthy success in combating the appeal of the Viet Cong and winning popular support for the Saigon regime. To quote him, "Pacification has if anything gone backward."[18] He recommended that the US force level in South Vietnam should be stabilized at 470,000. A new and significant note sounded by the Secretary related to placing emphasis on the objective of limiting further infiltration from the North. This

[17] Ibid., p. 49.
[18] Ibid., p. 82.

was a defensive approach whose spirit was sharply at variance with that underlying the demand of the JCS for additional troops. The Secretary suggested that between ten thousand and twenty thousand men of the force level suggested by him might be put in charge of constructing and maintaining an infiltration barrier. A small group of eminent scientists, constituted by the Defence Department, had recommended in early September 1966 the installation of an electronic barrier as an anti-infiltration move.[19] Apparently the Secretary was impressed by the possibilities that such a venture could open up, especially in view of his misgivings concerning bombing, as the means of combating infiltration. McNamara then went on to refer to an extremely sensitive issue— *a negotiated settlement*.[20] He urged that efforts should be made for creating a better environment for negotiations. He recommended that steps should be taken to increase the "credibility of our peace gestures in the minds of the enemy." The US might totally stop the bombing of North Vietnam or confine it only to the "zone of infiltration," he suggested. The Secretary proposed that the US should make efforts to split the Viet Cong away from Hanoi and develop a "realistic plan" which could offer a role to the Viet Cong in future negotiations and government of South Vietnam.[21] It could, thus, be seen that significant differences had emerged on major issues between the Secretary and his military advisers.

The JCS made no secret of their disagreement over the force level suggested by the Secretary and the feasibility and efficacy of the proposed anti-infiltration barrier. They also disagreed with the Secretary's view that the US should make fresh offers to induce the enemy to come to the negotiation table. Any fresh offer in this direction, they feared, would tend to betray American weakness.[22]

The 14 October memorandum marked a great change in the Defence Secretary's attitude towards the Vietnam was McNamara's reservations about the war, which were implicit in his 5 August memorandum were made explicit in the 14 October

[19] Ibid., p. 83.
[20] Ibid., p. 87.
[21] Ibid., p. 88.
[22] Ibid., pp. 92-4.

memorandum. The most important aspect of the latter was the importance he assigned to "negotiations" and his support for a role to the Viet Cong. From this time onwards, the Secretary was to continue to push this line. The "gut" question is how this change occurred in McNamara. The misgivings that he had voiced in his 5 August 1966 memorandum had sharply "escalated" by October. The Secretary perceived that the military escalation had failed to produce the kind of results that he had anticipated. He was probably deeply concerned over the implications of further and deeper involvement with no certainty of an early and favourable outcome. Signs were not lacking that the prolongation of the war, the mounting toll of casualties, and the receding mirage of "victory" were triggering increased criticism from the Congress and the public. The Secretary reposed considerable faith in the value of specialized studies as a tool of decision-making. He had before him the so-called JASON study which brought out the inadequacy of the results attained both by bombing and in ground war.

It is noteworthy that the members of the JCS were not unanimous in their opposition to the concept of anti-infiltration barrier. While the Chairman was inclined to favour experimenting with such a barrier, his other colleague in the JCS and the CUMUS-MACV were very doubtful about its utility and about the propriety of diverting resources for its installation.[23]

It was not long before the JCS could perceive that the Secretary would turn against them, in respect of future requests for additional troops, using the same devices that he had consistently used in his arguments with them over weapons procurement policies. He would let loose his system analysis men to subject their figures and requirements to critical and minute analysis. But the trump card that the military possessed was the fact that the President had not been touched seriously by the kind of misgivings that McNamara had. They were also emboldened by the further fact that McNamara showed no disposition to press his point of view unambiguously and forcefully on the President at this point. McNamara was not ready at this point to push matters to a point where his separation from the Administration might be the inevitable culmination. Probably his intention was to initiate efforts

[23] Ibid., Book 5, IV.C.6(b), p. 40.

to find allies and make converts in other agencies before initiating
further moves.

Another round of civil-military encounter took place in the
first half of 1967 on the question of sending more men to South
Vietnam—later known as "200,000 requests." In a message to
JCS on 18 March, General Westmoreland outlined two strategies
for ground deployment, namely, "minimum" and "optimum"
strategy.[24] The minimum strategy would need an additional
two and one-third divisions—roughly 100,000 men—"as soon as
possible but not later than 1 July 1968." The optimum strategy,
he said, would require four and two-thirds divisions in all—
201,250 more troops. Westmoreland's request was recommended
by the JCS to the Defence Secretary on 20 April. Amongst other
things, the Chiefs proposed a reserve call-up in spite of the
President's known opposition to it.[25] The military again pressed
for this reinforcement when Generals Wheeler and Westmoreland
met the President on 27 April 1967.[26] This push by the military
actors invited strong retaliation by their civilian colleagues in the
Defence Department.

One of the sharpest attacks on Westmoreland's 18 March
request was made by Alain Enthoven, Assistant Secretary of
Defence for Systems Analysis. It may not be accidental that the
studies made by the talented systems analyst generally tended
to be supportive of McNamara's views. After a thorough examination of this request, Enthoven observed:

. . .(a) VC/NVA (Viet Cong/North Vietnamese Army) losses
don't go up in proportion to our forces, they haven't in past
18 mos.
(b) even if they did, additional 200,000 U.S. forces wouldn't
put VC/NVA losses above their ability to sustain or their
willingness to accept.
(c) Our studies indicate VC/NVA control their losses, within
wide limits. They start most fights. Their losses go up when
they're attacking.[27]

[24] Ibid., pp. 61-3.
[25] Ibid., p. 75.
[26] Ibid., pp. 82-3.
[27] Ibid., p. 113.

He further pointed out that the deployment of additional forces would damage the economy of South Vietnam. He expressed his concern that it would result in eroding the incentives of South Vietnamese people to help themselves. It might give a wrong signal to Saigon, he argued, that "We will carry any load, regardless of their actions." In conclusion, he said, moving more men to South Vietnam would be a step in the wrong direction.[28] He recommended that additional forces for Southeast Asia should not be approved. Another of his recommendations was that the MACV be directed to submit plans by 1 August 1967 to increase the effectiveness of the forces of South Vietnam and those of the US and other "Free World Military Allies." The thrust of the Enthoven study, was that it would be futile to place reliance on additional reinforcements and that the military-leadership should concert measures to make the better use of forces already available.[29]

The military request was also severely attacked by another civilian adviser of Secretary McNamara. McNaughton, Assistant Secretary of Defence for International Security Affairs, seemed to have been disenchanted with the Vietnam war since the beginning of 1966. As early as 19 January 1966, he had stated that the US was engaged in an "escalating military stalemate." He had expressed his serious concern about the creeping American entanglement in Vietnam." At each decision point we have gambled; at each point, to avoid the damage to our effectiveness of defaulting on our commitment, we have upped the ante. We have not defaulted, and the ante (and commitment) is now very high." He had even recommended that the US should be prepared to accept, as a condition of settlement, a coalition government including Communists.[30] His growing uneasiness and pessimism about South Vietnam may be inferred from notes he made a conversation with an official who had just returned from Saigon. His notes read:

"Place (VN) is unholy mess.

"We control next to no territory.

[28] Ibid., p. 122.

[29] Ibid., p. 124.

[30] *DOD Documents*, Book 6, IV.C.7(a), vol. 1, p. 42; and Neil Sheehan, ed., *The Pentagon Papers*, published by the *New York Times* (1971), p. 483.

"Fears economic collapse.

"Militarily will be same place year from now.

"Pacification won't get off ground for a year.[31]

McNaughton's disenchantment with the ongoing escalation policy seems to have considerably increased by the time 200,000-more request was under consideration. In a DPM (Draft Presidential Memorandum), dated 5 May 1967, he pointed out the failure of Rolling Thunder. As regards sending more troops, he was not prepared even to accept the suggestion that Westmoreland might be given 80,000 men instead of 200,000 he had requested. It is not clear from the documents who in the Defence Department had initiated this suggestion. McNaughton asserted that provision of additional troops would be compounding the mistakes that had been made during the previous three years. It would be futile to argue to yield to the request for more troops and to pray that they would properly be used while some constructive diplomatic action was initiated. He asserted that time had come for fighting out the issues of exactly what "philosophy" the war was supposed to rest on. The President should, in his opinion, give General Westmoreland his "limit" as President Truman had done to General MacArthur at the time of the Korean war.[32]

Apparently the Defence Secretary's appraisal of the situation was reinforced by the view of such trusted civilian associates as McNaughton and Enthoven. It is equally possible that they too were not unaware of the shift that had been taking place in McNamara's own thinking. No indication of a similar stand is to be found in the available documents in the reactions of the Service Secretaries at this stage. In the absence of any reports of serious divisions or conflicts in the civilian component of the Defence Department it is perhaps reasonable to infer that the Service Secretaries were ready to go alone with McNamara or at least that the Secretary was not confronted by any noteworthy challenge from the Service Secretaries.

The climax of effects by the civilian elements of the Pentagon to contain the policy of escalation so fervently favoured by the

[31] Sheehan, ibid., p. 485.

[32] *DOD Documents*, n. 23, p. 147; and Sheehan, n. 30, p. 546.

military elements, was reached with the preparation of the DPM, dated 19 May 1967. It represented the broad range of thinking on the part of the civilian elements of the Pentagon regarding the war.[33] Though it appeared to be directly based on McNaughton's 5 May note, it also reflected McNamara's increasing pessimism which had been earlier expressed, though not in such a strong manner. The Secretary and his Assistant Secretary argued that the deployment of 200,000 more men in South Vietnam would require call-up of reserves which, in turn, was likely to lead to intense political polarization at home. The memorandum provided for a small increase of 30,000 men. For the first time the Defence civilians challenged the usefulness of sticking to the objective set forth in a basic document of the war—NSAM 288 of 17 March 1964. NSAM 288 had set forth as the American objective in Vietnam the establishment of "an independent non-Communist South Vietnam."[34] The civilians were prepared to accept a much more limited objective in order to bring about the termination of American involvement and they offered a rationalization of such a course. Their memorandum argued that the American commitment was only to see the people of South Vietnam were permitted to determine their own future. That commitment would cease to be operative if South Vietnam ceased to help herself.[35] The United States need not regard herself as irrevocably committed to ensure that any particular person or group remained in power in South Vietnam. She was not committed to guarantee that a government chosen by the South Vietnamese themselves should necessarily be non-Communist. It was not incumbent on the United States to insist that an independent South Vietnam ought to remain separate from North Vietnam. These views marked a radical break with what had all along been regarded as the official line flowing out of NSAM 288.

The reaction of the JCS to the 19 May DPM was very sharp. Within four days they wrote four memoranda in which they repeated their plea for 200,000 more men.[36] On 31 May they charged that the "drastic changes" in American policy advocated by the Defence Secretary, would seriously undermine the rationale

---

[33] *DOD Documents*, ibid., pp. 146-66.
[34] For the text of NSAM 288, see Sheehan, n. 30, pp. 291-3.
[35] Ibid., p. 595.
[36] *DOD Documents*, n. 23, pp. 165-71.

for American presence in South Vietnam. They urged that the 19 May DPM should not be forwarded to the President (The JCS did not know that the President had already gone through it twelve days back).[37] This phase of the rift between the civilian and military elements of the Pentagon in regard to 200,000-request came to an end when McNamara and Westmoreland, during the former's visit of Saigon, 7-12 July, agreed on a compromise figure of 45,000-man increase.[38] This figure was closer to the position of the civilian than to that of the military elements. In this sense, this marked a victory for the former, though not decisive, over the latter. The military lost a battle *vis-a-vis* the civilian elements of the Pentagon, but not yet a war.

Before the year 1967 was over, the civilian and military elements of the Defence Department disagreed on yet another issue relating to the ground war in Vietnam. On 1 November, McNamara addressed to the President a long memorandum with the title "Outlook if Present Course of Action is Continued." After making a gloomy prognosis of the future of the American war in Vietnam, he recommended that the US should announce the stabilization of her military operations both in the South and North and indicate that there would be no increase in the size of her combat forces beyond those already planned.[39] Besides seeking the advice of his other advisers, official and non-official, the President referred McNamara's memorandum to Westmoreland. The General did not challenge at that point the 525,000-man limit, but he did not agree with McNamara's suggestion that the US should announce it. It would be "foolish" to do it, the General asserted.[40] On 18 December, the President put his own thoughts on this issue in a memorandum for the permanent files. He did not find it advisable then to increase the number of American ground troops in South Vietnam. He expressed his opposition to the idea of announcing a policy of stabilization, as urged by McNamara.[41] It is important to note that the President's views exactly coincided with those of General West-

[37] Ibid., p. 177.
[38] Ibid., p. 209.
[39] Lyndon B. Johnson, *The Vantage Point: Perspectives of the Presidency 1963-1969* (Delhi, 1972), p. 372.
[40] Ibid., p. 376.
[41] Ibid., pp. 377-8.

moreland whereas they were at variance with the views of the Defence Secretary. On this point the President moved away from the Defence Secretary and toward the military.

The last round of the conflict between the civilian and military actors of the Pentagon in relation to the Vietnam war was played in the wake of the Tet Offensive. Of course, by that time, McNamara might have lost some of his influence within the Administration because of the official announcement, already made, that he would step down from his office on 1 March 1968. Nevertheless he continued to fight till the end; there was hardly any indication in his actions that his leverage *vis-a-vis* the military had been greatly eroded or that he was constrained to function as a lame-duck Defence Secretary. There were conflicting appraisals of whether the almost simultaneous attacks carried out by the Viet Cong on a number of places indicated the failure of the American military effort. Administration apologists tried to argue that the Viet Cong had engaged in a desperate gamble and having suffered serious casualties had been left weaker than before. The argument did not sound convincing to many who sought to draw an unfavourable contrast between earlier claims of the Administration concerning the progress in the war and the extensive onslaughts that the Viet Cong succeeded in mounting. Kissinger was to subsequently point out that the Tet Offensive mounted by Communists marked a great "political and psychological defeat" for the US, though not a military one. And in a guerilla war, the psychological aspect is the most important one.[42] The question of further expansion of American ground involvement in South Vietnam which seemed to have been shelved was reopened, with rival factions in the Pentagon sticking to their guns.

Both the *Pentagon Papers* and President Johnson's *The Ventage Point* indicate that on 12 February 1968, General Westmoreland asked for the earliest possible assigment of six manoeuvre battalions (about 10,000 men).[43] In their work *Roots of Involvements*, published in 1971, CBS correspondents Marvin Kalb and Elie Abel refer to messages that allegedly passed between President

---

[42] Henry A. Kissinger, *American Foreign Policy* (London, 1969), p. 106.
[43] Johnson, n. 39, pp. 385-6; and *DOD Documents*, Book 6, IV.C.7(b), vol. 2, p. 148.

Johnson, General Wheeler and General Westmoreland before Westmoreland made his request.[44] The President and the JCS, if Kalb and Abel are to be relied on, suggested to Westmoreland that he could go ahead and make the request. Before Westmoreland made his request for new reinforcements, General Wheeler seems to have tried to convince the President that such reinforcements were very urgent but Westmoreland would not make a request to that effect because of the fear of its rejection by the Secretary. Wheeler appears to have succeeded in procuring from the President some sort of a promise that "Westy's" request for more troops would be honoured. And the Chairman might have duly passed over this assurance from the President to CUMUSMACV. This understanding among the President, Wheeler and Westmoreland was apparently reached over the head of McNamara. One thus gets the impression that the President and the military actors were moving in the same direction at this point while the Secretary of Defence who was unable to share that approach was on his way out. The President's drift toward the military and away from the Defence Secretary had reached its culmination.

The Tet Offensive provided an opportunity for the JCS to push their proposal of reserve call-up. After hearing from General Westmoreland, they developed three plans each of which, they said, would make the strategic reserve in the US so thin that it would affect its worldwide commitments. They recommended to the Secretary that, if such a course was adopted, the decision to send more men to South Vietnam might be deferred. However, they added, preparatory measures should be taken then in anticipation of the possible dispatch of the 82nd Airborne Division and two-thirds of a Marine Division air wing team.[45] Perhaps the Chiefs were playing a smart game. They were probably aware that the President was going their way and was disinclined to "bow out" of South Vietnam. The President might buy their proposal for reserve call-up which would be a preparatory step for expanded action in the future. But the JCS received a jolt on 13 February when McNamara, without recom-

---

[44] Marvin Kalb and Elie Abel, *Roots of Involvement* (London, 1971), pp. 209-12.
[45] Sheehan, n. 30, p. 608.

mending a reserve call-up, approved immediate deployment of 10,500 men which raised the total of American troops above the 525,000 ceiling.[46]

On 28 February, the President decided to form a small group under the chairmanship of Clark Clifford to advise him on the issue. Clifford was an old name in Washington. He had been around the town for a pretty long time. He was a White House "counsellor" during the Truman Administration. He assisted President Kennedy in managing governmental affairs when the latter took over the office from Eisenhower. Reputed as a trouble-shooter and a hawk, Clifford was named by Johnson as McNamara's successor. The President, who was having a tough time with his advisers already divided amongst themselves on Vietnam, might have hoped that the new Defence Secretary would support his strong posture in Vietnam and put the house in order.

On 4 March, the Clifford group submitted its report to the President. It recommended that nearly 23,000 men might be immediately sent to South Vietnam and that the decision on the rest of 205,000 package requested by Westmoreland and supported by the JCS might be made on the basis of week-by-week examination of requirements. The Committee also recommended a reserve call-up of about 245,000 men.[47] Thus, the report of the Clifford group further consolidated the position of the military over the Secretary of Defence on the issue concerned. Both the main proposals of the military were accepted. The 205,000 package remained valid and a big reserve call-up was approved. One is not clear to what extent President Johnson's own preferences would have influenced the recommendations of the Committee headed by a man who was soon to step into McNamara's shoe.

THE EFFICACY OF THE AIR WAR AND THE ISSUE: "BOMBING PAUSES"

The Pentagon expected that the application of American air power could produce results in softening the enemy by making

---

[46] Ibid., pp. 608-9.
[47] Ibid., pp. 611-7.

him aware of the price that he may have to pay for continuing his ways. It was felt that if he was slow to respond to the message respresented by initial selective strikes, he could be made to realize his folly by graduated escalation of bombing. Even though, on the basis of studies made of effects of the bombing of Germany during the Second World War, some elements in the civilian component and, perhaps, even of the Army might not have been able to share completely the optimism of the Air Force in regard to the efficacy of bombing, there was apparently not much controversy about the initiation of the air war, and over the acceptance of the principle of graduated escalation.

When Operation Rolling Thunder launched on 2 March 1965 failed to yield the expected results, McNamara recommended to the President on 1 July 1965 stepped up offensive military operations including the sharp escalation in bombing operations. The Secretary argued for a total quarantine of the movement of war supplies into North Vietnam by sea, rail and road. In order to achieve the objective, he recommended that all ports of North Vietnam including Haiphong should be mined, all rail and road bridges connecting China and North Vietnam be bombed and fighter airfields and SAM sites in North Vietnam be destroyed.[48] These recommendations were immediately supported by the military. The JCS, in their memorandum of 2 July, emphasized the urgency of the mining of ports, and attacks on POL targets and SAM sites.[49]

After a lapse of nineteen days, however, McNamara modified his position. Now he recommended the mining of North Vietnam's harbours as a possible "severe reprisal should the VC or DRV commit a particularly damaging or horrendous act." He, however, urged that the number of strike sorties against North Vietnam be raised from 2,500 per month to 4,000 or more with the caveat that strikes on population and industrial targets, not very much connected with North Vietnam's supply of war materials to the Viet Cong, be avoided.[50] McNamara's 20 July memorandum indicated his continuing support for escalation but with a difference. The interposition of many

[48] *DOD Documents*, n. 30, p. 9.
[49] Ibid.
[50] Ibid., pp. 11-2.

qualifications and restrictions in that memorandum signified some change in McNamara although this change was not so big as to indicate a major reversal of his stand on the air war. Why did this change, though small, take place in McNamara's thinking? Why did he fail to go all out for the "kill" although his optimism was at an all-time high? He might have sensed some opposition to his position as laid down in his memorandum, dated 1 July 1965. McNaughton had advocated on 13 July that population targets, targets close to China's border and SAM sites should not be bombed.[51] These reservations were included in the Secretary's 20 July memorandum. It is, therefore, reasonable to argue that McNaughton's 13 July memorandum might have exercised some influence on the Defence Secretary. It is not clear if other "Vietnam principals" put some pressure on McNamara to change his earlier stand. The possible role of Under Secretary of State, George Ball, will be discussed in the next chapter. The other variable which might have acted upon McNamara was his visit of South Vietnam, 14-20 July 1965. During this tour, he found the situation in South Vietnam "worse" than before.[52] Nevertheless the Secretary was optimistic about the final outcome and ready to recommend a major escalation. Perhaps it reflected his appraisal of the trend of Johnson's thinking. Perhaps each reinforced the other's view. The Secretary could also confidently count on support for his course of escalation from the JCS.

In regard to American bombing of North Vietnam, the issue of attacking POL (Petroleum, Oil and Lubricants) targets of North Vietnam generated more controversy than any other issue. More specifically, it continued to divide the civilian and military elements of the Pentagon till McNamara's exit. As time passed, it became the symbol of civil-military conflict and both parties tended more and more to consider it as a prestige issue. This rift did not remain confined for long to the original adversaries. In course of time, different segments of the three "concentric circles" took sides.[53] The battle royal was fought in the spring

---

[51] Ibid., p. 11.

[52] *New York Times*, 21 July 1965.

[53] The phrase "three concentric circles" has been coined by Roger Hilsman, discussed in the Introductory Chapter.

of 1967 when Secretary McNamara confronted the Preparedness Investigating Subcommittee of the Senate Armed Services Committee in August 1967.

On 2 September 1965, the JCS recommended air strikes against the POL and other lucrative targets of North Vietnam. They argued that the destruction of POL targets would seriously cripple Hanoi's capacity to supply war materials to the Viet Cong. This proposal was not accepted by McNamara on the ground that it was too dangerous an escalatory step. Before the year expired, the Joint Chiefs again pressed their proposal for POL attacks.[54] No decision on this proposal was taken at the higher level before the 37-day bombing pause began on 24 December.

Before the year 1965 ended, the civilian and military elements of the Pentagon were again ranged in opposite camps—this time on the question of a bombing pause. As early as 20 July 1965, the Defence Secretary had argued for a pause.[55] He implicitly repeated it in his 30 July memorandum in which he advised, "Minimize the loss of DRV 'face'." According to him, it would be politically easy for North Vietnam to come to the negotiation table and/or to make concessions at a time when her territory was not currently bombed.[56] McNamara pushed this proposal with much vigour in the month of November. In two memoranda, written on 3 November and 30 November (just after his return from South Vietnam), the Secretary advocated a bombing pause. He added that if there was no favourable response from Hanoi, the ground operations in the South and the bombing of the North might be greatly intensified.[57] It is important to note that while in his 20 July memorandum the Secretary had argued for a 6-8 week pause, in his 30 November memorandum he proposed a three-to-four week pause. It appears that these two gestures on the Defence Secretary—his warning that the war could be greatly escalated if Hanoi failed to favourably respond, and his recommendation for a 3-to-4 week instead of 6-8-week pause—were concessions to his bureaucratic adversaries, in the

---

[54] *DOD Documents*, n. 30, p. 64.
[55] Ibid., p. 20.
[56] Ibid., p. 21.
[57] Ibid.

present context, the military and other civilian actors, to elicit their agreement to his proposal.

The 37-day pause began on 24 December 1965. Soon after this, there ensued a debate on whether the pause served any tangible purpose and on the shape of operations in the future. First the controversy centred round how one was to know that the "pause" failed. At what point would the US be satisfied that North Vietnam accepted or rejected her conditions for negotiations? In other words, how much concessions did Washington expect of Hanoi? McNamara, in his 3 November 1965 memorandum, stated that under a "hard-line" pause, the US was strongly determined to resume bombing if Hanoi failed to meet America's declared terms. "Under a soft-line pause," he added, "we would be willing to feel our way with respect to termination of the pause with less insistence on concrete concessions by the Communists." McNamara added that a "soft line" pause implied that the US was prepared for a "compromise" settlement. He hastened to add that he himself stood on the side of a "hard-line" pause.[58] By opting for the stronger dose, the Secretary seemingly sought to pre-empt, in the bureaucratic game, the moves by his competitors who were known to be taking a hard line—especially the JCS and other military actors.

The second point on which the opinion in Washington was divided was on the nature of bombing operations, if a decision to resume bombing were to be taken. Should it resume with a "bang" or should it move slowly? McNamara and his Assistant Secretary for International Security Affairs, McNaughton, pleaded that the resumption of bombing should not begin with a "dramatic strike." It should begin at a low level and then gradually escalate.[59] McNamara's advocacy of the "pause" and of resumption of bombing at a low level, if the pause failed to yield results, gave rise to the inference that some reservations on the escalation, *albeit* embryonic, had begun to form in the Secretary's mind. McNamara's views, on starting at a low level of air strikes, was not accepted by the military. They not only wanted that bombing should be resumed quickly, but also urged

---

[58] Ibid., pp. 26-7.
[59] Ibid., p. 28.

that it be fast and aggressive. They urged that from the very beginning of resumption, the US should go for strategic bombing. They recommended that the US should attack the POLs of North Vietnam, interdict all LOCs (Lines of Communication) from China and close all her posts.[60] The Secretary sought to buttress his position *vis-a-vis* the JCS by indicating that he too was for a "hard line" ultimately but not as a starter when the pause ended.

The bombing was resumed on 31 January 1966, but not in a dramatic fashion. Thus the President apparently sought to maintain balance between the civilian and military elements of the Pentagon by resuming bombing—a view strongly urged by the military—but deciding in favour of an initial "soft-line" resumption which was advocated by the civilian actors of the Pentagon. But the POL controversy was not set at rest. The JCS began to push their proposal for attacks on POL targets. On 1 March the JCS recommended to McNamara that POLs and LOCs should be bombed and North Vietnam's harbours mined. After ten days they repeated this recommendation with the addition that it had the approval of Ambassador Lodge and Admiral Sharp.[61] On 23 March the Secretary asked General Wheeler certain specific questions relating to bombing. One of his queries was whether POL attacks would produce significant results if not accompanied by mining of North Vietnamese ports.[62] This query indicates the direction in which the Secretary was thinking. It seems that he had by this time made up his mind to agree to the proposal of striking POLs if the JCS would not insist on the mining of harbours. By now the Secretary had probably come to believe that the mining of harbours was potentially very dangerous. Both McNamara and McNaughton had earlier pointed out that this step might provoke Moscow and Peking to get in. Sensing that the Secretary might be induced to go part of the way, the military made a concession. In response to the Secretary's query, General Wheeler said that the Chiefs attached the highest importance to the POL

[60] Ibid., pp. 32-3.
[61] Ibid., pp. 85-6.
[62] Ibid., p. 87.

operation, *"even if enemy harbors remained open."*[63] The Chiefs also strongly recommended attacks on adjoining industrial targets and LOCs. In late March McNamara recommended to the President that seven out of nine POL storage facilities in the Hanoi-Haiphong area should be bombed. He also proposed attacks on some plants, roads, bridges and railroads.

Thus, the late-March Pentagon recommendation on POL attacks was the product of mutual concessions made by the civilian and military elements of the Pentagon. For the time being the military withdrew their insistence on mining harbours and the Defence Secretary changed his earlier opposition in regard to attacking POLs. It is in line with our hypothesis stated at the outset that each decision in a bureaucratic process is not only a "compromise" among competitive actors, but also "incremental" in nature. A decision is the cumulative product of many successive steps taken earlier. When the JCS first pressed for POL attacks, the Defence Secretary tried to satisfy them by recommending the intensification of bombing—an increase in the level of bombing from 3,000 sorties per month to 4,000 sorties per month. For the time being he put aside the POL decision, but could not kill it. On the other hand, by yielding a few inches to the military he prepared the ground for the next move by the military. It was not a surprise that the military's next move was again POL attacks and mining of harbours. Secretary McNamara this time yielded on the POL question and postponed a decision on mining harbours. But again the Secretary paved the ground for the next higher bid by the military. Thus, in such an escalatory process, each bureaucratic decision contains within it the seeds of the next decision, the next increment. Each rung in an incremental ladder has its own mementum which spills over to the next higher rung.

Some time toward the third week of June 1966 the decision was taken at the highest level to attack POLs and on 29 June strikes were launched. Official reports were very optimistic. McNamara congratulated the field commanders involved in planning and executing the strikes. But this jubilation was short-lived. Soon the Secretary was to discover that the strikes

---

[63] Ibid.

had failed to pay dividends. Toward the end of July, the CIA reported that while the recent POL strikes had destroyed over 50 per cent of North Vietnam's petroleum storage capacity, substantial stocks still survived. North Vietnam would be able to import sufficient fuel to keep at least the essential military and economic traffic moving.[64] This discouraging report might have had some impact upon the Secretary in shaping his attitude towards bombing. But the stronger force which brought about a decisive change in him in this respect was the JASON study report, referred to earlier in connection with the issue of installing an electronic infiltration barrier.

Under the sponsorship of the Defence Department, a group of eminent scientists had been constituted in the summer of 1966 to study the results of Rolling Thunder. They submitted their report on 29 August 1966. The report stated that the bombing of North Vietnam including the recent POL strikes had not substantially affected the ability of North Vietnam to support the military operations in the South at the current level. The damage done to North Vietnam had been more than compensated by the increased flow of aid from her "allies," the USSR and China. Despite the bombing, the flow from the North to the South had been accelerated. Indeed, bombing had led to strengthened unity of the people of North Vietnam and improved relationship of Hanoi with Moscow and Peking. After making these appraisals of bombing, the study group went on to suggest that an anti-infiltration barrier be introduced as a substitute for bombing.[65]

The views of the study group probably served to resolve for McNamara the dilemma that he had wrestled with for some time. It was too the kind of report that he wanted to receive at that time in view of his own misgivings over the continuance of the bombing campaign. The device of "study group" is not infrequently resorted to by a leading player to strengthen his own hand. Not infrequently the members selected to constitute "study groups" are conscious of or are subtly made aware of the role expected of them. Taking advantage of such a situation the leading elements in a study group may put in "plugs"

---

[64] Ibid., p. 143.
[65] Ibid., pp. 150-60.

for a few subsidiary courses in which they are interested, while providing a justification for the course which the player commissioning the report is believed to favour. It is not argued here that this was what actually happened in respect of the JASON study. Evidence was not encountered bearing on this aspect. The scenario is mentioned as one of the possibilities.

From that time onwards McNamara took a decisive stand against expanded bombing operations pressed for by the JCS. Within the Administration he emerged to be the most persistent critic of their demands. He was vigorously supported by his civilian colleagues of the Pentagon in this direction. In the second week of October 1966, McNamara, along with McNaughton, Wheeler, and Katzenbach, the Under Secretary of State, visited South Vietnam. After his return he wrote to the President that the bombing had failed to stop infiltration. He proposed an anti-infiltration barrier, as recommended by the JASON study group. He also proposed a bombing pause which might improve the climate for negotiations.[66]

The JCS strongly disagreed with McNamara's memorandum. They believed that bombing was yielding results. They opposed any reduction in bombing or a pause. They did not believe that a pause would enhance the prospect for negotiations. They argued that bombing was one of the two trump cards that the President could play against the "Communists" (The other being the presence of American troops in South Vietnam). "It should not be given up without an end to the NVN aggression in SVN." On the other hand, the JCS urged, the US should give a "sharp knock" to North Vietnam's military targets.[67] Though McNamara had taken Wheeler along with him to South Vietnam, the latter, apparently, did not share the Secretary's appraisal. The JCS closed ranks and a near-complete cleavage between them and the Secretary appeared to exist on the issue. The President did not authorize the expansion of the air war which was strongly advocated by the military. But the President did not completely alienate his military advisers. He authorized an increase of B-52 sorties from 600 to 800 in February 1967, but it was a very small gesture on his part to keep the military on

[66] Ibid., pp. 163-6.
[67] Ibid., pp. 167-8.

board. The Defence Secretary, as in earlier rounds, won over the military this time too.

To the discord between civilian and military elements of the Pentagon on a bombing pause, another element came to be added early in 1967. The Secretary of Defence supported another Tet truce hoping that it would improve the climate for negotiations. All the segments of the military—the JCS, the CINCPAC and the CUMUSMACV—strongly opposed it. The President sided with the Secretary and the Tet truce was observed. The second issue on which the Secretary and JCS were at odds related to the mining of internal waterways in North Vietnam. The JCS sought to repeat the tactic of scaling down an earlier demand. Resiling for the time being from their old proposal for the mining of all the harbours of North Vitenam, they recommended selected inland waterways and selected coastal areas to be mined in interdict internal water transportation in North Vietnam.[68] That meant that Haiphong and some other strategic ports of North Vietnam were to be excluded but other "waterways" were to be fair game. It is not clear whether McNamara supported their recommendation or not. However, on the basis of the past behaviour of the Secretary, one may hazard the guess that he would have agreed to go along with a scaled down demand in order to avoid widening the breach with the military. The President approved of the aerial mining of internal waterways of North Vietnam on 22 February.

The Secretary might have yielded to the JCS on the issue of mining the internal waterways. But it did not mean that he had withdrawn his effort to undermine the basic position of the military "adversary." The effort took the form of the preparation of a DPM by Assistant Secretary McNaughton. His DPM of 5 May, (referred to also in the earlier section on the escalation of the ground war) challenged the domino theory and sought to reformulate American objective in Vietnam. It implied the replacement of the objective spelled out in NSAM 288 by efforts towards a political solution. McNaughton suggested that the US should be mentally prepared to accept in Saigon a coalition government consisting of Communists. In

---

[68] *DOD Documents*, Book 6, IV.C.7(b), vol. 2, p. 8.

regard to bombing, McNaughton argued that the bombing of the interior of North Vietnam was entailing heavy losses of civilian lives. He feared that the mining of ports would involve a risk of confrontation with the Soviet Union. He voiced doubts on whether American bombing could irreparably damage the ability of North Vietnam to send economic and military aid to the Viet Cong. He approvingly cited Consul-General Edward E. Rice [of Hong Kong] to the effect that "we cannot by bombing reach the critical level of pain in North Vietnam and that below that level, pain only increases the will to fight."[69] In view of these considerations, the Assistant Secretary recommended that the US should concentrates her strikes on the lines of communication south of 20°—the "funnel" through which the flow of men and materials passed from the North to the South. McNaughton's draft apparently reflected the Secretary's own thinking at this time. His views were substantially reproduced in McNamara's DPM of 19 May. He recommended a bombing programme involving concentration of effort on the infiltration routes near the south of North Vietnam. He added that all of the sorties should be flown in the area between 17° and 20°.[70]

On 20 May the JCS stated that the bombing of North Vietnam had so far failed to achieve the objectives fully because of the "restraints" imposed on it. They demanded that those restraints should be removed.[71] On 24 May General Wheeler argued that a complete or partial cessation of bombing would help the enemy immensely. Such a step could be "an aerial Dien Bien Phu," he warned.[72] The JCS memorandum of 1 June which was a reply to the DPM of 19 May was even more sharp in its tone. The Chiefs charged that the concept of a "funnel" was misleading, since the flow of aid to the South was coming from all sides. They argued that the restraints imposed upon bombing would, instead of creating favourable conditions for negotiations, spoil the prospects for negotiations. The de-escalation of the war in the North and the South was "conceptually

---

[69] Ibid., pp. 31-2.
[70] Ibid., p. 49.
[71] Ibid., p. 54.
[72] Ibid.

questionable," they asserted. The JCS bluntly declared that the Secretary's DPM "lacked adequate foundation for further consideration," and recommended that the DPM not be forwarded to the President."[73]

Many memoranda circulated within the Pentagon, representing the positions of different actors on the bombing debate initiated by the DPM of 19 May. The most important of them was another DPM written by the Defence Secretary on 12 June. It posited three alternatives. Alternative A required intensive attack on the Hanoi-Haiphong base. Under this alternative, all ships entering North Vietnam and going out of her would be attacked. Specifically, harbours would be mined, and foreign shipping would be "shouldered out" of Haiphong by air strikes. Under alternative B, emphasis would be put, not on preventing materials from coming into the North, but on preventing men and materials from going out of the North into the South. Alternative C was a compromise between alternative A and B. Secretary McNamara, Deputy Secretary Vance and the Secretary of the Navy supported alternative B. The JCS endorsed alternative A while the Secretary of the Air Force supported alternative C. It is thus clear that no other actors of the Pentagon except the JCS stood for alternative A.[74] This indicates the near unanimity among the civilian elements of the Pentagon in regard to the rejection of the actions envisaged under alternative A—actions that the JCS regarded as necessary and desirable.

When a dispute on a major issue between more or less equally powerful actors reaches an acute stage, it does not long remain a secret confined to the organization concerned. One or the other or both the principals may tend to project the issue outside the organization into an arena in which its position can be promoted. Apart from inspired newspaper "leaks," Congressional hearings are sought to be harnessed for the purpose. Congressional Committees too are usually on the look-out for such issues which provide them opportunities to project themselves in the decision-making process. Sometimes one side or the other involved in the conflict in the

Executive takes the initiative to stimulate Congressional interest in the matter. The side concerned will understandably stimulate that Committee which it expects to be favourable to its own point of view.

Hearings were called by the Preparedness Investigating Subcommittee of the Senate Committee on the Armed Services. Most of the members of the above Subcommittee including its Chairman Senator Stennis (Dem., Mississippi) were known to be strong defenders of the Air Force and ardent supporters of the military *vis-a-vis* the civilians. The witnesses invited to give testimony for this hearing were Secretary McNamara, the members of the JCS and Admiral Sharp, the CINCPAC. The Subcommittee first heard the military actors and the Defence Secretary subsequently. It is noteworthy that on 9 August—the day the hearings started—the military were authorized to bomb sixteen additional targets, six of which were within the 10-mile range of the inner circle of Hanoi.[75] This authorization appeard to be a pre-emptive step on the part of the Defence Secretary in order to take away a good deal of wind out of the sails of the military. It might also have been meant to soften up elements in the Committee that were known to favour increased pressure on the enemy.

In the course of the hearings the Generals tried to make three points. They stated that the bombing had done serious damage to North Vietnam. It had considerably reduced the flow of men and materials from the North to the South. The argument put forth by McNamara in earlier Congressional hearings held in the beginning of the year that if ports were mined, North Vietnam could still import adequate materials through rail lines and roads, and that she could send aid to the South by "bicycles, and back-packs," was strongly rebutted. The Chiefs argued that the bombing programme could have become more effective but for the "doctrine of gradualism." Because of the slow nature of bombing, the "enemy" could find sufficient time to report its losses, they contended. They asserted that the application of air power against North Vietnam was going to contribute in the overall to the "shortening

[75] Ibid., p. 91.

of the war."[76]

McNamara appeared before the Subcommittee on 25 August. He must have been aware that he was likely to face tough and hostile questioning. The military had had their say and their testimony was hostile to the course that he favoured. Given composition of the Subcommittee and the known views of several of its members, McNamara could hardly have been optimistic that he could make his views prevail. But with daring and skill, he formulated his replies in such fashion that regardless of the immediate outcome, they could have a longer-term impact on the Administration, the Congress, and the American public.

McNamara argued that bombing had not succeeded in breaking the morale of North Vietnamese. The people of North Vietnam were accustomed to live in difficulties and no amount of damage done by bombing would bring them to a level where they would be unable to keep on sending war supplies to the South. Nor would it make them withdraw their support for the Hanoi regime, the Secretary added. "There is nothing in the past reaction of the North Vietnamese leaders that would provide any confidence that they can be bombed to the negotiating table."[77] The Defence Secretary declared that the bombing of North Vietnam had always been considered as a supplement to and not a substitute for an effective counter-insurgency operations in South Vietnam. Obviously aiming at the military actors as well as other critics of "our present bombing policy," McNamara said :

Those who criticize our present bombing policy do so, in my opinion, because they believe that air attack against the North can be utilized to achieve quite different objectives. These critics appear to argue that our air-power can win the war in the South either by breaking the will of the North or by cutting off the war-supporting supplies needed in the South. In essence, this approach would seek to use the air

[76] US Senate, Cong. 90, sess. 1, Preparedness Investigating Subcommittee of the Committee on Armed Services, Hearings, *Air War Against North Vietnam*, part 1 (Washington, D.C., 1967), pp. 8, 19, 35, 152.
[77] Ibid., part 4, pp. 275, 325, 335.

attack against the North not as a supplement to, but as a substitute for the arduous ground war that we and our allies are waging in the South.[78]

In spite of his skilful performance, the Defence Secretary failed to convince the Subcommittee. The report of the Subcommittee, released a few days later, contained scathing criticisms of McNamara. (These aspects will be discussed in greater detail in the fifth chapter dealing with the Congressional interaction with the Pentagon on Vietnam.)

The McNamara-military rift on bombing continued till he left office at the end of February 1968. The final issue on which they differed related to military's advocacy of bombing Phuc Yen airfield near the Chinese border and bombing and mining Haiphong and other harbours of North Vietnam. The Defence Secretary was opposed to these steps. Eventually, however, a compromise was reached. The decision was taken to hit Phuc Yen and some targets in Haiphong, but not to mine the Haiphong port.[79] In a conflict situation, an adversary may retreat, step by step, from its initial position and may progressively move towards the position of the opponent. But a point may be reached representing what may be described as "irreducible minimum demand" of the actor. He may be fearful that if he permits himself to be pushed beyond this point, his viability as an actor might suffer grievous damage since the cause he believes in would, in his opinion, suffer grievously. McNamara was placed at that time in a similar situation in relation to the mining of Haiphong. McNamara believed that the cause advocated by the JCS might greatly increase the danger of Chinese and Russian intervention. Intelligence reports appeared to confirm this fear. Though the JCS could wring a partial concession from the Secretary on the eve of his departure, their victory was to prove to be pyrrhic. The Secretary with whom they had developed sharp disagreements was to make his exit. The JCS remained in position. But their common principal, the President, had finally moved towards an acceptance of the views of the departing Secretary and away from the

[78] Quoted in *DOD Documents*, n. 68, p. 95.
[79] Ibid., p. 105.

position of the JCS. Johnson continued to refuse the military's demand for mining Haiphong and set his course in the direction of ending the operations that had so sharply divided not merely the Pentagon but the nation itself.

THE ROLE OF EXTRA-PENTAGON VARIABLES

In evolving its approach to an issue, the Defence Department has to reckon not only with the President, and rival federal actors in other agencies, but also with Congress, the media, various interest groups, and "public opinion." The interaction of the Department with the federal actors and with Congress are dealt with in Chapter IV and Chapter V respectively. A brief discussion of the other variables may appropriately be attempted at this point.

Given the general disposition of the American public to rally round the President and the Armed Forces in a period of crisis and especially in the initial phase when US troops are involved in actual fighting, the Pentagon usually encounters little difficulty in receiving very substantial support from the media, service associations, veteran organizations, organized labour and other interest groups, and the general public. Indeed, to a substantial extent, the volume of public support probably has significant impact on the entities that have been referred to. It is noteworthy that the Vietnam venture continued to receive significant public support during the whole period under review, even though some erosion had set in the later phase.

Both the civilian and military components of the Department have a common stake in mobilizing and retaining, to the maximum extent possible, the support of the public as well as other entities for the national effort as well as the Department's own role in support of the effort. They, therefore, tend to work in harmony, in pursuance of that objective. When criticisms began to appear and to intensify in the media, they sought to evoke appraisals favourable to their point of view and to utilize service associations, veteran organizations, and other interest groups to stimulate public support. The situation became somewhat complicated when major differences developed within the Department itself between the civilian and military components. In that context, the same tactics of mobilizing support were sought to be employed by each group with some care being taken to avoid undue injury to the basic objective that they shared as well as the prestige and integrity of the military establishment, and constitutional provisions and conventions relating to the lines of authority in decision-making.

The reaction of the general American public towards the policies in respect of Vietnam was influenced by the information that was made available to them by the media and by the exposition of issues by governmental and other political leaders. The perception of Communist danger to the "free world" led by the United States and endorsed and propagated over the years by both the civilian and military actors in Washington had produced a situation in which the general public largely believed in the existence of the threat and the necessity of responding militarily to it whenever necessary. A nation-wide poll conducted by Gallup soon after the American air attack on North Vietnam in early February 1965 pointed out that 67 per cent of the respondents approved of the American action, 15 per cent expressed disapproval while 18 per cent were undecided.[80] A Harris survey conducted in late April of the same year revealed that 57 per cent of the respondents supported President Johnson's military policy in Vietnam.[81] As the Vietnam war escalated resulting in increased American casualties, there was gradual increase in the number of the people who felt that the American involvement in Vietnam was a mistake and who became highly critical of Johnson's handling of the war. In August 1965, a Gallup poll showed that 23 per cent of the respondents were of the view that the American involvement in Vietnam was a mistake. The number of people who shared this view in October 1967 was exactly doubled.[82] In August 1965, 57 per cent of the respondents, in a Gallup poll, approved of the President's conduct of the war. This number was reduced to 40 per cent in December 1967.[83] In spite of the increased criticism of Johnson's handling of the war, and the

---

[80] *Washington Post*, 16 February 1965.
[81] Ibid., 26 April 1965; and *New York Times*, 27 April 1965.
[82] *New York Times*, 9 October 1967.
[83] Cited in Larry Elowitz and John W. Spanier, "Korea and Vietnam: Limited War and the American Political System," *Orbis* (Philadelphia, Penn.), vol.58, Summer 1974, p. 525.

growing feeling that sending troops to Vietnam was a mistake the view that the US should withdraw from Vietnam did not enjoy the support of the majority of those polled till February 1968. In November 1967 when Johnson had reached the lowest point in his popularity in poll surveys,[84] a Gallup poll found out that 59 per cent of the respondents favoured continuing American military efforts and 55 per cent advocated an increase in the American military involvement in Vietnam.[85] While by the beginning of 1967 the civilian elements of the Pentagon had started to be disenchanted with this policy, they had still to reckon with the state of public opinion which could not be changed overnight. The continuing public approval of the "militaristic" solution of the Vietnam problem perhaps strengthened the hands of the military *vis-a-vis* the civilians of the Pentagon in relation to Vietnam. Its case began to suffer when its differences with the civilians began to surface and when the public began to be perplexed by reports that harmony and unity no longer prevailed at the very top in the Pentagon on the right course to be adopted to promote American interest.

The second variable which influenced the interaction between the civilian and military elements of the Pentagon were the media of mass communication. Hardly any newspaper took a critical look at the Vietnam policy in 1964 and 1965 when the active military involvement began. Some like the *New York Herald Tribune* favoured the use of force in South Vietnam. On 4 February 1965, it warned against the "defeatist talks" in Washington and expressed suspicion that President Johnson was preparing "to run up the white flag in expectation of another Dienbienphu."[86] On 18 February the same newspaper charged that those who were urging "negotiation" were really asking the American people to "surrender."[87]

Except Walter Lippmann and perhaps James Reston, no other nationally known columnist joined issue with the admini-

---

[84] *New York Times*, 14 November 1967.

[85] Ibid., 11 November 1967.

[86] "Confusion over Vietnam," editorial *New York Herald Tribune*, 4 February 1965.

[87] "The Semantics of Surrender," editorial, ibid., 18 February 1965.

stration's Vietnam policy during this critical phase. On the other hand, several of them ardently supported the policy of the Administration, and, at times, advocated even more hawkish course. Important among them were Joseph Alsop, William S. White, and Roscoe Drummond. Alsop tried to whip up nationalist emotions by presenting before the American people the bleak prospect of the impending American defeat in Vietnam.[88] He warned on 4 January 1965, "...if the loss of China poisoned American public life for a decade, *this defeat that looms ahead* will poison our public life for a generation."[89] On 21 April 1965, he accused Senator Fulbright and Professor Hans J. Morgenthau of suffering from "pompous ignorance."[90] (Fulbright and Morgenthau were at that time arguing for a negotiated peace.) From time to time White and Drummond continued to attack the "doves" and defend the Administration policy in Vietnam.[91] Even the group of young American newspaper reporters in Saigon whose critical comments on the Saigon regime created considerable sensation among the American public in 1963 and 1964 were not really opposed to overall American *policy*, but only to the American *tactics*. In 1965, David Halberstam, the *New York Times* correspondent stated that the US could not agree to a neutral Vietnam which could create a "vacuum" for Communist "subversion." American withdrawal from Vietnam would encourage Communists to attempt "Vietnam-type insurgencies" throughout the world, he added.[92] In 1966, Neil Sheehan said that there was no alternative to the American strategy of continuing to prosecute the war with the hope that enough killing would force the enemy's collapse through exhaustion and despair.[93] (Subsequently the two correspondents turned very critical of US policy.) Halberstam's

[88] Ibid., 1 January 1965.
[89] Ibid., 4 January 1965.
[90] *Washington Post*, 21 April 1965.
[91] Roscoe Drummond, "Vietnam Study: Senate Inquiry Needed," ibid., 8 January 1965; and William S. White, "Negotiation? U Thant's View on Vietnam," ibid., 26 February 1965.
[92] Quoted in James Aronson, "The Media and the Message," in Noam Chomsky and Howard Zinn, eds., *The Pentagon Papers* (Boston, 1972), vol. 5, p. 46.
[93] Neil Sheehan, "Not a Dove, But No Longer a Hawk," *New York Times Magazine*, 9 October 1966.

book, *The Best and Brightest*, a biting expose of American policy-making on Vietnam, won for him the coveted Pulitzer prize. Sheehan edited for the *New York Times* the *Pentagon Papers* which disclosed the internal story of American decision-making on Vietnam. The changed tone of the so-called "Young Turks" in 1965 and 1966 indicates a general lack of an effort on the part of "opinion elites" to challenge the main thrust of American course in Vietnam.

However, as the war progressed and "victory" appeared to be elusive, the "opinion elites" began to be divided in regard to Vietnam. While some of them continued to support the ongoing policy and/or advocated a deeper American military involvement in Vietnam, some others began to take a critical look at it. The latter began to express their concern against the escalation of the Vietnam war. The most consistent and prominent members of the former group were Joseph Alsop and Hanson W. Baldwin, the military correspondent of the *New York Times*. From time to time, Alsop stated in his syndicated columns that Communists were facing defeat in Vietnam and that American policy was a success. At times he would reflect the military's views regarding the need of further escalation both in ground involvement and aerial attacks on North Vietnam. Similar was the stand taken by Baldwin on Vietnam.[94] In regard to the civil-military conflict within the Pentagon on Vietnam, Baldwin took the side of the military. In February 1966, he strongly supported the military's demand for the limited mobilization of reserve forces which was then opposed by McNamara.[95] On 27 February 1966, he wrote a major article in the *New York Times Book Review* which sought to advocate the case of the escalation of the Vietnam war. He said:

> It is my conviction that the President has relatively little choice; the enemy controls escalation as well as we. Given the present situation in Vietnam and our other commitments throughout the world, it is high time—more than time—that Congress declare a state of national emergency, that there be a limited mobilization of reserves, the appropriation of more

[94] *New York Times*, 10 February 1965.
[95] Ibid., 21 February 1966.

billions for the war, a major increase of United States strength in South Vietnam, and intensification of the bombing of North Vietnam.[96]

Baldwin echoed the military's demand for 600,000-700,000 US troops in South Vietnam in order to spur the pacification programme.[97] When the civilian and military elements of the Pentagon were fighting over the question of increasing the tempo and the scope of the bombing of North Vietnam, Baldwin asserted that bombing was very effective. When Harrison Salisbury's report from Hanoi, published in the front page of the *New York Times* charged that the American air attacks on Hanoi were resulting in large civilian casualties, Baldwin was quick to echo the line of the military. He countercharged that Salisbury's reports were "grossly exaggerated."[98] It was not a surprise that the military also strongly attacked Salisbury's reports.

National Review edited by the conservative columnist William F. Buckley, Jr., consistently advocated a policy of escalation in Vietnam. It would even urge a nuclear attack on North Vietnam if that would expedite American victory in Vietnam.[99] The weekly charged that Fulbright and others who advocated negotiated settlement really wished "unconditional surrender" by the United States.[100] James Burnham, a regular writer in the weekly, severely attacked the restrictions imposed on the bombing of North Vietnam by the US. He took to task "the appeasers within his [President's] official family" who stood for an "inhibited Vietnam strategy."[101] He lamented that the military actors were not given a free hand in conducting the war. He said, "This is the first war that has been fought according to the prescriptions of the game theorists." Lending his support for the military's demand for an offensive role for the Army, Burnham urged that it should be encouraged to spring a "sur-

---

[96] Hanson Baldwin, "The Case for Escalation," *New York Times Book Review*, 27 February 1966, Section VI, pp. 22, 79, 80, 81 and 82.
[97] *New York Times*, 12 November 1966.
[98] Ibid., 30 December 1966.
[99] *National Review* (New York), 9 August 1966, p. 757.
[100] "Unconditional Surrender," ibid., 4 October 1966, p. 968.
[101] Ibid., 28 June 1966, p. 612.

prise," instead of being "pinned down to enclaves" as advocated by Lt. Gen. James M. Gavin.[102]

On the other side, some columnists and intellectuals began to shift their position and started to criticize the escalation of the war, especially the "ascendancy" of the military. Joseph Kraft, a liberal columnist based at Boston, stated on 30 December 1966, "McNamara has been put on the defensive. The military has gained the whip hand over the Secretary of Defence. The last resort of the civilian authority is at the mercy of the soldiers."[103] James Reston of the *New York Times* who had first expressed his misgivings about the American involvement in Vietnam in 1965 began to urge that the US should unilaterally stop bombing and seek to settle the Vietnam problem by political means.[104] C.S. Sulzberger of the *New York Times* who, as late as in early 1967 supported the Administration's "firm" policy in Vietnam,[105] began to change his tone as the war escalated. At the height of the escalation debate both within the Administration and in public, Sulzberger advocated that there should be a "pause," in bombing and efforts should be made to reach a political settlement. James Wechsler of the *New York Post* warned against the increasing dominance of the military in policy-making of Vietnam.[106]

It is not certain if there was any tacit alliance between these columnists and the civilian elements in the Administration who were advocating a similar approach as the former in regard to Vietnam. But the campaign of these columnists against escalation might have helped the cause of McNamara and his supporters *vis-a-vis* the military.

As is usually the case, when major differences develop between powerful contending factions in agencies, an effort is made to reach initially the "attentive public" by both contenders. What begins as discreet floating of rumours soon escalates to enlisting the services of friendly newspaper writers to support one's point of view and knock down that of the contender. As

---

[102] Ibid., 22 February 1966, p. 151.

[103] *Washington Post*, 30 December 1966.

[104] *New york Times*, 20 February 1966; 22 March 1966; 1 July 1966 and 14 May 1967.

[105] Ibid., 29 January 1967.

[106] *New York Post*, 29 December 1966.

the battle warms up, both sides leak even secret and confidential materials for self-serving purposes. Very often, the faction which believes that it may lose the contest "leaks more profusely than the other." General MacArthur took recourse to such device more than once when his recommendations were rejected by Washington. The Navy also reportedly leaked many secret data to the press during the "admiral's revolt" in 1949.[107] Similar leaks were made during the Thor-Jupiter controversy.[108] In the present case, when the differences between civilian and military elements of the Pentagon became serious, the latter, as on similar previous occasions, sought recourse to mobilizing extra-Pentagon pressures in its favour. Hanson Baldwin's regular front-page reports in the *New York Times* advocating the points of view of the military *vis-a-vis* the civilians of the Pentagon seemed to have been inspired by the leaks made by the military. His charge that the military was running short of arms and weapons, his advocacy of the escalation of war and his opposition to a pause in bombing[109] constituted the kind of support that the generals relished—and probably sought to inspire. Neil Sheehan and William Beecher who was later appointed as the spokesman of the Defence Department seemed to take the side of the civilians as against the military.[110] By "leaking" such inside information as the military's pressure to intensify the bombing of North Vietnam, they appeared to warn the civilian elements of the Pentagon and other actors both in the government and outside to counter this pressure. The civilians probably had as much interest in "inspiring" such sympathetic reporters as the military in its Baldwins and Alsops.

The continual screening of scenes of war, the toll of casualties, and the agony of the local people on the television, had perhaps a very significant cumulative effect. Optimistic statements by the Administration and its supporters came to have diminishing impact as the fighting continued. They probably evoked growing disquiet among an increasing circle of citizens.

---

[107] Jack Raymond, *Power at the Pentagon* (New York, 1964), p. 200.

[108] Michael H. Armacost, *The Politics of Weapons Innovation: The Thor-Jupiter Controversy* (New York, 1969).

[109] *New York Times*, 9 October 1966; 12 October 1966 and 30 December 1966.

[110] Ibid., 3 July 1966.

Even though a substantial number continued to support the Administration's course in Vietnam, the enthusiasm of the initial phase was greatly reduced. Perhaps it led to the undermining of the cause of the military actors who favoured continued escalation.

The Air Force, Navy and Army have their respective service associations to articulate their interests. The Air Force Association, the Navy League and the Association of the United States Army exercise considerable pressure on behalf of the military *vis-a-vis* the civilian actors of the Pentagon. In the present case, they launched strong offensives against McNamara for having "downgraded" and "muzzled" the military. *The Journal of Armed Forces*, which seeks to champion the cause of all the branches of the military, scored the Department of Defence of being increasingly "civilianized"—obviously at the cost of the military. It said, "Top Brass Civilians within the Defence Department have mushroomed like an atomic cloud during the tenure of Secretary Robert S. McNamara."[111] This military journal also supported the military *vis-a-vis* the Secretary of Defence in relation to the question of ABM deployment.[112] In a sharp rebuke to the Defence Secretary, the *Air Force and Space Digest* which is the spokesman of the Air Force Association, reported Admiral H. Rickover having said, "our society is threatened by any man who knows method but not meaning, technique but not principle." Adm. Rickover snipped at the man who tried to operate in a professional field in which he was unqualified, any man who depreciated wisdom, experience, and intuition. He further charged, "*cost effectiveness has become the modern superstition. The Christian notion of the possibility of redemption is incomprehensible to the computer.*"[113]

Dennis Joseph Donogue who has made a content analysis of the publications of the service associations from 1960 to 1969 observes, "The service associations as a group were critical of the civilian personnel in the Department of Defence throughout 1960s." He asserts that the combined editorial and article find-

---

[111] Louis Stockstill, "The Big DOD Build-up," *Journal of Armed Forces* (Washington, D.C.), 5 August 1967, pp. 1, 8 and 9.
[112] Ibid., 13 May 1967, pp. 1 and 31.
[113] *Air Force and Space Digest* (Washington, D.C.), August 1967, p. 16. Emphasis added.

ings support such a conclusion. He further says, "Statistically, the service associations were as strongly critical of the civilians in the Pentagon in the first half of the decade as in the second half. . . ."[114]

The service associations carried on similar attacks against the Secretary of Defence with regard to Vietnam. This attack gradually increased in intensity as the civil-military confrontation within the Pentagon on Vietnam began to escalate. They scored the restrictions imposed by the Secretary on conducting the war. They tried to "sell" to the American public the military's version that the United States was winning the war in Vietnam and could bring the task to a successful conclusion if only the military was not hamstrung by various restrictions imposed by the civilian authorities. John B. Spore, the editor of *Army*, visited South Vietnam in the first quarter of 1966 and wrote, in two parts, his observations on the progress of war. He asserted that the enemy had suffered defeats unprecedented in its experience since the Americans were committed to action.[115] William Beecher, the *New York Times* correspondent in South Vietnam, wrote in *Army* of January 1967 that the American military officers in South Vietnam were bitterly critical of the restraints imposed on the conduct of military operations.[116] In a symposium on "The Air War against North" organized by the Air Force Association's 21st anniversary convention, Major General Gilbert L. Meyers, who had retired from active duty, urged that restrictions on the air war against the North should be lifted. (Gen. Meyers was the Deputy Commander of the Seventh Air Force in Vietnam from July 1965 to August 1966.) He urged that in that case the American interdiction efforts would be more successful and the American forces would be less exposed to a combat environment.[117] The *Journal of the Armed Forces*, in its editorial of

---

[114] Dennis Joseph Donogue, The Military Interest Groups: The Political Attitudes of the Service Associations (Ph.D. Thesis, Miami University, Oxford, Ohio, 1972), p. 121.

[115] John B. Spore, "The U.S. Army in Vietnam," pt. 1, *Army* (Washington, D.C.), vol. 16, May 1966, pp. 28-32, 80-6; pt. II ibid., June 1966, pp. 66-74.

[116] William Beecher, "Vietnam Reports from the Battle-Fields: Crisis of Confidence," *Army*, vol. 17, January 1967, p. 45.

[117] Maj. General Gilbert L. Meyers, USAF (Ret.), "Why Not More

2 September 1967, bitterly accused McNamara of having imposed restrictions on the air war. The Secretary had stated that there were only 57 targets recommended by the JCS against which strikes had not yet been authorized. In a sharp criticism of this statement, the *Journal* editorially said, "What we do question is the number-game. Number of targets might be less important than six or a dozen of the fifty seven rejected tragets."[118] In an editorial, the following week, the *Journal* again attacked the Secretary for having allegedly tried to misguide the Congress with regard to the bombing of the North. It added:

> If the Secretary of Defence has learned nothing else about Congressional relations during his almost seven years in office, he should have learned that it is next to impossible to present 'selected' information to a House or Senate Committee. All of the facts eventually came to the surface, and the witness whose testimony is overstated invariably ends up looking rather silly, if not downright dishonest. . . .[119]

One of the most vehement attacks against McNamara was made by C. W. Borklund, the editor of *Armed Forces Management*. He vigorously supported the JCS' criticism of the Secretary regarding the restrictions on the air war against North Vietnam. He charged that the general failure of the Johnson Administration to heed more carefully the advice of military experts had led and might continue to lead to many of the "security aches and pains."[120]

Apart from the service associations, some other associations having connection with the military actively campaigned on behalf of the military *vis-a-vis* the civilian elements of the Pentagon. The most important of them was the American Legion which extended strong support to the continuing American

Targets in the North?," *Air Force and Space Digest*, vol. 50, May 1967, pp. 74-8.
[118] Louis Stockstill, "The Approved List," Editorial, *Journal of Armed Forces*, 2 September 1967, p. 13.
[119] Louis Stockstill, "Truth in Packaging," ibid., 9 September 1967, p. 13.
[120] C.W. Borklund, "Strategy by Semantics," *Armed Forces Management* (Washington, D.C.), vol. 14, no. 13, December 1967, p. 19.

policy of escalation in Vietnam. Its invitation to President Johnson and Secretary Rusk to address its annual convention of 1966 indicated its position of Vietnam. The contingent of 8,500 American Legionnaires present at the convention applauded the President for his vows of firmness. More thunderous was the applause when their national commander, L. Eldon James, hailed Johnson as a "fighting" American and thanked him for his military intervention in both Vietnam and the Dominican Republic.[121] (In 1965, President Johnson sent the American marines to Santo Domingo in order to prevent a "Communist" government from taking office there.) More significant was the Legion's invitation to Richard M. Nixon as one of the guest speakers at the convention. Nixon at that time was not in any important political position. The ex-Vice President who lost the presidency by a very small margin in 1960 and who had the mortification of being defeated in California's gubernatorial race in 1962, was attempting a comeback in national politics. Since 1965 Nixon began to talk more and more on Vietnam. He emerged to be one of the strongest critics of the US policy, which, in his opinion, was too "soft" to contend with Communists. Addressing the Legion's national convention, he warned that if Vietnam fell, the Pacific would be transformed into a Red Ocean and the road would be open to a third world war. He urged that the Johnson Administration should cut off by 95 per cent North Vietnam's oil and other supplies which came by sea. He also advocated that the strength of American ground troops in South Vietnam should be increased by 25 per cent.[122] It may be mentioned that the military actors were, at that time, advocating similar measures.

The pro-escalation stance of the American Legion, expressed in the national convention of 1966, was repeated the next year. The personalities invited to address the national convention of 1967 were known to be ardent supporters of an escalation policy. General Wallace M. Greene, Jr., Commandant of the Marine Corps, urged the Legionnaires to take to the people the message that the Vietnam war was the nation's "most pressing problem." Senator John Stennis, the Chairman of the Defence Prepared-

[121] *New York Times*, 31 August 1966.
[122] Ibid., 1 September 1966.

ness Investigating Subcommittee of the Armed Services Committee, and known to be a great friend of the military, said, "Never before as a nation have we stopped in the middle of a war to debate how we got there, or why. We should not do so now."[123] Gerald Ford of Michigan, the Republican leader in the House and a member of the House Defence Appropriations Subcommittee, was more direct in his attacks on the civilian elements of the Pentagon. He charged that McNamara was "a disciple of defeat." He further charged that nearly half of the significant military targets of North Vietnam had not yet been authorized.[124]

The Legion itself in a series of resolutions passed in the annual convention, pressed for the intensified bombing of North Vietnam. It demanded the removal of the restrictions imposed by the civilian actors upon the attacks against the strategic targets in North Vietnam. It also advocated that the port of Haiphong should be closed "by whatever military means are considered most feasible."[125] These demands touched upon the main point of contention between the civilian and military elements of the Pentagon which was going on at that time.

The Association of Jewish War Veterans also extended consistent support to the military as against the civilian actors on Vietnam. Their motivation mainly seemed to be the linkage between the American policy in Israel and the same in relation to Vietnam. Israel went to war with the Arabs in 1967 for the third time in her history and that year was the peak period of civil-military confrontation on Vietnam. Many Jews—veterans in particular—in their efforts to insure American support for Israel against the Arabs, felt impelled to support the policy of escalation in Vietnam.

All during this period, the Department as well as the Administration could count on a very substantial volume of support from the leadership of the American Federation of Labour, Congress of Industrial Organization (AFL-CIO). Its president, George Meany, was a staunch anti-Communist and consistently lent powerful support to the Administration's course. The International Brotherhood of Teamsters, the largest union outside

[123] Ibid., 31 August 1967.
[124] Ibid.
[125] Ibid., 1 September 1967.

the fold of AFL-CIO, was also a vigorous supporter of the American military effort. The AFL-CIO adopted a resolution on 24 August 1966 which commended President Johnson for "demonstrating to the world that our country is neither irresolute politically nor weak militarily while it is ever ready to negotiate the war's end."[126] It also took a decision to boycott the ships which would be having trade with North Vietnam.[127]

While some individual leaders in the AFL-CIO hierarchy might have had certain reservations, no challenge to the Meany-line materialized during the period. Leaders of some locals in a few trade unions were associated with anti-war elements, but they were unwilling to push their efforts beyond a certain point. It is generally believed that unlike among intellectuals and white-collar elements, support for the Administration remained substantially higher among blue-collar workers. Vociferous support for the war and criticism of anti-war groups emanated from those elements of workers who came to be characterized as hardhats.

As the war debate intensified, other segments of the American public got themselves aligned on rival sides. Many teachers and students protested against the escalation of the war. Sit-ins were organized in several campuses and protest marches were held in big cities. Draft cards were burnt, ROTC centres in several university campuses were attacked and there was angry demonstration by anti-war protestors before the Pentagon building. Never before in American history were seen thousands of students marching in big cities in protest against American involvement in a war. Some of the intellectuals, apart from addressing anti-war gatherings, expressed their views in writings. In this connection one may cite the articles of Professors John Kenneth Galbraith, Arthur Schlesinger, Jr., Hans J. Morgenthau, and Henry Commager. All four of them were noted for their liberal views and the first two of them had served the Kennedy Administration. Some other Kennedy officials like Roger Hilsman and Richard Goodwin also took an active role in the anti-war movement.

The number of teachers and students who supported the

---

[126] Ibid., 25 August 1966.
[127] Ibid., 23 February 1966.

escalation policy was very small in comparison to others who opposed it. Young Americans for Freedom was one of the few student organizations which extended support to the ongoing policy in Vietnam. The Administration, however, got support from other *ad hoc* groups which were organized to countervail the anti-war pressures. One of them was the Free Society Association for Stronger Action whose honorary chairman was Sen. Barry Goldwater. On 5 April 1967, it adopted a resolution urging the Administration to take stronger action in Vietnam.[128] The other important group that was formed with a view to supporting the policy of escalation was the Citizens Committee for Peace with Freedom on Vietnam. Two ex-Presidents—Harry Truman and General Eisenhower, the only other surviving "five star" general and Second World War "hero" Omar Bradley, and an important ex-Senator, Paul H. Douglas (Dem., Illinois) were some of its original members. On 25 October 1967, the committee gave strong endorsement to the Administration's policy of escalation.[129] Moreover, Eisenhower and Bradley favoured the military's demand for "hot pursuit" into North Vietnam, Laos and Cambodia.[130] The civilian elements of the Pentagon were opposed to the demand.

The preceding discussion suggests that in the initial phase of the American military involvement in Vietnam, the civilian and military components of the Defence Department were able to carry along with them the media, service associations, veteran organizations and other interest groups. The majority of the American people supported the main American military objectives in Vietnam throughout the period under study, even during the period when the existence of conflict between the civilian and military elements of the Defence Department came to be known. Towards the end, there was some erosion in this support, but apart from the anti-war student demonstrators, there was no menacing scourge of sentiment among the public against the Defence Department or the Administration's course in Vietnam. The civilian and military actors of the Pentagon sought, when differences on issues occurred between them, to bring to their

---

[128] Ibid., 6 April 1967.
[129] Ibid., 26 October 1967.
[130] Ibid., 29 November 1967.

respective support not only other federal actors and Congressional members, but other variables like the media, service associations, veteran organizations, and other articulate segments of the American public. "Leaks" were occasionally made by both sides to push forth their respective points of view. But neither side chose to push such tactics to a point that might have endangered the basic tasks to which both were dedicated. The game was played with some broad implicit understandings on the part of both players about the need to avoid any hurt to American objectives, to uphold the prestige and integrity of the military establishment and to maintain civilian control of the military.

CHAPTER FIVE

COMPETITION AMONG FEDERAL ACTORS TO INFLUENCE FOREIGN POLICY-MAKING

In the American system the President is the ultimate decision-maker on defence and foreign policy. He has a team of advisers to help him in determining the national security policy. The most prominent among them are the Secretary of State, the Secretary of Defence, the National Security Assistant, the JCS and the CIA Director. He also consults other members of his cabinet, when necessary. The National Security Council is the formal body which provides the forum for these advisers to meet and exchange their views on national security. They present to the President alternative courses of action on any issue under review. The President may also meet them separately outside the NSC. President Johnson reportedly used to discuss more important national security issues in his "Tuesday Lunches."[1] Moreover, the President may seek the advice of his unofficial advisers and Congressional leaders. He generally makes up his mind after hearing these people. However, his official advisers are his main advisers irrespective of where issues are discussed.

The President's advisers compete amongst themselves to reach his ear.[2] They have their personal and organizational interests involved. Moreover, each actor is psychologically motivated to exercise power, and power, here, is the ability of each actor to influence others including the President to accept his viewpoint. The chance of the viewpoint of any agency prevailing upon others may depend upon how well it has been articulated and developed inside the agency, the extent of unanimity that exists in its support in the agency, and how effectively and skilfully it is presented by

---

[1] Henry F. Graff, *The Tuesday Cabinet* (Englewood Cliffs, N.J., 1970).

[2] Merton H. Halperin, *Bureaucratic Politics and Foreign Policy* (Washington, D.C., 1974).

the head of the agency concerned in inter-agency meetings, formal or informal.[3] Other important variables which influence the degree of success of any agency in this regard is the Presidential style and the personal equation of the actor concerned with the President. Indeed, a main topic of conversation in Washington is who is "in" with the President now.[4] Dean Rusk probably meant the same thing when he talked of "confidence" that "flows down from the President."[5] Another factor that helps one in the bureaucratic competition of decision-making is the drive for power. One has to fight with his colleagues both inside his department and outside. This was probably in his mind when Secretary of State, Dean Acheson mentioned "The Killer Instinct" as the quality that a Secretary of State should possess.[6] Thus, from our point of view, the Secretary of Defence, in advocating his point of view, has to contend with five forces, namely, his civilian colleagues in the Department, the military, other federal actors, the President and Congress. In the last two chapters the interaction between the Secretary of Defence and the JCS was discussed. The next chapter will deal with the inter-relationship between the Secretary and Congress. The present chapter proposes to examine the interaction of the Defence Secretary *vis-a-vis* other federal actors in the realm of policy-making on Vietnam.

The State Department and the Defence Department are the principal agencies dealing with national security policy. As the Jackson Subcommittee on Governmental Operations said, they constitute the "central partnership" in national policy machinery. They are mainly responsible for advising on and executing national security decisions.[7] Thus the final outcome of any decision in this field is largely influenced by the personal and

[3] Adam Yarmolinsky, "Bureaucratic Structures and Political Outcomes, *Journal of International Affairs* (New York), vol. 23, no. 2, 1969, p. 232.

[4] Halperin, n. 2, p. 219.

[5] Dean Rusk, "Mr Secretary on the Eve of Emeritus," *Life* (Chicago), vol. 66, 17 January 1969, p. 62.

[6] Quoted in Joseph Kraft, *Profiles in Power : A Washington Insight* (New York, 1966), p. 178.

[7] Sen. Henry M. Jackson, ed., *The National Security Council : Jackson Subcommittee Papers on Policy-making at the Presidential Level* (New York, 1966), p. 9.

organizational equations between these two departments.

In order to insure that its views are properly reflected in the making of foreign policy, the Defence Department sought to set up a new bureau inside it. The result was the creation of the Office of the Assistant Secretary of Defence for International Security Affairs (ISA). It was primarily intended to enable the Defence Department to play its cards better in its competition with the State Department and in its dealings with Congress.[8] But if unity did not exist in the Pentagon, it would then be inclined to side with the Defence Secretary *vis-a-vis* his military opponents. Its internal organization on the basis of geographic subdivisions is largely similar to that of the State Department. It is often referred to as the "mini-State Department" of the Defence Department. The Assistant Secretary of Defence (ISA) is required to maintain active liaison for the exchange of information and advice with the military departments, the JCS and other Defence Department agencies. He is also required to coordinate relations between the Defence Department and the State Department "in the field of his assigned responsibility." Some of the functions of his office are as follows:

1. Monitor Department of Defence participation in National Security Council affairs. . . .

2. Assist the Secretary of Defense . . . and other agencies of the government in establishing defense policy by:

  a. Determining . . . the current and emerging international problems of major significance to the security of the United States, and analyzing the range of possible political-military actions for dealing with the long-term aspects of such problems.

  b. Identifying the national security objectives of the United States and developing the international political-military and foreign economic implications. . . .

  c. Initiating appropriate actions and measures within the Department of Defence for implementing approved National

---

[8] The discussion here on the Office of the Assistant Secretary of Defence (ISA) is mainly based on Donald F. Bletz, *The Role of the Military Professional in U.S. Foreign Policy* (New York, 1972), pp. 95-108.

Security Council policies. . . .

The Office of the Assistant Secretary of Defence (ISA) and its supporting staff is thus a Pentagon device to develop its own resources in terms of expertise that would be mobilized as it bargains with other federal actors and also as it presents its case to Congress. The State Department, which had earlier set up its own Policy Planning Council, sought to reinforce its position by creating the Office of Assistant Secretary for politico-military affairs. The office was created by the State Department to "look at politico-military problems on a world-wide basis. . . and provide a central point of focus and coordination, as required, for the politico-military activities being carried on by the geographical bureaus of the Department." This office was abolished in 1969 by the Nixon Administration. But this does not affect the present study which deals with the Kennedy and Johnson Administrations. The Policy Planning Council also deals with politico-military problems. But it is purely a planning body. It does not come in the operational channel.[9] A study of the record leads one to conclude that the Office of the Assistant Secretary of Defence (ISA) which combines both planning and operation, probably played a more important role than its State Department counterpart.

Other important actors in decision-making on foreign policy are the National Security Assistant to the President and the CIA. The National Security Assistant acts as a "filter."[10] He organizes and coordinates the views of other concerned agencies and presents them systematically to the President. When required, he also tenders his own advice to him. After the President makes up his mind, the Special Assistant is to communicate the President's decision to the concerned agencies. The Special Assistant's position assumes crucial significance because often it is he who decides how much of the views of what department is

---

[9] However, this formal limitation does not preclude the head of a Council from influencing decision-making by the force of his personality and/or his personal equation with the key actors in the policy process. A Kennan or a Rostow may play a more active role than what he is formally required to do.

[10] David Halberstam, "The Very Expensive Education of McGeorge Bundy," *Harper's* (New York), vol. 239, July 1969, pp. 21-41.

to be sent to the President. The CIA has primarily two functions.[11] It gathers intelligence on foreign countries and feeds
them to the President and the National Security Council. Second,
it engages in covert activities in other countries, in "the interest
of American national security." From time to time it has been
subjected to heavy fire of criticism on the ground that on its
own initiative, it often engineers covert activities in other countries and then faces Washington with a *fait accompli*. It has been
described as a "state within a state."[12] The Defence Department has to reckon with the strength and influence that the CIA
may be able to bring to bear on decision-making on issues of
vital concern to the former.

An attempt will be made in the present chapter to study how
different bureaucratic actors tried to influence Presidential
decisions on Vietnam and where the Pentagon stood. To what
extent was the Pentagon able to make its view prevail upon
other competitors? How far was it influenced by their postures?
To what extent did it succeed in stamping its imprint on
Presidential decisions or moderate its own views in line with
known Presidential wishes?

KENNEDY'S DECISION TO INCREASE THE
NUMBER OF MILITARY ADVISERS

Some time around the middle of November 1961 President
Kennedy took the decision to increase the number of military
advisers in South Vietnam. Hilsman suggests that Kennedy was
not in favour of sending American ground forces to Vietnam.[13]

---

[11] Allan Dulles, *The Craft of Intelligence* (New York, 1963); Harry
Howe Ransom, *The Intelligence Establishment* (Cambridge, Mass.,
1970); Lyman B. Kirkpatrick, Jr., *The US Intelligence Community*
(New York, 1973); and Victor Marchetti and John D. Marks, *The
CIA and the Cult of Intelligence* (London, 1974).

[12] Expressing concern over the activities of the CIA, President Truman
said in 1963, "For some time I have been disturbed by the way CIA
has been diverted from its original assignment. It has become an
operational and at times a policy-making arm of the government."
Washington Post, 22 December 1963; see also David Wise and Thomas
B. Ross, *The Invisible Government* (New York, 1964).

[13] Roger Hilsman, *To Move a Nation : The Politics of Foreign Policy in
the Administration of John F. Kennedy* (New York, 1967), pp. 536-7.

Schlesinger records that Kennedy told him in November 1961 that sending troops to Vietnam was like an alcoholic's first drink. "They want a force of American troops. . . . But it will be just like Berlin. The troops will march in; the bands will play; the crowds will cheer; and in four days everyone will have forgotten. Then we will be told to send in more troops. It's like taking a drink. The effect was off, and you have to take another,"[14] Kennedy said, according to Schlesinger. On the other hand, it has been alleged that the Kennedy Administration transformed the "limited-risk gamble" of the Eisenhower Administration into a "broad commitment" to prevent Communist domination of South Vietnam.[15] Within three months of coming to office, the President decided to send 400 Special Forces troops and 100 other American military advisers to South Vietnam. It was in violation of the Geneva Accords which limited the American presence in Saigon to 685-man contingent. The United States had promised to abide by them although she had not signed them. At the same time President Kennedy initiated a number of covert military operations against North Vietnam.[16] These operations included: dispatching agents to North Vietnam for intelligence gathering; infiltrating teams under light civilian cover to south-east Laos to locate and attack Vietnamese Communist bases and lines of communications, forming networks of resistance, covert bases and teams for sabotage and harassment in North Vietnam; conducting overflights for dropping of leaflets to harass the Communists and to "maintain morale of North Vietnamese population," and "increase gray [unidentified source] broadcasts to North Vietnam for the same purpose," and training "the South Vietnamese Army to conduct ranger raids and similar military actions in North Vietnam as might prove neces-

---

[14] Arthur M. Schlesinger, Jr., *A Thousand Days : John F. Kennedy in the White House* (London, 1965), p. 476.

[15] Neil Sheehan, ed., *The Pentagon Papers*, published by the *New York Times* (New York, 1971), p. 86.

    M.S. Venkataramani says that Kennedy's decisions of November 1961 in regard to Vietnam led to the launching of the first phase of the "Americanization" of the war in Vietnam. M.S. Venkataramani, "The United States and Thailand: The Anatomy of Super Power Policy-Making, 1948-1963," *International Studies* (New Delhi), vol. 12, no. 1, January-March 1973, p. 98.

[16] Sheehan, ibid.

sary or appropriate." By the end of the Kennedy Administration, the number of American troops—disguised as military advisers— had risen from 685 to roughly 16,000.

When Kennedy came to power, the major American problem in Southeast Asia was Laos, not Vietnam. The Pathet Lao forces were advancing. The stability of the Vientiene regime was in danger. The outgoing President, General Eisenhower, told Kennedy that Laos would pose the most serious challenge to the US. He advised that if necessary, American forces should be deployed to "save Laos from Communism."[17] The situation in South Vietnam, from the American point of view, was deteriorating. Pessimistic reports were being sent home from South Vietnam by American reporters, important amongst them being David Halberstam of the *New York Times* and Neil Sheehan of the UPI.

Washington continued to be under the spell of the alleged continuing Soviet threat which Walt Rostow described as the third year of the "post-sputnik offensive." In January 1961 there was considerable talk about "closing the missile gap,"— an alleged problem to which Kennedy had devoted a great deal of attention during the election campaign. In the same month, Nikita Khrushchev, the Soviet leader, announced his pledge to support "wars of national liberation." He also threatened to sign a separate peace treaty with the East Germans.

The Kennedy Administration began with a whimper. The Bay of Pigs invasion proved to be a big disaster for the US. The ill-fated adventure, instead of discouraging the Kennedy Administration from undertaking any so-called counter-insurgency efforts, seemed to encourage it. The major actors in Washington appeared to be in search of a spot where they could be tough with the Communists and regain prestige for their country. Either Laos or South Vietnam would perhaps provide a right

---

[17] Memorandum of Conference on January 19, 1961, between President Eisenhower and President-elect Kennedy on the subject of Laos, by Clark Clifford. Sent by Clifford to President Lyndon B. Johnson, 29 September 1967, US House Committee on Armed Services, Committee Print, *United States-Vietnam Relations 1945-1967 : Study Prepared by the Department of Defence* (Washington, D.C., 1971), vol. 10, pp. 1360-4. This major source will hereafter be described as *DOD Documents*.

place. Another factor that might have prompted Kennedy to take a tough stand against "Communists" at that time was his bitter encounter with Khrushchev at Vienna in June 1961. The "rookie" President had a tough time with the veteran Communist leader. "Roughest thing in my life," Kennedy told James Reston of the *New York Times* soon after the meeting was over. He felt that Khrushchev "mistook" him as immature and inexperienced. He would have to give him a stand somewhere and make the American power credible. And for that "Vietnam looks like the place," he told Reston.[18] The Bay of Pigs and the Vienna encounter seem to have influenced Kennedy and his advisers to follow an activist policy against "Communists" in Southeast Asia.

When Kennedy began making his initial moves in Vietnam he did not anticipate any serious domestic opposition to his course. There was no organized opposition within the Executive, Congress, or among the public at large to efforts ostensibly aimed to "help" South Vietnam to safeguard herself from Communist "aggression" and subversion. If the effort called for a certain modest American involvement the country was, by and large, apparently willing to go along. J.W. Fulbright (Dem., Arkansas), the Chairman of the Foreign Relations Committee, threw his weight on 4 May 1961 on the side of sending troops to Vietnam. He was one of the two persons in Washington—the other one was Chester Bowles—who had advised President Kennedy against the Bay of Pigs adventure. Fulbright's support for the deployment of ground troops in South Vietnam might have given an impression to the President that sending troops to Vietnam would not face any serious challenge in Congress.

W.W. Rostow, a senior White House specialist on Southeast

[18] David Halberstam, *The Best and Brightest* (New York, 1972), pp. 76-7; Chester Bowles, Under Secretary of State in the Kennedy Administration, recalls that "following the Bay of Pigs, his confrontation with Khrushchev in Vienna and the resumption of nuclear testing by the Soviets, I sensed that *subconsciously at least, he* (Kennedy) *was searching for some issue on which he could prove at a relatively low cost that he was, in fact, a tough President who could not be pushed around by the soviets, the Chinese or anyone else.*" Chester Bowles, *Promises to Keep* (Bombay, 1972), p. 408; Emphasis added.

Asia, and Brig. General Edward G. Lansdale who was in charge of "special operations" for the Pentagon were probably the first within the Administration to make moves in relation to Vietnam. The general, referred to in Chapter II, was a reputed military activist on counter-insurgency operations. He was also an old hand on Vietnam. Rostow, who was to emerge as one of the most important actors in the Vietnam drama, represented an approach that subsequently came to be characterized as "hawkish." In order to understand his role, one should go back to his Fort Bragg speech of April 1961. He said that "modernization" was a revolutionary process and a transitional society was vulnerable to the guerilla attack. According to him, the Communists were the "scavengers of the modernization process." His conclusion was that the best way to win a guerilla war was to prevent it from happening. Extending his logic, Rostow said, it might be necessary to "seek out and engage the ultimate source of aggression."[19] Rostow, in his memorandum of 12 April 1961 to the President, proposed "gearing up the whole Vietnam operations."[20] He suggested that a visit to South Vietnam by the Vice President and a visit to the US by Nguyen Dinh Thuan, acting Defence Minister of South Vietnam, should be arranged. More important, he proposed that the number of American military advisers in Saigon should be increased. This simply meant that some way should be found to get into Saigon an undetermined number of ununiformed U.S. military personnel. Anticipating the possibility of diplomatic difficulty in initiating such a course, Rostow stated that "an alternative way" might be introduced into the Vietnam operation a substantial number of "*Special Forces* types."[21] It is important to note that many of these suggestions were soon accepted by the President.

Rostow and Lansdale, the respective counter-insurgency experts of the White House and the Defence Department, met on 13 April and the product of their discussion was a paper which recommended that the President set up a task force for

---

[19] W.W. Rostow, *View from the Seventh Floor* (New York, 1964), pp. 92-120.
[20] *DOD Documents*, Book 2, IV.B.I, p. 23.
[21] Ibid.

Vietnam. This paper seems to have reached their supervisors, probably including the President. On 20 April Secretary McNamara asked his Deputy Secretary, Roswell Gilpatric, to take the help of other agencies in preparing a report which would contain the current situation and Communist activities in South Vietnam and recommendations to "prevent Communist domination of that country."[22] McNamara's memorandum was in line with the Rostow-Lansdale paper. Thus the Defence Department took the initiative in having a report prepared and other agencies were to contribute their inputs to its report.

The task force, headed by Gilpatric, submitted its report on 27 April 1961. It recommended an increase of 100 men in the American Military Assistance Command in Saigon (MACV), more arms and aid for the South Vietnamese Civil Guards and sending General Lansdale, the Operations Officer for the Task Force, to South Vietnam immediately after the programme received the Presidential approval.[23]

In the meantime the situation in Laos had taken a dramatic turn. On 26 April reports reached Washington that the Pathet Lao forces were moving rapidly and most of Laos would fall to them before a ceasefire was enforced. On 27 April—the day the Gilpatric Task Force Report was submitted—Washington was in the grip of a crisis situation—the principals meeting to devise means for facing the Laotian crisis. For the time being, Vietnam was again relegated to the second place. The possibility seemed to exist that the situation in Laos might have "spill over" effects in Vietnam. So on 28 April, an annexe was added to the Gilpatric Report which recommended an increase of 3,600 men in the MAAG ceiling, instead of the original recommendation for a 100-man increase.[24]

On 29 April, with Washington still struggling through the Laotian crisis, Kennedy took action on the original report of the Gilpatric Task Force submitted on 27th. He ordered an increase of 100 men in the American advisory mission ceiling.[25] No

[22] Ibid., p. 19.
[23] Task Force Draft, 26 April 1961, *DOD Documents*, Book 11, V.B.4, pp. 42-57.
[24] Second Draft "Laos Index" to Task Force Report, 28 April 1961, ibid., pp. 58-61.
[25] *DOD Documents* Book 2, IV.B.1, pp. 29-30.

action was taken on the Laotian annexe of 28th. At this point the State Department sought to get into the act. Up to this point the ball appeared to be passing among McNamara, Gilpatric, Lansdale, and Rostow. On 1 May, a significant revision was made in the Laos annexe. It provided that "the US should be prepared to intervene unilaterally in fulfilment of its commitment under Article IV, 2 of Manila Pact. . . ."[26] The 1 May draft was circulated among the various concerned agencies.

The State Department's revised draft made some significant changes in the Gilpatric report. It recommended that Lansdale's special role—Operations Officer of the Task Force—be deleted and the Gilpatric Task Force, having completed its assignment, be dissolved. A new task force should take its place, with Under Secretary of State George Ball acting as its coordinator. Moreover, the State Department wanted the "unilateral intervention in Vietnam" clause of the original report to be substituted by a "new bilateral arrangement" with South Vietnam.[27] This change was also retained in the final Gilpatric report.

These changes suggested by the State Department are likely to imply that the State Department was taking a more cautious stand as contrasted with the Defence Department. But the reasons cited by it for concluding a defensive alliance with South Vietnam seem to give a different picture. It argued that the Geneva Accords had been violated with impunity by the Communists, but they had so far prevented the US from taking any "dramatic actions" on behalf of South Vietnam and other Southeast Asian countries against the Communists. It, therefore, urged that these inhibitions should "not prevent our action" in future. Hence arose the necessity of joining with South Vietnam in "a clear-cut defensive alliance which include *stationing of US forces on Vietnamese* soil."[28] Thus the State Department was no less in favour of increased military involvement in Vietnam than the Defence Department. The "bilateral arrangement" provision was suggested to meet diplomatic and procedural problems that might otherwise ensue. It is natural that it was the State Department, the diplomatic arm of the government, rather than any

[26] Ibid., p. 34.
[27] Ibid., pp. 36-7.
[28] Ibid., pp. 37-8; Emphasis added.

other agency which took this aspect into account. Getting the
concurrence of Saigon for a "defensive alliance" would not
have been deemed to be difficult. The changes suggested by the
State Department, apart from other aspects, were clearly intended to put the Department squarely in the picture in regard to
policy-making on Vietnam.

In the second week of May 1961 President Kennedy sent his
Vice-President Lyndon Johnson on a whirlwind tour of some
Asian countries, South Vietnam included. On 12 May LBJ,
during his talks with President Diem, broached the possibility
of American troops in Vietnam. The South Vietnamese leader
did not seem to be very interested about getting American
troops at present. He would, however, have them "only in case
of overt aggression." Diem also did not show any interest in
signing a "defensive alliance" with the US.[29]

In his report Johnson stated that American troops would not
be welcomed in Asia except on training missions. Because of
recent colonial experiences, Asians would tend to view with
suspicion the return of Western troops, he argued. However,
the major thrust of the Vice-President's report was interventionist. "The battle against Communism must be joined in Southeast Asia with strength and determination to achieve success
there—or the United States, inevitably, must surrender the
Pacific and take up our defenses on our own shores." Johnson
concluded his report in a tone of urgency. "The basic decision
in Southeast Asia is here. We must decide whether to help
these countries to the best of our ability or throw in the towel
in the area and pull back our defenses to San Francisco and [a]
"Fortress America" concept. . . ."[30]

In the month of June, the Washington principals did not
seem to be in a mood to send ground troops to South Vietnam.
In spite of the "lobbying" of pro-troops elements—General
Lansdale, General McGarr and perhaps Frederick E. Nolting,
Jr., the US Ambassador in Saigon—the proposal to send ground
troops to Vietnam did not gain much support. However, there

---

[29] Ibid., Book 11, n. 23, p. 152.
[30] Subject: "Mission to Southeast Asia, India and Pakistan," Memoran
   dum from the Vice-President to the President, 23 May 1961, ibid.,
   pp. 159-66.

was growing sentiment for substantial preparatory work looking towards possible eventual intervention. A note from Rostow to Secretary McNamara on 5 June probably reflected the dominant attitude in the high echelons of US policy-makers. Because of the importance of the letter, it may be reproduced in full:[31]

> Bob:
> We must think of the kind of forces and missions for Thailand now, Vietnam later.
> We need a guerrilla *deterrence* operations in Thailand's northeast.
> We shall need forces to support a counter-guerrilla war in Vietnam.
> aircraft
> helicopters
> communications men
> special forces
> militia teachers
> etc.
>
> WWR

This letter was important in the sense that recommendations contained in it were exactly the courses later approved by the President. It is doubtful whether such a development was because of Rostow's personal influence on or standing with Kennedy. Rostow was not that important an actor at that time. The more probable reason was that Rostow represented the prevailing mood of Washington at that time, and the President, because of the Laotian situation and the possible reactions at home and abroad, was not prepared to take the risk of deploying American combat troops in South Vietnam. The letter also indicated the somewhat low place to which Vietnam had perhaps been relegated in America's perception at that time. Thailand was accorded a "higher" place than Vietnam. Vietnam was not in the centre; it had been pushed to the periphery. But at least some of those who were favouring giving Vietnam a peripheral place at this time probably did so in the hope that it was the most feasible

---

[31] Ibid., Book 2, n. 20, pp. 67-8.

way of eventually moving her to the centre. Rostow might also have thought that his present recommendations—sending special forces to South Vietnam—might be pace-setters; they might finally lead to the deployment of American combat troops in Vietnam.

No significant movement was made with regard to Vietnam till October when Rostow and Taylor were sent to Saigon. In the meantime, however, the situation in South Vietnam had considerably deteriorated. The Viet Cong were reportedly increasing their strength. Theodore H. White, a noted American journalist with access to Kennedy, was sending "alarming" reports from South Vietnam to the White House.[32] In September, the Viet Cong dealt a stunning blow to the Saigon regime when they seized Phuoc Thanh, a provincial capital only 55 miles away from Saigon, publicly beheaded the provincial chief and left the town before the South Vietnamese forces arrived. These developments might have had some impact upon Washington and might have moved back Vietnam into the centre of the stage. By the month of October, there were four proposals relating to Vietnam to be considered by the National Security Council. One was the JCS plan which advocated sending American ground troops to Laos. Another was the "Rostow Proposal" which favoured the deployment of a SEATO force of 25,000 men in South Vienam. The JCS rejected the Rostow proposal and submitted a supplementary note which stated that 40,000 US military personnel would be required to mop up the Viet Cong and 128,000 additional men would be needed to fend off possible North Vietnamese and/or Chinese intervention.[33] The third proposal came from U. Alexis Johnson, Deputy Under Secretary of State. It was a combination of the first and second.[34]

The last proposal pending for consideration by the NSC was sent by William P. Bundy, the Assistant Secretary of Defence (ISA) who frequently sought to feed his inputs into policy-making on Vietnam (he is the elder brother of McGeorge Bundy,

---

[32] Ibid., p. 72.
[33] Ibid., pp. 75-6; for the JCS' rejoinder to Rostow's proposal, see JCS Memorandum for Secretary of Defence, JCSM 716-61, 9 October 1961, *DOD Documents*, Book 11, V.B.4, pp. 297-9.
[34] Ibid., Book 2, pp. 77-8.

the National Security Assistant). William Bundy was not unfamiliar in Washington before he joined the Kennedy Administration. His father, Harvey Bundy, was a close friend of Henry Stmson, one of the great patriarchs of the Eastern Establishmeint. Bundy's father-in-law, Dean Acheson, who was the Secretary of State during the Truman Administration, was still a force to be reckoned with both in Washington and in the Democratic Pa rty. Bundy had worked for the CIA during the Eisenhower period. Known to be a favourite of Allen Dulles, the CIA Director, he survived McCarthyite witchhunting because of the timely intervention on his behalf by his boss. Bundy joined the Kennedy Administration as the Deputy Assistant Secretary of Defence (ISA), but he was soon promoted when the Assistant Secretary Paul Nitze, was moved up as the Secretary of the Navy. With these connections with some of the big names of the Establishment, and with his younger brother, McGeorge Bundy in the White House as the National Security Assistant, Bundy was to play the role of an influential insider during both Kennedy and Johnson Administrations.

In a note to McNamara on 10 October 1961, described in chapter II, William Bundy stated that "it is really now or never" if the Viet Cong gains were to be arrested. He pointed out that the Viet Cong movement was spreading and they would certainly exploit the "back-the-winner sentiment" as they did against the French in 1954. He advocated "an early and hard-hitting operation" which had, according to him, 70 per cent chance of success. He warned that if a month passed by, it would come down to 60-40, 50-50 and so on.[35]

It is precisely on such occasions that the CIA's input tends to assume considerable importance in decision-making. The immediate prior record of success or failure of an agency tends to have some effect on the appraisal that it may make on another emergency situation having serious implications. It may tend to make the agency more cautious. A National Intelligence Estimate (NIE), dated 5 October 1961, of the possible impact of the deployment of a SEATO contingent of troops in South Vietnam upon the insurgency that had been prepared for the

---

[35] Bundy Memorandum for Secretary McNamara, 10 October 1961, *ibid.*, Book 11, p. 312.

NSC's consideration did not reflect the same confidence as indicated in Bundy's note. It stated that the Viet Cong would mount guerrilla tactics and harass the SEATO forces. The flow of the North Vietnamese "irregulars" into the South would be intensified, it added.[36] The tone of the NIE was in contrast to that of the interventionist proposals of Rostow, the JCS, Johnson and Bundy.

In accordance with the decision of NSC meeting, dated 11 October 1961. General Taylor and Walt Rostow were sent to South Vietnam to make an appraisal of the situation there and to make necessary recommendations.[37] It was originally proposed that Rostow alone would visit South Vietnam. Rostow was known as a "hawk" whose mind was already set on intervention. To mollify those within the Administration who favoured a balanced appraisal of the situation it would be desirable to add another senior person whose views could command confidence. The man to take the lead in pressing the case for an expanded team was Chester Bowles, the Under Secretary of State. Bowles had serious reservations concerning the thrust towards intervention that Rostow and several others in the Administration represented.

Unlike many others in the Administration, Bowles had his independent political constituency as a veteran liberal and former Governor and Congressman. His sympathy for third world countries was well-known. One of the original candidates for the post of the Secretary of State, he accepted the number two post hoping that he would be enabled to play a responsible role in areas of special interest to him. The number one in State being a "status quo man" with strong views on holding back the "Communists," strain between the two was inevitable. Bowles was one of the few in Washington to have expressed strong concern over the Bay of Pigs adventure. From the very beginning of the Kennedy Administration, he expressed his opposition to any increased American involvement in Vietnam. At the time when the Rostow mission was to be dispatched, he

[36] "Block Support of the Communist Effort Against the Government of Vietnam," Special National Intelligence Estimate Number 53-2-61, ibid., pp., 291-4.

[37] Gilpatric Memorandum for record, 11 October 1961, ibid., pp. 322-3.

reportedly pressed that a senior man from the State should accompany it but Rusk was apparently not prepared to get his department involved at that stage.[38] However, the upshot of Bowles' fight was the inclusion of General Taylor in the mission to Saigon. Taylor, a member of the so-called "Never Again Club"—a phrase, used in the context of the American war in Korea—, seemed to be a counter to "hawkish" Rostow and, therefore, was not unacceptable to liberals like Bowles. Two lesser officials of the State Department named Sterling J. Cottrell and William J. Jorden were included in the team—a gesture towards Bowles, the "protester."

The Taylor-Rostow team visited South Vietnam, 18-24 October. They had two meetings with Diem and his advisers. The questions of deploying American ground troops in South Vietnam, and Washington and Saigon signing a military agreement, on the initiative of the American side, were discussed. Diem expressed his interest in the first, but seemed to be cool towards the second. In his cable "Eyes Only" for the President from the Philippines on 1 November 1961, Taylor recommended that the US should "provide a US military presence capable of raising national morale and of showing to Southeast Asia the seriousness of the US intent to resist a Communist takeover."[39] He further recommended that the US should conduct logistical operations in support of military and as he put it, "flood relief operations." He also recommended such "combat operations as are necessary for self-defense and for the security of the area in which they are stationed." (Taylor's report has been referred to in Chapter II).[40] Taylor was aware of the risk that such a commitment would involve. "If the first contingent is not enough to accomplish the necessary results, it will be difficult to resist the pressure to reinforce." At a certain point, there would be "no limit to our possible commitment. . . .,"[41] Taylor warned. However, he argued that these risks would be outweighed by the benefits that such a commitment would lead to. The introduction of American troops in South Vietnam, Taylor

[38] Halberstam, n. 18, pp. 155-6; see also Bowles, n. 18, pp. 361, 408.
[39] "Top Secret: Eyes Only for the President from General Taylor," 1 November 1961, *DOD Documents*, Book 11, n. 23, pp. 337-42.
[40] Ibid., pp. 339-40; Emphasis added.
[41] Ibid., p. 338.

reiterated, would best convey the American seriousness of purpose and would best give "a much needed shot in arm to national morale."

The two State Department officials who had accompanied the visiting team expressed some doubts about sending American ground troops to South Vietnam. Cottrell, head of the inter-agency Vietnam task force in Washington, stated in a memo-randum dated 27 October that "since it is an open question whether the GVN can succeed even with the US assistance, it would be a mistake for the U.S. to commit itself irrevocably to the defeat of the Communists in SVN." But his position was confused because he added that if the combined efforts of the US and South Vietnam failed in the South, the US should punish North Vietnam by graduated bombing.[42] Jorden report-ed that many government officials and military officers "have lost confidence in President Diem and his leadership." He advis-ed that the US should not identify herself "with a man or a regime."[43] It may be relevent to point out that as contrasted with the views of these State Department officials, some elements of the Defence Department—the JCS and William Bundy, the Assistant Secretary of Defence (ISA)—advocated at that time that the US should send ground troops to South Vietnam.

The Secretary of State was away from the capital when the "Eyes only" cables of Taylor were hitting the White House. But he was not kept in the dark about what was happening in regard to Vietnam. Dean Rusk was not a big name in the Demo-cratic Party. But he was not a stranger to Washington—unlike his colleague McNamara—when he joined the Kennedy Administration. In the Truman Administration he had worked under Dean Acheson as Assistant Secretary of State for Far Eastern Affairs. In the aftermath of the "fall of China," when the "fall" of South Korea to Communists looked probable, Rusk was an advocate of "tough" posture against the Communists. He con-tinued to maintain broadly a "hard-liner" stance after he be-came the Secretary of State. But, from time to time, as at this point, he adopted a cautious approach. As early as 29 April 1961 he advocated that American and Thai troops should be

[42] Ibid., Book 2, n. 20, pp. 105-6.
[43] Ibid., pp. 103-4.

placed in Laos.[44] On 4 May he told news reporters with regard to Vietnam, "If you don't pay attention to the periphery, the periphery changes. And the first thing you know, the periphery is the center."[45] But the very next day, the Secretary's tone was restrained and cautious. In a meeting held at the State Department, he said, "We should not place combat forces in South Vietnam *at this time*."[46] He recommended that the MAAG in Saigon should be augmented in small increments. However, Great Britain, a member of the International Control Commission, should not be informed of it, he added. The Secretary would approve of "small violations" of the Geneva Accords, care being taken to maintain *secrecy*. He was not, in principle, against sending American troops to South Vietnam. He would not approve of it just yet because of diplomatic factors—probably keeping the Geneva talks on Laos in view. However, he recommended that the deployment of additional US forces should receive further study and consideration.[47] Rusk's enthusiasm for sending troops to Thailand and his reluctance to do so in the case of South Vietnam probably stemmed from the fact that Thailand was covered by the main provisions of the Manila Pact whereas South Vietnam formed a part of its protocol. Thus, introducing American troops in Thailand could be defended better diplomatically than the same in relation to South Vietnam, Rusk might have reasoned. Once in Thailand, such troops would be conveniently at hand if needed later in Vietnam.

Rusk was visiting Japan when he was informed of Taylor's recommendations. He seemed to be unhappy with Diem's regime which was constantly being charged with nepotism and favouritism. He wished that Diem would bring about some reforms before Washington committed itself to his defence. Otherwise, he stated in a cable from Japan dated 1 November that he would be "reluctant to see US make major additional commitment [of] American prestige to a *losing horse*."[48]

Further opposition to Taylor-Rostow's recommendations in favour of sending American troops to South Vietnam came from

---

[44] *DOD Documents*, Book 11, pp. 63-6.
[45] *New York Times*, 5 May 1961.
[46] *DOD Documents*, Book 11, n. 23, p. 67.
[47] Ibid.
[48] Ibid., Book 2, n. 20, p. 118.

the intelligence community. A National Intelligence Estimate (NIE) dated 5 November, stated that the proposed step would lead to further increase in the level of Hanoi's support for the Viet Cong. It predicted that bombing of the North—which was being discussed in Washington as a possible course of punitive actions against North Vietnam—would have no significant impact on the nature of the flow of help from the North into the South.[49] This pessimistic report would have made the Washington principals have second thoughts over the proposals of introducing ground troops into South Vietnam and bombing North Vietnam.

Before November 1961 the Defence Secretary does not seem to have come in a big way in decision-making on Vietnam. This was to some extent true of Secretary Rusk too. While Rusk's role did not markedly expand subsequently, McNamara emerged to be the most dominant actor in policy-making on Vietnam. The relatively quiet role played by McNamara during this period may be mainly attributed to two factors. Firstly, he was a stranger to the Washington community and he might have been carefully orienting himself to the intricacies of how the game was being played. Moreover, he might have felt that initially Rusk should have the opportunity to play the traditional lead role of a Secretary of State. If there was a vacuum in this respect, McNamara was not the kind of man to hold himself back. McNamara also perhaps thought it wise to give first priority to setting his own house in order. After he established his mastery there, he would be ready to deal with his competitors.

On 8 November 1961, McNamara, Gilpatric and the JCS, in a memorandum to the President, stated, they were "inclined to recommend" that the US should commit herself to the objective of "saving" South Vietnam.[50] As pointed out in Chapter II, the document may be deemed to represent the consensus in the Pentagon. In regard, however, to the question of when, how, in what manner and in what numbers and for what missions US military personnel were to be introduced in South Vietnam, the

---

[49] Ibid., pp. 120-1.
[50] Secretary of Defence Memorandum for the President, 8 November 1961, ibid., Book 11, p. 343.

Secretary of Defence had apparently to work out an agreed position with his counterpart who headed the State Department. A joint memorandum, dated 11 November 1961, signed by both McNamara and Rusk reiterated the Pentagon consensus that the US should "take the decision to commit ourselves to the objective of preventing the fall of South Vietnam to Communism..."[51] The Rusk-McNamara memorandum, as pointed out earlier, recommended for the time being, the introduction of American "advisory" and "support" forces in South Vietnam.[52] The question of injecting American combat forces in South Vietnam was deferred. However, the report did not rule out the possibility of such an eventuality.

Though the time-gap between both the memoranda was only three days and though McNamara was the common signatory to both of them, there were some significant differences between the McNamara-Gilpatric-JCS memorandum of 8 November and the Rusk-McNamara memorandum of 11 November. While the latter recommended categorically that the US should commit herself to the defence of South Vietnam against Communists, the former had some reservations regarding it. The 8 November memorandum stated that McNamara and co-signatories were "inclined to recommend...." Thus, in so far as the American commitment to the objective of "saving" South Vietnam from Communists was concerned, the 11 November memorandum of Rusk-McNamara was more categorical and forthright than the other. On the other hand, in regard to the deployment of American troops in South Vietnam, Rusk-McNamara memorandum was weaker than the other. While the latter had recommended that an American military task force consisting of both "combat" and "support" forces be, without delay, deployed in South Vietnam, the former recommended that only support forces should be sent. The 11 November memorandum appears to have been the product of mutual concessions made by Rusk and McNamara. Rusk was already known to have been an advocate of American commitment to the defence of South Vietnam against Communists. But he had not earlier committed

---

[51] State/Defence Memorandum to the President, 11 November 1961, ibid., pp. 359-67.
[52] Ibid., p. 363.

himself to the sending of American troops to South Vietnam. Only ten days back he had cabled Washington from Japan warning against the unilateral deployment of American troops in South Vietnam. Thus his support, stated in 11 November memorandum for sending American support troops to South Vietnam was a concession on his part. McNamara who had not catogorically committed himself in 8 November memorandum, to the objective of saving the Saigon regime from Communists, did it on 11 November. On the other hand, he came down a little bit in regard to the actual American military commitment in South Vietnam. He agreed to the alternative of sending only "support" troops instead of combat troops which he had recommended on 8 November. It is a different question whether McNamara earlier believed or did not believe in the American commitment to the political objective of defending South Vietnam against Communists. It is possible that his reservation in this regard on 8 November was a deliberate bureaucratic ploy to be used for bargaining with Rusk whose position on this was, by and large, clear.

Was there any other compulsion, besides the bureaucratic compromise, which might have influenced Rusk and McNamara in taking the stand that they took on 11 November? Could they also have taken into account the acceptibility of Taylor's recommendations for sending ground troops to South Vietnam by other actors in Washington including President Kennedy? Does an actor in a policy-making process take into consideration not only his personal and organizational interests, but also the degree of chance of his position being accepted by his competitors and more importantly, by his supervisors?

The President was the man to take the decision. Memories of the Bay of Pigs and Vienna meeting were undoubtedly fresh in his mind. The President, in his desire for projecting himself as a tough President, was in need of taking a tough stand in Southeast Asia. He was aware of the rift between Moscow and Peking. He could also rely upon the calculation that the Soviet Union, because of her desire to maintain "detente" with the US, would avoid intervening in Southeast Asia against the US. At the same time, he was conscious of the fact that any miscalculations on his part concerning the Soviet response might lead to dangerous consequences. He was aware that the Soviet Union possessed the capability to create complications for him elsewhere if he were to offend her unduly in Southeast Asia. A crisis in Berlin, for instance, of the type that had taken place a month earlier, was not a happy prospect. Even in respect of Southeast Asia, on the international scene, the US, under his leadership, had taken the public posture of seeking a settlement through negotiations that were then in progress in Geneva. Any action in South Vietnam at that stage involving the projection of American military pressure could run counter to his proclaimed effort in the direction of peaceful settlement in Southeast Asia. Because of these considerations, the President might have been led to conclude that the US' objective should be to "save" South Vietnam against the "Communists," but it was not the opportune time for the US to send military troops to South Vietnam. On 13 November Kennedy accepted all the recommendations of Rusk and McNamara except the one which required the US' unqualified commitment to the goal of saving South Vietnam from Communism. Diem was to be informed that the Pentagon was preparing contingency plans for sending soon combat-support troops to South Vietnam. But he was required to broaden his government and undertake some social and political reforms before the US troops were deployed in South Vietnam.[53]

Inferences

By and large, the President, Secretary Rusk, Secretary Mc-Namara and the National Security Assistant McGeorge Bundy subscribed to the "domino" theory. They agreed that the "loss" of South Vietnam to Communists would lead to the spread of Communism in the rest of Southeast Asia. There was no conflict on the perspective.

Concerned agencies of the Executive vie amongst themselves to influence the President's decision-making on defence and foreign policy. Each one of them is alert to ensure that another agency does not steal a march on it in this regard. Whenever one agency feels that its prerogatives are usurped by another agency, it would tend to fight back for their restoration. The

[53] Sheehan, n. 15, p. 112.

dissolution of the Gilpatric Task Force on Vietnam and its substitution by a new task force headed by George Ball, the Under Secretary of State, was a good illustration of it. Another such example was the concern of the State Department about original Rostow Mission to South Vietnam. It deemed it derogatory to its position that Rostow, a member of the White House advisory staff, was selected to head the mission.

Neither Rusk nor McNamara seemed to have been the prime moving spirit in policy-making on Vietnam during this period. The reasons for this were manifold. It was the first year of the Kennedy Administration. Both the Secretaries gave first priority to the reorganization of their respective departments and allowed their deputies to carry on dealing with Vietnam in a routine manner. Moreover, in the beginning, the Administration was gripped with more immediate problems like the Bay of Pigs, Berlin and Laos than Vietnam. But once Rusk and McNamara felt that an important decision on Vietnam was about to be taken, they sought to take the reins themselves. In the month of November, they emerged as the prime moving spirits in policy-making on Vietnam. Between the two, one gets the impression that Rusk had an edge over the other. He seemed to be "more equal" than McNamara and other principals in Washington in regard to policy-making on Vietnam.

The 11 November memorandum was a compromise between Rusk and McNamara. Both of them had to give in something in order to reach an agreement. But this compromise was within the general framework of the options left to the President. In a policy-making process, an actor tends to keep in mind not only how much his competitor or competitors can move toward his viewpoint, but also the forces that the helmsman—the final decision-maker, here the President—has to reckon with. The higher an official is placed, the more seriously he is likely to take this aspect into account. That may explain the parallel difference between the positions of McNamara and the JCS, and between those of Rusk and, Bowles and Ball.

AMERICAN INVOLVEMENT IN THE COUP AGAINST DIEM

The interaction between the civilian and military elements of the Pentagon in regard to the overthrow of the Diem regime was discussed in Chapter II. It is proposed here to deal with the competition among federal actors including the Defence Department to influence the policy to be adopted regarding Diem's continuance.

Discontent against Diem was smouldering in South Vietnam for some time. It was exploded by the Buddhist crises of May and August 1963. Plans for a coup against the Diem regime were being prepared by some top military officers in Saigon. They knew that they could not implement them unless they had indication that the United States could not be averse to their course. Matters began to move fast with the arrival of newly appointed Ambassador, Henry Cabot Lodge, in Saigon on 22 August 1963. Within a few hours of his arrival there, Lodge cabled the State Department that American support of a coup would be a "shot in the dark."[54] This message which reached Washington on 24 August resulted in what became one of the most "controversial" actions in the Kennedy Administration.

On 24 August 1964, the State Department sent the Ambassador a reply signed by Acting Secretary George Ball. It began by saying that the United States could no longer go along with the powerful role played by Nhus.

> We wish to give Diem reasonable opportunity to remove Nhus, but if he remains obdurate, then we are prepared to accept the obvious implication that we can no longer support Diem. You may also tell appropriate military commanders we will give them direct support in any interim period of breakdown of central government mechanism.[55]

This message was drafted by Roger Hilsman, Assistant Secretary of State for Far Eastern Affairs, W. Averell Harriman,

---

[54] Embassy Saigon Message 316, Lodge to Hilsman, *DOD Documents*, Book 3, IV.B.5, p. 14.
[55] State Message 243, State to Lodge, ibid., p. 15.

Under Secretary of State for Political Affairs, Michael V. Forrestal, White House Specialist on Vietnam and Southeast Asia, and George Ball. President Kennedy, Secretary Rusk, Secretary McNamara, General Taylor, the Chairman of the JCS, and CIA Director John A. McCone were out of the town. Hilsman's account says that the cable was cleared by Kennedy and Rusk through several telephone conversations. Roswell. L. Gilpatric, the Acting Secretary of Defence, cleared it for the civilian side of the Defence Department. The Acting Director of CIA approved of it, deciding not to disturb his chief's vacation. Taylor cleared it while out to a dinner.[56]

However, a slightly different account of the event has been given by Schlesinger and Trewhitt.[57] They suggest that the clearance of the cable was affected by "misunderstanding" among the actors, Schlesinger reports,

The draft was cleared through all the relevant departments but not at the top level. Defence accepted it because it understood that the cable had already gone; McNamara, if he had been consulted, would have opposed it. So also would McCone. No one is sure what Rusk's position would have been. The President saw the draft at Hyannis Port without realizing that the departmental clearances did not signify the concurrence of his senior advisers.[58]

This would suggest that there was a "communication failure." All the accounts including that of Hilsman suggest that perhaps the shape of the cable might have been different if the principal

---

[56] Hilsman, n. 13, p. 488.

[57] Schlesinger, n. 14, p. 844; Henry L. Trewhitt, *McNamara* (New York, 1971), p. 204. (Trewhitt says that he had several rounds of talks with McNamara while writing this book. He had also worked for McNamara's book, *The Essence of Security*. One wonders if Trewhitt's account is really the one given by McNamara himself to him. For the view that there was some sort of "conspiracy" against Diem in the State Department, and the 24 August message of the State Department was manipulated by the interested few, see Marguerite Higgins, *Our Vietnam Nightmare* (New York, 1965), pp. 189-201.

[58] Schlesinger, ibid.

actors had been present in the town.[59] This is the kind of situation bringing out the importance of a point connected with the model 2, mentioned in our theoretical discussion—the importance of "communication flow" in policy making. It is true that a consensus was reached in the next day NSC meeting in favour of the policy was spelled out in the cable, but that does not mean that an identical consensus could have been possible in a meeting earlier than 24 August. It is more difficult to oppose a policy after it has been decided upon than before.

In an NSC meeting held on 27 August Frederick E. Nolting, Jr., the retiring American Ambassador in Saigon, strongly defended Diem. He expressed his pessimism about the capacity of the Vietnamese generals to rule.[60] The President decided to ask Lodge, the new Ambassador and Harkins (MAAG Chief) to express their views. Later it was discovered that the JCS had sent a telegram to Harkins through their own channels soon after the above NSC meeting which appeared to suggest to him how he should answer the questions put to him by Washington.[61] This suggests the critical role that the military leadership can play in a situation involving tugs with the State Department and the Defence Secretary to influence policy-making. Another instance of interdepartment differences was revealed in the NSC meeting of 28 August. Rusk was sceptical of an approach to Diem. He feared that Diem and Nhu could indulge in "irrational acts." McNamara favoured such an approach because he thought that there was no visible alternative to Diem in Saigon.[62]

Another incident would reveal near-polarization of views in the Administration on Vietnam. It was an NSC meeting on 31 August 1963. The President was absent. Secretary Rusk, who chaired the meeting in his absence, called for considering Lodge's cable of the same day suggesting that Nhu should go.

[59] Hilsman says, "Back in Washington, General Taylor began to have misgivings. He communicated them to McNamara when he returned, and McNamara shared them. So did John McCone." Hilsman, n. 13, p. 490; Schlesinger asserts that McNamara would have opposed it. So also would McCone. Schlesinger, ibid.

[60] *DOD Documents*, Book 3, n. 54, p. 19.

[61] Hilsman, n. 13, pp. 492-3; and Halberstam, n. 18, p. 271.

[62] Hilsman, ibid.

He said, he felt that it was unrealistic to start off by asserting that Nhu must go. McNamara supported him. Hilsman, supported by a State Department official, Paul M. Kattenburg, who headed the Vietnam Inter-Departmental Working Group, argued that the United States should not continue supporting a Nhu-dominated regime because it would have a disastrous effect on the war. They also pointed to the growing disaffection and restiveness of middle level bureaucrats and military officers which Secretary McNamara and General Taylor did not seem share. Kattenburg stated that if the US would continue to support the Diem regime, she would be "thrown out of the country in six months." He proposed that at that juncture it would be better for the United States to "get out honourably." Rusk commented that Kattenburg's recital was "largely speculative." He emphasized that the United States would not pull out of Vietnam until the war was won and that Washington would not run a coup. McNamara, Taylor, Vice-President Johnson and Nolting, the ex-Ambassador to South Vietnam, agreed with him.[63]

The rift between some elements of the Pentagon and those of the State Department was further revealed when General Krulak and Mendenhall, after their visit to South Vietnam, reported back to the NSC on 10 September 1963. Being seriously concerned over the division within his Administration in regard to Vietnam, Kennedy sent on 6 September General Krulak, the Pentagon's top-ranking expert in counter-guerrilla warfare and Joseph A. Mendenhall of the State Department who was a former "political counsellor" in the Saigon embassy. Mendenhall talked to people in Saigon whereas Krulak went to the field. On their way back they were accompanied, as instructed by Harriman, by John Mecklin, head of the USIA (United States Information Agency) in Saigon and Rufus Philips who was in charge of the strategic hamlet programme in South Vietnam. Krulak told the NSC that the war was running well. Mendenhall reported that the political situation in Saigon was very bad. On listening to both, the President was provoked to ask, "You two did visit the same country, didn't you?"[64] Mecklin,

---

[63] *DOD Documents*, n. 54, p. 82.
[64] Ibid., pp. 25-6.

who, as a news reporter in Saigon in 1950s, was trying to sell Diem to Americans, now recommended a change in government. He also proposed that the US should, if necessary, send combat troops to South Vietnam to "save her from Communists."[65] The last to report to the NSC was Phillips who challenged Krulak's view that the war was going on well. He said that the Viet Cong forces were making rapid progress in the Delta.[66] This was a very confusing picture—the representatives of the State and Defence Departments challenging each other's view and the members of other civilian agencies attacking the Pentagon line. Had the President hoped to get a clearer view of Vietnam, he would have been terribly disappointed by the Krulak-Mendenhall mission.

How much voice the man on the spot would have in Washington would largely depend upon who he is. Normally an Ambassador is the representative of the State Department on the spot, and he would normally be bound by the instructions of the State Department. But, in some cases, the standard equation may not hold true. An Ambassador may prove to be more than something to be taken for granted by his Department. A Nolting may be somewhat of a light weight in Washington game, but a Lodge or a Taylor is not. Lodge was a top Republican leader with a solid base at home. Moreover, the President would take him seriously for the sake of projecting his Administration as bipartisan. Taylor was already an experienced, principal player in Washington before he was appointed as Ambassador in Washington. In peace-time, such an Ambassador would try to be the real master of his house. He would keep all the components of his mission—both civilian and military—under control. But once shooting starts, the picture may change. With war on, the military man-on-the-field tends to be more powerful than before. His equation with his civilian head on the spot—the ambassador—would tend to change. Washington, in such situations, would be inclined to heed more to the field commander than to the ambassador. Even a Lodge or a Taylor would find it difficult to check the

[65] Ibid., p. 27; see also John Mecklin, *Mission in Torment* (New York, 1968), pp. 208-9.
[66] Halberstam, n. 18 pp. 278-9.

increasing power of the field commander. But unless and until a shooting has started, the former is a safe rider. That was the situation in the American mission in Saigon in the middle of 1963.

When Ambassador Lodge joined his post on 22 August 1963, American officials in Saigon were divided amongst themselves in regard to South Vietnam and Diem. The American embassy, the American military mission in Saigon and the Central Intelligence Agency station were the important American agencies which were actively involved with the anti-Diem coup, at its various stages. Richardson who was the head of the American intelligence branch in Saigon was recalled on 6 October 1963. General Harkins, the head of American Military Assistance Command, Vietnam, was there throughout the coup period. Ambassador Lodge arrived at a time when plans for the coup were going on and his attitude towards the Diem regime worked as the catalyst for coup-plotters. Richardson, who was a witness to the August-phase of the coup that ended in a failure, had to leave Saigon when the October phase had taken off the ground. Lodge, for helping those who were planning a coup against Diem, allegedly took the initiative which led to Richardson's recall from Washington at a crucial time. The anti-Diem Generals of South Vietnam were suspicious of the apparent friendship between Diem and Richardson. They feared that the American intelligence chief of Saigon might leak in advance the coup news to Diem.

The CIA's role in South Vietnam around that time was twofold, namely, intelligence-gathering and covert political operations. In hindsight, its estimates, made from time to time, were mostly accurate. They were not as optimistic as those reported by the military. The Viet Cong danger was still there and the situation remained "fragile," a national intelligence estimate—the CIA being the dominant component—said in April 1963. In the aftermath of the Buddhist-Pagoda crisis, another NIE stated that unless the President and the Buddhists came to an agreement, chances of a coup against Diem would further brighten. But a coup, if staged, would adversely affect the war effort, it added. As differences among American officials both in Washington and Saigon sharpened over the advisability of supporting a coup against Diem, the CIA sent a special officer to Saigon to make an independent assessment. His conclusion was that the suspension of aid to South Vietnam by American Government would not have any constructive results, a coup against Diem should not be encouraged and a "business as usual" policy should be followed. Richardson, the Chief of CIA station, Saigon, was also opposed to coup efforts against President Diem.

It is important to note that when the CIA special officer from Washington advised against supporting any anti-Diem coup attempts, some segments of the CIA station in Saigon were already intimately involved in such efforts. In this connection, special mention may be made of Lieutenant Colonel Lucien Conein, an Indo-China veteran who had first come to Vietnam for the Office of Strategic Services (OSS), the forerunner of the CIA. Under Lodge's instructions, he maintained contacts with Major General Tran Van Don, the acting chief of staff of the armed forces and Lieut. General Duong Van Minh, the military adviser to President Diem. He acted as the go-between between Lodge and the anti-Diem generals, passed over to the latter vital intelligence regarding the pro-Diem forces, and took part in coup-planning. The fact that he was in their midst at Vietnamese General Staff headquarters when the coup was staged indicates the extent of association the CIA had with the coup promoters.[67]

The CIA station in Saigon too was stricken with internal cleavages—some of the CIA personnel there supporting the coup, and others opposing it. Ambassador Lodge and Richardson, the CIA Chief of Saigon, did not see eye to eye in regard to the coup. But the main antagonists in Saigon were Ambassador Lodge and General Harkins, the respective heads of American diplomatic and military missions in Saigon. Henry Cabot Lodge, a Boston Brahmin, was an important Republican leader with national appeal. A former Senator and a Vice-Presidential candidate in 1960, he had an independent political constituency of his own before he accepted Kennedy's offer of Ambassadorship to South Vietnam. A man of decision and determination, he fought doggedly to effect a

---

[67] Robert Shaplen, *The Lost Revolution: The US in Vietnam, 1946-1966* (New York, 1966), pp. 203-4.

governmental change in Saigon once he was convinced that it was right. His voice appeared to weigh heavily in Washington. On the other hand, General Harkins who was known to be close to President Diem, had, in course of time, developed some vested interest in the survival of his regime. He argued that the anti-Diem generals were themselves greatly divided amongst themselves and there was little prospect that a successful coup against Diem would be followed by political stability. On these grounds he continued to oppose till the end the idea of any coup against the Diem regime. In the process his relationship with Lodge deteriorated.

In the last week of August 1963, when a coup against Diem seemed to be imminent, the differences between Lodge and Harkins became very sharp. Lodge wrote to the Secretary of State:

> We are launched on a course from which there is no respectable turning back: the overthrow of the Diem regime. There is no turning back in part because US prestige is already publicly committed to this end in large measure and will become more so as facts leak out. In a more fundamental sense there is no turning back because there is no possibility in my view, that the war can be won under a Diem administration....[68]

Harkins, on the other hand, had his reservations about the desirability of supporting this. He proposed that at least as a final effort Diem should be approached and induced to make the desired reforms.[69] However, the coup-plan was shelved for the time being because the plotters could not be convinced of the genuineness of the American support for them.

When the coup attempt was revived in the beginning of October, differences again occurred between Lodge and Harkins more intensely than ever before. Harkins continued to express his scepticism about the anti-Diem generals who were a mix of many groups. "Though I am not trying to thwart a change in government, I think we should take a good hard look at the

[68] *DOD Documents*, n. 54, p. 20.
[69] Ibid.

group's proposals to see if we think it would be capable of increasing the effectiveness of the military effort," the general warned Washington in the last week of October.[70] This was not liked by the Ambassador who took exception to Harkin's reservations about a coup and arguing for a policy of "not thwarting."[71]

Differences between Lodge and Harkins tended to slide towards a crisis. The Ambassador seemed to lose his confidence in the MACV. The general was cut off by the Ambassador from the chain of communications relating to the coup between Washington and Saigon. Secretary McNamara and the JCS were seriously concerned about this lack of coordination and the failure of communication between these two high American officials in Saigon. They apparently took the issue to the President and prevailed upon him to interfere on behalf of Harkins as against Lodge. After the NSC meeting on 29 October, Lodge was directed to show Harkins the relevant cables and to insure that he was kept fully aware of the coup plans. The Ambassador was further instructed to ask Harkins to officiate for him during his absence.[72] This case indicates how differences at lower levels could spill over to higher levels. It also points out that whenever there is an external challenge to an organization, its members, in spite of their internal rifts, tend to unite and fight for the common cause—the interests of the organization as a whole.

Ambassador Lodge and General Harkins continued to sharply differ almost till the day the coup took place. While the former apparently took all possible steps to insure that the coup succeeded, the latter continued to make the plea that a last approach to Diem should be made and he should not be "ditched." The prospect of a successful coup being followed confusion and disorder continued to disturb General Harkins. Generals thereafter would fight one another, he feared. In a cable to General Taylor on 30 October, he said, "I have seen no batting order proposed by any of the coup groups."[73] He

---

[70] Ibid., p. 44.
[71] Ibid., p. 45.
[72] Ibid., p. 47.
[73] Ibid.

suggested that the US should not try to "change horses too quickly."[74] On the other side, Lodge made a fervent plea, in his message to the White House on the same day, that the plotters should not be interfered with. The coup was purely a Vietnamese affair and they should be given a free hand, the Ambassador pleaded. In testifying to the force of character of coup leaders, he argued, "I do not know what more proof can be offered than the fact these men are obviously prepared to risk their lives and that they want nothing for themselves."[75] This indicates the high degree of emotional commitment of the Ambassador to the cause of the success of the anti-Diem coup,

It is thus a confused picture that one obtains regarding the circumstances surrounding the overthrow of President Diem. Neither McNamara nor the JCS nor General Harkins seem to have supported the immediate ouster of the South Vietnamese President. Perhaps General Harkins went much further in advocating the continuance of Diem than his supervisors in Washington. This was probably due to the fact that he was the man on the spot, confronted with the seemingly implacable opposition of Ambassador Lodge to Diem. There was no direct conflict between the Secretary of Defence and the Secretary of State because the latter too was not an enthusiast in favour of the immediate overthrow of Diem. However, other subordinates of Rusk, some with access to the President, felt that the American objectives in South Vietnam could be attained only if Diem were removed from the scene. The State Department's man in Saigon, Lodge, was convinced that Diem should go.

In the Central Intelligence Agency, the chiefs in Washington were apparently not convinced whether the mere ouster of Diem would provide a panacea in Saigon. The CIA man in Saigon, Richardson, was somewhat equivocal on the issue of Diem's outser. Within the CIA set-up in Saigon itself, there was elements which were strongly committed to the idea of supporting a coup against Diem. The principal figure among them was Conein. A high ranking American diplomat who prefers to remain unidentified told the present writer that Conein

[74] Ibid., p. 48.
[75] Ibid., p. 49.

worked very closely with the coup-group.[76] Out of this confusing welter of circumstances, the only inference that one can possibly hazard is that the Pentagon was probably not the prime mover in instigating the ouster of Diem.

Inferences

The Kennedy Administration's policy towards the Diem regime is a good example of "governmental politics" outlined in Model 3. There were interagency cleavages—the conflicting reports of General Krulak and J.A. Mendenhall: differences in the State Department (Rusk vs. Harriman, Hilsman and Kattenburg) and in the CIA (McCone vs. Richardson). The US missions in Saigon reflected these differences and to some extent contributed to them. There was no love lost between Lodge and Harkins. At the broader plane, there seemed to be existing two polarized groups (Rusk, McNamara, Taylor McCone vs. Harriman, Ball, Hilsman and Forrestal). Because of his increasing number of statements on Vietnam and visits to South Vietnam and Hawaii, McNamara started to be identified more and more with the American policy in Vietnam. Both the civilian and military elements of the Pentagon had almost the same perception of Vietnam. They believed that from the American point of view, Diem was indispensable in Saigon. They would not accept the suggestion that was lurking in some corner of the State Department in lower levels that the US should "honourably" withdraw from South Vietnam. There is no evidence that there was any friction between them on Vietnam and the Pentagon's cable to Harkins by its private channel shows the anxiety of the Pentagon to influence the policy-making on Vietnam. It sought to oppose American encouragement to the coup group, *but it did not push its opposition to a critical point*. This leads one to hazard the inference that perhaps the Pentagon read the signs and believed that the President himself had lost faith in the usefulness of continued US support to the Diem regime. A similar appraisal probably lent encouragement to elements in other agencies who believed

---

[76] Interview with a well-informed former US Foreign Service Officer in Vietnam who did not want his name to be revealed.

that "it is time for a change" in Saigon.

THE TONKIN GULF INCIDENT : THE PREPARATION FOR
THE LAUNCHING OF ROLLING THUNDER

Within a few days after Diem's overthrow, President Kennedy was assassinated. Ambassador Lodge who was in San Francisco on his way to meet Kennedy heard the sad news. He was asked by McGeorge Bundy to proceed to Washington because the new President was more in need of consultation with him than Kennedy was. Other principal advisers were present when the Ambassador briefed Lyndon Johnson on Vietnam. He stated that "hard decisions" would be necessary to "save" South Vietnam. "Unfortunately, Mr President, you will have to make them," he added. The President's reported response was, "I am not going to lose Vietnam. I am not going to be the President who saw Southeast Asia go the way China went."[77] Thus, barely forty-eight hours after he had taken the oath, the "accidental President" committed himself to the "defence" of South Vietnam.

Johnson was a great parliamentary politician. A veteran of the House of Representatives and Senate, he knew where the levers of power lay in Washington and how to manipulate them. Like any successful politician, he was a man of the Centre.[78] Give something to this faction and give something to the other faction and do not fully alienate any group. This was the main tactic of Lyndon Johnson as Senate Majority Leader, and President Johnson would continue to follow it. He was a "practical" man and he "knew" what the people would accept and what they would not. In 1954, just before the fall of Dien Bien Phu, he vehemently opposed the plan of the Eisenhower Administration to intervene militarily on behalf of France. He was afraid that the American people would react sharply to the prospect of another land war in the wake of the Korean war. But both during the Truman and Eisenhower Administrations,

---

[77] Halberstam, n. 18, p. 298; and Tom Wicker, *JFK and LBJ, The Influence of Personality upon Politics* (New York, 1968), p. 205.

[78] Philip Geyelin, *Lyndon B. Johnson and the world* (New York, 1966), p. 33.

he was a good friend of the military—especially of the Air Force. It was usually profitable on the part of a member of the House or the Senate to be an ally of the military: one could wrap the flag around and, at the same time, do good "pork barrel" politics. Johnson was very good at that. But the White House and the Capitol were two different places. He would no longer have to deal with only fellow Americans. His adversaries would be foreigners—Russians, Chinese, Vietnamese etc. The game had changed, but he continued to cling to his old rules. If he got into a scarp with the Vietnamese Communists, he knew how to mobilize the support of Congress and country behind him. He did not harbour any serious doubt that he would succeed in his enterprise and he probably believed that he might go down in American history as a great President like Abraham Lincoln, Franklin D. Roosevelt and other Presidents who had led the country successfully in wars. He failed to realize that if the Vietnamese adversaries showed no disposition to knuckle under, if his anticipated "victory" remained elusive, and if the toll of American lives and treasure continued to mount, his support among the public and in Congress might be seriously eroded. There perhaps lay his failure.

The first priority of Lyndon Johnson was to make himself a "real President". The next November he would have to face an election. He declared that he would continue with "Kennedy policies" in the hope that the Kennedy people would not leave him. The "best and the brightest" men of Kennedy would be retained so that he could fight the election wearing the "Kennedy mantle." A skilled political strategist, he knew his objectives well and he tailored his strategies to those objectives.

Johnson did not have much knowledge of Vietnam. Kennedy had apparently not regarded his Vice President's trip to Saigon as an assignment of crucial importance. Johnson's Saigon trip would better be remembered for the hyperboles he used— "Diem, Churchill of today," "folding back to Fortress America" etc.—than for any significant impact it had upon America's Vietnam policy. But President Johnson sought to use Vietnam as one of his election instruments. He would allow Rusk, McNamara, and McGeorge Bundy to take charge of Vietnam while he would take care of his election, but both would move in unison. Throughout the campaign, he would portray himself and would be treated as the "man of peace" and "man of prudence." At times, he would not be seriously taken because the other man—Rupublican candidate Barry Goldwater gave an impression during the campaign that he would not hesitate to go for nuclear strikes, if necessary. Thus, in the 1964 election, Vietnam became the trump card; after four years, it would be his graveyard.

Johnson was a Southerner—a Texan. He was hardly at ease with Easterners. During the Kennedy Administration he felt that he was an "outcast."[79] After he came to the White House he reportedly said that McNamara was the "ablest" man he ever met. He praised McGeorge Bundy, the "intellectual administrator." He was enthusiastic over Dean Rusk, the Secretary of State.[80] Rusk was another "outcast" during the Kennedy Administration. Rusk had built his base in the East, but he had his roots in the South. He liked Johnson's style of government. The President liked to discuss issues in a closed circle of his top advisers rather than in the NSC or inter-department meetings consisting of second or third level government officials. This new style was to the taste of Rusk who did not like his subordinates arguing with him in the President's presence, or, at times, bypassing him and going straight to the President, as Hilsman often used to do during the Kennedy days. Johnson and Rusk develped mutual liking which proved lasting. Rusk continued in office till the end of Johnson's term whereas both Bundy and McNamara left earlier.

With the broad consensus among his principal advisers in favour of some vigorous moves the new President was in agreement. This lent momentum to preparations which by their nature were military in character. The initiative was thus increasingly taken by the President and the steps that were evolved in the Pentagon have been described in Chapter II.

Contingency planning for bombing operations against North Vietnam seem to have started soon after 17 March 1964 when the NSC accepted McNamara's recommendations for preparing

[79] Wicker, n. 77, p. 198.
[80] Ibid.

two types of plans to launch bombing—one within 72 hours and the other within 30 days.[81] In a closed session of the House Appropriations Subcommittee on Foreign Aid, William P. Bundy, the Assistant Secretary of State for Far Eastern Affairs, stated, "We are going to drive the Communists out of South Vietnam" even if that eventually involved a choice of "attacking the country to the north"—North Vietnam.[82] By 23 May 1964 Bundy and McNaughton, the Assistant Secretary of Defence (ISA), were able to prepare a 30-day programme leading to the full-scale bombing of North Vietnam.[83] Although its scenario was not later implemented in full, some of its elements formed the components of the Tonkin scenario. Rung 4 of the 23 May escalation ladder said, "Obtain joint resolution approving past actions and authorizing whatever is necessary with respect to Vietnam."[84] A draft of a Congressional resolution was prepared by William Bundy on 25 May. The Executive Council of the NSC, consisting of Rusk, McNamara, McGeorge Bundy and McCone, the CIA Director, after an examination of the 23 May scenario, decided to recommend only a few of its elements. Important amongst them was the move for a Congressional resolution.[85]

Meanwhile, the situation in South Vietnam was going from bad to worse. Big Minh who was one of the coup-leaders against Diem was himself overthrown on 30 January 1964. General Khanh who succeeded Minh seemingly failed to arrest the erosion of political stability. Viet Cong elements were reportedly improving their strength. Communists were doing still better in Laos. On 17 May the Pathet Lao launched a severe assault which threatened the existence of Souvanna Phouma's government, supported by the US. These developments must have disturbed American policy-makers. At home, the election campaign was in full swing. Republicans were attacking the "no-win" policy of the Johnson Administration. Both Goldwater and Nixon were urging that the US should

---

[81] *DOD Documents*, Book 3, IV.C.1, pp, 46ff.
[82] *New York Times*, 19 June 1964.
[83] *DOD Documents*, Book 3, IV.C.2(a), pp. 22-4.
[84] Ibid., p. 22.
[85] Ibid., p. 26.

bomb the North.[86] Against this background, all the main actors except the President met at Honolulu to review the Vietnam policy on 1 and 2 June 1964. The new face in the conference was General Westmoreland who had replaced General Harkins as the head of the Military Assistance Command, Vietnam (MACV).

The two subjects that received the main attention in the Honolulu meeting were the bombing of North Vietnam and getting a Congressional resolution passed expressing its support for the President to take actions in Southeast Asia in the interest of American security. Ambassador Lodge stated some "counter-terrorism measures" against North Vietnam would result in diminishing her support for Viet Cong. Admiral Felt, the CINCPAC, shared this view. But the principal presidential advisers—Rusk, McNamara and McCone—did not favour any immediate action against North Vietnam. They would like to have first a Congressional resolution in the President's pocket which might serve as a "blank cheque" for American military actions in Vietnam. They were not opposed to taking military steps against North Vietnam as such. They would rather first try to build up the "mood" of the nation for the contingency and in the meantime take preparatory military steps.[87]

While Washington was getting ready to take the plunge, Johnson asked a pertinent question to the CIA, "Would the rest of Southeast Asia necessarily fall if Laos and South Vietnam came under North Vietnam's control?" The CIA's reply on 9 June 1964 was a refutation of the "domino theory." It said that with the possible exception of Cambodia, no other nation in Southeast Asia would come under Communist control as a result of the fall of South Vietnam and Laos.[88] This analysis seems not to have been accepted by other actors including the President. Rusk, McNamara, McGeorge Bundy, Taylor, Rostow and the JCS, all believed in the validity of the domino theory.

Two second level officials in the Administration, Rostow

---

[86] *New York Times*, 19 March 1964, 10 April 1964, 17 April 1964, 12 May 1964, and 25 May 1964.

[87] *DOD Documents*, n. 83, p. 31.

[88] Ibid., p. 36.

and William Bundy, the Assistant Secretary of State for Far Eastern Affairs, worked hard during these critical months for launching the bombing of North Vietnam. In order to allay the fears and suspicions agitating Washington at that time, Rostow argued that the enemy—North Vietnam and the Viet Cong—was afflicted with anxieties and complications that the Administration tended to under-estimate. He urged that the US should behave like the greatest power in the world.[89] On 12 June 1964 William Bundy, in a memorandum, stated that the Administration was immediately in need of a Congressional resolution which would provide it with enough firmness and flexibility to deal with Southeast Asia in near future.[90] In spite of his denial that the Administration was planning to move soon against North Vietnam, it was not difficult to predict in which direction Washington was moving at that time. The last move in Washington to take punitive measures against North Vietnam was apparently made by the JCS. A command and control study of the Tonkin Gulf episode done by the Defence Department's Weapons System Evaluation Group in 1965, reveals that on 25 July 1964, the JCS urged that air strikes by unmarked planes flown by non-Americans against North Vietnam targets should be conducted.[91] This proposal was sent by McNaughton to Secretary Rusk on 30 July, the very day on which the first shot leading to the Tonkin Gulf incident was fired.

One may ask why William Bundy, McNaughton, the JCS and Ambassador Lodge strongly favoured punitive actions against the North whereas Rusk, McNamara, and Mac Bundy were very reluctant to do so. Both at the NSC Executive Council meeting of May and the Honolulu Conference of June 1964, the latter decided against taking such actions forthwith. On the other hand, when the *Maddox* was attacked in the Tonkin Gulf on 30 July, they "unanimously" recommended that the US should retaliate by bombing North Vietnam.

The election day was round the corner. Johnson was campaigning on a "peace platform" whereas his challenger, Gold-

[89] Sheehan, n. 15, p. 264.
[90] Ibid., p. 265; and *DOD Documents*, Book 3, IV.C.1, p. 83.
[91] Cited in Sheehan, n. 15, p. 266.

water, appeared to the public as a "war-monger". Johnson sought to maintain this image till November. His best strategy would be to avoid resorting to any escalation in Vietnam. His principal advisers must have been aware of it, as also their deputies. But this awareness tends to be lower as one goes down in the hierarchy. The lower an official is placed, the more he is inclined to be influenced by the organizational interests, bureaucratic rivalry and his personality. The higher an official is placed, the more he tends to take into account, besides the above variables, the domestic and external forces that the helmsman will have to reckon with. The principal advisers of the President appear to have felt that any attack on the North before a "serious incident" would spoil the "dovish image" of Johnson. The "incident" occurred on 4 August. Then the advisers were agreed that inaction on the part of the US after the alleged North Vietnamese attack on the *Maddox* would damage his prospect because he would be subjected to Republican charges that he could not stand up to the Communists.

Inferences

All the main actors except the CIA continued to subscribe to the "domino theory." The CIA refuted it. It also predicted that the bombing of North Vietnam would not succeed in stopping the flow of men and materials from the North to South.

The overwhelming concern of the principal advisers was the Presidential election in November. At lower levels, this consideration was less. There was some difference over Vietnam between McNamara and his deputies—McNaughton and the JCS. There was similar difference existing between Rusk and his deputies—William Bundy and Ambassador Lodge. So also did McGeorge Bundy and Rostow differ between themselves.

McNamara had emerged to be the "star actor" in regard to Vietnam. It was the Secretary of Defence and not the Secretary of State or the Director of Central Intelligence Agency who could claim to have made several visits to South Vietnam for "on the spot" examination of the situation. At the Honolulu meetings, it was the Secretary of Defence who set the stage for discussion of future courses of action with the JCS, the CINCPAC and the

Chief of the MACV. At these meetings the State Department's representation was on a lower level. Apart from McNamara's personality, the other factor that was responsible for his playing a leading role was perhaps the momentum of onrushing military preparation. In any politico-military preparation, as the imminence of military action increases, the lead would progressively pass from the diplomatic branch to the military branch. The debate, if any, at such a time tends to take place within the Defence Establishment. At this point, such differences as existed between the civilian and military components of the Pentagon were of relatively minor order. The Secretary of Defence was clearly seen to be the master in his own house and he had also succeeded in establishing very satisfactory equation with the President.

THE US ENTERS THE WAR: THE LAUNCHING OF
ROLLING THUNDER

Operation "Rolling Thunder" was approved on 13 February 1965. But a "general consensus" for bombing North Vietnam some time in future had already been reached in a White House strategy meeting on 7 September 1964. Prior to this, Ambassador Taylor had cabled on 18 August 1964 for "a carefully orchestrated bombing attack on North Vietnam, directed primarily at infiltration and other military targets" with "1 January 1965, as a target D-Day." On 26 August, the JCS sent to the President a memoradum which concurred with Taylor's cable and which was the first "provocation strategy" for the Administration's consideration. The course suggested by the Ambassador who was a former Chairman of the JCS, was endorsed by the JCS and had the support of the Defence Secretary. Other agencies fell in line and there was virtually no opposition from their heads. The reason why the policy-makers, on 7 September meeting, did not immediately go for bombing the North, apart from the major issue of the national election was, as expressed by McNamara at that meeting, that there was a "clear hope of strengthening the GVN." But he went on to urge that "the way be kept open for stronger actions" even if South Vietnam did not improve or in the event the war was widened by the Communists.[92] The NSAM 214, issued on 10 September, contained some "interim measures" to boost the morale of South Vietnam. It also clearly stated that, if "larger decisions" were required at any time by a change in the situation, they would be taken.[93] It was also decided that the US "should be prepared" to launch Tonkin-type "tit-for-tat" reprisal air strikes, if necessary, against North Vietnam.

The "general consensus" was reached among the principal advisers in 7 September NSC meeting regarding the decision to bomb North Vietnam starting some time after the election. To that course there was one important dissenter in the second level of the State Department—George Ball, the under Secretary of State. Ball had strong doubts about the wisdom of the course. The Under Secretary, who had continued to look after European affairs after Johnson succeeded Kennedy had not been actively concerned about Vietnam as Harriman and Hilsman were in the beginning of the Johnson Administration. However, after Harriman and Hilsman were "purged" from the Vietnam decision-making scene, Ball took increasing interest in Vietnam. On 5 October 1964, he sent a long memorandum to Rusk, McNamara and McGeorge Bundy in which he argued that the Saigon regime was capable neither of winning the broad support of the South Vietnamese people nor of undertaking successful military operations against the Viet Cong. On the other hand, he recommended a course of action which would allow a political settlement without direct American military involvement.[94] He sounded a sharp warning against increased US military involvement. He argued that once entangled, it would be very difficult for the US to withdraw. He stated succinctly, "Once on the tiger's back we cannot be sure of picking the place to dismount."[95] Ball's arguments seemed to make little impact upon other key men in Washington who believed that force would work.

The Viet Cong attack on the American air base at Bien Hoa took place on 1 November 1964. The JCS, ignoring the domestic

[92] *DOD Documents*, Book 4, IV.C.2(b), pp. 26-7.

[93] For the full text of NSAM 214, see Seehan, n. 15, pp. 368-9.

[94] Henry Braudou, *Anatomy of Error, The Inside Story of the Asian War on the Potomrc, 1954-1939* (Boston, 1969), p. 37.

[95] Quoted in Halberstam, n. 18, p. 498.

political scene, urged a B-52 attack on North Vietnam. Ambassador Taylor cabled for a more restrained response consisting of "retaliation bombing attacks on selected DRV targets" using both American and South Vietnamese planes.[96] The civilian advisers, especially Rusk and McNamara, as pointed out by Lyndon Johnson in *Vantage Point*, were opposed to the immediate bombing of the North.[97] In view of the "continuing unsteadiness of the South Vietnamese Government and military assistance" and the concern for safety of US dependents in Saigon, the President decided against a retaliatory attack. But, probably the more compelling reason, which Johnson does not mention in his book, was that the election was only two days away.

An interagency working group, unofficially known as the Bundy Working Group, which the President appointed on 1 November, developed three options for direct action against North Vietnam. These options, which have been described in Chapter II, were described as A, B and C.[98] On the basis of available documents, it has not been possible to determine the positions pushed by the various actors in this group or the manner in which the three options were evolved. Option B, of course, went the farthest in terms of the military action and appears to be in consonance with the JCS' recommendation of B-52 attacks on targets in North Vietnam. Option C was the only one not envisaging immediate strikes against North Vietnam even though that option contemplated significant ground involvement in South Vietnam. It is noteworthy that the point of view articulated by Ball did not figure at all as a possible option to deal with the situation. Perhaps the signal from above as interpreted by the Bundy Group pointed in the direction of some vigorous actions and they appear to have spelled out the options in that framework.

At the meeting of a select committee of the NSC on 24 November, the options put forth by Bundy Group were discussed. McNamara shared Rusk's concern about the chaos in South

---

[96] *DOD Documents*, Book 4, IV.C.2(c), p. 4.
[97] Lyndon B. Johnson, *The Vantage Point*: *Perspectives of the Presidency 1963-1969* (New York, 1971), p, 121.
[98] *DOD Documents*, n. 96, pp. 18-23.

Vietnam, but warned that the condition would worsen if no additional steps were taken to reverse the trend.[99] In reply to Ball's query whether bombing North Vietnam could improve the situation in South Vietnam, McNamara said that it could not unless the "bombing actually cut down infiltration into the South."[100] The Pentagon analyst infers that Ball probably favoured Option A whereas Wheeler, the Chairman of the JCS and, possibly McCone went for B. Option C was favoured by McNamara, McNaughton, Rusk and the Bundy brothers. However, the Pentagon analyst adds that McGeorge Bundy and McNamara stood for a "firm C" whereas the other three preferred a more restrained, incremental approach.[101]

On 27 November 1964, Ambassador Taylor expressed his doubt whether bombing would definitely have a favourable effect in South Vietnam. Others including McNamara agreed with him. However, McNamara pointed out that "the strengthening effect of Option C could at least buy time, possibly measured in years."[102] Taylor then recommended the adoption of "Option A plus the first stages of Option C" strategy; others agreed.[103]

The opinion of the intelligence community on bombing the North was ambiguous and it contained perhaps elements of contradiction. On the one hand they challenged Rostow's thesis that the destruction of her industries would be a great blow to North Vietnam. "DRV leaders. . . would probably be willing to suffer some damage to the country in the course of a test of wills with the US over the course of events in South Vietnam," they stated. On the other hand, they pointed out that the interdiction of imports into the North and the destruction of her industries would seriously affect the capability of the North to supply men and matrials to the South.[104] This analysis strengthened the hand of the pro-bombing elements, who, at that time, were seeking to inflict more "pain" on North Vietnam, with a view to inducing her to change her course. Moreover, the prediction of the intelligence community that Russia and China were

[99] Ibid., p. 46.
[100] Ibid., p. 39.
[101] Ibid., p. 42.
[102] Ibid., pp. 42-6.
[103] Ibid., p. 46.
[104] Ibid., p. 8; and Sheehan, n. 15, pp. 340-1.

very unlikely to directly intervene if the North was bombed was a further fillip to these elements. Thus, in the immediate context, the "pessimistic" part of the report was outweighed by its "optimistic" one.

On 20 December, Saigon faced another political crisis. The High National Council, acting as legislature, was dissolved by General Khanh. On Christmas eve, two Americans were killed in Saigon by a bomb explosion. The US Mission in Saigon immediately sent a "joint message" to Washington urging the bombing of North Vietnam.[105] The President continued to deliberate. He did not authorize immediate bombing of the North in spite of strong recommendations from Taylor and the JCS. Meanwhile the Administration was trying to "educate" the public by leaking out stories to newspapers on infiltration of the North Vietnamese into South Vietnam.

At this critical point the Secretary of State apprently voiced some serious reservations concerning early intensification of air attack. In such a situation the player representing the Pentagon may feel constrained to take urgent action to induce the President to accept the course strongly urged by his organization, especially if he himself is convinced of the utility of the course. He may seek to reinforce his effort by securing a high ranking and influential ally from outside his organization. In the present situation, the Defence Secretary found such an ally in National Security Assistant, McGeoge Bundy. Bundy sent a memorandum on 27 January 1965 to the President indicating that its contents represented his thinking as well as that of McNamara. The memorandum sought to counter the kind of opinion that Rusk might have expressed to the President. The memorandum stated that Bundy and McNamara had reached a "critical moment" in their thinking. They argued that the time had come to "move out of the middle course" and to use more power than had thus far been employed. Acknowledging that Rusk did not agree with them, they said that Rusk believed that the consequences of both escalation and withdrawal were so bad that they must find a way of making the existing policy work. " This would be good if it is possible. Bob and I do not think it is," it added.[106]

---

[105] *DOD Documents*, ibid., pp. 72-3.
[106] Johnson, n. 97, pp. 122-3.

It was one of the decisive points in the history of the American military involvement in Vietnam. Two of the most important actors in Washington joined hands on the side of the use of force. Their alliance was too big a pressure for Rusk to withstand for long. Rusk, of course, was not an opponent of the use of force. His hesitation to go with Bundy and McNamara in favour of immediate air operation was, perhaps, due to his concern over the diplomatic implications of the projected course and the warning signals sent by his deputy, George Ball. The President seemed ready to buy the Bundy-McNamara line. Bundy appears to be the key figure at this point. The President sent Bundy to South Vietnam to assess the position. McNamara could not have been concerned over it because Bundy's line was his own too.

On 6 February 1965, a Viet Cong attack on the US base at Pleiku took place. From Saigon Bundy recommended that the US should go ahead with air strikes at once. When the issue was discussed at a White House meeting, all participants except Senator Mike Mansfield (Dem., Montana) were for the air strikes, President Johnson claims.[107] The President authorized the strikes the same day. On 13 February he decided to launch Operation Rolling Thunder, initiating air war against North Vietnam. The only other forces that might have had some impact on the President in taking 13 February decision were McGeorge Bundy's report on his return from South Vietnam in which Bundy had recommended "a policy of sustained reprisal," and Ambassador Taylor's messages to the President on 11 and 12 February. Bundy's key role at this point is also brought out by Johnson's comment in his memoirs that he was "impressed by its [Bundy report's] logic and persuaded strongly by its arguments."[108]

Mac Bundy, while recommending retaliation, was not very optimistic that success would be early or certain.[109] He thought that while it was possible that at some future time a neutral non-Communist force might emerge in South Vietnam, no such force existed at that time. He warned, "At its very best the struggle in Vietnam will be long." He sought to make it very clear that there was no short cut to success in South Vietnam. His tone of

---

[107] Ibid., p. 125.
[108] Ibid., p. 128.
[109] *DOD Documents*, Book 4, IV. C.3, pp. 31-5

diffidence was further revealed when he said, ". . .even if it fails, the policy will be worth it. At a minimum, it will damp down the charge that we did not do all that we could have done, and this charge will be important in many countries, including our own. . . ."[110] This indicates the deep concern of decision-makers regarding the public opinion in their own countries. It may be mentioned that overwhelming support for the Pleiku retaliation was expressed in a Gallup poll held soon after that.

At about the time McGeorge Bundy's recommendation reached the White House, Ambassador Taylor, in a message to the President on 11 February, urged the latter to take "a measured, controlled sequence of actions" against North Vietnam in reprisal for the attack on Pleiku.[111] In this respect his recommendation was similar to that of Bundy who had presumably consulted the Ambassador only a few days earlier in Saigon before sending his recommendation to the President. However, they differed in respect of the objective of bombing. Bundy sought to influence the course of the struggle in South Vietnam, because he thought that the bombing of the North would boost morale in Saigon and provide unity and cohesion to it. Taylor's main objective was to apply more pressure on Hanoi so that it would "cease intervention" and would be amenable to talks for a political settlement.

Inferences

The Harriman Group was almost out of the "power centre." Its views were contrary to the dominant current. George Ball, the lone dissenter, was hardly in a position to influence the rest. His pessimistic assessment of the situation in South Vietnam and of the utility of air strikes probably did not carry much weight exept for a while with the chief of his own organization. All other principal actors including the President seemed to be in favour of bombing North Vietnam. While the JCS favoured launching immediate attacks on the targets in North Vietnam, including the strategic ones in Hanoi and Haiphong, Rusk, Mc-Namara, Mac Bundy, Taylor, McCone, W. P. Bundy and

---

[110] Ibid., p. 38.
[111] Ibid., pp. 40-1.

McNaughton were not ready to go as far as the JCS in this regard. They supported the bombing of North Vietnam, but they favoured sparing for the time being strategic targets in Hanoi and Haiphong. While McNamara and Taylor appeared to tilt somewhat in the direction of the JCS, Rusk seemed to oscillate back to the centre.

In the overall perspective, McNamara seemed to be the lead man, though at a critical point he was content to let McGeorge Bundy to carry the ball in order to counter Rusk's diffidence. He appeared to be a more powerful actor than Rusk. In respect of influencing the President on Vietnam, the Defence Secretary was closely followed by McGeorge Bundy and Taylor in that order. However, in the immediate context of President's February decision to launch Rolling Thunder, Mac Bundy seems to have been the most influential actor.

THE BEGINNING OF US COMBAT ROLE IN VIETNAM

There was a substantial measure of agreement between the civilian and military elements of the Pentagon regarding the deployment of ground troops in South Vietnam by the time the first batch of Marines landed at Da Nang on 8 March 1965. From that time till the middle of June 1965 when there was a sharp escalation in the ground war, this harmony between them, broadly speaking, continued to exist. The main opposition to the rise in the level of ground involvement came mainly from George Ball, the Under Secretary of State, and General Taylor, US Ambassador in Saigon. It is interesting to see that General Taylor who, in October 1961 was the first to propose the sending of US military personnel to South Vietnam under the cover of "flood relief operation" was the one who very strongly opposed the increasing US ground involvement in 1965. It is also significant to note that as the shooting intensified, the military man on the field began to exercise more influence than before and his leverage *vis-a-vis* other players in Washington tended to increase.

The timing of a decision on military involvement abroad, however, is not solely dependent upon the situation on the field in the foreign territory concerned. Significant changes may take place on the field and the military man on the field may request authorization of increased military activity; but it would be difficult to take a decision to that effect if the domestic climate is very unfavourable for taking such a step. The principals in Washington cannot overlook that factor, least of all, the President. But if there is a broad consensus among the principals in favour of adopting an interventionist policy and if the opinion at home is either in its favour or at least not strongly opposed to it, and if the field commander urges the Administration for sending American troops to the field of operation, it becomes relatively easy for the Administration to take a decision to that effect. At the beginning of 1965, such a broad consensus existed among Washington players and with the elections over and the President returned by a landslide such an opinion prevailed among American people. As a result, the momentum towards an increased ground involvement by the US continued to mount in spite of the strong opposition from Ball and Taylor.

The beginning of American combat involvement in South Vietnam was mostly a continuous battle between Ambassador Taylor and Westmoreland, who headed the American Military Assistance Command, Saigon. Taylor and Westmoreland were two of the brightest West Pointers in the post-war period. They were good friends. In fact, Westmoreland was Secretary of the General Staff under General Taylor when the latter was the Chief of Staff of the Army. Before they were sent to Saigon, the American missions in Saigon were strife-ridden; Ambassador Lodge and General Harkins often were on the "war-path." It was hoped that the atmosphere would change with the change in personnel there, especially with the appointment of two persons who had worked in harmony in the past. Such hope was belied. Sharp differences in relation to men and strategy arose between Taylor and Westmoreland. The problem was complex because though Taylor had put on a civilian cap, he was still regarded in Washington as a brilliant military strategist. Perhaps because of their different constituencies, the general-turned-ambassador and the general on active duty tended to perceive things differently.

When Marines landed at Da Nang, Rolling Thunder had been authorized and was about to be launched. There was some hope that America could succeed in "bombing Hanoi to the negotiating table." That was probably why Taylor did not express much concern over the arrival of Marines charged with the mission of base security. Rolling Thunder did not yield the expected dividends. Westmoreland, supported by the CINCPAC and the JCS, soon started pressing for more men. He also planned an "aggressive strategy" which would later emerge as "search and destroy" strategy. McNamara extended "qualified support" for Westmoreland's request for more men. Taylor, who was in Washington at the end of March, spoke strongly against these demands. The NSAM 328 which contained the President's decision, made during the NSC meeting of 1-2 April, was a compromise.[112] Johnson approved only two Marine battalions, not all that Westmoreland had asked for. While not accepting the "aggressive strategy," he was not content to retain unchanged the old strategy of base security. "The President approved a change of mission for all Marine battalions deployed to Vietnam to permit their more active use under conditions to be established and approved by the Secretary of Defense in consultation with the Secretary of State."[113] In other words, the American ground troops could now be used for offensive missions. The thrust of the new mission was discernible—to move forward to a certain extent, not to stay pat. Thus was initiated the so-called "enclave strategy."[114] Taylor could derive some consolation that the military, because of his opposition, had not succeeded in getting all that they wanted. But, in the bargain, he had to give in something too. In order to kill the "search and destroy strategy," he had to agree to the "enclave strategy" which, as events were to prove, was one step towards the former. The military actors were on offensive and, given the circumstances, it was increasingly difficult to beat down their demands.

Hardly was the ink of the NSAM 328 dry when the CUMUSMACV began his new "push" for more troops—this time for the 173rd Airborne Brigade.[115] To further compound the discomfiture of Taylor, a joint State/Defence message with the blessing of the "highest authority" in Washington was issued to

---

[112] Ibid., IV.C.5, pp. 59-60.

[113] For the text of the National Security Action Memorandum 328, 6 April 1965, signed by McGeorge Bundy and addressed to the Secretary of State, the Secretary of Defence and the Director of Central Intelligence, see Sheehan, n. 15, pp. 452-3.

[114] *DOD Documents*, n. 112 pp. 67-70.

[115] Ibid., p. 64.

Taylor on 18 April. It recommended the introduction of more ground troops in South Vietnam for "counterinsurgency" purposes.[116] (The phrase "highest authority" apparently included the Secretaries of State and Defence, and the President.) The phrase "counterinsurgency" must have been disturbing to Taylor, because it would include sending American troops beyond the perimeter of enclaves.

A conference of American civil and military officials was held at Honolulu on 20 April. The military again pressed for the adoption of the "search and destroy" strategy, but they were successfully challenged by Taylor. The "enclave strategy" was retained, but a big rise in the level of American ground troops in Vietnam was approved—from 33,500 to 73,500.[117] Taylor was the lone fighter in the Honolulu meeting against further escalation in ground involvement, but his days as an effective player were numbered. At Honolulu, General Westmoreland emerged as the most influential impressive player.

A look at the persons who attended the Honolulu meeting would suggest that the military was beginning to gain ascendancy in the policy-making on Vietnam. The participants were McNamara, Secretary of Defence, William P. Bundy, Assistant Secretary of State for Far Eastern Affairs, John McNaughton, Assistant Secretary of Defence (ISA), General Wheeler, Chairman of the JCS, Adm. U.S. Grant Sharp, the CINCPAC, Ambassador Taylor and General Westmoreland, the CUMUSMACV. Out of seven, three were active military men, one—Taylor—, a retired JCS Chairman, two, top civilians of the Pentagon and the seventh one—Bundy—was till recently, in the Pentagon service. One may hypothesize that the input of the Defence Department *vis-a-vis* the State Department into decisions having important foreign policy implications tends to increase as a war escalates. At the Honolulu meeting, Taylor won only a partial success in winning approval for the continuance of the "enclave strategy" as against a more aggressive strategy advocated by the military. But the Ambassador could have had little doubt that pressure from the military would continue and increase.

The intra-Administration reactions to the Honolulu recom-

[116] Ibid.
[117] Ibid., pp. 71-8.

mendations were primarily of three kinds. The dominant group consisting mostly of elements of the State and Defence Departments supported them. The CIA led by Director McCone expressed its reservation about them. The United States would get herself "mired down" in the Vietnamese jungle and it would be difficult for her either to win or get out, McCone had warned on 2 April. He assessed that the US might go for ground war only if it was supplemented by air war.[118] He repeated the same warning in a personal memorandum to the President on 28 April.[119] McCone was not a dove. He would prefer the application of force if the US was willing to employ such force as was adequate to realize her objective—a view not dissimilar to that of the JCS.

The only opposition to the Honolulu recommendations came from George Ball, the "devil's advocate" within "Johnson's court." He argued that sending more American GIs to South Vietnam would be matched by more men from the North to the South. He reportedly warned that the US was at a "threshold" and it was the time for a pause and trying some diplomatic means.[120] Ball's scepticism was clearly expressed, but it was contrary to the perception of McNamara and other important actors. McNamara approved of the Honolulu recommendation on 30 April.

In May 1965 Viet Cong forces resumed offensive and dealt severe blows to the South Vietnamese forces. The American officials in Saigon were seriously concerned over the prospect of a total collapse of the Saigon forces. Quick action was needed to stave off the Viet Cong progress. It appeared to be a crises situation from the American point of view and Taylor could no longer argue that South Vietnam was not in the grip of a crisis as he had contended earlier. Thus Taylor was at last caught in the web; he was willing to adjust himself to circumstances in Saigon as well as Washington. As an experienced player he knew well how far he could move and where he should stop if he were to remain as a player on the board. Beyond a point, opposition might reduce his usefulness and even cost him his

[118] Ibid., pp. 115-6
[119] Ibid.
[120] Halberstam, n. 18, pp. 579-81; and Brandon, n. 94, pp. 53-4.

position. Deteriorating conditions in South Vietnam might have
served to reinforce such coordination and to lead Taylor to the
conclusion that the time had come for him to switch. Taylor
joined Westmoreland and Alexis Johnson, his deputy in Saigon,
in recommending to the State Department on 5 June that in view
of the impending collapse of the South Vietnamese forces, the
US ground troops might be committed to action.[121] Unlike the
previous month, the American mission in Saigon appeared to be
united, all going the same way—at that point, Westmoreland's
way.

By the first week of June, there was virtual unanimity among
the principal advisers except Ball as to the advisability of escalating the American ground war in Vietnam. The time was propitious for Westmoreland to make the next move. On 7 June, he
sent the "44-battalion request." He asked for 35 battalions to be
immediately deployed in South Vietnam. He identified other nine
battalions which could be sent later. He argued that the US
troops could "successfully take the fight to the VC" and the
Viet Cong would be convinced that they could not win. It was
exactly the language of the "victory strategy" which was the
consensus reached among the conferees in the Honolulu meeting
of 20 April.[122]

While the "44-battalion request" was under active consideration in Washington, Westmoreland was authorized to commit
American forces to battle in support of Saigon forces "in any
situation . . . when, in CUMUSMACV's judgement, their use is
necessary to strengthen the relative position of GVN forces."[123]
The US forces were no longer required to sit tight in the perimeter of enclaves. They could move beyond them in offensive
operations against Viet Cong. The "enclave strategy" was buried
and the "search and destroy" strategy was born.[124] Henceforward,
the battle would be waged not regarding strategy, but on the
number of men to be sent to South Vietnam.

Towards the end of June and the beginning of July, the 44-
battalion debate was raging up in Washington. The military

---

[121] *DOD Documents*, Book 4, IV.C.5, p. 25.
[122] *DOD Documents*, n. 112, pp. 90ff.
[123] Ibid., p. 104.
[124] Ibid., pp. 116-24.

members were in a confident mood that things would go their way. The principal civilian advisers to the President, Rusk and McNamara, were relatively quite. Even George Ball did not remain unaffected. His opposition to the military was not complete. He was prepared to go half the way. He would go with the programmed 15 battalions and 72,000 men made public in mid-June by McNamara. But there the US should stop and try for a diplomatic settlement, Ball urged. Otherwise, the US faced the risk of "a costly and indeterminate struggle," he warned in a memorandum to the President on 28 June.[125] By going half-way, he sought to appease the military and its allies. But he could not succeed.

On the same day, William Bundy, the key man in the State Department on Vietnam, wrote a memorandum to the President. His strategy was to hold on without risking a major disaster. His recommendation was to bring the American strength in South Vietnam to 18 manoeuvre battalions and 85,000 men. Bundy was again in the middle.[126] A skilled bureaucratic player, he too tried to bring about a "consensus," because the President was essentially a "consensus man."

McNaughton, the Assistant Secretary of Defence (ISA), did not appear to be active in the beginning of the American ground involvement as he was when decisions were being made on beginning the bombing of North Vietnam. However, towards the end of the game, he too made a move which reflected the "action-oriented" mood of that particular time. As has been stated earlier, on 13 July, he recommended to Secretary McNamara that the US should introduce 44 battalions in South Vietnam and be prepared to send more in future.[127] Of three possible courses, namely, success for US/South Vietnam, inconclusive results for either side, and a South Vietnamese collapse and concomitant US defeat, McNaughton indicated that the US should opt for the first. This was the highest point of hawkishness that McNaughton was to touch in relation to military involvement in Vietnam. His recommendation which was hardly different from what the JCS had advocated probably facilitated the acceptance of the

---

[125] Ibid., p. 105.
[126] Ibid., p. 106.
[127] Ibid., p. 127.

JCS point of view by McNamara and by the President a week latter. One interesting question arises—why was the usually ebullient Secretary of Defence not as active as he usually was? Others appeared to be having their say while he had not apparently chosen to show himself as the dominant figure.

McNaughton's memorandum appears to have been inspired by his awareness of the position of Defence Secretary on Vietnam. McNamara too was in favour of the American ground involvement in Vietnam. But, with things developing in a manner satisfactory from his point of view, he himself did not probably seek to appear as the leader of the pack because of the opposition of Ambassador Taylor with whom his personal equation was very good. Moreover, he might have been concerned about the silence of Rusk on this question. Rusk, by background, was an advocate of strong American military posture abroad as an instrument of her foreign policy. His position on Vietnam so far was not contrary to this image. However, he too was not as vociferous as some other actors in Washington for speedy American military involvement in Vietnam. He was conscious of his responsibility as the head of the diplomatic organ of the government. He would opt for diplomatic settlement, of course, only on American terms. He would go for virtual military solution only if negotiations had no prospect of success. Moreover, his own "house"—the State Department— was somewhat divided on Vietnam. While William Bundy was in favour of American ground involvement, George Ball was opposed to it. It was, thus, not easy for Rusk to decisively throw his weight on any side. On the other hand, it was not difficult for his bureaucratic competitor—McNamara, for example—to neutralise him by not provoking him to choose a side. McNamara probably deemed it prudent to get the desired decision by allowing the battle to be fought at a lower level, instead of raising it to a higher pitch. By adopting personally a low profile he sought to avoid provoking senior players like Rusk from entering the field, thereby making the outcome uncertain.

Inferences

There does not appear to be any basic change in the JCS

position. They continued to urge for sending more American forces for South Vietnam. However, the demand for more troops was voiced with increasing vigour by the military commander in the field, Westmoreland. Ball and Taylor continued to oppose the ground involvement, although they, to some extent, modified their stand after some time. Taylor, unlike the military who wanted fast buildup, preferred slow and gradual buildup.

The CIA's McCone was opposed to the buildup of ground forces not so much because he was against the American military involvement in Vietnam, as due to his fear that the US would be "mired down" in Vietnam if combat operations on the ground were not sufficiently supported by heavy bombing and mining of North Vietnamese harbours. William Bundy and McNaughton were for the "middle way." Rusk does not seem to have figured significantly in the present case. He seems to have been largely on the sidelines. The Defence Department appears to have played a more predominant role than the State Department in the field of policy-making on Vietnam. McNamara himself shrewdly kept a low profile, allowing others to perform in the arena.

As actors manoeuvre for the acceptance of their respective positions, there sometimes occurs a situation when the general climate becomes so action-oriented that doubters and 'nay'-sayers tend to go along rather than risk possible isolation. Such a situation appears to have developed at this point in respect of the demand vigorously pushed forward by the JCS and General Westmoreland. General Taylor and George Ball are seen in such a context to modify their position and McNaughton is seen willing to endorse what the military sought.

ESCALATION AND DE-ESCALATION: PULL AND HAUL WITHIN

With the launching of Rolling Thunder in March 1965 and that of the "search and destroy" strategy in June 1965, American military involvement in Vietnam became very evident. The Rubicon was crossed. The debate within the Administration would no longer revolve round the question of whether to get in or not to get in. Henceforward the debate within the Administration was on whether it was wise to raise the level of

American military involvement in Vietnam or not. The interaction within the civilian and military elements of the Defence
Department in regard to the question of escalation was discussed in Chapter III. To what extent the role of other federal
actors in regard to escalation affected the Pentagon's posture,
and equation between the civilian and military components of
the Pentagon over that question will be discussed here.

It is important to note that other federal actors—especially,
the State Department, the CIA and the National Security
Assistant—were apparently more concerned over the air than
over the ground war. The number of memoranda that flowed
within the Administration in relation to air operations is much
larger than that of memoranda touching on land operations.
The dramatic and potentially critical nature of air operations
might have accounted for the difference in the response of
federal actors to the ground and air wars in Vietnam.

In July 1965 both the civilian and military elements of the
Pentagon favoured the intensification of American military
involvement in Vietnam. As has been said earlier, McNamara
advocated "total quarantine" of the North. Secretary Rusk
gave full support to McNamara for escalation. "The integrity
of the U.S. commitment is the principal pillar of peace throughout the world," Rusk said. If "the US commitment" were
found unreliable, the risk of a general war would increase, he
argued.[128]

But the State Department itself was divided over escalation.
The principal opposition to escalation came from George Ball,
the Under Secretary of State. In a memorandum sent to other
"principals" in Washington on 1 July 1965, Ball argued against
escalation. He warned that any large-scale American involvement
on land would be a "catastrophic error" and would bring humi-
liation on the United States. He advised that the US should withdraw or go for a limited involvement which could be supported by
her capabilities. "This is our last clear chance to make this decision," he asserted.[129] William Bundy, the Assistant Secretary of
State for Far Eastern Affairs, took a different stand. He did not
side fully either with Rusk or with Ball. He sought to take a

---

[128] *DOD Documents*, Book 6, IV.C.7(a), p. 8.
[129] Ibid. pp. 6-8.

"middle way" between them. He was for the intensification of American military involvement in Vietnam, but he would not urge it at present. Some time should be allowed to prepare the American public to accept the fact that the US was engaged in an intense war in Vietnam, Bundy agrued.[130] McNamara did not agree with Bundy's plea for delay in bombing on the ground that the situation in South Vietnam was too serious to afford the "luxury of delay."[131]

The intelligence community's assessment was not a very clear-cut assessment. As SNIE on 23 July stated that attacks on military targets in the Hanoi-Haiphong area and the interdiction of supplies along the China border would hurt North Vietnam, but it would not have a "critical impact" upon her capability to help the South. Only severe attacks on POLs might inflict substantial damage upon North Vietnam and induce her to agree to negotiate.[132] The thrust of the estimate seemed to favour the intensification of the bombing of North Vietnam.

Towards the end of 1965 there ensued a debate within the Administration whether the US should stop bombing North Vietnam for some time. As noted earlier, McNamara and McNaughton argued for a pause on the ground that it might induce North Vietnam to seek negotiation. The military strongly opposed the move. The proposal for a pause faced stiff opposition from the State Department. In a memorandum to the President on 9 November 1965, the Department pointed out that the US, having stopped bombing the North, would have played the "very important card" without any substantial return. A pause may not win Saigon's acceptance and it might adversely affect the solidarity of the Saigon regime, the State Department argued. If the pause failed, it would be difficult to resume bombing because of the obstacles put in the meantime by Hanoi.[133] The State paper, speaking for Rusk, recommended that the pause should not be undertaken at the present time.[134] Thus, the main difference between the position of the State

---

[130] Ibid. p. 9.
[131] Ibid.
[132] Ibid., pp. 10-1.
[133] Ibid., p. 22.
[134] Ibid., p. 23.

Department and that of the civilian elements of the Pentagon over the question of a pause was that whereas the former argued that the bombing of North Vietnam was an important card which could be played only once, the latter said that this card could be played several times.[135]

The position of the State Department regarding a pause appears to have changed by the first week of December. William Bundy and Alexis Johnson, in a joint memorandum to the President on 6 December, stated the pros and cons of a pause and then recommended that the President should approve a pause as soon as possible.[136] As the memorandum was addressed to the President, it seems that Rusk had, by that time, dropped his objection to the proposed pause and the memorandum of Bundy and Johnson had the implicit support and approval of the Secretary. In fact the day after Bundy and Johnson sent their memorandum to the President, Rusk, McNamara and Mac Bundy met with the President in his ranch in Texas and tried to prevail upon him to order a pause.[137] President Johnson, in his memoirs, says that he was still sceptical of the utility of a pause. On 18 December, the President again discussed the matter with his principal associates along with two of his trusted personal advisers, Clark Clifford and associate Justice, Abe Fortas. Rusk argued that by observing a pause the President would be able to fend off the domestic criticism that he was not doing enough to reach a peaceful settlement. McNamara, Mac Bundy, Ball and U.A. Johnson supported Rusk. On the other hand, Clifford and Fortas advised against a pause.[138] Eventually as noted earlier, the President decided in favour of a pause and it started on 24 December 1965 and lasted till 31 January 1966.

A significant aspect of the pause debate was the reason why Rusk and McGeorge Bundy who were initially opposed to the pause proposal later changed their mind and vigorously worked for a pause. A possible factor was the signal they received from two important diplomatic sources. One day late in

[135] Ibid.
[136] Ibid., p. 26.
[137] Johnson, n. 97, p. 235.
[138] Ibid., pp. 235-6.

November Soviet Ambassador Anatoly Dobrynin, assured McGeorge Bundy that a pause of "twelve to twenty days" would lead to "intense diplomatic activity."[139] A Hungarian diplomat told Rusk that a pause "for a few weeks would be enough" to start negotiations.[140] The other possible factor was the concern of Rusk and Bundy for getting a bureaucratic consensus. They perhaps did not perceive, by going for a pause, any serious threat to the ongoing Vietnam policy to which they were wedded. On the other hand, they could, by conceding a little at present, hope to wring some substantial concession from McNamara in future in the bureaucratic game.

During the pause there began a debate within the Administration as to the nature of the resumption of bombing if the pause failed to achieve its objective. As pointed out earlier, the military elements of the Pentagon advocated that the bombing should be resumed with a "bang" whereas the civilian elements of the Pentagon argued for a slow start—bombing in a low key. As in many other cases, this intra-Pentagon debate too spilled over to other segments of the Executive, especially the State Department. Writing on 15 January William Bundy extended support to the civilian elements of the Pentagon by proposing that the bombing should not resume in a dramatic fashion. He argued that the resumption of bombing with a bang would add fuel to the charge that the Communists would most likely make that the pause was meant to make way for more fierce and hard strikes by the US.[141] The available data do not help us in knowing the thinking of Secretary Rusk at that time. However, a few days before the expiry of the pause, the second highest official of the State Department came out hard against Rolling Thunder. In a memorandum to the President on 25 January, Ball said "that a sustained bombing program acquires a life and dynamism of its own."[142] He argued that the American "philosophy of bombing requires gradual escalation." He stated that the fundamental assumption of American bombing was that it would one day force

---

[139] Ibid., p. 235.
[140] Ibid.
[141] *DOD Documents*, n. 128, p. 28.
[142] Ibid., p. 47.

Hanoi to stop the war. As long as Hanoi did not stop fighting, the US would have to continue to strike more and more sensitive, strategic targets in the hope that the resultant pain to Hanoi would induce her to stop the war and start talks. This reasoning would lead the US to bomb strategic targets near the Chinese border and those in Hanoi and Haiphong.[143] Ball warned,

> Quite clearly there is a threshold which we cannot pass over without precipitating a major Chinese involvement. We do not know—even within wide margins of error—where that threshold is. Unhappily we will not find out until after the catastrophe.[144]

Over the question of the resumption of bombing, the State Department did not present a unified stand. There is no evidence to indicate any discord within the Department in so far as the officials in the head office—Washington—were concerned. The Saigon embassy, however, took an opposite position. Ambassador Lodge stood solidly with the military in urging hard hitting tactics after the pause expired.[145] The difference between the attitude of Ball and Bundy on the one hand and that of Lodge on the other was partly due to their locations. An Ambassador would tend to be more concerned over the happenings in the field and getting a favourable outcome at the earliest than by international diplomacy and domestic debate that are far removed from his immediate environment.

The bombing of the North did not resume in a dramatic manner. The resumption was in a low key as urged by the civilian elements of the Pentagon and their supporters in other agencies of the Executive. The military members were soon provoked to demand the intensification of bombing including strikes of POL targets which they had been urging since the middle of 1965. McNamara and his civilian colleagues in the Defence Department opposed the move for POL strikes.

[143] Ibid., pp. 47-8.
[144] Ibid., p. 49.
[145] Ibid., p. 30.

The POL question led to some hectic movements within the Executive till 22 June 1966 when the decision was taken to hit the POLs. During this period, the intelligence community filed several memoranda touching on the benefits to be accrued from bombing and hitting the POLs in particular. The intelligence estimates on bombing were apparently not consistent. Sometimes they were optimistic; some other times they were pessimistic. In reports to the Defence Secretary on 28 November and 3 December 1965, the intelligence community said that the attacks on POL targets would do substantial damage to the North, but not to that extent as to make it impossible for her to support the Viet Cong.[146] This assessment of the impact of POL strikes might have been of some encouragement to the civilian elements of the Pentagon. But the intelligence estimate seemed to pull the rug from under their feet by further stating that the attack on POL targets was unlikely to provoke China and Russia to intervene. The intelligence community provided further fillip to the military elements of the Pentagon by asserting towards the end of December 1965 that North Vietnam was fast dispersing the POL facilities and unless the US bombed them soon, there would hardly be any POL facility vulnerable to bombing.[147] The intelligence estimates of February 1966 were similar to those of November and December 1965.[148] On balance, the intelligence reports seem to have strengthened the military *vis-a-vis* the civilian members of the Pentagon.

While the POL debate was in full swing, an interagency group consisting of Deputy Secretary Vance and McNaughton of Defence, Ball, Bundy and Leonard Unger of the State Department, and George Carver of the CIA met at the White House on 9 April 1966 to formulate alternative courses of action in Vietnam. Carver recommended that the current strength of American ground troops in South Vietnam should be maintained and the authorized number should be deployed. He further recommended that, in general, population centres like Hanoi and Haiphong should be spared bombing, but he added that major POL storage depots should be destroyed and

[146] Ibid., p. 69.
[147] Ibid., p. 85.
[148] Ibid., p. 76.

the Haiphong harbour should be mined.[149] Thus, in line with the earlier recommendation of the CIA, Carver supported the military's plea for bombing POLs. Unger took a middle stand. He would support a modest rise in ground forces, but no step-up in the air war.[150] Broadly, McNaughton was in agreement with Unger in regard to his military recommendation.[151] Ball's recommendation, which was, in a sense, the opposite of Carver's, was based upon the need for "cutting our losses."[152] He said that the US should put a brake of the deployment of additional US GIs in South Vietnam and reduce the level of bombing on the North. There was no element of surprise in Ball's recommendation. However, the tone of de-escalation present in the recommendation of Unger supported by McNaughton, and that of Ball appeared to prepare the ground for the alliance between the State Department and the civilian elements of the Pentagon *vis-a-vis* the military in future in regard to Vietnam.

But the "point of convergence" among the civilians as opposed to the military was yet to come. Some elements of the State Department were taking a line which was directly or indirectly helping the position of the military. Important amongst them was William Bundy who, on 16 April 1966, reiterated, in a different name, the domino theory which had virtually disappeared from the lexicon of the civilian elements of the Pentagon. He warned that the US failure in South Vietnam would result in the spread of "shock waves" in all "free countries" of Southeast Asia and the Far East.[153] The military seems to have relished this language very much. It is important to note that on the same day—16 April—McNaughton, in another inter-agency meeting circulated a paper in which he repudiated the so-called domino theory. He stated that "Except for its psychological impact, withdrawal from Vietnam would not affect the present line of containment from its Korean anchor down the Japan-Ryukyus-Taiwan-Philippines Islands chain."[154]

In March 1966, after months of hesitation, McNamara accept-

[149] Ibid., p. 94.
[150] Ibid., pp. 95-6.
[151] Ibid.
[152] Ibid., p. 97.
[153] Ibid., p. 103.
[154] Ibid., p. 106.

ed the military's demand for bombing the POL targets and accordingly sent a memorandum to the President. But the President did not immediately approve the proposal. It was probably difficult for him to order the attack on POL storages when President De Gaulle of France and U Thant, the UN Secretary-General, were engaged in efforts to find out some avenue for a peaceful settlement in Vietnam. He faced pressures from within the country and outside to observe another pause which might induce Hanoi to start talks. The hearings held by Fulbright's Foreign Relations Committee in February highlighted sentiment in favour of de-escalation and a pause.[155] The ongoing policy seemed to lose support in the press and, to some extent, among the general public.[156] Hard pressed by these factors, the President might have found it difficult to order fresh escalation. At this critical point, however, the President was persuaded by three of his principal advisers to take a tough posture in Vietnam. In a memorandum to the President on 27 April 1966, Maxwell Taylor urged him not to order the cessation of bombing unless there was a reciprocal action on the part of Hanoi. He argued that bombing was a valuable "blue chip" which should not be thrown away unless and until it was accompanied by a corresponding concession by Hanoi and the Viet Cong—for example, cessation of the flow of men and materials from the North to the South and reduction of fighting by Viet Cong.[157] On 4 May, William Bundy, in a memorandum to Rusk, lent staunch support to Taylor's "blue chip" thesis and advised that the US, while going for a pause, must ask for a "price" from Hanoi and the Viet Cong. He said, ". . .I have myself been more inclined to an asking price, at least, that would include both a declared cessation of infiltration and a sharp reduction in VC/NVA military operations in the South. . . ."[158] The President, in finally deciding to order the

---

[155] *The Vietnam Hearings*, with an Introduction by J. W. Fulbright, Chairman, United States Senate Committee on Foreign Relations (New York, 1966).

[156] Larry Elowitz and John W. Spanier, "Korea and Vietnam: Limited War and the American Political System," *Orbis* (Philadelphia, Penn.), vol. 18, Summer 1974, pp. 510-34.

[157] *DOD Documents*, n. 128, p. 113.

[158] Ibid., pp. 114-5.

bombing of the POL targets, was probably influenced by his new National Security Assistant Walt Rostow who had replaced McGeorge Bundy on 1 April 1966. In a memorandum to Rusk and McNamara, Rostow urged that the US should immediately attack the oil reserves of North Vietnam. He said:

> With an understanding that simple analogies are dangerous, I nevertheless feel it is quite possible the military effects of a systematic and sustained bombing of POL in North Vietnam may be more prompt and direct than conventional intelligence would suggest.[159]

The persuasion by these three influential advisers to the President seems to have had tilted the scale in favour of attacking the POL targets and the President took the decision to that effect towards the end of May. But the decision could not be implemented because of renewed diplomatic efforts at different levels for starting peace negotiations. On 7 June a Canadian diplomat, Chestor A. Ronning flew to Hanoi to know its mind regarding negotiations. This mission had the approval of the State Department. Rusk who was at that time in Paris immediately cabled to the President to postpone bombing POLs until the Ronning mission was over.[160] Rusk, left to himself, would prefer a tough posture. But because of mounting pressures from within his Department and outside for a settlement, he advocated the postponement of POL strikes in the hope that peace talks might start or at least no escalation should be initiated until various other possibilities were adequately explored and shown to be unproductive. It suggests that Rusk would opt for a negotiated settlement whenever it was possible on American terms. But failing that, he would choose a military solution. As the peace initiatives did not pay any dividends, the US launched strikes on POLs on 22 June despite a pessimistic report filed by the CIA on 8 June regarding the results of such strikes.

The attacks on POL storages did not prove to be effective and the Secretary sought to take a fresh look at the bombing programme. In the meantime the military was pressing hard for

[159] Ibid., p. 119.
[160] Ibid., pp. 123-4.

sending more ground troops to South Vietnam and for hitting more sensitive targets like the power plants in Hanoi. As mentioned earlier, the Secretary paid a visit to South Vietnam in the middle of October 1966 and on his return wrote a memorandum to the President. He proposed the stabilization of Rolling Thunder and a small increase in the number of American ground troops in South Vietnam. He also recommended that the US should observe another "pause" some time in future to prepare an atmosphere for the beginning of fresh efforts at negotiation.[161] All these suggestions were bitterly opposed by the military. It is not known how the Secretary of State and the National Security Assistant reacted to this new round of the rift between the civilian and military components of the Pentagon. Katzenbach, the Under Secretary of State, seemingly supported the recommendations of McNamara.[162] The CIA disagreed with most of these recommendations. Carver, writing for the Director of the CIA, disagreed with McNamara's indirect assertion that changes in the bombing programme would not be effective. On the other hand, he asserted that the mining of Haiphong and the destruction of rail lines between China and North Vietnam would have a significant impact.[163] Carver did not accept the Secretary's proposal for a pause and initiation of talks. Thus whereas the State Department tended to gradually accept the viewpoints of the civilian elements of the Pentagon, the CIA continued to be pro-escalation in its tone—thereby siding with the military in the intra-Pentagon rift on Vietnam.

Before the year drew to a close, McNamara filed another memorandum in which he repeated his recommendations of October. He repudiated the military's assertion that the war was going well for the US.[164] As pointed out earlier, the Secretary's views invited sharp reaction from the military members who repeated their old arguments against him. As in the case of the October debate, in this case too, Rusk's reaction is not known. The CIA which had reacted to the October memorandum of the Secretary remained silent this time. On the other

---

[161] Ibid., pp. 162-3.
[162] Ibid., p. 169.
[163] Ibid., pp. 169-70.
[164] Ibid., pp. 174-6.

hand, Rostow who had not taken part in the October debate joined issue with McNamara in November, expressing his disagreement with the Secretary's gloomy view of the war.[165] McNamara seemed to have succeeded in virtually winning the support of the State Department. But the National Security Assistant and the CIA were not willing to go along with him.

The beginning of 1967 witnessed mounting opposition to the war at home and a flurry of actions within the Administration with many alternative courses in Vietnam coming up for consideration. The line between the civilian and military elements of the Pentagon had been drawn; they continued to oppose each other's course. While the former favoured a truce, the latter opposed it. At this point, W. Bundy, one of the most active actors on Vietnam, threw his weight in favour of a pause. In a memorandum to Katzenbach on 21 January, he strongly urged the Under Secretary to oppose anything that would compromise the scheduled suspension of operations against North Vietnam.[166] Soon after the pause, which began on 8 February and expired on 14 February, the military elements renewed their efforts for further intensification of the war both on land and in the air. In March, Westmoreland made his 200,000 men request, which dominated the intra-Executive movements for the whole of the year.

Gradually the pro-de-escalation forces gained strength inside the Administration. William Bundy made another turn toward de-escalation in February by expressing his disagreement with the military's request for mining Haiphong. But his switch toward de-escalation was not complete. He said, on the other hand, that the US might mine North Vietnam's coastal waterways which were not used by Soviet ships.[167] Bundy's proposal won the approval of the President the next day. Johnson deferred his decision on mining Haiphong. Besides William Bundy who again registered his opposition to mining Haiphong on 1 May,[168] another recruit to the anti-escalation group was Robert Komer, the special assistant to the President who was in charge of

---

[165] Sheehan, n. 15, p. 534.
[166] *DOD Documents*, Book 6, IV.C.7 (b), pp. 4-5.
[167] Ibid., p. 13.
[168] Ibid., pp. 23-5.

"pacification." He stated that stepped up bombing and mining would raise the level of pain for the North, but would not force her to give up fighting. According to him, Hanoi was unlikely to start negotiations in the near future. Thus, he argued, the fate of the war would be determined in South Vietnam. The critical variables affecting the war would be the erosion of the strength of the Viet Cong and the strength of the Saigon regime.[169] Against this background of the slow increase in the number of supporters of the de-escalation course, McNamara and McNaughton wrote the 5 May DPM in which they strongly argued against any intensification of the war.[170] They reiterated their views against escalation in another DPM on 19 May.[171]

These DPMs led to an increased flow of memoranda within the Administration, some of which joined issue with the views expressed in them, and others, supporting them. The sharp reaction of the military to these memoranda has been described earlier. The first amongst the non-Pentagon actors to react was W.W. Rostow, the National Security Assistant. On 6 May, he observed that there were three bombing options before the US which he described as "closing the top of the funnel," "attacking what is inside the funnel," and "concentration on Route Package 1 and 2." The first option required blocking the supply lines through which war material moved into North Vietnam. It would involve attacks on major harbours and the rail lines between Hanoi and China. The second option would include bombing supplying dumps, stockpiles, and fuel storage areas, as well as bridges, railroad yards, and other targets in the Hanoi-Haiphong area. The third option would call for attacking the lines of communication and infiltration routes in Southern North Vietnam and through Laos. After weighing the cost and effectiveness of all the options, he, on balance, favoured the third option while adding that the second option should be kept open.[172] Thus he was now virtually in agreement with McNamara and McNaughton regarding bombing as opposed to the military. Rostow's support for de-escalation was an important development in

---

[169] Ibid.
[170] Ibid., pp. 22-3.
[171] Sheehan, n. 15, pp. 589-97.
[172] *DOD Documents*, n. 166, pp. 33-7.

policy-making on Vietnam. He had long been fervently advocating stepped-up bombing of North Vietnam. His continued support for the strategic bombing of the North would have been a great obstacle to the de-escalation forces within the Administration. Because of his key position as the National Security Assistant, he was well-placed to significantly influence the President's decisions in regard to Vietnam. His changed position on bombing was a great gain for McNamara and his allies who were arguing for de-escalation.

On 8 May William Bundy circulated a memorandum amongst other actors in which he reiterated his opposition to the mining of Haiphong. After weighing the pros and cons of five options, he expressed his preference for the option D which called for hitting mainly the targets around the 20th parallel.[173] This was in broad agreement with the recommendation of 5 May DPM on bombing except that Bundy would recommend a re-striking of some significant targets north of the 20th parallel whereas McNamara had proposed to concentrate fire only to its south. The CIA which was equivocal and ambiguous in earlier stages in its views on bombing seemed finally to take a clear stand against the intensification of bombing. On 12 May it pointed out that the bombing of the North for 27 months had neither significantly undermined the morale of North Vietnamese nor had it substantially eroded their capability to help the Viet Cong.[174] With Rostow, Bundy and the CIA in their side, the civilian elements of the Pentagon might have felt encouraged to continue their efforts more vigorously against escalation.

As said earlier, the 19 May DPM which restated with more vigour the de-escalation arguments contained in the 5 May DPM, invited bitter criticism of the military.[175] Taking sharp exception to these arguments, the JCS said, "The DPM not be forwarded to the President." William Bundy, who had a few days back supported McNamara's views on bombing, disagreed with some elements of 19 May DPM. As contrasted with the pessimistic tone of the DPM, Bundy asserted that American involvement in Vietnam had succeeded in containing Communism in

---

[173] Ibid., pp. 37-41.
[174] Ibid., pp. 41-2.
[175] Sheehan, n. 15, p. 550.

Southeast Asia and laid the foundation for progress in South Vietnam. Taking issue with the DPM, he argued that the US objective was not only to drive North Vietnamese out of South Vietnam but to insure that "the political board in South Vietnam is not tilted to the advantage of the NLF."[176] The shift in Bundy, however, was more apparent than real; it was rather half-hearted in tone. Bundy was careful enough to avoid touching on the specific recommendation of DPM on bombing. On the other hand he accepted the general thrust of the DPM in stating that the massive US intervention in Vietnam had resulted in a significant adverse effect in that South Vietnamese tended to think, "Uncle Sam will do their job for them." Indirectly he criticized the military's 200,000 men request on the ground that an additional deployment of such a large number of ground troops in South Vietnam would not make much difference in the war.[177] Thus Bundy's continued support for de-escalation might have further encouraged the civilian elements of the Pentagon who were locked in a grim fight with the military on the issue.

Another actor to give a helping hand to McNamara and his civilian colleagues in the Defence Department was Katzenbach, the Under Secretary of State. He said that the war, from the US point of view, was not going on well, and that the "pacification" programme was in a bad shape. He claimed to take a "middle" road between those who favoured sending 200,000 more GIs to South Vietnam and others who advocated that the existing strength of US troops in South Vietnam should be maintained. Katzenbach recommended an increase of 30,000 more ground troops in South Vietnam. Regarding the war against North Vietnam, he favoured an anti-infiltration barrier and proposed that the US should concentrate bombing on lines of communication throughout North Vietnam and not hit strategic targets.[178] Katzenbach was thus not taking a middle course as he asserted. McNamara himself recommended an increase of 30,000 troops. Similarly, Katzenbach's recommendation on bombing was quite similar to McNamara's. He was virtually one with the civilian elements of Pentagon in arguing

---

[176] *DOD Documents*, n. 166, p. 60.
[177] *DOD Documents*, Book 5, IV.6(b), pp. 180-1.
[178] Ibid., pp. 183-9.

for de-escalation.

Faced with the heavy fire of criticism from the military, the Secretary had requested Richard Helms, the CIA Director, to make his assessment of the bombing of North Vietnam. Helms said that bombing would not be able to reduce the level of the flow of men and materials from the North to the South nor to considerably dampen the spirit and determination of Hanoi to continue to fight.[179] Thus by the middle of June 1967, there was a broad consensus amongst the civilian advisers as to the desirability of de-escalation as opposed to the military advisers who were pressing hard for further intensification of the American involvement in the war. The President sought to adopt a middle course between the contrary views of the rival factions. He approved only a 45,000 increase of ground troops which was closer to McNamara's figure than the military's. On the other hand, he decided that besides the supply lines around the 20th parallel, the other areas of North Vietnam except the air targets within 10 miles of Hanoi would be subject to bombing.[180] Within a short period he ordered attacks on some targets which were within 10 miles of Hanoi. Thus, in respect of the air war, the President went closer to the military than to the civilians in the Pentagon and other agencies.

The Communist offensive in South Vietnam in September 1967 and the urgent appeal by Westmoreland to the President for quick reinforcement on 28 September led to another round of intra-Executive moves in Washington. McNamara was probably concerned over the implications of a possible gradual tilt towards the military on the part of the President. On 1 November he recommended that the United States should announce the stabilization of her efforts—not expanding her bombing programme and not increasing the size of her ground troops. Moreover, the Secretary proposed that the US should go for another bombing pause before the end of 1967.[181] Rostow, the National Security Assistant, broadly agreed with McNamara's recommendation. He, however, did not think it prudent on the part of the US to observe an unconditional bombing halt which,

---

[179] *DOD Documents*, n. 166, p. 62.
[180] Johnson, n. 97, p. 370.
[181] Ibid., pp. 372-3.

according to him, would signify American weakness.[182] Maxwell Taylor, a special consultant to the President, disagreed with both the recommendations of the Defence Secretary. In a memorandum to the President on 3 November, he described McNamara's proposals as a "pull-back" strategy which would "probably degenerate into an eventual pull-out."[183] Clifford and Fortas, Johnson's personal friends and advisers, conveyed to the President their total disagreements with McNamara.[184] Taylor, Clifford and Fortas did not strictly constitute a part of the Executive, but they were important figures in Washington, and were known to be considerably influential with the President. Their stand against McNamara seemed to have been a great asset to the military elements of the Pentagon and, coupled with Rostow's reluctance to totally support McNamara at this point, might have helped to widen the distance between the President and the Defence Secretary.

The last to enter the debate was the State Department. It was surprisingly this time not Bundy, who, during the previous years, was very active in the field of policy-making on Vietnam. The number one and number two men in the State Department communicated their views to the President in the second half of November. Katzenbach prescribed a "limited" role for the US in Vietnam in providing "military cover and non-military assistance." Responsibility for the military effort should be increasingly transferred to South Vietnam, he said. He expressed his broad agreement with McNamara regarding a pause. He favoured a "qualified but indefinite halt in the bombing." By "qualified" he meant that the US should hit North Vietnam if she tried to expand the re-supply to the South or attempted troop concentrations near the de militarized zone.[185] Katzenbach thus did not falter in his continued support for the course of de-escalation advocated by the civilian elements of the Pentagon.

Dean Rusk preferred to put his views to the President in their private meetings. In official deliberations, he was not conspicuous in his participation. However, he was probably the most active defender of the Administration's policy in Vietnam. He had

---

[182] Ibid., pp. 373-4.
[183] Ibid., p. 374.
[184] Ibid., pp. 374-5.
[185] Ibid., pp. 375-6.

always been a believer in tough posture. In the past, he compromised here and there, in order to come to terms with the other powerful actors within the Administration and outside. But he hardly effected a major switch as his chief bureaucratic competitor McNamara did. He seldom put his thoughts in writing; but whenever he did, it indicated that the issue involved considerable importance. Because of his official position and personal equation with the President, Rusk's view at that stage might have weighed heavily with the latter. On 20 November, Rusk informed the President of his support for McNamara's proposal for the stabilization of US efforts in Vietnam, but he disagreed with his suggestion of announcing it publicly. He also opposed "an extended pause." He did not think that Hanoi would be persuaded to start talks by a bombing halt.[186] Thus Rusk took a "middle course," as did Rostow, but with a difference. Both of them supported stabilization, and opposed an unconditional pause. Rusk opposed the public announcement of stabilization whereas Rostow remained silent on that. Moreover, Rostow favoured attacking only the supply lines whereas Rusk advocated that the US should hit the northern part of North Vietnam to put extra-pressure on her for beginning negotiation. However, the thrust of the viewpoints of both these actors was the same partial support for the civilian elements of the Pentagon and partial support for the military.

The State Department spoke with more than one voice. Katzenbach differed from his Chief in some respects, but it was not something new in the Department with Rusk as its head. Katzenbach's predecessors, Harriman and Ball, had often acted in similar fashion. Unlike Bundy, Katzenbach was relatively new to the Department. He did not have much past involvement in Vietnam policy from which he had to dissociate himself. It might have been difficult for Bundy to directly disagree with Rusk because of their long association with policy-making in regard to Vietnam and because of the fact that they had long been taking, more or less, the same stance. Soon after he joined the State Department, Katzenbach extended support to the McNamara group and he continued to do so subsequently. That was perhaps the cause of division within the State Depart-

186 Ibid., pp. 376-7.

ment and the silence of Bundy during this round of debate on Vietnam policy.

In the midst of the welter of conflicting advice from his principal advisers stood President Johnson, the ardent believer in consensus. The differences between the civilian and military elements of the Pentagon had gone too far; the political costs were heavy; Congressional critics were increasingly strident; "world public opinion" was turning hostile. The Administration needed to present a unified image of itself in the election year of 1968. Divisions in the country caused directly and indirectly by the prolonged war appeared to increase progressively. Johnson probably felt increasingly impelled to see his way through to some course that could reverse the adverse trends and command increasing public confidence and support. He had tilted towards the military often in his decisions. He had no complaints against the JCS and he believed that American officers and soldiers had fought and sacrificed valiantly. He had no respect for "doves" and "nervous nellies," but he was a political realist. Escalation appeared less and less to be the course that could reverse the trend. If de-escalation was to be the course, the President had to bring it about in such fashion as not to offend the military unduly.

With a political decision of his own in his offing; the President moved with caution and with his customary skill. Since he believed that the Secretary of Defence was increasingly moving in a different track, he prepared the ground for his exit. This step, among other things, was probably intended by the President to soften up the JCS for subsequent actions he might have to make. The President probably took note of the fact that Rusk and Rostow had not fully identified themselves with the point of view represented by McNamara. He could count on them to stay the course with him. In a memorandum for the record that he wrote on 18 December 1967, Johnson expressed his opposition to the proposal for stabilization and for an unconditional bombing halt. In the context of the intense conflict between McNamara and the JCS at that time, the President's disagreement with the proposal of stabilization and an unconditional pause might have encourged the military elements to continue, with more vigour, their fight against the Secretary and might have signalled to McNamara about the direction in which the President was moving.

The civilian and military elements of the Pentagon continued to oppose each other in the beginning phase of 1968 even though McNamara, by that time, had been reduced to be a lame-duck Secretary. In the wake of the Tet offensive which took place on 31 January, the military actors pushed for more reinforcements in South Vietnam and for a call-up of reserves. McNamara did not concede much to the military. He continued to oppose their demand to the very end. On 1 March 1968, Clark Clifford replaced McNamara as Secretary of Defence. Available materials do not tell us the role that the civilian actors of other agencies might have played during this phase. The role of the Clifford group which was formed in the last week of February and which submitted its report in the first week of March does not come under the purview of the present study.[187] However, to provide perspective, a brief reference to it has been made in Chapter III.

Inferences

In a bureaucratic game the players keep in mind the personal values, preferences and choices of the ultimate decision-maker. They would, to a considerable extent, tend to attune themselves to the perceived stance of the latter. Rusk and Rostow who, since the beginning of the Kennedy Administration had been favouring a tough posture in Vietnam, later began to tone themselves down as they perceived that McNamara and his civilian associates of the Pentagon advocated a de-escalation course which the President seemed willing to consider and accept in part. Rostow, in May 1967, quite unlike his earlier stance, argued for restricted bombing of the North. Rusk chose to remain silent. He did not explicitly support McNamara, but he did not oppose him and that was a significant gain for the Defence Secretary. As Johnson seemed to express his doubts about McNamara's course, the Secretary of State and the National Security Assistant tended to swing back to their earlier position. The inclination of these two important actors either to "tilt" towards the military, or at least not to fully side with McNamara was a serious obstacle to him. The President would have faced a serious dilemma had

---

[187] *DOD Documents*, n. 166, pp. 150-71.

all the civilian actors aligned themselves against the military in regard to Vietnam. What finally accounted for the "defeat" of McNamara in the bureaucratic fight over Vietnam were the personal preferences of President Johnson which were similar to those of the military and the failure of McNamara to receive the full support and cooperation of his civilian colleagues in other agencies when the chips were down.

In peace time the State Department's input in decision-making in foreign policy is, of course, quite substantial and significant. But as the tension increases in an area and when military preparations are undertaken at a high pitch the Defence Department's input into policy-making tends to increase. In the Department of Defence the role of the JCS assumes greater significance and its respresentative in the area of tension is increasingly heard. Once the shooting starts, the role of the Defence Department—both civilian and military elements of the Department—in policy-making becomes quite significant. The JCS and the commander in the field tend to be more insistent in their demands since their personal and organizational interests are profoundly at stake. If the Secretary of Defence does not go along with them, a conflict situation emerges. The search will commence on both sides to influence the President and to enlist the support of other federal actors and external allies. That was broadly the pattern to developments in regard to Vietnam policy since 1965.

Extra-Pentagon federal actors, while trying to promote their own views, were often influenced by their perception of what the President's inclination was in respect of given issues. If they perceived that the President was tilting towards the view urged by the military, rather than by that of the Secretary of Defence, they did not remain uninflunced, and *vice versa*. There were, of course, exceptions. Only very few like George Ball displayed the courage and determination called for in propounding a course that can clearly be seen to run counter to the dominant thinking of major actors and even of the President. When in course of time things do not work out as planned, more actors find it possible to muster some courage, though it is usually mixed with caution. They tend to bear in mind the prevailing direction of the wind in their own organizations and in the White House as they cautiously make their suggestions indicating some support for modifications in an ongoing policy.

CHAPTER SIX

THE INTERACTION BETWEEN THE PENTAGON AND CONGRESS IN RELATION TO VIETNAM POLICY

The present chapter will deal with how the role of Congress in foreign policy-making influenced the role of the Pentagon in decision-making on Vietnam. In this connection, the interaction between Congress and the Pentagon in defence matters and their impact on the field of foreign policy will be examined. It is also proposed to examine whether there are any constraints on Congress in playing its role relating to defence and foreign policy and whether they affected its role in decision-making in Vietnam.[1]

THEORETICAL FRAMEWORK

According to the American Constitution, Congress has the power to authorize and appropriate funds for government operation, to raise and maintain the Army and Navy, and to "declare war." It also provides that the President is the Commander-in-Chief and that the executive power is vested in him. Thus, foreign policy-making, constitutionally, is a joint exercise to be done by the President and the Congress. The Constitution provides for separation of powers, but not

---

[1] For a general discussion of Congress-Pentagon interaction, see Edward A. Kolodziej, *The Uncommon Defense and Congress, 1945-1963* (Columbus, Ohio, 1966); Adam Yarmolinsky, *The Military Establishment: Its Impacts on American Society* (New York, 1971), pp. 38-52; Samuel P. Huntington, *The Common Defense: Strategic Programs in National Policy* (New York, 1961), pp. 400-28; and Alton Frye, *A Responsible Congress: The Politics of National Security* (New York, 1975).

separation of functions.[2] As in many other fields, in the field of defence too, there is a great deal of sharing and overlapping between the Executive and Congress. Practice, however, seems to be rather different. Foreign policy appears to be almost the exclusive domain of the President, with Congress playing a minor role. The traditional pattern of Executive dominance in the field of foreign policy-making was considerably strengthened in the post-Second World War period due to severral factors.[3] The onset of the Cold War, the consequent bipolarization of world politics, and recurrent international crisis intensified the security problem of the United States (as well as that of her adversary, the Soviet Union). It was a state of affairs that called for a high state of preparedness and quick political, diplomatic and strategic decisions. The rapid advance in science and the revolutionary improvement in the weapons technology resulted in the overarching threat of nuclear war. It was argued that the possibility of a surprise nuclear attack by the adversary could not be ruled out. The situation demanded the maintenance of the highest degree of secrecy relating to defence and foreign policy matters, it was generally agreed.

The Executive was better equipped than Congress to play the dominant role in the field of defence and foreign policy primarily because of two factors. It had vastly greater amount of "information" at its disposal than Congress. It could dole out to Congress such information as it deemed fit to suit its purposes. "Secrecy" in the name of "national security" became the watch-word in Washington. Only a few senior Congressional leaders had access, on a very limited basis, to classified materials. Congress did not have at its disposal adequate expertise to deal with highly technical and complex matters relating to defence and foreign policy. Congressional Committees examining defence and foreign policy issues had small staffs of experts while the resources of the Executive departments in this respect were vast.

[2] Samuel P. Huntington, *The Soldier and the State: The Theory and Politics of Civil-Military Relations* (Cambridge, Mass., 1959), pp. 400-2.

[3] Lewis Anthony Dexter, "Congressman and the Making of Military Policy," in Raymond E. Wolfinger, ed., *Readings in Congress* (Englewood Cliffs, N.J., 1971), pp. 378-87.

Congress is handicapped by other limitations, namely, partisanship, sectionalism, and inter-House and inter-Committee cleavages.[4] Some degree of competition and "jealousy" between the Senate and the House of Representatives has always existed.[5] It is the former which has, often, in the post-Second World War period, stolen a march over the other in the field of foreign policy-making. But, in so far as decision-making on defence policy is concerned, the game seems to be evenly-balanced. Both are zealous of their powers and prerogatives, and neither would like to play second fiddle to the other. Even in the field of foreign policy, the equation seems to be in flux. The Foreign Affairs Committee (now, International Relations Committee of the House) wants to demonstrate that it can play as important a role as the Senate Foreign Relations Committee in this area. Thus, the institutional competition, often carried to the level of rivalry, is a factor affecting Congressional action on defence budgets. The inter-Committee cleavage includes both the rivaly between the two Committe es of the two Houses on the same subject—say, Senate and House Defence Appropriations Subcommittees—, and also the rivalry among the Committees of the same chamber—i.e., the Foreign Relations Committee, the Defence Appropriations Subcommittee and the Armed Services Committee of the Senate. The members of the Military Committees (the Armed Services Committees and the Defence Appropriations Subcommittees of both Houses), in general, are prone to voting for large defence budgets. The constituencies of some of the very influential members of these Committees tend to be favoured by the Pentagon with military installations.[6]

[4] See Edward Eugene Bozik, National Defense and Congressional Behavior: Congressional Action on Authorizing and Appropriating Legislation for Military Budgets and Military Construction, 1951-1966 (Georgetown University, Ph.D. Thesis, 1968), pp. 221-38.

[5] Holbert N. Carrol, *The House of Representatives and Foreign Affairs* (Boston, Mass., 1966), pp. 285-9.

[6] For instance, over a period of several years the Pentagon appeared to find Charleston, South Carolina, a most suitable place for locating military installations. It so happens that Charleston was the constituency of Congressman Mendel Rivers, Chairman of the House Armed Services Committee. It used to be said in Washington that Charleston might sink if the Congressman's enthusiasm for the city persisted.

By and large, in the post-Second World War years (until recently), Congress had tended to yield the lead to the Executive in the domain of policy-making on defence and foreign policy. To be more specific, if the foreign policy process involves four stages—initiation, deliberation, implementation and evaluation—then the Executive dominates the first and third, and Congress, the second and fourth.[7] The first and third stages are very important; in respect of the second and fourth, greater control of information and exploitation of a climate of crisis enables the Executive to influence the role of Congress significantly.

The pre-eminence of the Executive in foreign policy making is not to suggest that the role that Congress has played or can play is insignificant. By various means it tries to influence decisions in this field by the Executive.[8] The Chairman or a member of a Military Committee may sound officially or privately to the Pentagon his concern about a particular strategic programme. In this connection one may refer to the initiative taken by Senator Brien McMahon (Democrat, Connecticut), the Chairman of the Joint Committee on Atomic Energy, in 1949 in asking the Pentagon to take an interest in the production of the hydrogen bomb. The Pentagon would give due consideration to such an expression of interest. Secondly, Congress may conduct investigation into any programme. Hearings by a Committee where members of the Pentagon, civilian and military, normally give testimony, are bound to have some impact upon the Executive. Hearings by the Symington Subcommittee on Air Force levels in 1956, by Senator Johnson's Preparedness Investigating Subcommittee on the Missile Gap in 1958, and, by the McClellan Subcommittee on the TFX in 1963 are important cases in this regard. The third method by which Congress influences the Administration's defence policy is authorization and appropriation. Any defence programme has first to be authorized by Congress, then to be followed by appropriation. Authorization and appropriation

---

[7] William C. Olson, "The Role of Congress in Making the Foreign Policy of the United States," *The Parliamentarian* (London), vol. 56, no. 3, July 1975, pp. 151-8.

[8] Huntington, n. 1, pp. 135-45.

hearings are conducted by the Armed Services Committee and Defence Appropriations Subcommittees of both the Houses respectively.

These hearings provide an opportunity to the Pentagon to display a united approach when there is harmony and consensus in the organization. But hearings may also provide scope for military actors to air discreetly their differences with the Secretary of Defence and other civilian actors on defence and foreign policy matters. Concerned Committees arrange executive sessions if any witness is unwilling to reveal some information in open hearings and requests a secret hearing. The rival testimonies by the members of the Air Force and Navy in B-36 hearings, of the supporters and opponents of the "New Look" before Defence Appropriations Subcommittees, and of the civilian and military actors of the Pentagon before the McClellan Subcommittee are some of the leading examples on this score. Another important aspect of these hearings is that a Congressional group can exploit the intra-Pentagon differences to its advantage. So also may the Executive exploit the intra-Congress differences.

The defence policy and foreign policy of any country are intimately inter-related. The military capability of a country would affect its external relations and the former would have to be attuned to the latter. This inter-relation is prone to vary in proportion to the difference in the military power of states. The more powerful a country is, the more extensive and intensive its external involvement is likely to be. (Its reverse, however, is not necessarily and always true. A country which is military weak, may in some special circumstances play, and may be permitted by stronger countries for their own reasons to play, an important role in international politics.) In this perspective, one may presume the strong inter-relationship between the defence and foreign policies of the United States. This pattern became clearer in the post-war period as the US emerged to be the most powerful nation with world-wide politico-economic-security interests.

Apart from this general link between the defence and foreign policy, there might be some specific factors influencing the Pentagon-Congress interaction in this regard. There is an apparent alliance between the military actors and several members of Congress regarding the procurement of weapons. If this alliance suffers some recurrent and major disappointments at the hands of the civilian members of the Pentagon, then the consequent strain in their relationship in this field may tend to affect their equation in foreign policy making. Disagreement between the military and civilian elements of the Pentagon in regard to the procurement of weapons and other defence-related matters, and their agreement on the basic premises of foreign policy are not incompatible. Perhaps the former would not strain the latter except under very extraordinary circumstances. But if the civilian and military components of the Pentagon have disagreement with regard to both defence and foreign policy matters, then the former would tend to exacerbate the latter.

At this point it is in order to posit some hypotheses which may be tested below.

(1) Defence policy and foreign policy are intimately related to each other.

A corollary of this hypothesis is:

The interaction between Congress and the Pentagon on defence matters influences their equation in the realm of foreign policy, and *vice versa*.

(2) The Congressional role in the field of defence and foreign policy is affected by inter-House, inter-Committee and intra-Committee conflicts.

(3) Hearings provide an opportunity to Congress to elicit information and views from civilian and military representatives of the Pentagon that might indicate the existence of unity or differences between the civilian and military elements. They may also indicate the existence of unity or differences within each of the two groups.

A corollary of this hypothesis is:

If internal cleavages are seen to exist in the Pentagon, Congress will try to exploit them to its own ends; if they exist in Congress, the Pentagon will exploit them similarly.

II

CONGRESS' ATTITUDE TOWARDS VIETNAM IN 1950s

The interest of Congress in Vietnam during the period 1950-1953 was very meagre. That was probably because the US then faced politico-military issues that loomed much larger than the situation in Vietnam. The establishment of a Communist Government in China in 1949 and the outbreak of the Korean War the following year dominated the attention of Congress till 1953 when in the course of hearings of the Defence Appropriations Subcommittee of the Senate in the years 1950, 1951, 1952 and 1953, the Pentagon witness, both civilian and military, were put many questions on Korea, Formosa and Japan.[9] Issues relating to Indochina were hardly raised during the hearings.

In the year 1954 some concern over Indochina was expressed in Congress. From the American point of view, the events in Indochina were perceived to be of significance in their implications as the Communists appeared to be moving towards a military victory over French forces. Washington was considering a contingency plan of intervening in Vietnam in order to save Dien Bien Phu. However, the amount of interest shown by Congress was small in comparison to the intensity of the debate within the Executive branch over Indochina. During the hearings of a House Defence Appropriations Subcommittee in the beginning of the year, Robert L.F. Sikes (Dem., Florida), while questioning Defence Secretary Charles E. Wilson, expressed his concern over the Communist progress in Vietnam. The latter shared this concern only "in part." He asserted that some of

---

[9] Us Senate, Congress 81, Session 2, Subcommittee of the Committee on Appropriations, Hearings, *Department of Defence Appropriations for 1951* (Washington, 1950), pp. 69-70; US Senate, Cong. 82, sess. 1, Subcommittee of the Committee on Appropriations, Hearings, *Department of Defence Appropriations for 1952* (Washington, D.C., 1951); US Senate, Cong. 82, sess. 2, Subcommittee of the Committee on Appropriations, Hearings, *Department of Defence Appropriations for 1953* (Washington, D.C., 1952), pp. 336, 356, 359 1194, 1210, 1213; and US Senate, Cong. 83, sess. 1, Subcommittee of the Committee on Appropriations, Hearings, *Department of Defence Appropriations for 1954* (Washington, D.C., 1953), p. 35.

the newspapers reporting on Vietnam was exaggerated.[10]

However, it much be said to the credit of Congress that in an hour of "crisis," it effectively played its role. As the fall of Dien Bien Phu appeared imminent, the Executive was gripped with the question whether to intervene on behalf of France or not. Secretary of State John Foster Dulles was the main advocate of a policy of intervention. He was even prepared to consider the use of nuclear weapons if that was warranted to avert an impending French defeat. He tried his best to prevail upon President Eisenhower to accept his advice. The President insisted that the American decision to militarily intervene in Dien Bien Phu be preceded by the fulfilment of two conditions, namely, the acquiescence of Britain and France in the proposed course of action and its advance acceptance by Congrees. Dulles failed in the first. London did not agree with the idea of intervention.

The Secretary of State met the same fate in regard to the second. Accompanied by Admiral Arthur W. Radford, the Chairman of the Joint Chiefs of Staff on 3 April 1954, he met in a conference seven Congressional leaders. They sought to convince the latter of the need of immediate American military intervention in Indochnina. In the course of discussion, Earle C. Clements (Dem., Kentucky), asked Radford, "Does this plan have the approval of the other members of the JCS?

"No," replied the Admiral.
"How many of the three agree with you?"
"None."
"How do you account for that?"
"I have spent more time in the Far East than any of them and I understand the situation better."[11]

Radford's explanation failed to convince the Congressional

[10] US House of Representatives, Cong. 83, sess. 2, Subcommittee of the Committee on Appropriations, Hearings, *Department of Defence and Related Independent Agencies*: *Appropriations for 1955* (Washington, D.C., 1954), p. 104.
[11] Chalmers M. Roberts, "The Day We Didn't Go to War," *Reporter* (Madison), 14 September 1954, pp. 31-5; and Dwight D. Eisenhower, *Mandate for Change, 1953-1956* (London, 1953), p. 347.

leaders. The fact that other members of the JCS did not agree with the Chairman probably made the latter's case somewhat weak in their estimation. A unified position presented by the JCS enhances the prospect of Congressional approval; evidence of lack of unity lessens the prospect. The Congressional leaders told Dulles and Radford that the US must have the support of her allies in militarily intervening in Indochina. And the President was adamant that the approval of Congress was indispensable before he approved of the use of American forces in Indochina.[12]

Between 1954 and 1960 there occurred many significant developments in Southeast Asia in general and Vietnam in particular. This was also the period during which the United States got substantially involved in Vietnam. The Southeast Asia Treaty Organization which came into existence in September 1954 was mostly the creation of John Foster Dulles. As a part of the containment policy which had already been introduced in Europe, he succeeded in selling it to some countries of the region. An American Military Assistance Advisory Group was set up in Saigon in the last part of 1954. Its declared objective was to impart military training to South Vietnamese troops. As discussed earlier, with the active encouragement of the United States, the Diem Government of South Vietnam did not allow an election in the whole of Vietnam, scheduled to be held in the year 1956, as had been agreed at Geneva in 1954. As the American intelligence reports testify, Communist insurgency in a large form took shape in South Vitenam as a direct result of Saigon's refusal to hold the general election.

While such important developments were taking place in Vietnam and in the American policy in regard to the area, Congress got itself preoccupied with other issues which produced more noise and distraction in the US than Vietnam did. The vehement opposition of the Army led by General Ridgway and then by General Taylor to the "New Look" of the Eisenhower Administration generated excessive heat in both Congress and the press. The Army feared that its role was in danger of being eroded and undermined by the introduction of the "New Look."[13] While this controversy seemed to have subsided after

---

[12] Eisenhower, ibid., p. 346.
[13] Ridgway, Metthew B., *The Memoirs of Matthew B. Ridgway* (New

the exist of General Taylor from the scene, another issue with considerable politico-military implications cropped up towards the end of 1950s. The fear that the Soviet Union had stolen a clear missile lead over the US aroused grave concern in Congress.[14] The issue was dramatized because of its link with the Presidential election politics. In the process, Congress failed to keep track of what was happening in Vietnam and what the US Executive was planning and doing in that country. So far as Congress was concerned, for the most of the 1950s, Vietnam was somewhat of a minor, side-issue, though the Executive had begun to take a steadily growing interest in it.

III

INITIAL CONGRESSIONAL ASSESSMENT OF MCNAMARA

At the beginning of McNamara's tenure as the Secretary of Defence, there was no doubt expressed by any Congressional member as to his capability to run the Pentagon, even though he was relatively young and inexperienced in governmental affairs. Within a short time of his appointment, he was able to win the acclamation of many important members of Congress as a very effective Secretary of Defence. A presentation that he made before the House Armed Services Committee shortly after becoming Secretary drew a fulsome tribute from Carl Vinson, Chairman of the Committee. Vinson said:

I want to say this. I say it from the very bottom of my heart. I have been here dealing with these problems since 1919. I want to state that this is the most comprehensive, most factual statement that has ever been my privilege to have an

York, 1956); Gavin, James M., *War and Peace in the Space Age* (New York, 1958); and Taylor Maxwell D., *The Uncertain Trumpet* (New York, 1959).

[14] For example, Senate Appropriations Subcommittee on Defence in 1959 was mostly concerned over the so-called "missile gap." US Senate, Cong. 86, sess. 1, Subcommittee of the Committee on Appropriations, Hearings, *Department of Defence Appropriations for 1960* (Washington, D.C., 1959).

opportunity to receive from any of the departments of Government.

There is more information in here than any Committee in Congress has ever received along the line that it is dealing with. It is so full of information all one has to do is just study it. You dealt with both sides of the problem. When you reach a decision, you set out the reasons why you reached that decision. You point out why—it probably could have been done the other way, but the other facts were superior and therefore you followed the method you did.

It is a magnificent statement.[15]

On the same occasion, Vinson observed:

You made a superb witness. You know every phase of the Department of National Defense in the most remote detail. It is indeed refreshing to have a witness like you that can answer all the questions that run through the minds of 37 members of the Committee.[16]

The powerful Chairman of the Senate Committee on Armed Services, Richard Russell, praised McNamara on 13 August 1961, as "one of the great cabinet members of history."[17] These words from two of the most influential members of Congress signified the degree of esteem in which Congress held the Secretary of Defence at that time.

IV

McNAMARA AND CONGRESS FIGHT OVER HARDWARE

During the period 1961-1968, there were several issues on which the Pentagon and Congress interacted. They may be grouped into two categories, namely, defence and foreign policy. The former included questions regarding weapons policies and

---

[15] US House of Representatives, Cong. 87, sess. 1, Committee on Armed Services, *Hearings on Military Posture* (Washington, D.C., 1962) p. 3306.

[16] Ibid., p. 3345.

[17] *New York Times*, 14 August 1961.

military production and procurement. The latter related to the military, political and diplomatic dimensions of American policies in foreign countries. Thus Vietnam constituted one of several issues that came in between the Defence Department and Congress, and their interaction on Vietnam might have been influenced by their interrelationship in regard to other issues.

Apart from Vietnam, the other issue on which there cropped up sharp disagreements between the Secretary of Defence and Congress related to military hardware. Conflicts arising out of weapons were not peculiar to the McNamara period. Many times in the past, intra-Government differences on weapons policies had reached critical points. Moreover, these periodic conflicts are not completely independent of each other. One of them might have led to another. The conflicts of the McNamara period on military hardware were, to some extent, the continuation of those which had originated during the Eisenhower Administration. The main difference was that while in the 1950s the Services often fought amongst themselves over roles and missions, during McNamara's days they mostly closed their ranks and unitedly fought against him.

The members of the military, while appearing before Congressional Committees on defence appropriation, always tend to ask for new and more sophisticated weapons. If the Secretary of Defence goes along with them in this respect, then the latter are happy with him and there is broad harmony between the Secretary and the military. If, on the other hand, the Secretary takes the lead in asserting that the need for the weapon requested by the military does not exist and/or there should be some reduction in the amount requested by them, the military elements are prone to be unhappy with him. The strain between the Secretary and the military caused thereby may affect their interaction in other respects. Secretary McNamara, with his own approach to the decision-making on defence policy, tended often to differ from the estimates of the military regarding the procurement of weapons. It so happened that the period of strain between the Secretary and the JCS over matters relating to the procurement of hardware was also the period during which the escalation of American involvement in Vietnam took place. It is therefore appropriate that the equation between McNamara and the JCS over weapons matters be briefly discussed.

In the very first year of the so-called "McNamara monarchy," sharp differences cropped up between the Defence Secretary and many pro-military members of Congress over the questions of B-52 and B-58 bombers, the Nike-Zeus missile and Skybolt missiles. These issues continued to strain the McNamara-Congress relationship throughout the former's tenure as the Defence Secretary. Two other important issues which were later added to this list were those of the TFX and ABM (Anti-Ballistic Missiles). It is significant to note that on these issues some important elements of Congress and the military stood on the same side as against the Secretary of Defence.

During the hearings held by the House Defence Appropriations Subcommittee in April 1961, Chairman Mahon (Dem., Texas) expressed his concern over the rift between the civilian and military elements of the Pentagon. He asked the Secretary to comment on the "reports of the JCS being bypassed on major [defence] decisions."[18] He cited a report in the *Chicago Sun Times* of 12 March 1961 of a confidential memorandum to the Secretary submitted on 2 March 1961 by the Army Chief of Staff, Gen. Lyman L. Lemnitzer. The General had complained that McNamara had rushed through an important decision in February without giving the JCS enough time to reach a considered judgement. The General reportedly was resentful that the decision gave the Air Force a virtual monopoly over the development of space weapons. The Secretary did not deny. Instead of touching on the particular episode, the Secretary proceeded to emphasize that he had succeeded in building a strong relationship between the civilian and military authorities.[19] Gen. Lemintzer was also evasive in his response to the query of Mahon. He did not deny the existence of the memorandum at issue. He regretted that the "so-called rift" had been exaggerated in the news media.[20] This incident shows up not only the occurrence of a conflict between McNamara and the military soon after he took over as the Secretary of Defence but also the immediate

---

[18] US House of Representatives, Cong. 87, sess. 1, Defence Subcommittee of the Committee on Appropriations, Hearings, *Department of Defence Appropriations for 1962* (Washington, D.C., 1961), part 3, pp. 31-2.

[19] Ibid., p. 33.

[20] Ibid.

concern expressed by Congress over it.

As regards the rift centring round B-52s, McNamara argued that the utility of bombers had been considerably reduced as a result of the development of missiles. The rate of survivability of a bomber was less than that of a missile. The Secretary urged that the B-52 and B-58 bombers should be phased out over a period of five to ten years and should be replaced by missiles.[21] The Secretary's views were not palatable to his military colleagues. It is noteworthy that most of the members of Military Committees did not respond favourably to the Secretary's appraisal. They were reluctant to accept his judgement as against that of the military professionals. General LeMay, the Chief of Staff of the Air Force, observed, "With a missile system, no matter how good they are, you only have two choices. You press the button and you are at war—and in a nuclear war—or you are off the button and you are at peace. There is nothing in between."[22] Many members of Military Committees concurred with this criticism. Senator Russell, the Chairman of the Armed Services Committee, expressed his concern that McNamara's decision on the question of bombers *vis-a-vis* missiles was a "long gamble."[23] Senator Stuart Symington (Dem., Missourie), a member of the Defence Appropriations Subcommittee and Foreign Relations Committee, charged that the Secretary's decision amounted to "an awful lot of eggs in one basket."[24]

McNamara's decision to postpone the production of RS-70s, an advanced manned bomber which had been decided upon by the Eisenhower Administration, incurred the displeasure of the military and its allies in Congress. During the hearings of the House Armed Services Committee in the year 1962, Carl Vinson,

[21] US Senate, Cong. 88, sess. 1, Defence Subcommittee of the Committee on Appropriations, Hearings, *Department of Defence Appropriations for 1964* (Washington, D.C., 1963), p. 178; and US Senate, Cong. 89, sess. 1, Defence Subcommittee of the Committee on Appropriations and the Committee on Armed Services, Joint Hearings, *Department of Defence Appropriations for 1966* (Washington, D.C., 1965), p. 16.

[22] US Senate Cong. 88, sess. 1, Subcommittee of the Committee on Appropriations, Hearings, *Department of Defence Appropriations for 1964* (Washington, D.C., 1963), pp. 178, 353.

[23] Ibid., pp. 349, 357.

[24] US Senate, Defence Subcommittee of the Committee on Appropriations and the Committee on Armed Services, n. 21, p. 239.

its powerful Chairman, tried to impress upon the Secretary of Defence the urgency of the production of RS-70s which the latter did not share. This provoked Vinson to write a report which included the following statement:

> . . .the Secretary of the Air Force, as an official of the Executive branch, is *directed, ordered, mandated* and *required* to utilize the full amount of the $492,000,000 authority granted to proceed with production planning and long lead-time procurement for an RS-70 weapon system.[25]

The impasse, however, was resolved by the intervention of President Kennedy who persuaded Vinson, during a much-publicised stroll in the White House Rose Garden, not to hasten a confrontation with McNamara. The particular issue was settled, but the strain it had created in the meantime was not fully healed. The very next year the Secretary was subjected to further criticism by the military and its supporters in Congress over RS-70s. General LeMay, while recommending the continuation of the B-70 programme, alleged that the US' "strategic superiority" over the Soviet Union was "slipping a little, a little bit." He stated that more effort should be put into the strategic field than before.[26] This concern was shared by Senator Russell.[27] Launching a bitter attack on McNamara's stand on the RS-70, Sen. Gordon L. Allott (Rep., Colorado), said that the US was going to face about a "10-year conceptual delinquency" in the strategic field.[28]

McNamara's cancellation of the Skybolt airborne missile project was another irritant in the interrelationship between the Secretary of Defence and the military and the latter's allies in Congress. Appearing before the Senate Armed Services Committee in 1963, the Secretary argued with remarkable cogency and lucidity that Skybolt would combine the disadvantages of the bomber with those of the missile, and that the substitution of

[25] Jack Raymond, *Power at the Pentagon* (New York, 1964), pp. 296-8.
[26] US Senate, Cong. 88, sess. 1, Defence Subcommittee of the Committee on Appropriations, n. 21, p. 349.
[27] Ibid.
[28] Ibid., p. 357.

Skybolt by the Hound Dog missile would save $2 billion.[29] The military actors did not agree with the Secretary. Against McNamara's facts and figures, they and their Congressional allies could only assert that the Skybolt decision would diminish US military capacity. The military members felt that they were being ignored and undermined by their civilian colleagues in the Pentagon. Their "allies" in Congress went with them and criticized the Secretary for being obsessed with cost-effectiveness considerations and not being guided by military factors deemed important by seasoned soldiers. Sen. John C. Stennis, the Chairman of the Preparedness Investigating Subcommittee of the Senate Armed Services Committee, bluntly told McNamara that he found his exposition unconvincing.[30]

The Secretary faced considerable difficulties with Congress in regard to the so-called TFX affair. For a long time the Air Force and the Navy had been pressing the Administration for accepting their respective versions of new fighter planes. Two powerful industrial giants, General Dynamics and Boeing, developed the models of a single dual-purpose aircraft, as sought by McNamara, for their respective clients—the Air Force and Navy. Both corporations were engaged in lobbying for support in the Executive as well as the legislative branches. However, after some time, the alliance-pattern underwent a big change. Both the Air Force and Navy came round to accept the Boeing version whereas the Secretary of Defence preferred the TFX model developed by its competitor, General Dynamics. The TFX sought to meet the needs of both the Air Force and Navy. Neither of the services felt that the TFX was capable of doing that. General LeMay alleged that it lacked sufficient penetrative capacity to get through modern defences. He pointed out that it might do a fine job in a tactical role but in the strategic role it was "just not big enough to do it."[31] In spite of the unanimous recommendation of the

---

[29] US Senate, Cong. 88, sess. 1, Committee on Armed Services, Hearings, *Military Procurement Authorization Fiscal Year 1964* (Washington, D.C., 1963), p. 4.

[30] Ibid., p. 97.

[31] US Senate, Cong. 88, sess. 2, Defence Subcommittee of Committee on Appropriations and the Committee on Armed Services, Joint Hearings, *Department of Defence Appropriations, 1965* (Washington, D.C., 1964), p. 715.

JCS to the contrary, the Secretary went ahead with his decision to develop and procure TFXs.

The Secretary's action in the face of the unanimous view of the JCS provided the Secretary's Congressional detractors a big stick to beat him with. They expressed their serious misgivings about the wisdom of McNamara's decision. They renewed the criticism that he was downgrading and bypassing the JCS even on purely military matters. During the hearings on the defence appropriations for 1964, Senator Barry Goldwater (Rep., Arizona), subjected the Secretary to intense and critical questioning on the TFX issue.[32] Sen. McClellan (Dem., Arkansas) conducted long, intensive and, at times hostile hearings on the TFX affair. The Secretary and the JCS took contrary positions.[33] Adm. Anderson, Chief of Naval Operations, besides asserting that the JCS had unanimously recommended Boeing to be awarded the contract, charged that there was lacking mutual belief in the Pentagon between its civilian and military components. He further alleged that non-military, rather than military, considerations were the determining factors in taking decisions on weapons matters. The military view was shared by Sen. McClellan and some other members of the Subcommittee. The Secretary, however, bravely weathered the storm. He denied the charge that some of his civilian subordinates had influenced the TFX decision in favour of General Dynamics because of their business links with the company. Some influential members of the Congress extended strong support to the Secretary. Rep. Mahon, the Chairman of the House Appropriations Committee, stated that the Secretary, in awarding the contract to General Dynamics, believed that it was in the "best interest of defence and taxpayer." "The Secretary must have believed, as I do, that the Boeing design would have been even more difficult to develop,"[34] Mahon added. McClellan and his supporters failed to censure Gilpatric, the Deputy Secretary of Defence, for his role in the

---

[32] US Senate, Cong. 88, sess. 1, Defence Subcommittee of the Committee on Appropriations, n. 21, p. 201.

[33] US Senate, Cong. 88, sess. 1, Permanent Subcommittee on Investigation of the Committee on Government Operations, Hearings, *The TFX Contract Investigation* (Washington, D.C., 1963); and Robert J. Art, *The TFX Decision: McNamara and the Military* (Boston, 1968).

[34] *Facts on File* (New York), pp. 333, 420.

TFX award. Gilpatric got a 5-4 "vote of confidence" from the members of the Subcommittee. Thus, while the TFX controversy highlighted the civilian-military conflict in the Pentagon on matters relating to hardware, and pushed the Secretary into the defensive, it could not vanquish him. Though ruffled, he came out of the ordeal creditably.

McNamara's views on the necessity and desirability of the deployment of Anti-Ballistic Missile System (ABM) differed from those of the JCS. The dissatisfaction voiced by the JCS was loudly echoed in Congress. The Secretary argued that the ABM system, Nike X, did not seem to provide substantial protection against an offensive attack by the Soviet Union. It was within the capacity of the Soviet Union to add to her arsenal of offensive weapons to counter any damage limiting measures taken by the United States. Thus the deployment of ABM would tend to intensify the arms race and increase the defence expenditure instead of providing any substantial protection to the US against a Russian strike, the Secretary argued.[35] The JCS argued, on the other hand, that the deployment of ABM by the US would force Moscow to make economic and technological expenditures to counter it. As a result, the latter would have to divert a lot of their resources from other high-priority programmes. The JCS further pointed out, "deterrence is a combination of forces in being and state of mind." If the Russians came to believe that their ballistic missile defence, coupled with a nuclear attack on the United States, would limit damage to the Soviet Union herself to an "acceptable" level, the American forces would fail to deter.[36]

The members of Military Committees, in general, supported the military *vis-a-vis* the Secretary on the question of ABM. During the joint hearings of the Senate Defence Subcommittee

---

[35] US Senate Defence Subcommittee of the Committee on Appropriations and the Committee on Armed Services, n. 31, p. 45; US Senate, Cong. 89, sess. 2; Defence Subcommittee of the Committee on Appropriations, Hearings, *Department of Defence Appropriations for Fiscal Year 1967* (Washington, D.C., 1966), pp. 702, 726; and US Senate, Cong. 90, sess. 1, Defence Subcommittee of the Committee on Appropriations, Hearings, *Department of Defence Appropriations for Fiscal Year 1968* (Washington, D.C., 1967), pt. 1, pp. 236, 238.

[36] US Senate, Cong. 90, sess. 1, ibid., p. 251.

of the Committee on Appropriations and the Senate Committee on Armed Services on 24 February 1965, Senator Strom Thurmond (Rep., South Carolina) demanded that the Nike X production be started immediately. The Secretary deferred the decision till the next year, because he felt that the system was not fully developed. However, the Senator succeeded in forcing McNamara to reveal that the JCS had unanimously recommended the immediate production of Nike X.[37] The Senator repeated his performance the next year by drawing the disclosure from the Secretary that the latter was opposing the unanimous recommendation of the JCS for the production of Nike X.[38] McNamara, however, stuck to his guns and did not yield to the demand of the supporters of Nike X for its immediate manufacture. In retaliation, Congress approved $11.8 million for the development of Nike X and an advanced manned bomber which had not been requested by him. The authorized funds were not utilized by the direction of the Secretary. During the hearings of the House Defence Appropriations Subcommittee on 20 February 1967, the Secretary was bitterly attacked for having impounded the funds which Congress had appropriated for the production of ABM in 1966. "What gives the Department of Defence this great and uncontrollable authority and what gives the Department of Defence the right to be as loose in handling the money that Congress appropriates to it, and why can't we, as members of Congress, have a better idea and a better control over Department of Defence money?" Rep. Glenard P. Lipscomb (Rep., California) asked. He lamented, "It appears to me that we have lost control as a Congress over the Department of Defence appropriations."[39]

It is thus seen that while McNamara inspired awe and respect in Congress by his formidable mastery over facts and figures and

---

[37] US Senate, Cong. 89, sess. 1, Defence Subcommittee of the Committee on Appropriations and the Committee on Armed Services, Joint Hearings, *Department of Defence Appropriations, 1966* (Washington, D.C., 1965), pp. 355-6.

[38] US Senate, Subcommittee of the Committee on Appropriations, n. 35, p. 726.

[39] US House of Representatives, Cong. 90, sess. 1, Defence Subcommittee of the Committee on Appropriations, Hearings, *Defence Supplemental 1967* (Washington, D.C., 1967), p. 239.

analytical skills, his views on several major questions relating to weapons development, production, procurement, and deployment encountered stiff opposition in Congress. The opposition was fierce whenever it came to be known that his appraisals differed from those of the military; it was most fierce whenever members of Congress concluded that his decisions were unanimously opposed by the JCS. During the hearings, several leading members of Congress expressed sympathy and support for the JCS. The way in which, at times, they elicited information unpalatable to the Secretary indicates that they had probably been privately briefed by the military before the hearings began. Even some special hearings were held perhaps with a view to exposing the sharp differences between the Secretary and the military over the above questions and to push the former to the corner. The Secretary at times was subjected to offensive and hostile interrogation by the allies of military in Congress. Disaffection with the Secretary on the part of a number of Congressional critics on issues relating to weapons probably influenced, to some extent, their attitude towards decisions relating to Vietnam on which civilian and military elements of the Pentagon were known to be or believed to be at odds.

V

HARMONY AND DISCORD IN THE PENTAGON: IMPACT ON CONGRESS

Apart from the speeches and statements of the President and the Executive actors, the more important members of Congress get briefings from representatives of the Pentagon, the State Department, and the CIA on politico-military developments in respect of foreign relations. Congressional Committees also receive further information in the course of hearings conducted by them, during which they have ample opportunities to question witnesses both in executive and open sessions. Except when things are going wrong for one reason or another, Congressional hearings provide a good opportunity to both the civilian and military representatives of the Pentagon to present information in such fashion as to mobilize the maximum possible support.

In regard to the US course in Vietnam, the skilful presentations of McNamara, backed by vigorous supporting statements from the military representatives, were favourably received in Congress and contributed to winning support for the Administration. In time, however, when there were indications from the military side that opinion in the Pentagon was somewhat less than unanimous, Congressional critics, friendly to the military, tended to address some sharp questions to the Defence Secretary on whether the views of professional soldiers were being given due weight. Eventually when differences with the Secretary were brought into the open in Congressional hearings by the military representatives, criticism from the Congressional elements tended to become sharper and, in time, produced reactions from others holding a different approach. As will be described below, the impact that the Defence Department was able to make was maximum when the civilian and military elements were able to present a united front to Congress.

Secretary McNamara began his involvement with Vietnam by reaffirming the US's faith in the validity of the "domino" theory. He stated that the "forces of freedom and communism" were locked in armed struggle over the future of Vietnam.[40] He pointed out that Communists were making similar efforts to "destroy freedom" in other parts of the world, namely, Berlin and Laos. In support of his charge, he alluded to the call of Khrushchev for "popular revolts" or "national liberation movements." He asserted that the future of Vietnam would affect the security of the whole "free world." "The survival of an independent government in South Vietnam is so important to the security of all of Southeast Asia and to the free world that we must be prepared to take all necessary measures within our capability to prevent a Communist victory."[41] Year after year, he repeated the pattern of waving the "domino" theory as the basis of the American policy in Vietnam. In spite of his later disenchantment with the ongoing Vietnam policy and his effort at the Executive level to reverse it, he could not disown this

---

[40] US House of Representatives, Cong. 87, sess. 2, Defence Subcommittee of the Committee on Appropriations, Hearings, *Department of Defence Appropriations for 1963* (Washington, D.C., 1962), pt. 2, p. 2.

[41] US Senate, n. 21, p. 97.

theory while appearing before Congressional Committees. His dilemma in this regard was revealed by his attempt to use the word "ripple" in the place of "domino." In an answer to Rep. William E. Minshall's (Rep., Ohio) question whether he went along with the "so-called domino theory," the Secretary said:

> I don't like to use the word "domino" in relation to the actions that will follow because I do not think they would be that immediate or that automatic. . .but they are like "ripple" effects which could stem from the loss of Laos and South Vietnam.[42]

Till 1964 McNamara continued to maintain that the US did not intend to send ground combat troops to South Vietnam to fight against "Communist guerilla." "It is a guerilla war that must be fought by Vietnamese countering the local Viet Cong guerillas," he said during the hearing of the Senate Committee on Appropriations on 22 January 1964.[43] The United States would give South Vietnamese soldiers military training and provide them with advice and assistance. It could not take on the combat task for them, the Secretary asserted. He argued on another occasion that South Vietnamese forces would fare better than American forces in the task of driving out "guerillas."[44]

Until 1966 military witnesses in their testimony before Congressional Committees did not express any disagreement with their civilian colleagues in the Pentagon on Vietnam. Asked by Melvin R. Laird (Rep., Wisconsin) on 6 February 1963 whether the military members were duly consulted in preparing the defence budget, General Maxwell Taylor, the Chairman of the JCS, replied that the JCS participated more on the preparation of that budget—Department of Defence Appropriations for 1964—than

---

[42] US House of Representatives, Cong. 89, sess. 2. Defence Subcommittee of the Committee on Appropriations, Hearings, *Department of Defence Appropriations for 1966* (Washington, D.C., 1965), pt. 3, p. 338.

[43] US Senate, Cong. 88, sess. 2, Committee on Appropriations, Hearings, *Foreign Assistance and Related Agencies Appropriations for 1965* (Washington, D.C., 1964), p. 218.

[44] US Senate, Defence Subcommittee of the Committee on Appropriations, and the Committee on Armed Services, n. 31, p. 74.

was ever the case previously.[45] When an important question like the Tonkin Gulf Resolution was discussed in the first week of August 1964 in the House Foreign Affairs Committee and the Senate Foreign Relations Committee, General Wheeler, the JCS Chairman, accompanied McNamara to Capitol Hill and expressed the military's support for the resolution. It is important to note that since the very beginning, the JCS did not hesitate to differ from McNamara on matter relating to the production and procurement of weapons. In so far as Vietnam was concerned, the military since the last part of 1963 started pressing the Defence Secretary for hitting significant targets inside North Vietnam. In spite of their repeated failure to get his approval for this, they did not carry their internal difference to Congress. The matter remained confined to the bureaucratic actors in Washington—both the military and civilians. Perhaps the military leaders were hopeful till the end of 1965 that they would ultimately be able to prevail upon McNamara in that regard. Only when they were finally disillusioned in 1966, did they begin to air their differences with the Secretary before Congressional Committees with the hope that their allies on Hill would put pressure on him to buy their demand for bombing North Vietnam and sending more American ground troops to the South.

In January 1966, for the first time, the military actors expressed before Congress their differences with the civilian elements of the Pentagon on Vietnam. In the course of the hearing of the Senate Defence Subcommittee of the Committee on Appropriations, held on 26 January 1966, Mahon, the Chairman of the Committee, asked General Wheeler whether the JCS were in accord with the ongoing policies in South Vietnam. The latter replied, ". . .generally speaking we are, sir, with some variations of belief as among the individual chiefs."[46] The civil-military conflict on Vietnam, by this time, was still at a low key. The Generals preferred to express the military's reservations about the Vietnam policy in a subdued form instead of indicating their dimensions.

---

[45] Defence Subcommittee of the Committee on Appropriations, n. 41, p. 342.

[46] US House of Representatives, Cong. 89, sess. 2, Defence Subcommittee of the Committee on Appropriations, Hearings, *Department of Defence Appropriations for 1967* (Washington, D.C., 1966) pt. 1, p. 34.

The military actors do not seem to have reached complete unanimity by the end of 1966 in their opposition to the civilian elements of the Pentagon on Vietnam. Probably there was some tension between the Army and Air Force on matters relating to the strategy and tactics to be followed in Vietnam. Each one of them was interested in upholding the importance of its own role in the Vietnam theatre. While testifying before the Senate Defence Subcommittee of the Committee on Appropriations on 26 January 1967, General Johnson, the Chief of Staff of the Army, expressed his support for the policy of limited bombing of North Vietnam. In spite of repeated questions of Sen. Thurmond, the General did not change his stand. He did not accept the Senator's contention that the destruction of all millitary and industrial facilities in North Vietnam would alter her capability to provide substantially the same level of support that she then did to South Vietnam.[47] About the contention that the bombing of all strategic targets in North Vietnam would expedite the resolution on the war, he said:

> I think there could be a question about it, about the resolution of the war. It would bring additional pressure on them, and it would cause additional interference with what they are doing in the south. But I wouldn't join in the opinion that it would hasten the resolution of the war. On the other hand, I wouldn't argue that this might not happen. We just don't know.[48]

The Army Chief did not initially accept the view of the Air Force on bombing the strategic targets in North Vietnam. But, under the pressure of Thurmond's apparently partisan questioning, he faltered. He withdrew from his position, but he did not reverse it. He did not accept the argument that the bombing of strategic targets of North Vietnam would bring about an early end of the war. He remained non-committed on this controversy.

Even though by this time there were several reports of civil-military rift on Vietnam in newspapers and even though many

---

[47] US Senate, Defence Subcommittee of the Committee on Appropriations, n. 35, pt. 1, p, 575.
[48] Ibid., p. 576.

Congressmen expressed their grave concern over it, the military members of the Pentagon were apparently reluctant initially to face the Secretary headlong during Congressional hearings. They chose to keep their disagreements with him in public to the minimum and to express them, whenever they did, indirectly. While testifying before the joint sessions of Senate Defence Sub-committee of the Committee on Appropriations and the Committee on Armed Services held on 23 January 1967, McNamara stated that the bombing of North Vietnam had so far not significantly reduced the actual flow of men and material to South Vietnam. He conceded that the bombing might have restricted, to some extent, the supply from the North to the South, but he emphasized that it was not "below the level necessary to support the force in the South at the present time."[49] He asserted that this trend was not likely to change in future. Opposing the demand for the bombing of the petroleum storage depots of North Vietnam, the Secretary argued that it would not be effective in stopping the flow of petroleum and if it was, North Vietnamese would move it by bicycles and back-packs.[50]

In his testimony during the same hearing, General Wheeler gave a slightly different picture of the effects of the bombing of North Vietnam. He asserted that it had reduced the flow of men and materials from North Vietnam to South Vietnam.[51] But he did not respond to the most significant part of the Secretary's arguments against bombing—it had not *significantly* reduced the flow of men and materials and it had not reduced it below a certain level. He tried to skirt around the point: "Now when we start talking about whether it will reduce it below a certain level and a fairly small level, that is another thing, and I can't give you a judgement on that. . ."[52] The reluctance of the military at that time to directly challenge the Secretary in regard to their difference on the question of bombing North Vietnam was perhaps due to their desire to avoid a frontal confrontation

---

[49] US Senate, Cong. 90, sess. 1, Defence Subcommittee of the Committee on Appropriations, and the Committee on Armed Services, Joint Hearings, *Supplemental Defence Appropriations and Authorizations, Fiscal Year 1967* (Washington, D.C., 1967), p. 57.

[50] Ibid., p. 70.

[51] Ibid., p. 137.

[52] Ibid., p. 70.

with him until they had fully mobilized their forces—all the elements of the military and their supporters outside, especially in Congress.

The reluctance on the part of the military to have a face-to-face confrontation with the Defence Secretary over Vietnam persisted for some time more. In the course of the hearings of the House Defence Subcommittee of the Committee on Appropriations, held on 20 February 1967, Mahon asked a pointed question to General Wheeler regarding the extent to which the civilians were "running the war and making decisions and the extent to which the military were running the war and making the decisions."[53] Probably he wanted to know the relative role of the civilian and military elements of the Pentagon in the formulation of the broad policy and strategy regarding Vietnam and in taking tactical decisions in the field. The General touched only the second part of the question and evaded the first part. He stated that as regards the combat actions in South Vietnam, General Westmoreland had a free hand. But he did not say anything regarding Westmoreland's request to Washington for sending more ground troops to South Vietnam and the response of the Administration to it. In fact this was one of the causes of the civil-military conflict and this was being highlighted by the press. Similarly, regarding the bombing of North Vietnam he was not very clear and forthright in his criticism of the Defence Secretary. He said that the air was against North Vietnam was controlled on the military side by Admiral Sharp, the CINCPAC. He, of course, pointed to some "additional restrictions imposed by Washington" on the attack in the "high priority targets" in North Vietnam. But he avoided going into the details of the civil-military strain on the issue. In order to further soft-pedal his difference with McNamara on Vietnam, he asserted that there was a "high degree of unanimity between the military and civilian leadership as to the conduct of the war."[54] He refrained from referring to the degree of cleavage between the civilian and military actors which might have been narrow in range, but was deep in nature.

---

[53] US House of Representatives, Defence Subcommittee of the Committee on Appropriations, n. 39, p. 28.

[54] Ibid., pp. 28-9.

A few days after the above hearing, Gen. Wheeler, while testifying before the House Defence Subcommittee of the Committee on Appropriations, exhibited similar hesitation in revealing the civil-military rift over Vietnam before Congress. He supported McNamara's statement that the differences between the JCS and others in the government as to the conduct of the war were "quite small." He added that it was only a "matter of degree, the matter of the amount of pressure and the timing of the pressure."[55] It may be remembered that at that time the military actors were putting heavy pressure on McNamara for escalating the war in Vietnam and the latter was strongly resisting it. It is again important to note that the JCS had already expressed their unanimous opposition to the Secretary on some weapons procurement issues such as ABM before the concerned Congressional Committees. The reason why they hesitated to directly challenge the Secretary is regard to Vietnam during the Congressional hearings was probably because of their belief that they were more strongly placed in the field of weapons production and procurement than in that of Vietnam having direct and major foreign policy implications. It is also possible that they deemed it prudent preparing the ground by initially merely hinting at differences and thereby alerting friendly elements in Congress to the need for probing matters further.

The apparent inhibition on the part of the military to face the Secretary head-on over Vietnam was overcome towards the middle of 1967. One of the reasons for this seemed to be the Draft Presidential Memorandum (DPM) of 19 May 1967 addressed by Secretary McNamara to the President. The Memorandum, discussed in Chapter III, suggested that the Secretary was vehemently opposed to any further escalation of the war and he favoured negotiated settlement. It might have dashed any lurking hope in the JCS for concessions to be made by the former in regard to escalating further the American involvement in the war. By that time too military actors could perceive clear indications from their Congressional allies that they would receive strong support in their posture *vis-a-vis* the Secretary. Thus,

[55] US House of Representatives, Cong. 90, sess. 1, Defence Subcommittee of the Committee on Appropriations, Hearings, *Department of Defence Appropriations for 1968* (Washington, D.C., 1967), pt. 2, p. 258.

when the Senate Preparedness Investigating Subcommittee held hearings in August on the air war in Vietnam, the JCS unanimously criticized the ongoing policy favoured by the Secretary. Point by point, they sought to refute the Secretary and in this they got strong support and encouragement from the members of the Subcommittee.

These developments weakened the position of the Secretary without necessarily strengthening that of the military. Evidence of discord in the Pentagon tended to lessen its capacity to mobilize support in Congress for the Administration's course. It served as a stimulus to the efforts of non-Pentagon actors in the Executive who disliked the posture of one or the other of Pentagon factions. It also served to sharpen hostile criticism in Congress itself.

The differences between the civilian and military elements in the Pentagon on certain issues were serious. However, since on fundamentals relating to the national posture they were able to present to Congress a substantial degree of unity, no danger developed during the entire period under review of opposition in Congress reaching such a level as to constitute a serious threat to the Administration's course. This raises the issue of how effectively or vigorously Congress sought to subject the basics of the Administration's policy, as expounded by the Pentagon, to critical scrutiny.

VI

PENTAGON FAILS TO SUPPLY ACCURATE INFORMATION TO CONGRESS

The Pentagon, both the civilian and military elements included, did not provide accurate information on Vietnam to Congress. Sometimes the information that it chose to dole out to Congress in this connection was distorted and misleading. As a result Congress was put in a difficult position to properly appraise the situation in Vietnam. However, it may be pointed out that Congress initially was disposed to believe what it was told and was not inclined to ask probing questions.

From time to time Secretary McNamara presented before

Congressional Committees conflicting pictures of the situation in South Vietnam. While the intelligence reports at his disposal pointed to the rise in the Communist influence in South Vietnam, the Secretary told a joint sitting of the Senate Defence Subcommittee of the Committee on Appropriations and the Committee on Armed Services on 3 February 1964 that the Communist influence in South Vietnam was gradually decreasing.[56]

McNamara told the House Armed Services Committee on 27 January 1964 that the situation in South Vietnam continued to be grave. He described the situation in Laos as "precarious." But the next day he stressed in a press conference that there "has been a very noticeable improvement" in the conduct of the war and that he was "encouraged by the progress of the last two weeks."[57] The apparent contradiction in these remarks invited very strong criticism from the press. The *Washington Post*, in an editorial titled "Retreat from Candor" asserted bluntly, "Verbal ambiguity is an old story on Vietnam. . . Isn't it time for the Administration to show more faith in the intelligence and good sense of the American people?[58] James Reston, one of the most respected journalists in Washington, observed: "The first casualty in every war is truth, and the war in Vietnam has been no exception. . . ."[59]

The Pentagon hid some information and distorted some others while requesting Congress to adopt the Tonkin Gulf Resolution in August 1964. It did not tell Congress that the US had already been undertaking for some time covert operations against North Vietnam. It did not disclose that the De Soto patrol off the coast of North Vietnam by the *Maddox* was a part of the provocative strategy already determined by Washington. Nor did it reveal that the De Soto patrol and 34-A Operations undertaken by South Vietnamese were coordinated efforts and the *Maddox* was aware that South Vietnam fired on two coastal villages of North Vietnam while it was getting closer to the latter's coast in the Gulf of Tonkin. Worst of all, it did not

---

[56] US Senate, Defence Subcommittee of the Committee on Appropriations and the Committee on Armed Services, n. 31, pt. 1. p. 84.
[57] *New York Times*, 29 January 1964.
[58] "Retreat from Candor, " ed., *Washington Post*, 28 January 1964.
[59] James Reston, "McNamara Adds to Viet Confusion," *New York Times*, 29 January 1964.

tell the latter that a draft of the proposed Tonkin Gulf Resolution had already been prepared a few days before the incident occurred. One is not sure of how Congress would have reacted had all these facts been disclosed to it, especially when the President was appealing to it to stand with him to defend American lives and property. But the truth is that the Pentagon seemed to have deliberately kept Congress in the dark about some of the most relevant facts regarding the Tonkin Gulf incident.

VII

FAILURE OF CONGRESS TO SUBJECT PENTAGON PRESENTATION TO CRITICAL SCRUTINY

The members of Congress often failed to critically examine the role of the Pentagon in regard to Vietnam. They hardly made any serious effort to put to intensive scrutiny some of the basic assumptions of American policy in Vietnam. The witnesses of the Pentagon, for example, continued to cite, year after year, the so-colled "domino theory" as the principal basis of American involvement in Vietnam. Hardly did a member of Congress take a serious look at this theory during the period under review. At times, some members of Congress outdistanced the Pentagon witnesses in selling the domino theory.

It has been pointed out earlier that in the first year of the Kennedy Administration, Vietnam hardly caught the attention of Congress. No member of the Senate Defence Appropriations Subcommittee evinced any interest in American policy in Vietnam. Nor did any member show any interest about any other country in Southeast Asia—especially Laos which at that time was a tension area. The same was true of the Senate Committee on Armed Services. Only during the hearings before the House Defence Appropriations Subcommittee was some amount of time devoted to the US's Southeast Asian policy. Chairman Mahon expressed concern over the possibility of escalation of war in Laos if major powers intervened. He did not raise any question about South Vietnam.[60]

---

[60] US House of Representatives, Defence Subcommittee of the Committee on Appropriations, n. 18, p. 133.

During the following year there was no great surge of Congressional interest in Vietnam, but many members spoke of the Communist threat to Southeast Asia. Senator Dodd (Dem., Connecticut) said that the Communist conquest of Southeast Asia would produce a serious shift in the world balance of power and threaten the security of the United States.[61] Senator Hubert Humphrey (Dem., Minnesota) advocated American economic and military assistance to South Vietnam and acknowledged, it might involve a great risk. However, he asserted that the greatest risk was "Communist aggression, Communist conquest, and Communist advance. That we cannot permit, if it is humanly possible to stop it."[62] No inquiry was made as to the nature of regime ruling in Saigon to which the US was to be economically and militarily committed. Nor was any concern expressed about the fact that the US had sent the previous year 16,000 so-called "military advisers" to South Vietnam.

The pattern of a lack of determination on the part of Congress to take a hard look at Vietnam persisted in the year 1963. In 1964, a few members expressed concern over the reported decline in the control of the Saigon regime over the people of South Vietnam. During the defence budget hearings Senator Milton R. Young (Rep., North Dakota) asked the Secretary of Defence whether the reports of Communists gaining the increased support of the local people in South Vietnam were true. The Secretary denied it.[63] Senator Clifford Philip Case (Rep., Illinois) scored the Secretary for his "over-optimistic reports" on South Vietnam from time to time.[64] But there was no discussion on the implications of American involvement in Vietnam.

The way the Tonkin Gulf Resolution was adopted by Congress further illustrates the lack of willingness and determination on the part of Congress to subject the Pentagon witnesses to a critical scrutiny and to take a serious look at American policy in Vietnam. The so-called attack on the *Maddox* was highly dramatized by the Pentagon. A virtually hypnotized Congress believed that North Vietnam had launched an unprovoked

---

[61] *Congressional Record* (Washington), vol. 108, part 7, 1962, p. 8770.

[62] Ibid., vol. 108, part 3, 1962, p. 3861.

[63] US Senate, Defence Subcommittee of the Committee on Appropriations and the Committee on Armed Services, n. 31, part 1, p. 84.

[64] US Senate, Committee on Appropriations, n. 43, p. 152.

attack on an American patrol ship in international waters. It did not care to examine the resolution thoroughly. The "mood" of the nation and skilful news management by the Executive, especially the Pentagon had their clear impact on Congress. The retaliatory action ordered by President Johnson against North Vietnam was almost universally hailed. The Republican Presidential candidate, Senator Barry Goldwater, extended his wholehearted support to the President in the hour of "crisis." Against this backdrop, the resolution was brought to Congress.

The Congressional hearings on the Tonkin Resolution were just a routine affair.[65] Rusk and McNamara appeared on 6 August 1964 before a joint session of the Senate Foreign Relations and Armed Services Committees. Fulbright who presided over the hearings did not ask a single question, although he had already been informed by Morse of his doubts about the version of the *Maddox* story as narrated by the Executive. Saltonstall (Rep., Massachusetts), the ranking Republican member in the Foreign Relations Committee, also remained silent. The general "mood" of the Committee—for that matter, of Congress—was expressed by Senator Russell Long (Dem., Lousiana) when he said: "As much as I would like to be consulted with on this kind of thing the less time you spend on consulting and the quicker you shoot back the better off you are."[66] Others who asked some questions only sought from the witnesses some minor details. None of them except Morse appeared to take a critical look at the Executive's account regarding the *Maddox* incident nor did any one of them try to understand the longrange implications of the proposed resolution for the Vietnam policy.

Morse carried on a lone battle against the resolution. He had been told on August 5 by a Pentagon man that the *Maddox* was not on a routine patrol; it was a spy ship and had some connection with the South Vietnamese attack on North Vietnamese islands around the time in which the *Maddox* was fired at. The Senator agreed with McNamara that North Vietnam was indulging in subversive activities against the South. But he

[65] See John Galloway, *The Gulf of Tonkin Resolution* (Madison, 1970).
[66] US Senate, Cong. 88, sess. 2, Committee on Foreign Relations and Armed Services, Joint Hearings, *A Joint Resolution to Promote the Maintenance of International Peace and Security in Southeast Asia* (Washington, D.C., 1964), Appendix 6 to Galloway, Ibid., p. 209.

deplored that the Secretary had never provided the Committee (Foreign Relations) with all necessary information to that effect.[67] At the other end of the table, Senator Strom Thurmond of South Carolina asked for stronger American actions against North Vietnam. He demanded that the US should "strike at the heart of the trouble. . . or get out."[68] The hearings lasted for one hour and forty minutes and, except Morse, all other members voted in favour of the resolution. The same day, Rusk, McNamara and Gen. Wheeler appeared before the House Armed Services and Foreign Affairs Committees. This time the whole business was over within less than an hour and the passage of the resolution was unanimous—29 to 0.

Before the resolution came to the floor of Congress for discussion, some journalist had started to express their suspicions about the whole incident.[69] The Executive, in spite of its well-prepared dramatic performance, seemingly failed to have satisfied the whole of the press. Murrey Marder of the *Washington Post* suggested that the South Vietnamese attack on the North Vietnamese islands might have provoked the attack on the *Maddox*.[70] On 4 August, the *New York Times* said that the American "destroyers on patrol have sometimes collaborated with South Vietnamese hit-and-run raids on North Vietnam's port cities, though the destroyers themselves stay in international waters." James Reston, in his 7 August column, observed, "May be, this [the resolution] is what the country wants and there is a good case to be made for it, but even in the hurry to get the resolution passed there shouldn't be much objection to looking at what it says and what it doesn't say." All these doubts and suspicions, expressed by some elements of the "prestige papers" which are considered to be very influential with foreign policy matters, seemed to have fallen flat on the majority of the members of Congress.

The resolution received a similar treatment, as in the Committees, on the floor of Congress. Apart from Morse, some other liberals expressed their misgivings about the import of the

---

[67] Ibid., p. 204.
[68] Ibid., pp. 219-22.
[69] Galloway, n. 65, pp. 81-2.
[70] *Washington Post*, 4 August 1964.

resolution. Senator Albert Arnold Gore (Dem., Tennessee), Senator McGovern (Dem., South Dakota), and Senator Javits (Rep., New York) wanted to be sure that the resolution was not an approval in advance of any radical change in the American mission in Vietnam. Morse again carried on his virtually lone but strong fight against the proposed resolution. He argued that the American officialdom in the Pentagon and the State Department knew that the South Vietnamese bombardment of the North was going to take place *Maddox* and *Turner Joy* entered the North Vietnamese coast. Being challenged by Senator Frank J. Lausche (Dem., Ohio), that "there was not a syllable of such testimony in the record," the Senator from Oregon retorted, "Get permission of the State Department or the Pentagon to publicly release the whole of the transcript without a single word deleted, and let the country know what they said."[71] Senator Gaylord A. Nelson (Dem., Wisconsin) expressed his concern about the increase in American troops in Vietnam from 1,000 in 1960 to around 16,000 in 1964. To insure that Washington was not seeking, through this resolution, any intensification of the present military conflict, he moved an amendment, which read:

> Our continuing policy is to limit our role to the provision of aid, training, assistance, and military advice, and it is the sense of Congress, that except when provoked to greater response, we should continue to avoid a direct military involvement in the Southeastern Asian conflict.[72]

It was opposed by Fulbright on the ground that it would delay matters and "cause confusion."[73] That a man like Fulbright should have expressed such sentiments shows how difficult it is for a member of Congress to raise critical questions or seek detailed clarification when the Administration, with the Pentagon out in front, succeeds in creating a mood of crisis in the country. It calls for great courage for a Congress to risk the charge of "delaying matters" or "creating confusion" at such a

[71] *Congressional Record*, vol. 110, part 14, August 1964, p. 18425.
[72] Ibid., p. 18459.
[73] Ibid.

time. Even reservations and misgivings are voiced in cautious and indirect fashion. Thus it came to pass that the Senate adopted the resolution 88-2 (Morse and Gruening, Rep., Alaska, voting against). The House vote was 416-0.

The Tonkin Gulf story illustrates that Congress rallies overwhelmingly to support the Executive when the latter, waving the Stars and Stripes, makes an appeal to the whole nation to stand with it in defending American lives and property. A crisis situation, real or imaginary, has got its own momentum and once it erupts, it is likely to galvanize the decision-makers in Washington and force them into immediate action. It would be extremely difficult for Congress to take any step which might delay the action on the part of the Executive to meet the "crisis."

Another instance of the reluctance of Congress to critically examine the American policy in Vietnam was the way it voted the Supplemental Appropriation for the Defence Department 1965, Emergency Fund, Southeast Asia. On 5 May 1965, the President asked Congress, in a special message, to grant $700 million for conducting effectively the Vietnam war. He made it very clear that Congress, in approving of his request, would reaffirm the Tonkin Gulf Resolution of August 1964. To quote him in length:

> This is not a routine appropriation. For each member of Congress who supports this request is also voting to persist in our effort to halt Communist aggression in South Vietnam. Each is saying that the Congress and the President stand united before the world in joint determination that the independence of South Vietnam shall be preserved and Communist attack will not succeed.[74]

This was again emphasized by McNamara in his testimony before the Senate Committee on Appropriations and Armed Services during their joint hearings on the Supplemental Appropriation for the Defence Department 1965. He stated that the objective of the appropriation was to "allow the Congress an

[74] *Congressional Record*, vol. 111, part 7, 1965, p. 9492.

opportunity to reappraise the U.S. policy in Southeast Asia."[75]

The opportunity was given. But Congress did not take advantage of it to take a fresh, hard look at the course in Vietnam. The Senate Defence Appropriations Subcommittee and the Armed Services Committee did not do justice to their job. The hearings jointly held by them started at 10 A.M on 5 May 1965 and recessed at 12.05 P.M. on the same day. There was hardly any discussion on policy issues. Senator Case said, "it does raise the question that there is a little more than just an appropriations operation, as far as nuts and bolts and other things are concerned. That is why I think it is appropriate to ask one or two questions along the line of policy, and strategy, and what not, if I may . . . ."[76] But even he did not follow up with any question on policy. Questions relating to "bolts and nuts" were discussed. On the whole, the members of these two Committees showed hardly any interest in critically examining the Pentagon officials in regard to the American policy in Vietnam.

The Bill had received similar treatment in the House Armed Services Committee which endorsed it on 4 May 1965 by a vote of 37 to 0. The 50-member House Committee on Appropriations not only passed the Bill unanimously but made a proud assertion in its report. ". . .It will also provide Congress an opportunity to again make known to our friends and foes alike that the people of the United States have every intention of standing firm in their opposition to Communist aggression."[77]

The pattern of the Congressional treatment of the Bill was not much different when it was debated in both Houses. On July 6, Senator Saltonstall said that the defeat of the Bill would be tantamount to the repudiation of the earlier joint resolution of August 1964.[78] In the House Mendel Rivers observed that the appropriation was a "simple reaffirmation of

---

[75] US Senate, Cong. 89, sess. 1, Defence Subcommittee of the Committee on Appropriations and the Committee on Armed Services, Joint Hearings, *Supplemental Appropriation for Department of Defence 1965, Emergency Fund, Southeast Asia* (Washington, D.C, 1965,) p. 21.

[76] Ibid.

[77] Cited in *Congressional Record*, n. 74, p. 9519.

[78] Ibid., p. 9495.

the action taken on 10 August 1964."[79] Thus Congress was well aware of the implication of the passage of the Bill for the American military involvement in Vietnam.

Some members of Congress like Senators Gore, Nelson and Javits who had expressed their misgivings on the Tonkin Gulf Resolution were put in a tight corner while voting on the Defence Supplemental, 1965. Their support for it would be tantamount to reaffirming the Tonkin Gulf Resolution and the policy of escalation. Opposition to it, they feared, would be read as their failure to stand by the said of the American soldiers fighting in South Vietnam. In that case, they would be dubbed as "unpatriotic." They resolved the dilemma by supporting the Supplemental with the assertion that Congress should be consulted if the war escalated. This was just a pious hope on their part. On the other hand, the overwhelming support of Congress for the Defence Supplemental further strengthened the hands of the executive to pursue the Vietnam policy as it liked. A confident President and an ebullient Secretary of Defence had boldly asked the members of Congress to reappraise the policy if they so desired. But the latter backed away from any such effort. This is another illustration of the reluctance on the part of Congress to subject the Pentagon witnesses to critical scrutiny in regard to Vietnam in the early phase of escalation.

The Defence Supplemental, 1966, was largely treated by Congress in the same manner as that in the previous year. A few members tried to raise some basic issues relating to the American involvement. A few more had their misgivings about the policy of escalation but not to the extent of being provoked to come out openly against the ongoing policy. The overwhelming majority extended its support to the Administration's course. Many legislators who had long been advocating a hawkish policy in Vietnam (to be discussed later) propagated the logic that there was no time to discuss the very origin of American involvement in Vietnam; what was needed was to make the best fight out of the present. Senator Stennis (Dem., Mississippi) delivered on the floor of Senate, a long talk with

[79] Ibid., p. 9520.

the title, "we must start from where we are."[80] He said that the
question of how the US got into Vietnam had long since passed.
The question might have been relevant, but that was not the
issue then, because the US had always been there since 1954,
he added. The same line was taken by Rivers, the Chairman
of the House Armed Services Committee. He stated that the
debate on how the US got in there might be carried on at a
different time, but the immediate job was to vote for supplying
weapons to the soldiers fighting in South Vietnam.[81]

Congress came to deal with the nub of the problem when it
tried to determine whether sanctioning appropriations for
defence programmes related to the Vietnam war amounted to
making policy on Vietnam. Senator Morse and Senator
Gruening believed so. They felt that such authorizations and
appropriations gave to the Executive a "blank check" for
expanding the war into Laos and Thailand. As Senator Morse
put it, "The pending Bill, S 2791 is the most open ended invitation to the continued expansion and escalation of the Vietnam
war that could be requested by a war department or granted by
a Congress."[82] The same point was made by Rep. Ryan of
New York who carried a lone but grim battle in the House of
Representatives against this Bill. He observed that it was not a
routine authorization for a routine appropriation. He feared
that it was a request for another brick in the arch of Congressional support for the Vietnam policy. He also suspected that
through this authorization the Pentagon was seeking to
escalate the war in Vietnam.[83]

Many other members, however, took a different view. They
believed that such appropriations amounted neither to the
approval nor disapproval of the policy in Vietnam. What they
did seek was simply to supply arms and weapons to and stand
by the side of American soldiers fighting in that distant land.
According to Senator Russell, nothing in that legislation (S 2791)
could properly be construed as determining foreign policy, as
ratifying decisions made in the past or as endorsing new commit-

[80] Ibid., vol. 112, part 3. 1966, pp. 3382-4.
[81] Ibid., vol. 112, part 4, 1966, p. 4441.
[82] Ibid., vol. 112, part 3, 1966, p. 4145.
[83] Ibid., vol. 112, part 4, 1966, pp. 4434-7.

ments.[84] To him it was just the throwing of a rope to a man in the water.[85]

It is difficult to say which of these two arguments was right. It is true that such authorizations do not explicilty endorse the government's foreign policy. It is also true that the supplementary defence appropriations were urgent measures to meet emergency needs in Vietnam. The American soldiers were fighting in Vietnam in pursuance of a policy determined by Washington. To that extent, such appropriations might properly be construed as endorsement of the Vietnam policy. One could understand the difficulty of the members of Congress when called upon to vote on the Defence Supplemental, 1966. There was no shirking the fact that if they voted for the measure, they would be extending their support to the Vietnam policy, as determined and implemented by the Executive, with the Pentagon playing a very major role. This will perhaps be made clear from the following colloquy between Ford and Mahon:

> Ford—. . .An 'aye' vote in this Bill today means that one supports adequate military strength to meet successfully the challenge of Communist aggression in South Vietnam.
> Mahon—This, I believe, would be a fair interpretation of a vote in favour of the pending legislation. . . .[86]

The reaction of "doves" to the Defence Supplemental 1966 was the same as it was the previous year. They would not concede that their support for the Bill amounted to the support of the Vietnam policy. They believed that the commitment of US forces in Vietnam was a serious mistake, and would prove to be, as Senator Gore said, a "historic mistake." But they would not vote against the Bill because they perhaps feared that they would be indicted as having betrayed their brothers fighting in a foreign country. The Bill was passed on 1 March 1966 by the House, 392 to 4, and by the Senate, 93 to 2.

The inability of Congress to critically examine the Pentagon

[84] Ibid., part 3, p. 3135.
[85] Ibid., p. 3138.
[86] Ibid., vol. 112, part 5, 1966, p. 5804.

witnesses on Vietnam thus stemmed primarily from three factors. First, Congress would initially be reluctant to go deep into the matter if it relates to defence and foreign policy; it would better leave that to be dealt with by the Executive. Second, the reluctance of Congress in this regard would all the more increase if it were confronted with a "crisis" situation. It tends to believe that "crisis" demands promptness in decision and action which would be hampered by any delaying actions on its part. Thirdly, it becomes all the more difficult for Congress to subject the Executive to critical scrutiny if the "American boys are already in the field." It would normally not meddle with the policy pursued by the Executive unless it is compelled by circumstances to do so.

A similar lack of serious efforts on the part of Congress to have a critical look at the Vietnam policy while examining Pentagon officials during the hearings on the defence budget was demonstrated in the year 1967. The members of Military Committees, while questioning the Defence Secretary and the Chairman of the JCS, expressed their concern over strategies of the ongoing war rather than about the policy to be pursued. There was no attempt on their part at re-evaluating and reapprising the existing American military involvement in Vietnam. The domino theory was treated as very sacred and hence beyond discussion. None of the members tried to explore any means other than military ones for the settlement of the Vietnam conflict. Direct negotiations with the Viet Cong and North Vietnam as a means of settlement did not come to the discussion at all.[87] Most members took the Secretary to task for his failure to accept the military's recommendation for bombing and mining many important targests of Hanoi and Haiphong which will be discussed after a while.

---

[87] US Senate, Defence Subcommittee of the Committe on Appropriations and the Committee on Armed Services, n. 49; and US Senate, Cong. 90, sess. 1, Defence Subcommittee of the Committee on Appropriations, n. 35, part 1.

VIII

HAWKS AND DOVES IN CONGRESS

It has been pointed out that there was very little direct criticism in Congress of the course pursued by Kennedy and Johnson in Southeast Asia which was presented as an essential effort to prevent Communist expansionism. The overwhelming support accorded to the Tonkin Gulf Resolution marked the high point of Congressional support. There had, of course, been earlier instances where certain members of Congress advocated even more vigorous actions than the Administration appeared to be following. Gerald Ford, for instance, expressed unhappiness in 1962 over the progress of Communist forces in Laos.[88] Representative Minshall wondered whether the US was doing enough and he called upon McNamara to convince America's friends in Laos and South Vietnam that the US would support them effectively, "when chips were down."[89] These were the kind of elements in Congress that were subsequently to evolve into "hawks," supporting every increment in US military involvement, siding with the military whenever they suspected that the civilian elements of the Pentagon were overwhelming them and eventually subjecting the Defence Secretary himself to sharp criticism for not doing what was needed to be done for ensuring "victory."

The emergence of a "dovish" group in Congress was a much slower process. Little attention was paid to Senator Wayne Morse when he asked in 1963 why the US should have a "commitment to support a tyrant in South Vietnam."[90] On 12 September 1963, Senator Church asserted that all American assistance to Saigon should stop unless Saigon gave up its repressive policies.[91] As the months passed by, a few other Senators ventured to cast some doubts on McNamara's optimistic reports concerning developments in Vietnam. The Secretary answered firmly in the negative when Senator Young

---

[88] US House of Representatives, Defence Subcommittee of the Committee on Appropriations, n. 40, p. 239.

[89] Ibid., p. 248.

[90] *Congressional Record*, vol. 109, part 12, 1963, p. 15744.

[91] Ibid., p. 16824.

asked him whether the Communists were getting increased support in South Vietnam.[92] Sentor Case criticized McNamara for his "overoptimistic" reports.[93] But it was Wayne Morse who persisted in raising basic issues and accused the Secretary of giving to Congress inadequate and misleading information. On 25 April 1964 Morse charged that the military activity that American personnel had been engaging in were without any constitutional sanction. Pointing his finger at McNamara, he charged, "Well, at long last, we have smoked him out. We now have an admission from the Secretary of Defence that this Nation is engaged in war." He alleged bluntly that the Vietnam war was "McNamara's war."[94]

At that point the Secretary was less troubled by Morse's criticisms than by those of the hawks who stridently demanded vigorous measures to put an end to North Vietnamese support to the Viet Cong. During the Senate Committee on Appropriations hearings on the Foreign Assistance and Related Agencies for 1965, McClellan asked McNamara whether the US would drive the "North Vietnamese infiltrators" out of South Vietnam or whether she would just continue the "holding action," just to hold them off.[95] Senator Thurmond asked the Secretary on 3 February 1964 whether the United States would be able to win in Vietnam until she went into North Vietnam and destroyed the Communist elements there.[96] In the House, Gerald Ford indirectly criticized McNamara for insufficient militancy in dealing with the situation in Vietnam. He urged that the government make some hard choices.[97] Laird severely criticized the Secretary for his statement that the American aim in Vietnam was to prevent a Communist victory there. He attacked it as a "bad psychology" to say it that way. He said that

[92] US Senate, Defence Subcommittee of the Committee on Appropriations, and the Committee on Armed Services, n. 31, part 1, p. 84.
[93] US Senate, Committee on Appropriations, n. 43, p. 152.
[94] *Congressional Record*, vol. 110, part 7, 1964, p. 217.
[95] US Senate, Committee on Appropriations, n. 43, p. 217.
[96] US Senate, n. 31, p. 91.
[97] US House of Representatives, Cong. 88, sess. 2, Defence Subcommittee of the Committee on Appropriations, Hearings, *Department of Defence Appropriations for 1965* (Washington, D.C., 1964), p. 117.

preventing a Communist victory was not necessarily the same thing as achieving an American or a South Vietnamese victory.[98] Another strong advocate of this viewpoint was Clement J. Zablocki (Dem., Wisconsin), a prominent member of the House Foreign Affairs Committee. He observed on 3 March, "To me, our course in Vietnam is clear. We must stay and assist the South Vietnamese defeat the Viet Cong, no matter how long the fight, no matter what the commitment of resources. . . ."[99]

Thus as 1964 drew to a close, the basic thrust of the Administration was challenged by a mere handful in Congress. The overwhelming majority readily endorsed the Secretary's exposition of Administration's policies and even the hawks merely insisted that it should be prepared to act even more vigorously and effectively.

The decisive votes by which Congress voted Supplemental Appropriations for Vietnam in 1965 has already been mentioned. A small number of critics of the Administration's policy opposed escalatory measures but avoided giving any suggestions that they advocated any unconditional US withdrawal from Vietnam. They were probably influenced by the appraisal that the war was still "popular" with American public and it would be politically suicidal to be appearing to advocate unilateral withdrawal from Vietnam. Some of them did urge that the objective of the US should be to carry on the holding action and work to bring about a settlement through negotiation.

The hawks decried the plea for negotiations and at the same time renewed their criticism of the Secretary of Defence for not acting on the entire range of recommendations made by the millitary. Laird said:

> If our objective is a negotiated settlement, it is time to use other means than the needless sacrifice of American lives to attain that objective. Once American troops are committed in any situation, a top priority objective must be to take those steps necessary to protect American lives and minimize the number of casualties.

[98] Ibid., p. 364.
[99] *Congressional Record*, vol. 110, part 3, 1964, pp. 3226-7.

He added, "One such step, already long overdue, is to retarget our combing raids on more significant targets in North Vietnam."[100] By this time, as pointed out earlier, indications were available to Congress that differences had emerged between the JCS and the Secretary. The small and, by no means, cohesive group of "doves" did not give any credit to the Secretary for his effort to resist the demands of the JCS. They could see no real difference between the posture of the Secretary and that of the JCS; both appeared to the "doves" to be advocates of escalation. The "doves" were still too small to pose any headache to the Pentagon. The "hawks" made their routine points, but did not push their challenge to the Secretary beyond certain limits. For instance, they did not ask any pointed question on civil-military differences on Vietnam while interrogating McNamara during the defence budget hearings.

The war continued, the casualties mounted, and the draft was a looming spectre for young men. The end was not in sight. Such a state of affairs resulted in a steady erosion of support among the public for the Administration's course as 1966 advanced. A Harris Survey in February 1966 pointed out that the percentage of the so-called "doves" was only nine per cent. (Their percentage was also the same in the previous month.)[101] A Gallup Poll held in the month of May found out that 47 per cent of informants supported the Administration's policy whereas 35 per cent disapproved of it.[102] Another Gallup Poll conducted in the month of September, said that the number of supporters of the Administration's policy was 43 per cent, that of dissenters, 40 per cent, and 17 per cent had no opinion.[103] This suggests that although the number of domestic dissenters was very small in the beginning of 1966, it started to increase significantly in course of time. By the middle of the year, it had reached a substantial level. Such poll results might have had some impact upon the Congressional response to the role of the Pentagon in regard to Vietnam. They

---

[100] *New York Times*, 16 June 1965.
[101] *Washington Post*, 28 February 1966.
[102] *New York Times*, 22 May 1966.
[103] Ibid., 22 September 1966.

emboldened Congressional critics of the Administration, brought converts to their ranks, and made them into an invariably coherent and active group of "doves." The "hawks," on the other hand, reacted to the situation by stepping up their criticism of McNamara.[104] The Secretary's refusal to call up reserves as requested by the JCS brought on him the bitter displeasure of some members of Congress. The strongest attack on McNamara on this question was made in a Senate Committee by no less a person than Chairman Russell. While interrogating General Jonn L. Throckmorton, who was in charge of reserves, the Senator said:

> You understand that I am not critical of you. I stated at the very outset you gentlemen [the military] did not fix this policy. I cannot conceive of the military leaders of this country fixing any such policy. I think they would have used some of these Reserve units if they had an opportunity. I believe they would have. Some of them said so *in private conversation*, and I heard that they had made a recommendation to the Commander-in-Chief that they use some of them, but they were turned down.[105]

The "hawks" in Congress alleged that the US was not doing enough to win the war in Vietnam. They believed that the real source of danger to the Saigon regime lay in North Vietnam. They urged that the US should bomb the enemy's supply lines and the significant military targets in Hanoi and Haiphong.[106] Sikes asked the Secretary whether the US was not encouraging the build-up of enemy artillery of all types by not resuming the

---

[104] In reply to a question by Sikes, during the House Defence Appropriations Subcommittee Hearings, held on 14 February 1966, McNamara stated, "We have no present plans for calling Reserves or Guard personnel to active duty in association with Southeast Asia operations." US House of Representatives, Defence Subcommittee of the Committee on Appropriations, n. 46, p. 260.

[105] US Senate, Cong. 89, sess. 2, Defence Subcommittee of the Committee on Appropriations, n. 35, p. 59; Emphasis added.

[106] US House of Representatives, Defence Subcommittee of the Committee on Appropriations, n. 46, p. 128.

bombing attacks on North Vietnam.[107] Another member even went to the extent of suggesting that the US should use nuclear arms against North Vietnam.[108] Demands to mine Haiphong were also made on the floor of the Senate. Russell strongly urged the Administration to close the harbour at Haiphong:

> It seems to me it would be self-evident even to a lay mind that it would be more effective to close the stopper of a bottle than to pour out the contents and set the bottle back down to be refilled. That is all that would be accomplished by clearing the petroleum dumps, because the next day a tanker would come into Haiphong and replenish those dumps.[109]

Although the pro-military elements included both Democratic and Republican members, the latter were more vocal than the former. It was only the Republicans who singled out McNamara as their target whereas the hawks from among the Democrats were still hesitant to pinpoint their attacks on McNamara. Again and again, the Republican critics snipped at the Secretary publicly. On 30 April 1966, Gerald Ford, the Republican leader in the House of Representatives, accused McNamara of "mismanagement" of war.[110] On 18 May, Laird alleged that, in relation to Vietnam, the Secretary of Defence had been "consistently wrong."[111] Goldwater charged in the Senate that the big shortage of war materials in South Vietnam was a "national scandal." (At that time, supporters of the military both inside Congress and outside were holding McNamara responsible for this "shortage.") He scored the Secretary for calling his critics "irresponsible."[112] The reluctance of Democratic hawks to single out McNamara as the principal villain might have been due to the fact that the Presi-

---

[107] US House of Representatives, Cong. 89, sess. 2, Defence Subcommittee of the Committee on Appropriations, Hearings, *Defence Supplemental for 1966* (Washington, D.C., 1966), p. 39.

[108] Ibid., pp. 98-9.

[109] *Congressional Record*, vol. 112, part 5, 1966, p. 6460.

[110] *New York Times*, 1 May 1966.

[111] Ibid., 19 May 1966.

[112] Ibid., 6 May 1966.

dent still seemed to be nearer to the Secretary than to the JCS and their criticism against McNamara might be construed as a rebuke to the President and might hurt, thereby, their party in 1966 Congressional elections.

In 1966 Senator Fulbright, the Chairman of the Foreign Relations Committee, emerged as a prominent spokesman of the doves in Congress. It was a metamorphosis in him to have opposed the Vietnam policy, because in August 1964 he had piloted the Tonkin Gulf Resolution and he had supported the Defence Supplemental 1965, primarily meant for Vietnam. Disenchantment with the course of events and the Administration's course coupled with the American intervention in the Dominican Republic in April 1965 probably influenced Fulbright to reconsider his position. His Committee came across some information which were different from what the President had said in justifying the American action in Santo Domingo. With bitter indignation, he told the Senate that the US policy in the Dominican Republic was initially characterized by overtimidity and subsequently by overreaction. "Throughout the whole affair, it has been characterized by a lack of candor," he added.[113] He sensed a "similar lack of candor" in the Vietnam policy. The Dominican intervention, more or less, coincided with the escalation of the American military involvement in Vietnam. From the beginning of 1966 he started publicly airing his misgivings about the ongoing Vietnam policy and he made ample use of his Committee for that purpose.

On 24 January 1966, Fulbright urged a longer bombing pause and inviting the Viet Cong for talks. On 28 January, his Committee opened the "educational hearings" on Vietnam.[114]

---

[113] Fulbright was provoked to write later:

"The evidence is incontrovertible that American forces landed in Santo Domingo on 28 April 1965, not, as was and is officially contended, for the primary purpose of saving American lives but for the primary, if not the sole purpose of defeating the revolution, which, on the basis of fragmentary evidence and exaggerated estimates of Communist influence, was judged to be either Communist-dominated or certain to become so."

J.W. Fulbright, *The Arrogance of Power* (London, 1970), p. 88; see also Fulbright, *The Pentagon Propaganda Machine* (New York, 1970), p. 83.

[114] *New York Times*, 29 January 1966.

In the second week of February, the Foreign Relations Committee held public hearings on Vietnam in which leading critics of escalation like George F. Kennan and Lieutenant General James M. Gavin expressed their views.[115] The hearings provided a suitable forum for critics both inside Congress and outside to air their criticism of the policy of escalation in Vietnam. It proved to be an effective antidote to the pro-escalation offensives launched by "hawks" during the hearings of the Military Committees of both Houses. It placed Fulbright in the centre of the stage and hereafter he continued his campaign for the de-escalation of American military involvement in Vietnam with increasing vigour. In his television programme on 6 March 1966, he strongly opposed the mining of Haiphong. On 4 April, he charged that the US was interfering in a "civil war." In his interview to Eric Sevareid, published in *Look* of 19 April 1966, Fulbright asserted that "had we not struck our nose in the business, the problem would have long since been settled. . . ."[116] On 28 April, he charged that the US was suffering from "arrogance of power" leading to "over-extension of power and mission."[117] Fulbright had taken a stand and he did not waver subsequently.

The civil-military differences in the Pentagon over Vietnam reached their peak in 1967. McNamara himself had finally begun to favour slow de-escalation and negotiation with "Communists." The military was quite unhappy with his posture and the resulting tussle was reflected in the conflict between the hawks and doves in Congress.

By the end of the first quarter of 1967, the doves had succeeded in forming a solid bloc in Congress, especially in the Senate. Apart from Senators Morse and Gruening who had been fighting against the Vietnam involvement since 1964, other important recruits to this group were Senators Fulbright, Nelson, Church, McGovern, Gore, Javits, Aiken (Rep., Vermont), and Robert Kennedy (Dem., New York). It is pertinent to note that most of these Senators were members of the Foreign Relations Committee chaired by Fulbright. Kennedy, after some

[115] Ibid., 4 and 11 February 1966.
[116] Reported in *New York Times*, 20 April 1966.
[117] Ibid., 29 April 1966.

initial vacillation, finally broke with the Administration on 1 March 1967. He advocated an immediate step in the bombing of North Vietnam.[118]

Senator Mansfield (Dem., Montana), the Majority Leader, was still hesitating to decisively break with the Administration on Vietnam. He was the most well-known expert in Congress on Southeast Asia. In 1950s, the Senator had paid three visits to Vietnam. In December 1962, after his return from a visit to Southeast Asia, Mansfield gave a pessimistic report which was directly opposite to the optimistic reports of the Administration at that time. Again in 1965, he paid a visit to South Vietnam and recommended, in his report to Congress, against the deployment of US troops in South Vietnam. The next year he made another trip to South Vietnam and in his report to the Foreign Relations Committee, he urged immediate talks accompanied by ceasefire.[119] Gradually, his disaffection with the Administration's policy began to grow, but, till the end of the Johnson Administration, he did not completely break with it on Vietnam perhaps due to the fact that he was leading the party to which the President belonged.

Senator Clark (Dem., Pennsylvania) had moved an amendment to the war funds Bill which barred continued bombing of North Vietnam or increasing American troops beyond 500,000 without a declaration of war by Congress.[120] Senator Mansfield moved a compromise resolution, as a substitute for the Clark amendment. It expressed Congress support for efforts by President Johnson and "other men of goodwill" to prevent war extension, and reach a negotiated peace. This amendment was passed by the Senate.[121] It was interpreted as a setback for the hawks, but the military and hawkish Congress-

---

[118] Ibid., 2 March 1966.
[119] US Senate, Cong. 88, sess. 1, Committee on Foreign Relations, Report of Sen. Mike Mansfield, *et al*, *Vietnam and Southeast Asia* (Washington, D.C., 1963); US Senate, Cong. 89, sess. 2, Committee on Foreign Relations, Report of Sen. Mike Mansfield, *et al*, *The Vietnam Conflict: The Substance and the Shadow* (Washington; D.C., 1966); and US Senate, Cong. 90, sess. 1, Committee on Foreign Relations, Report of Sen. Mike Mansfield, *et al*, *The Rim of Asia* (Washington, D.C., 1967).
[120] *New York Times.*, 24 February 1967.
[121] Ibid., 25 February 1967.

men, who sought to extend the war to North Vietnam and who were opposed to any negotiation with the Viet Cong. It may be relevant to point out that the doves like Fulbright, Morse and Cooper supported the Mansfield amendment and the hawks, namely, Stennis, Russell and Thurmond voted against it.[122]

The "hawks" had also been well-organized in Congress. They intensified their criticism against McNamara for his "poor" handling of the Vietnam war. They charged that the American failure to win the war in Vietnam was due to the soft line taken by him. They accused him of "appeasing" Communists. During the hearings on the Defence Supplemental 1967, Senator Stennis asked McNamara why he did not accept General Westmoreland's recommendation for bombing strategically more important targets in Henoi and Haiphong.[123] The same question was also raised by Symington and Thurmond during the same hearing.[124] Senator Howard W. Cannon (Dem., Nevada) charged that the military had told him that they "had their hands tied" in so far as the bombing of the POL targets in North Vietnam was concerned.[125]

A similar pattern was repeated in the hearing on the same Bill by the House Appropriation Subcommittee on Defence. Representative Sikes stated that the US was condemning herself to a much longer war in South Vietnam if she continued to apply only low key pressure on North Vietnam.[126] The same point was made by Representative Mark Andrews (Rep., North Dakota). He reminded the Subcommittee that it had earlier been told by General Curtis LeMay, the retired Chief of the Strategic Air Command: "You can kill all the flies until : ou destroy the manure pile."[127]

In a sense, the counterpart of Senator Mansfield in the House of Representatives was Mahon, the highly respected Chairman

[122] Ibid.
[123] US Senate, Defence Subcommittee of the Committee on Appropriations and the Committee on Armed Services, n. 49, p. 51.
[124] Ibid., pp. 137 and 145.
[125] Ibid., p. 71.
[126] US House of Representatives, Defence Subcommittee of the Committee on Appropriations, n. 39, p. 77.
[127] Ibid., p. 53.

of the House Appropriation Committee. His role was not very clear-cut. He did not throw his weight decisively in favour of the either group—hawks or doves. He seemed to have developed suspicion regarding the validity of restrictions on bombing North Vietnam, but he did not take an extreme position along with other hawks over this issue. It is just possible that because of his long personal relationship with President Johnson who also belonged to Mahon's state—Texas—he did not want to break with the Administration. While questioning the Secretary on bombing restrictions, he also asked him whether, in reality, US security was involved in Vietnam.[128] By raising this question, although very late, he seemingly joined hands with the "doves" who had also started pressing this question. A "no" to this question would have undercut the major premise of "hawks" argument—the very basis of the American involvement in Vietnam.

The answers of Secretary McNamara and General Wheeler to Mahon's question were vague and obfuscating. General Wheeler tried to bring in a sharp distinction between the US "security" and her "long-term security interests." He stated, "I do not believe that our own security is involved, but certainly our security interests are involved."[129] McNamara said that besides the independence of South Vietnam which was at stake, it was the security of the United States, faced with political commitments worldwide, and faced with an interest in the preservation of peace in the major areas of the world that was at stake in Vietnam.[130]

One of the bitterest attacks on McNamara was made by Representative Jamie L. Whitten (Dem., Mississippi). He charged that the Secretary of Defence was violating the spirit of the Constitution. According to him, the post of the Secretary of Defence was created primarily to check the competitiveness of the services for dollars and arms and for organizing the war effort effectively. He complained that, never to his knowledge, was the Secretary of Defence supposed to "call the shots and run the war." He criticized the Secretary for "calling the targets" in

---

[128] Ibid., p. 64.
[129] Ibid., p. 65.
[130] Ibid.

Vietnam.[131] He implied that to run the war was the business of the military, not of the civilian leadership in the Pentagon. Another member who snipped at the Secretary was Congressman H.R. Gross (Rep., Iowa). On 15 February 1967, he charged on the Floor of House of Representatives that since the day McNamara began functioning as the custodian of the Pentagon, there had been an increased "muzzling" of the military. He alleged that the Secretary was trying to run the Congress of the United States.[132]

The attack on McNamara by the "hawks" reached its peak with the hearings by the Senate Preparedness Investigating Sub-committee of the Committee on Armed Services on the "Air War Against North Vietnam." It was a single-handed defence by McNamara against the joint criticism by his military colleagues of the Pentagon and the members of the Subcommittee chaired by Senator Stennis. One by one, all members of the JCS expressed, during their testimony before the Subcommittee, their sharp disagreements with the Secretary on the question of bombing North Vietnam. The pattern was set by Chairman Stennis who, in a statement before the hearings opened, asserted that a suspension or further restriction of the bombing would be "a tragic and perhaps fatal mistake."[133] Senator Thurmond complained that because of the delay in authorizing the POL strike, the enemy was able to disperse its fuel supplies.[134] He reminded the Subcommittee of the "domino" spectre, and desired to see America "win," not just pull out from Vietnam. He warned that if the United States withdrew from there, the whole of Southeast Asia would go to the Communists.[135] The Senator expressed his great disappointment with the statement of the Secretary in which he said that the primary objective of the US was to reduce the flow and/or to increase the cost of the continued infiltration of men and supplies from North to South Vietnam.

[131] US House of Representatives, Defence Subcommittee of the Committee on Appropriations, n. 55, p. 201.

[132] *New York Times*, 16 February 1967.

[133] US Senate, Cong. 90, sess. 1, Preparedness Investigating Subcommittee of the Committee on Armed Services, Hearings, *Air War Against North Vietnam* (Washington, D.C., 1967), part 1, p. 2.

[134] Ibid., p. 35.

[135] Ibid., p. 57.

He charged, "it is a statement of appeasing the Communists. It is a statement of no-win."[136] Senator Jackson (Dem., Washington) said that the fundamental problem was the Soviet Union; if the Soviets could be prevented effectively from supplying North Vietnam, the end of the war then could be predicted.[137] Senator Jack Richard Miller of Iowa observed that more effective use of the American air power and sea power could shorten the war.[138] The same point was made by Senator Symington in a more succint way. He said that what was needed was to attack the octopus in its head even though it might be only five per cent of the octopus.[139]

After three weeks of hearings, the Subcommittee urged President Johnson, in its report, to widen the air war against North Vietnam and discontinue the policy of "carefully controlled bombing."[140] It said that unless the air war was intensified, the US ground forces could not be asked to continue fighting in South Vietnam. Referring to the civil-military differences on the impact of bombing North Vietnam, the Subcommittee strongly supported the military's position. The report stated:

> The Secretary of Defense testified that he does not believe that such a campaign can stem the flow of supplies and goods sufficiently to prevent support of North Vietnamese and Viet Cong combat activity in South Vietnam at its present level. The Joint Chiefs and other military experts believe it can accomplish more—much more. It is their judgement that a less restricted air campaign which interdicts war material at the point of entry and the major arteries of supply will result in reduced support for aggression in South Vietnam and at the D.M.Z., curtailed activity by enemy units and reduced casualties for American and allied ground forces. As between these diametrically opposed views, and in view of the unsatisfactory progress of the war, logic and prudence require that the decision be with the unanimous weight of professional military judgement. From the record made before us, this appears to be the best and, very possibly, only hope for a

---

[136] Ibid., part 4, p. 297.
[137] Ibid., p. 299.
[138] Ibid., p. 311.
[139] Ibid., p. 335.
[140] *New York Times*, 1 September 1967.

successful end to the war as quickly as possible.[141]

The Stennis Subcommittee's attack on McNamara invited immediate reaction from the doves. They decried the way the hearing was conducted and the leakage of secret testimony given by the military representatives. They accused the Subcommittee of indulging in discrimination against Secretary McNamara. They charged that the Subcommittee invited only the generals and admirals who were already reported to have favoured intensified bombing of North Vietnam. It did not invite others who were known to be opposed to that view. Senator Stephen M. Young (Dem., Ohio) asked why the Subcommittee did not call Lt. Gen. James M. Gavin, Gen. Matthew B. Ridgway and Gen. David M. Shoup. The Senator held that the plea of the JCS for "unlimited bombing" in spite of the Secretary's statements was repugnant to the democratic process. "This is one more manifestation of the arrogant power which the Military Establishment has taken unto itself, and which threatens the vary basis of our Republic,"[142] the Senator declared. In the same vein, Senator Mansfield, the Majority Leader, observed that McNamara's statement (before the Preparedness Investigating Subcommittee) revealed again the wisdom of one of the most fundamental principles of the nation's constitutional structure—civilian direction of the Defence Establishment.[143] He was strongly supported by Senator Case.[144] Representative Don Edwards (Dem., California), said that there was a powerful coalition in Washington which seemed determined to escalate the war. This coalition, according to him, got the word from the military and fought for more bombs and more spending.[145]

One noteworthy feature in the posture of those who opposed the position of the military and its allies was their changed attitude towards the Secretary of Defence. While during the earlier phase they had been able to perceive no special merit in McNamara's reported efforts to hold on the demands of the military, they could now sense that the Secretary himself tended

---

[141] Ibid.
[142] *Congressional Record*, vol. 113, part 19, 1967, pp. 25388-9.
[143] Ibid., vol. 113, part 18, 1967, p. 24766.
[144] Ibid., p. 24768.
[145] Ibid., vol. 113, part 17, p. 22232.

to favour de-escalation and renewed efforts to seek a settlement. Thus whereas the hawks raised their criticism of the Secretary to a new height, their opponents adopted far milder attitude towards the Secretary, concentrated their fire on the military, and laid stress on the principle of the civilian control over the military.

While, in the month of August, the Stennis Subcommittee was conducting the hearing on the Air War in Vietnam, the Foreign Relations Committee was also having hearing on a "Sense of the Senate" Resolution introduced by Chairman Fulbright himself. It aimed at restoring a balance between the Executive and Congress in foreign policy-making. It said that any commitment of American troops abroad in future should be the joint action of the President and Congress.[146] It was passed by the Foreign Relations Committee by a vote of 14 to 0 on 16 November 1967. It was an indirect warning for the hawks— the military and its allies in Congress—who were then pressing for sending more American ground troops to South Vietnam. The news of McNamara stepping down from the post of Defence Secretary to accept the post of the President of World Bank was made public on 28 November 1967. It created a sensation in the United States. Some said that it was a victory of the military over the civilians within the Pentagon. Others believed that McNamara's "fall" was due to the civilian conspiracy—of those civilians having a vested interest in the continuation of the Vietnam war.[147] Those civilians allegedly included the members of the Military Committees and other civilian federal actors who were McNamara's competitors in the game of decision-making. Perhaps it was a combination of the military, the hawkish federal actors and the hawkish Congressional members who prevailed upon the "hawkish" President to take note of McNamara's changed attitude.

Even if it was certain in the beginning of 1968 that McNamara would leave office soon, his detractors in Congress missed no opportunity to subject him to their barrage to attacks. During the hearing by the House Defence Appropriations Subcommittee,

---

[146] *New York Times*, 17 November 1967.
[147] Gabriel Kolko, *The Roots of American Foreign Policy* (Boston, 1969), p. 47.

the Secretary met his old critics and faced the old questions on Vietnam. Chairman Mahon wanted to know how the decision-making with respect to Vietnam was being done in Washington. He inquired, in particular, about the alleged rift between the Secretary and the Military regarding the war. McNamara conceded that there was some disagreement between them, but he asserted that the "areas of disagreement" were "small."[148] Representatives Lipscomb and Minshall asked the Secretary why he was not recommending the mining of Haiphong. The Secretary replied, "it would not have a significant impact on the war."[149] Minshall adopted on old tactic of embarrassing the Secretary by asserting that no military man in the Pentagon shared his views on bombing. He asked the Secretary point blank, "who else shares your view about mining Haiphong on the military side?" McNamara declined to respond.[150]

A few days before he left office, McNamara was called to appear before the Foreign Relations Committee to clear an old record—his testimony in 1964 on the Tonkin Gulf incident. Because of increasing suspicion about the truthfulness of the account as supplied by the Executive at that time, the Committee decided to review the whole episode. As McNamara was the star witness in 1964 on the subject and as he continued to be the main actor till his exist from office, the Committee could not have found a better witness for the occasion. The only intriguing factor is the timing of the hearing. The Committee by this time must have been aware of the internal rift in the Pentagon over Vietnam. It must also not have been lost on Chairman Fulbright and those on the Committee who shared his views that the Secretary's position on Vietnam was at that time closer to theirs than to those of his own military associates. It was obvious that any attack on the Secretary at that time for his "mistakes" in the past was sure to strengthen the hands of their adversary—the military and other "hawks" in Congress. In spite of this risk, the Fulbright Committee went ahead with the hearings.

The most stringent attacks on McNamara were made by

---

[148] US House of Representatives, Cong. 90, sess. 2, Defence Subcommittee of the Committee on Appropriations, Hearings, *Department of Defence Appropriations for 1969* (Washington, D.C., 1968), part 1, pp. 50-8.

[149] Ibid., p. 116.

[150] Ibid., p. 117.

Senator Morse, Senator Gore and the Chairman himself. They argued very effectively that the De Soto patrols—the *Maddox* patrolling in the coast of North Vietnam—and, the 34A operations—the South Vietnam's attack on some villages of North Vietnam—were not unrelated. They were coordinated efforts and were directed by the same people in Saigon, it was argued. The De Soto patrolling was provocative in nature. It was electronic invasion of North Vietnam. The critics also pointed out that a draft or the Tonkin Resolution had already been prepared before this incident took place.[151] In spite of the vigorous rebuttals by McNamara, the Committee seemed to have won that round. In fact, the Secretary agreed to the compromise suggestion of Senator Symington toward the end of the hearing that the failure of the Executive—especially that of the Pentagon—to supply Congress some relevant information on the Tonkin incident involved no conspiracy by the Executive; it was an "innocent mistake."[152]

Inferences

During the period under review, the Administration presented to Congress and American public a picture of a "crisis situation" in Vietnam, followed by a course of action that involved successive doses of military escalation involving American forces in a shooting war in Vietnam. Since the course concerned security considerations and subsequent military actions in the field, the Pentagon emerged as the most prominent spokesman for the Administration before Congress. Heading the Department of Defence during the period was one of the ablest and sharpest men to have served in the cabinet since the end of the Second World War. Enjoying during much of the period the confidence of the President and having established by his innovative techniques and style his dominance over the department, including its military component, the Secretary was successful in getting Congressional approval for the Administration's course in whose

---

[151] US Senate, Cong. 90, sess. 2, Committee on Foreign Relations, Hearings, *The Gulf of Tonkin, The 1964 Incidents* (Washington, D.C., 1968), pp. 29, 31, 82-7, 100-3.
[152] Ibid.

formulation he himself had played a vital role. He claimed that the Administration's policy had the support and cooperation of the other elements of the Defence Department. The claim was not challenged before Congress by those elements even though the military representative cautiously expressed reservations, in the latter phase, over certain aspects. Despite a spate of criticisms, especially in the latter half of the period under review, from both "hawks" and "doves" in Congress, the Administration's policy, as expounded and endorsed by the Pentagon's civilian chief and his military associates, was not repudiated or even seriously mauled by any Congressional action during the period.

Over the years in the climate of Cold War and the "crusade against international Communism," Congress had become somewhat relaxed in the assertion of its powers and in submitting the appraisals of the Department, particularly those of the Pentagon to critical and detailed scrutiny. In an atmosphere of "crisis," and especially when a shooting war is in progress, the Congress tends to go along with the Administration and to deal gently with the Pentagon. When success is delayed and the costs mount, critics emerge in Congress and become increasingly vociferous. But, barring a few intrepid men, many of the critics themselves tend to be cautious to avoid giving the impression that their actions might endanger the national defence. Congress is particularly susceptible to the state of public opinion, and critics, particularly those who face re-election contests, tend to be doubly cautious in their voting, if not in their speeches.

During most of the period under review, the man in the White House was a Democrat who had been elected to a term on his own by a landslide in 1964. The Democratic Party had an overwhelming majority in both the Senate and the House of Representatives. The Secretary of Defence and the JCS were all appointees of the Democratic President. While some of the critics of the Administration and the Pentagon showed a disposition to put party considerations aside, a far greater number probably tended to avoid actions that might undercut the Administration and damage the political fortunes of the Party. The situation might have been different had the Republicans been in control of the two Houses by decisive majorities instead of the Democrats.

The emergence of differences between the Secretary of Defence and his military associates on a variety of issues pertaining to the Vietnam policy has been described in the present and some of the previous chapters. The possible interconnections of differences over weapons procurement, production and deployment with differences on Vietnam has also been indicated. At no time, however, did those differences, reach a point representing an extremely serious threat to the Administration or even to the facade of broad consensus on basic objectives as laid down by the President and Commander-in-Chief. The chain of authority was never subjected to extreme strain. Both the Secretary and the military representatives took care to represent themselves as carrying out the Administration's course as formulated by the President. And in the Pentagon itself no action of the military during this period could in any way be characterized as a challenge to the time-honoured concept of civilian control over the military. Within that situational framework the differences that did sprout up between the Secretary and Congress created some complications for both the components in their dealings with Congress.

As regards Vietnam, the Secretary and the JCS broadly shared some views till the middle of 1966. Both subscribed to the "domino" theory and both argued that American armed intervention was necessary to safeguard US security interests and to check Communist expansion. By the end of 1964, however, some minor differences had cropped up between the Secretary and the milittary. While the latter advocated a larger dose of American military involvement in Vietnam, the former stood for a comparatively smaller one. But the military leaders did not reveal their differences with the Secretary during Congressional hearings till the middle of 1966 though they might have "leaked" their misgivings to some sympathetic Congressional members. But when, towards the middle of 1966, they found that their breach with the Secretary had become serious, they began to differ from him while testifying before Congress. The civil-military conflict within the Pentagon over Vietnam reached its peak in August 1967 when the Senate Preparedness Investigating Subcommittee conducted hearings on the "Air War Against North Vietnam."

From 1964 to the middle of 1966, the military actors kept their differences with McNamara within the confines of the Executive. But the "hawks" in Congress had started criticizing the Secretary since 1964, though initially their complaints were kept on a low key. Their criticism of the Secretary began to mount in course of time and its zenith was marked by the hearings on Vietnam by the Senate Preparedness Investigating Subcommittee in August 1967. It seems that from 1964 onwards they were aware of the intra-Pentagon differences in regards to Vietnam and the source of this information were perhaps the "leaks" made by the military to their "allies" in Congress.

The discussion re-emphasizes the point that defence policy and foreign policy are interrelated; any change in one is likely to affect the other. It also suggests that the equation between Congress and the Pentagon in the field of defence policy is likely to influence their interaction in the realm of foreign policy. A cleavage between the Congress and the Pentagon on specific narrow issues of policy or strategy may not necessarily lead to severe strains in their interaction on the basic foreign policy approach. Here are mainly involved three leading actors, the Secretary of Defence, the JCS and the Committees concerned with military and foreign policy. Despite differences on specific issues, there was more or less broad endorsement of the basic objective of safeguarding and promoting American security interest. In articulating these interests, the Pentagon played a key role and the civil and military components, working in unison, were able, as pointed out earlier, to create a significant impact on the policy-making relating to Vietnam.

The viewpoints of Military Committees were found to be influenced to a great extent by the attitude and interests of the military than by the appraisal of the defence Secretary, especially if there were indications that the Secretary was not seeing eye to eye with the military. If there was a large degree of agreement between the Defence Secretary and the JCS on any foreign policy issue, the Military Committees went along with them, even if there was already some strain between the Secretary and Congress on some defence matters. On the other hand, in such cases where the relationship between Congress and the Secretary became somewhat strained due to their difference on defence matters, it got further exacerbated when there was a rift between the Secretary and the JCS. It is also pertinent to inquire if it is true the other way round—a rift on foreign policy heightening the strain due to differences on defence matters. It is plausible to argue that the disaffection with the Secretary among Congressional elements, especially hawks, over Vietnam sharpened the Congressional attack on McNamara in 1966 and 1967 on the ABM issue.

Defence budgets from 1961 to 1968 were overwhelmingly passed in both Houses. In this regard, one may look at the Supplementary Defence Appropriations, 1965-1967, which were primarily meant for the Vietnam war. The Defence Supplemental 1965 was passed by the House of Representatives by a margin of 408-7, and by the Senate, 88-3. In the case of the 1966 Supplemental, the margins in the House of Representatives and the Senate were 389-3, and 87-2 respectively. The 1967 first Supplemental was passed by the House of Representatives by a vote of 385-11, and also, by a wide margin by the Senate. Attempts by "doves" to insert amendments relating to Vietnam hardly received any support in either House. The Morse amendment of 1 March 1966 that the Tonkin resolution of 1964 should be repealed was defeated in the Senate by 92 to 5.[153] The Gruening amendment of 24 February 1966 that draftees should not be sent to Southeast Asia for combat without the consent of Congress was rejected by the Senate, 94 to 2.[154] The House of Representatives, by a vote of 123 to 2, rejected the Brown amendment which said that none of the funds appropriated in the 1967 first Defence Supplemental could be available for the implementation of any plan to invade North Vietnam with American ground forces "except in time of war."[155] The Morse amendment of 22 August 1967 which sought to cut the 1968 Defence Appropriation Bill by 10 per cent was defeated in the Senate by a margin of 85 to 5.[156] The record thus shows, as already mentioned, that basically the Administration was able to have its way decisively with Congress, between 1965 and 1967. The contribution of the representatives of the Defence Department in this respect was quite significant.

---

[153] *Congressional Record*, vol. 112, part 4, 1966, p. 4370.
[154] Ibid., vol. 112, part 3, 1966, p. 3956.
[155] Ibid., vol. 113, part 6, 1967, p. 6886.
[156] Ibid., vol. 113, part 18, 1967, p. 23471.

It brings out the reluctance of Congress to "knock" the Pentagon when American security is held to be involved and especially if a shooting war is in progress. Both Houses, with almost equal enthusiasm, followed the Pentagon's lead. They expressed their belief in the "domino" theory and overwhelmingly supported American military intervention in Vietnam. There was hardly interest shown by either of the Houses in appraising the validity of the "domino" theory and questioning the theory that important US security interests were involved in Vietnam. The effort made by a few "doves" in Congress at having a second look at the ongoing Vietnam policy could hardly make any headway. Once American boys are in the battlefield, it would require tremendous courage and determination on the part of a Congressional member to initiate a move to deny money sought by the Pentagon or to assert that the GIs have illegally been sent to a wrong place to fight a wrong war. So, when the chips were down, many "doves" themselves did not vote in favour of anti-war amendments moved by their more determined fellow-"doves." This phenomenon was noticed in both Houses alike.

As the civil-military conflict within the Pentagon intensified in correspondence to the escalation of the war, both adversaries tended to seek allies outside the Pentagon. It seems that the alliance between the military and the "hawks" in Congress was built on an organized basis. But one is not sure if the common stand taken by the civilian elements of the Pentagon and the "doves" in Congress against the escalation of the war was the result of any formal alignment between them. It is just possible that in the beginning, their common fight against escalation was accidental, but as the "dove-hawk" fight mounted in intensity, they became increasingly conscious of the need of co-ordinating their efforts aimed at de-escalating the war. During the second phase of this "alliance," the civilian elements of the Defence Department might have "leaked" some important information on the war to their "allies" in Congress.

The members of Congress tend to use Congressional Committees which they happen to control for propagating views that they champion. This was true both of "hawks" and "doves" in regard to Vietnam. The "hawks" who were in control of the Military Committees—the Armed Services Committees and Defence Appropriations Subcommittees of both Houses—made ample use of them to strongly criticize the Secretary and support the military over Vietnam. Senator Stennis' Preparedness Investigating Subcommittee which held a hearing on the "Air War Against North Vietnam" at the height of tension in August 1967, invited only those generals who were known to advocate a pro-escalation policy. It did not call in reputed generals like Ridgway and Gavin to testify before the Committee. At the other end, Senator Fulbright's Foreign Relations Committee which held several hearings on Vietnam invited amongst others George Kennan, General Ridgway and Lt. Gen. James Gavin who were known advocates of de-escalation. One is not sure if Committee membership tends to influence one's opinion on a foreign policy issue. But members, and particularly the Chairman, tend to make use of the Committe for propagating their viewpoint on any such issue.

Members of Congress would tend to go with their allies in the Pentagon so long as their interests, as they view them, are identical or compatible. But if there is conflict between the two, the former would not hesitate to do something which might endanger the interest of the latter. Chairman Fulbright and other "dovish" members of the Foreign Relations Committee were aware that their Committee holding a hearing on the Tonkin Gulf incident would weaken the position of civilian elements of the Pentagon led by Secretary McNamara who at that time were advocating de-escalation. But, nevertheless, they went ahead with the hearings probably because they were anxious to have the record show that their earlier actions, taken in good faith, were on the basis of inadequate, inaccurate, and at times misleading information made available to them by the Executive branch. It was thus part of an effort to explain the role of the legislature to the American public and, in respect of Fulbright and his allies, to justify their criticism of the course of the Executive, especially that of the Pentagon, in having "misled" them in the initial phase when escalation was decided on. In doing so they placed their perceived institutional interests as members of the Foreign Relations Committee higher than the interest of their "ally" in a common cause.

The increasingly Congressional division on Vietnam was marked more by "dove-hawk" cleavage than by partisanship. The coalition of hawkish Democrats (mostly from the South), and hawkish Republicans continued to hold together against the anti-war campaign by "doves" spearheaded by Fulbright. However, partisanship was not completely absent. Some top Republicans tried to reap partisan advantage out of the troubles that a Democratic Administration had led the country into. They hardly missed an opportunity to remind the American people that the Vietnam involvement started under a Democratic (Kennedy) Administration and that another Democratic (Johnson) Administration led the country into war. They attacked McNamara hard perhaps with the view thereby to undermining the credibility of President Johnson, as McNamara was considered the most influential member of his cabinet in respect of Vietnam policy. That such was the Republican tactic was not without its impact on the Democratic members, with the exception of the most determined critics of the Administration.

CHAPTER SEVEN

CONCLUSIONS

Among the conclusions that the present study points to, the following may be cited:

1. The Pentagon—the civilian and military components of the Department of Defence—was not a monolithic behemoth formulating its own course on policy-making relating to Vietnam and imposing it on the rest of the Executive branch of the United States Government.

2. The tradition of civilian control of the military never came under any severe strain as policy was formulated and implemented. The President's authority was never even remotely questioned or challenged by the Pentagon. Within the Pentagon the authority of the civilian Secretary of Defence was real and not nominal.

3. At no point did the Pentagon act as though it could take the legislative branch for granted. While using various techniques for influencing Congressional opinion, the Pentagon nevertheless functioned with a continual awareness of the constitutional powers of the legislative branch.

4. The Pentagon did not at any point act as though public opinion was an irrelevant factor. While employing various techniques of propaganda, public relations, and news management, it functioned with the awareness that public opinion would be of crucial importance in determining the future of a course favoured by it.

5. In the making of policy towards a foreign country or region, the Pentagon's role increases in a crisis situation and becomes even greater when the shooting starts.

6. The Pentagon has to reckon with other federal actors who influence foreign policy-making area including the State Department, the CIA, the White House Staff (especially the National Security Adviser), and other extra-Executive actors

including Congressional leaders and friends of the President whom he may bring in from time to time. Because of organizational rivalry, bureaucratic politics and clashing personal interests, the possibility exists of conflict among actors who eventually tend to reach compromises through bargaining.

7. If the Pentagon itself is in a position to achieve internal unity and harmony on a given issue, it is better placed to win acceptance for its point of view and to exploit possible differences among non-Pentagon agencies. The reverse becomes possible if the Pentagon is unable to present a united front.

8. The Pentagon itself may at times be a divided house. Rifts may develop between the civilian and military elements of the Pentagon. A rift on matters relating to the development, production and procurement of weapons may have spill over effects affecting their interaction in foreign policy.

9. The Secretary of Defence is in a strong position to deal with his non-Pentagon bureaucratic competitors when he is able to carry with him the whole organization—both the civilian and military components included. When he is able to maintain unity and harmony among the civilians subordinate to him, he is in a better position in his bargaining with the JCS. Similarly, the JCS will be on a good wicket in dealing with the Secretary when it achieves unanimity and commands the support of senior officers down the line.

10. During the entire period including the spells of sharp disagreement, no disposition was seen on the part of either of the components of the Pentagon to defy established constitutional procedures. That such was the case in the midst of a very trying, divisive national ordeal was a commentary on the stability of the American political system.

The Defence Department is a vast bureaucracy. The relationship between the civilian and military components of the Department of Defence may be strained either due to their differences relating to weapons matters or due to their conflicting approaches to some foreign policy issues with national security implications. As weapons policy and foreign policy are interrelated, the conflict between the civilian and military elements of the Pentagon in one area may spill over to the other area. Such conflicts may occur at several points and on several levels. There may arise a rift between one service and another service or more than one service. The civilian and military elements of one service may fight against the civilian and military elements of another service. Conflict may also spring up among the military branches themselves over roles and missions, rival weapons programmes and rival war strategies.

In regard to their role in shaping the foreign policy, both the civilian and military elements of the Pentagon have to compete with other federal actors. They have to take into account the attitude of the President and of Congress. At times the President, the ultimate decision-makers, himself becomes an adversary in the bureaucratic game of decision-making when he is seen to be tilting significantly towards a point of view advocated by a rival actor or coalition of actors. In such a case, the Pentagon, as an entity or that component that finds its point of view not getting the desired degree of acceptance by the President, seeks to mobilize whatever leverage it may be able to bring to bear in order to induce the President to reconsider his position. Sometimes the President retreats from his position and adjusts to a different viewpoint.

So long as there is a broad agreement between the civilian and military elements of the Pentagon regarding any issue, the prospects of the Pentagon having its way will be greater, with some accommodation in respect of the views of other major federal actors so as to evolve the appearance of a consensus. Only when there arises a rift between the two segments of the Defence Department, other federal actors tend to come in and utilize such differences to their advantage. However, if there is a broad consensus between the civilian and military elements of the Pentagon, the military actors do not tend to allow their differences, if any, over matters relating to the production and procurement of weapons, to vitiate that consensus. But when the military members find that the Secretary of Defence advocates a course in foreign policy much different from theirs, they might blend the two issues in indicating their divergence from the Secretary and thus laying the latter open to criticism from Congress, the media and from other federal actors as well.

When a conflict arises in the Pentagon between its civilian and military components, they tend to seek "allies" from the outside. They would compete for winning the co-operation of other federal actors, Congressional members, pressure groups, the press and others who are in a position to influence the decision-making. Extra-Pentagon actors, especially those with their interests at stake, sometimes volunteer their help and take sides in the conflict. The military elements have their "natural allies" in weapons-related industries, and service associations which are, in terms of men and money, powerful and well-organized. The civilian elements of the Pentagon also have the support of these entities, but when they develop differences with the military, the support is not forthcoming in similar measure. In such a situation, they do not have dependable, indentifiable allies. As a result, a pro-military campaign is launched quicker than the pro-civilian one. The elements which would rally behind the civilian components of the Pentagon are disparate, lacking existing unified organization.

When a serious breach occurs within the Executive, especially within the Pentagon, the adversaries tend to "leak" sensitive materials to outside friendly and sympathetic elements. As the conflict prolongs and one party seems to be winning over another, the latter would be inclined to be more active in "leaking" information selectively in order to reverse the trend of the game. During the period of the intensification of the conflict between the civilian and military elements of the Pentagon over the Vietnam war, "leaks" occurred frequently and the military which, at the outset, felt disappointed due to the resistance of the Defence Secretary to its move for escalation, seemed to have indulged more in leaking than the civilian elements of the Pentagon.

Apart from "leaks", the adversaries within the Pentagon tend, when matters advance beyond a certain point, to give indication of their differences and even use cautiously-phrased criticisms in Congressional forums. Friendly elements in Congress are inclined to make speeches on the floor in support of their respective allies in the Pentagon. They also tend to launch and run Congressional hearings in order to enable their allies to express their viewpoints in the most advantageous manner. Apart from the witnesses from the Pentagon, Congressional Committees generally invite persons from the outside who would support the dominant point of view, though an opposing point of view cannot be altogether shut off since unanimity is seldom achieved among all Committees themselves. When the rift between the civilian and military components of the Pentagon over Vietnam reached its nadir, the Senate Preparedness Investigating Subcommittee of the Armed Services Committee conducted, in August 1967, long, prolonged, and intensive hearings in which all but one (McNamara) were only military witnesses. Another example of this sort was a hearing on Vietnam conducted by Senator Fulbright's Foreign Relations Committee which invited, amongst others, George Kennan and Lt. Gen. James Gavin who were known to be opposed to escalation.

Continuity in service, better organization, and greater resources are factors that help the military in any duel with the civilian elements of the Pentagon, but they may not ensure the victory to the military. Because of the well-entrenched traditional civilian control they do not push their opposition to a point of no return. Other factors like the domestic and international public opinion, developments in the battlefield, the attitude of other federal actors, Congress and the President would finally determine the outcome of the duel.

In peace time the Pentagon plays second fiddle to the State Department in the field of foreign policy, but once a crisis situation involving national security is seen to develop and even more when shooting starts, the former tends to move increasingly to the centre in respect of decision-making. Before the shooting starts, the general on the field generally tends to follow the lead of his superiors in the Pentagon. But once the fighting starts, he tends to increasingly assert himself *vis-a-vis* the latter. As American soldiers in large numbers are deployed in the field and as the war escalates, his influence in policy-making tends to increase. General Westmoreland stood in the wings and the Washington players and Ambassador Taylor occupied the centre of the stage from the Tonkin incident of August 1964 to June 1965. Then Westmoreland made a big push for increased American ground involvement in South Vietnam. As the war escalated, the general exercised increased influence in policy-making in regard to Vietnam.

Federal actors, while taking decisions on foreign policy, keep in mind the "shared interest", i.e., the picture that the dominant persons in Washington have on a particular issue and also the public opinion at home concerning the issue. This hypothesis, however, is subject to two qualifications. The higher an official is placed, the greater is his awareness of these factors and *vice versa*. Secondly, an actor on the field abroad might tend to be less concerned about domestic public opinion than the actors in Washington.

Coming to the Pentagon, the Secretary and his civilian colleagues tend to give more weightage to the "shared interest," political constraints and compulsions, and the public opinion at home than his military colleagues both in Washington and on the field abroad. Among the military elements, the JCS tend to be more influenced by such considerations than those lower down. That was mainly responsible for the differences over Vietnam between McNamara and the military in general, and between the JCS and the CUMUSMACV in the initial phase of American military involvement in Vietnam—up to June 1965. Only after the war escalated and the civil-military line was drawn in the Pentagon, the JCS and Westmoreland bridged the distance between themselves and took a common stand against the civilian elements of the Pentagon. In this case, the JCS, as often happens, tended to support the assessment concerning reinforcements put forth by the field commander.

Decision-making is influenced by organizationalism. While taking a stand, an actor would tend to take into account the interest of his organization. But this awareness would progressively diminish upward. In other words, the higher an official is placed, the less he is affected by organizational consideration, the more he is inclined to be influenced by "shared image", personal interest and other extra-organizational considerations. The lower an official is placed in the organizational ladder, the more he tends to be bound by the interest of his organization. Secretary Rusk preferred to be a judge than a manager. He avoided being caught in inter-agency conflicts. He did not show much interest in assuming for his Department inter-agency leadership. But given Rusk's general attitudes, Kennedy increasingly looked for inter-agency leadership to the Defence Department headed by Robert McNamara who showed traits of dynamism and leadership. As a result, the task of defending the interest of the State Department fell upon Rusk's deputies like Bowles, Ball, Harriman and Hilsman. These officials were very much concerned over the constitution of a Vietnam Task Force under the chairmanship of Gilpatric, the Deputy Secretary of Defence. Immediately they made efforts for reconstituting the Task Force and within a short time succeeded in replacing Gilpatric by Ball as its chairman. Similarly these officials were disappointed when Rostow and Taylor were sent to South Vietnam in October 1961. They felt bad because such an important mission was not led,—indeed, did not even include— a high official of the State Department. For the most part of 1963 before the coup against Diem took place, Harriman and Hilsman of the State Department fought bitterly with the civilian and military members of the Pentagon.

Information is an important source of power. It is capable of significantly influencing the formulation of a policy. Besides access to information, the way it flows within an organization or among the various agencies constituting the decision-making machinery is of much importance. In order to play an active and vigorous role in policy-making, President Kennedy often bypassed the regular channels and tapped some lower officials to elicit information. When, in August 1963, the National Security Council decided to seek some information from the Saigon mission regarding the state of affairs in South Vietnam, the JCS immediately used their "back channel" to advise General Harkins, the head of the American Military Assistance Command, Saigon, the way he should answer some of the questions of Washington. Independent of the controversy over the manner in which the 24 August 1963 State message to Ambassador Lodge was cleared by some principal actors who were outside Washington on that day, the fact that such an important and controversial message could be cleared, in a short time, by the various agencies and sent to the American Ambassador in Saigon suggests the extent to which the control over information and communication-flow may influence the outcome of a policy. In August 1964 the Executive managed to win the quick approval of Congress for the Tonkin resolution by telling the latter only a part of the story and by suppressing some relevant, important information about the incident.

Policy-making is a bureaucratic game which involves conflict, bargain and compromise. Conflict occurs because of organiza. tional interests, bureaucratic politics, personal interests and cultural background of various actors. Conflict is accepted as a part of the game, but it is not overstretched, because it may endanger the game itself. Hence arises the need of compromise which is reached through bargaining. An actor has to concede some points in order that he may retain the rest of his package. He cannot bargain away something which he considers vital for him. The conflict-bargain-compromise process takes place not only within the Executive, but also inside each agency. Throughout the period under review there was a prolonged conflict between the civilian and military elements of the Pentagon in regard to weapons matters as well as to Vietnam, especially from 1965 to 1967. The more the military pressed for intensification of the war, the more the Secretary sought to restrain them. But at the end of each round, the decision was a compromise. Each time the military was offered a part of the package it had asked for which succeeded in keeping the military on board. Each concession to the military, however, had its own mmoentum—and the military leaders were conscious of it. In successive rounds the military was able to bring increased concessions from the Defence Secretary and the President. In other words, policy-making is incremental. Each policy is a cumulative product of a few successive decisions, each successive decision being increasingly closer to the final outcome.

The present study suggests that none of the three models described at the outset would, by itself, be able to explain the formulation of foreign policy. Systemic interaction, organizational interest, and bureaucratic politics, are important variables affecting policy-making. Sometimes one of these factors may alone be responsible for a policy, or it may be the most dominant factor influencing its outcome. But often a combination of these variables determines the emergence of a policy. An actor, while making his debut in policy-making, keeps in mind the broad national goals, the interest of his organization, his personal interest, the "shared image" dominant among Washington actors, the public opinion at home and abroad and the attitude of the ultimate decision-maker. It would be difficult to accurately predict the relative importance of these variables at any given point of time. The importance of any variable would vary from situation to situation, from time to time. In the present study, both the civilian and military elements of the

Pentagon were influenced, more or less, by the above forces while taking part in policy-making in regard to Vietnam. Secretary McNamara was perhaps not less ardent at the outset than any other federal actor in championing the domino theory and in advocating the mission of "containing international Communism." He was interested not only in asserting civilian supremacy in the Pentagon, but also in claiming for his Department an ever-increasing role, in relation to others, in the field of foreign policy-making. He might also have liked to build his personal image—a task which became increasingly easier for him. He had probably a clearer knowledge than others of the Kennedy mind, as for instance, the President's inclination in November 1961 to take a tough stand in Vietnam as well as his reluctance at that time to send American ground troops to that country. He also sought to bear in mind the state of domestic public opinion.

The military members of the Pentagon were also aware of political considerations, though not to the same extent as their civilian Secretary was. Several times, after stating first their "pure military" recommendations, they said that if those recommendations were not acceptable because of *political considerations*, they would propose a different modified package. The Defence Secretary is a political appointee, personally responsible to the President and at any time he may be fired by him. But the status of the military is different. They are "regular" officers in the military service, selected and promoted through established procedures, having tenure till the prescribed age of retirement. A general may be shifted from an important position to one less important if the President is not happy with him. But he cannot be thrown out of his job before his normal retirement age even if he gives indication of reservations about some policy of the Administration. The difference in the nature of the jobs of the civilian and military elements of the Pentagon is partly responsible for the difference in their susceptibility to be influenced by public opinion and political compulsions and constraints. It was, therefore, not a surprise that toward the end of 1966 and in the beginning of 1967 when American public got increasingly restive about the American military involvement in Vietnam, it was McNamara, not the JCS, who changed his tone regarding the war.

It is difficult for an actor to dissociate himself from an ongoing policy or to oppose it if in the past he had been intimately associated with it or strongly identified with it. McNamara started developing doubts about the Vietnam policy since the beginning of 1966 and he became disenchanted with it by the middle of that year, but he could not break with the policy overnight. In the public's eye, he was the main architect of the ongoing policy. It would have been very difficult for him to convince others of the rightness of any sudden change on Vietnam. Slowly he prepared the way for his final breach in May 1967 with the policy pursued by the Administration. Largely for this reason it was difficult for William Bundy in late 1967 to completely identify himself with McNamara's changed position in regard to Vietnam. On the other hand, it is relatively easier for an actor to challenge a policy if he had not been intimately involved in the past in its formulation. Ball was mainly pre-occupied with European affairs before he started taking keen interest in Vietnam. Similarly, Katzenbach did not have any association with Vietnam before he was appointed as the Under Secretary of State in place of Ball. As a result, these two actors did not face much psycological constraints in challenging the ongoing Vietnam policy during the period of escalation.

The present study does not susbstantiate either of the hypotheses that the military as a part of the "power elite" controls foreign policy and the military is a conduit for the civilians for representing the latter's interest in foreign policy. At no point of time during the period under review did the military control the policy-making in regard to Vietnam. Its importance in decision-making varied from time to time. Its influence gradually increased as the war escalated. But it was not even then the sole or even decisive controlling force. Many influential civilian actors in Washington also favoured escalation. Therefore it would be wrong to infer that the military dominated the making of Vietnam policy, even its escalation phase.

It would also be equally wrong to suggest that the military was just the instrument of civilians for ensuring the reflection of the latter's interest in foreign policy. The military is an independent entity with its own life and interest. It would co-operate with civilians as long as their interests are identical. When their interests clash, the military would tend to pay serious attention to its organizational interests. It will present its demands and place on record the implications of a refusal or reduction of its demands. It cannot afford to jeopardise the image of the organization and its future role. The military is not always a unified house. Nor are the civilians. Both houses may get divided on issues and several varieties of coalitions of the components of both sides take place. The military, in pursuance of its objectives, would join hands with military industries, service associations, and friendly elements of Congress having the same or similar interest. But in doing so, the military does not see itself as just serving the interest of these "allies". It enters into such an alliance only in the pursuit of its perceived interests. The military neither controls foreign policy-making, nor does it play simply the role of an instrument or a conduit for serving the interests of civilians. The truth lies somewhere between the two.

SELECT BIBLIOGRAPHY

Primary Sources

Government Documents

U.S. *Congressional Record* (Washington, D.C.), for the years 1960-1968.

U.S. Department of State, *Department of State Bulletin* (Washington, D C.), for the years 1960-1968.

US House of Representatives, Congress 83, Session 2, Defence Subcommittee of the Committee on Appropriations, Hearings, *Department of Defence and Related Independent Agencies: Appropriations for 1955* (Washington, D.C., 1954).

———, Cong. 84, sess. 1, Defence Subcommittee of the Committee on Appropriations, Hearings, *Department of Defence Appropriations for 1956* (Washington, D.C., 1955).

———, Cong. 85, sess. 1, Defence Subcommittee of the Committee on Appropriations, Hearings, *Department of Defence Appropriations for 1958* (Washington, D.C., 1957).

———, Cong. 87, sess. 1, Defence Subcommittee of the Committee on Appropriations, Hearings, *Department of Defence Appropriations for 1962* (Washington, D.C., 1961).

———, Cong. 87, sess. 2, Defence Subcommittee of the Committee on Appropriations, Hearings, *Department of Defence Appropriations for 1963* (Washington, D.C., 1962).

———, Cong. 88, sess. 2, Defence Subcommittee of the Committee on Appropriations, Hearings, *Department of Defence Appropriations for 1965* (Washington, D.C., 1964).

———, Cong. 89, sess. 1, Committee on Appropriations, Hearings, *Supplemental Department of Defence Appropriation for 1965* (Washington, D.C., 1965).

———Cong, 89, sess. 1, Defence Subcommittee of the Committee on Foreign Operations and Related Agencies Appropriations of the Committee on Appropriations, Hearings, *Foreign Assistance and Related Agencies Appropriations for 1966* (Washington, D.C., 1965).

——, Cong. 89, sess. 2, Defence Subcommittee of the Committee on Appropriations, Hearings, *Department of Defence Appropriations for 1966* (Washington, D.C., 1965).

————, Cong. 89, sess. 2, Defence Subcommittee of the Committee on Appropriations, Hearings, *Department of Defence Appropriations for 1967* (Washington, D.C., 1966).

————, Cong. 89, sess. 2, Defence Subcommittee of the Committee on Appropriations, Hearings, *Supplemental Defence Appropriations for 1966* (Washington, D.C., 1966).

————, Cong. 90, sess. 1, Defence Subcommittee of the Committee on Appropriations, Hearings, *Supplemental Defence Appropriations for 1967* (Washington, D.C., 1967).

————, Cong. 90, sess. 1, Defence Subcommittee of the Committee on Appropriations, Hearings, *Department of Defence Appropriations for 1968* (Washington, D.C., 1967).

————, Cong. 90, sess. 2, Defence Subcommittee of the Committee on Appropriations, Hearings, *Department of Defence Appropriations for 1969* (Washington, D.C., 1968).

————, Cong. 92, sess. 1, Committee on Armed Services, Committee Print, *United States-Vietnam Relations 1945-1967: Study Prepared by the Department of Defence* (Washington, D.C., 1971), 12 vols.

US Senate, Cong. 83, sess. 1, Defence Subcommittee of the Committee on Appropriations, Hearings, *Department of Defence Appropriations for 1954* (Washington, D.C., 1953).

————, Cong. 83, sess. 2, Defence Subcommittee of the Committee on Appropriations, Hearings, *Department of Defence Appropriations for 1955* (Washington, D.C., 1954).

————, Cong. 84, sess. 1, Defence Subcommittee of the Committee on Appropriations, Hearings, *Department of Defence Appropriations for 1956* (Washington, D.C., 1955).

————, Cong. 84, sess. 2, Defence Subcommittee of the Committee on Appropriations, Hearings, *Department of Defence Appropriations for 1957* (Washington, D.C., 1956).

————, Cong. 85, sess. 1, Defence Subcommittee of the Committee on Appropriations, Hearings, *Department of Defence*

Appropriations for 1958 (Washington, D.C., 1957).

————, Cong. 85, sess. 1, Committee on Appropriations, Hearings, *Mutual Security Appropriations for 1958* (Washington, D.C., 1957).

————, Cong. 85, sess. 2, Subcommittee of the Committee on Appropriations, Hearings, *Department of Defence Appropriations for 1959* (Washington, D.C., 1958).

————, Cong. 86, sess. 1, Defence Subcommittee of the Committee on Appropriations, Hearings, *Department of Defence Appropriations for 1960* (Washington, D.C., 1959).

————, Cong. 86, sess. 2, Defence Subcommittee of the Committee on Appropriations, Hearings, *Department of Defence Appropriations for 1961* (Washington, D.C., 1960).

————, Cong. 87, sess. 1, Defence Subcommittee of the Committee on Appropriations, Hearings, *Department of Defence Appropriations for 1962* (Washington, D.C., 1961).

————, Cong. 87, sess. 2, Defence Subcommittee of the Committee on Appropriations, Hearings, *Department of Defence Appropriations for 1963* (Washington, D.C., 1962).

————, Cong. 88, sess. 1 Defence Subcommittee of the Committee on Appropriations, Hearings, *Department of Defence Appropriations for 1964* (Washington, D.C., 1963).

————, Cong. 88, sess. 2, Defence Subcommittee of the Committee on Appropriations, and the Committee on Armed Services, Joint Hearings, *Department of Defence Appropriations for 1965* (Washington, D.C., 1964).

————, Cong. 89, sess. 1, Committee on Appropriations and Committee on Armed Services, Joint Hearings, *Supplemental Appropriations for the Department of Defence 1965, Emergency Fund, Southeast Asia* (Washington, D.C., 1965).

————, Cong. 89, sess. 1, Defence Subcommittee of the Committee on Appropriations, and the Committee on Armed Services, Joint Hearings, *Department of Defence Appropriations, 1966* (Washington, D.C., 1965).

————, Cong. 89, sess. 2, Defence Subcommittee of the Committee on Appropriations, Hearings, *Department of Defence Appropriations for Fiscal Year 1967* (Washington, D.C., 1966).

————, Cong. 90, sess. 1, Defence Subcommittee of the Committee on Appropriations, and the Committee on Armed

Services, Joint Hearings, *Supplemental Defence Appropria-tions and Authorizations, Fiscal Year 1967* (Washington, D.C., 1967).

————, Cong. 90, sess. 1, Defence Subcommittee of the Committee on Appropriations, Hearings, *Department of Defence Appropriations for Fiscal Year 1968* (Washington, D.C., 1968).

————, Cong. 90, sess. 2, Defence Subcommittee of the Committee on Appropriations, Hearings, *Department of Defence Appropriations for Fiscal Year 1969* (Washington, D.C., 1968).

US Senate, Cong. 87, sess. 1, Committee on Armed Services, Hearings, *Military Procurement Authorization Fiscal Year 1962* (Washington, D.C., 1961).

————, Cong. 88, sess. 1, Committee on Armed Services, Hearings, *Military Procurement Authorization Fiscal Year 1964* (Washington, D.C., 1963).

————, Cong. 90, sess. 1, Preparedness Investigating Subcommittee of the Committee on Armed Services, Hearings, *Air War Against North Vietnam*: Parts 1-4 (Washington, D.C., 1967).

————Cong, 86, sess. 2, Committee on Foreign Relations, *United States Foreign Policy: The Formulation and Administration of United States Foreign Policy, Study Prepared by the Brookings Institution* (Washington, D.C., 1960).

Other Documents

Department of State, *American Foreign Policy, 1950-1955: Basic Documents*, 2 vols., Washington, D.C., 1957.

————, *American Foreign Policy: Current Documents 1959*, Washington, D.C., 1963.

US Senate, Cong. 83, sess. 1, Committee on Foreign Relations, *Indochina: Report of Sen. Mike Mansfield on a Study Mission to the Associated States of Indo-China, Vietnam, Cambodia, Laos*, 27 October 1953, Washington, D.C., 1953.

————, Cong. 83, sess. 2, Committee on Foreign Relations, *Report on Indochina: Report of Sen. Mike Mansfield on a Study Mission to Vietnam, Cambodia, Laos*, 15 October 1954,

Washington, D.C., 1954.

———, Cong. 84, sess. 1, Committee on Foreign Relations, *Vietnam, Cambodia and Laos, Report by Sen. Mansfield 6 October 1955*, Washington, D.C., 1955.

———, Cong. 88, sess. 1, Committee on Foreign Relations *Vietnam and Southeast Asia, Report of Sen. Mansfield and others*, Washington, D.C., 1963.

———, Cong. 89, sess. 2, Committee on Foreign Relations, *The Vietnam Conflict: The Substance and the Shadow, Report of Sen. Mansfield and others*, Washington, D.C., 1966.

———, Cong. 90, sess. 1, Committee on Foreign Relations, *The Rim of Asia, Report of Sen. Mansfield*, Washington, D.C., 1967.

Books and Memoirs

Acheson, Dean, *Present at the Creation: My Years in the State Department*, New York, 1969.

Ball, George W., *The Discipline of Power: Essentials of a Modern World Structure*, Boston, 1968.

Bowles, Chester, *Promises to Keep: My Years in Public Life, 1941-1969*, New York, 1971.

Dulles, Allen, *The Craft of Intelligence*, New York, 1963.

Eisenhower, Dwight D., *The White House Years. vol. 1: Mandate for Change, 1953-1956*, New York, 1963.

Gavin, James M., *War and Peace in the Space Age*, New York, 1958.

Hilsman, Roger, *To Move a Nation: The Politics of Foreign Policy in the Administration of John F. Kennedy*, New York, 1967.

———, *The Politics of Policy-Making in Defence and Foreign Affairs*, New York, 1971.

Hoopes, Townsend, *The Limits of Intervention: An Inside Account of How the Johnson Policy of Escalation in Vietnam was Reversed*, New York, 1969.

Jackson, Henry M., ed., *The National Security Council: Jackson Subcommittee Papers on the Conduct of American Foreign Policy*, New York, 1964.

Johnson, Lyndon B., *The Vantage Point: Perspectives of the*

Presidency, 1963-1969, New York, 1971).

Lansdale, Edward Geary, *In the Midst of Wars*, New York, 1972.

Le May, Curtis E., *Mission with LeMay: My Story*, New York, 1965.

Lodge, Henry Cabot, *The Storm has Many Eyes: A Personal Narrative*, New York, 1973.

McNamara, Robert S., *The Essence of Security: Reflections in Office*, London, 1968.

Mecklin, John, *Mission in Torment: An Intimate Account of the U.S. Role in Vietnam*, New York, 1965.

Ridgway, Matthew B., *Soldier: The Memoirs of Matthew B. Ridgway*, New York, 1956.

Rostow, W.W., *The Diffusion of Power, 1957-1972*, New York, 1972.

Schlesinger, Arthur M., Jr., *A Thousand Days: John F. Kennedy in the White House*, Boston, 1965.

Sheehan, Neil, ed., *The Pentagon Papers*, published by the *New York Times*, 1971.

Sorensen, Theodore C., *Kennedy*, New York, 1965.

Taylor, Maxwell D., *The Uncertain Trumpet*, New York, 1959.

———, *Swords and Plowshares*, New York, 1972.

Articles

Ball, George W., "Top Secret: The Prophecy the President Rejected," *The Atlantic* (Boston) pp. 36-49.

Bundy, McGeorge, "The Presidency and the Peace," *Foreign Affairs* (New York), April 1964, pp. 353-65.

Carver, George A., "The Real Revolution in South Vietnam," *Foreign Affairs*, April 1965, pp. 387-408.

Hoopes, Townsend, "The Fight for the President's Mind," *The Atlantic*, October 1969, pp. 97-114.

———, "Legacy of the Cold War in Indochina," *Foreign Affairs*, July 1970, pp. 601-16.

Javits, Jacob K., "The Congressional Presence in Foreign Relations," *Foreign Affairs*, January 1970, pp. 221-34.

McNamara, Robert S., "McNamara Defines His Job," *The New York Times Magazine*, 26 April 1964, pp. 13 and 108-13.

Moyers, Bill, "Bill Moyers Talks about LBJ, Poverty, War, and the Youth," *The Atlantic*, July 1968, pp. 29-37.

Rusk, Dean, "Mr. Secretary on the Eve of Emeritus," *Life* (Chicago), 17 January 1969, pp. 56-62B.

————, "The US Commitment in Vietnam: Fundamental Issues," *Department of State Bulletin* (Washington, D.C.), 7 March 1966, pp. 346-56.

Thomson, James C., "How Could Vietnam Happen? An Autopsy," *The Atlantic*, April 1968, pp. 47-52.

Secondary Sources

Books

Allison, Graham T., *Essence of Decision*: *Explaining the Cuban Missile Crisis*, Boston, Mass., 1971.

Almond, Gabriel, *The American People and Foreign Policy*, New York, 1950.

Alperovitz, Gar, *Atomic Diplomacy*, London, 1966.

Alsop, Stewart, *The Centre*: *The Anatomy of Power in Washington*, London, 1968.

Ambrose, Stephen E., and James Alden Barber, Jr., eds., *The Military and American Society*, New York, 1972.

Armacost, Michael H., *The Politics of Weapons Innovation*: *The Thor-Jupiter Controversy*, New York, 1969.

Art, Robert J., *The TFX Decision*: *McNamara and the Military*, Boston, 1968.

Bletz, Donald F., *The Role of the Military Professional in U.S. Foreign Policy*, New York, 1972.

Branden, Henry, *Anatomy of Error*, Boston, 1969.

Caraley, Demetrios, *The Politics of Military Unification*: *A Study of Conflict and the Policy Process*, New York, 1966.

Carrol, Helbert N., *The House of Representatives and Foreign Affairs*, Boston, Mass., 1966.

Charlesworth, James C., ed., *Contemporary Political Analysis*, New York, 1967.

Clark, Keith C., and Laurence J. Legere, eds., *The President and the Management of National Security: A Report by the Institute for Defence Analyses*, New York, 1969.

Cohen, Bernard, *The Influence of Non-Governmental Groups in Foreign Policy-Making*, Boston, 1959.

———, *The Press and Foreign Policy*, Princeton, N.J., 1963.

Cook, Fred J., *The Warfare State*, London, 1963.

Cooper, Chester L., *The Lost Crusade: The Full Story of US Involvement in Vietnam from Roosevelt to Nixon*, London, 1970.

de Rivera, Joseph, *The Psychological Dimension of Foreign Policy*, Colombus, Ohio, 1968.

Destler, I.M., *Presidents, Bureaucrats, and Foreign Policy: The Politics of Organization Reform*, Princeton, N.J., 1972.

Deutsch, Karl W., *The Nerves of Government: Models of Political Communication and Control*, New York, 1963.

———, *The Analysis of International Relations*, New Jersey, 1968.

Donovan, James A., *Militarism, USA*, New York, 1970.

Dulles, John Foster, *War or Peace?* New York, 1950.

Duscha, Julius, *Arms, Money and Politics*, New York, 1965.

Eden, Anthony, *Toward Peace in Indochina*, Boston, 1966.

Ellsberg, Daniel, *Papers on the War*, New York, 1972.

Evans, Rowland and Robert Novak, *Lyndon B. Johnson: The Exercise of Power*, New York, 1966.

Fall, Bernard B., *Last Reflections on a War*, Garden City, N.Y., 1967.

Fitzgerald, Frances, *Fire in the Lake: The Vietnamese and the Americans in Vietnam*, Boston, 1972.

Frye, Alton, *A Responsible Congress: The Politics of National Security*, New York, 1975

Fulbright, J.W., *The Pentagon Propaganda Machine*, New York, 1970.

———, *The Arrogance of Power*, London, 1970.

Galbraith, John K., *How to Control the Military*, Signet, 1969.

Geyelin, Philip L., *Lyndon B. Johnson and the World*, New York, 1966.

Graff, Henry F., *The Tuesday Cabinet*, Englewood Cliffs, N.J., 1970.

Gurtov, Melvin, *The First Vietnam Crisis*, New York, 1967.

Halberstam, David, *The Making of a Quagmire*, New York 1965.

————, *The Best and the Brightest*, New York, 1972.

Halperin, Morton H., and Arnold Kanter, eds., *Readings in Foreign Policy: A Bureaucratic Perspective*, Boston, 1973.

Halperin, Morton H.. *Bureaucratic Politics and Foreign Policy*, Washington, D.C., 1974.

Hammond, Paul Y., *Organizing for Defence: The American Military Establishment in the Twentieth Century*, Princeton, N.J., 1961.

Huntington, Samuel P., *The Soldier and the State: The Theory and Politics of Civil-Military Relations*, Cambridge, Mass., 1957.

————, *The Common Defence*, New York, 1961.

Janowitz, Morris, *The Professional Soldier: A Social and Political Portrait*, Glencoe, Ill., 1960.

Kahin, George M., and John W. Lewis, *The United States in Vietnam*, New York, 1967.

Kahn, Herman, *On Escalation*, New York, 1965.

Kalb, Marvin, and Elie Abel, *Roots of Involvement: The U.S. in Asia, 1784-1971*, New York, 1971.

Kaufman, William W., *The McNamara Strategy*, New York, 1964.

Kissinger, Henry, *Nuclear Weapons and Foreign Policy*, New York, 1957.

————, *American Foreign Policy: Three Essays*, New York, 1969.

Kolko, Gabriel, *The Roots of American Foreign Policy: An Analysis of Power and Purposes*, Boston, Mass., 1970.

Kolko, Joyce and Gabriel, *The Limits of Power: The World and United States Foreign Policy 1945-1954*, New York, 1972.

Kolodziej, Edward A., *The Uncommon Defence and Congress, 1945-1963*, Colombus, Ohio, 1966.

Kraft, Joseph, *Profiles in Power: A Washington Insight*, New York, 1966.

Lifton, Robert J., ed., *America and the Asian Revolutions*, US, the place of publication not mentioned, 1970.

LeMay, Curtis E., *America in Danger*, New York, 1968.

Manning, Robert and Michael Janeway, eds., *Who We Are: Chronicle of the United States and Vietnam*, Boston, 1965.

Moe, Ronald C., ed., *Congress and the President: Allies and Adversaries*, Berkeley, Calif., 1971.

Morgenthau, Hans J., *Vietnam and the United States*, Washington, D.C., 1965.

———, *Politics Among Nations*, New York, 1970.

Neustadt, Richard, *Presidential Power*, New York, 1960.

Paige, Glen D., *The Korean Decision*, New York, 1968.

Plischke, Elmer, *Conduct of American Diplomacy*, Princeton, N.J., 1968.

Posvar, Wesley W., *et al*, *American Defence Policy*, Baltimore, Md., 1965.

Randle, Robert F., *Geneva 1954: The Setttement of the Indochina War*, Princeton, N.J., 1969.

Ransom, Harry H., *The Intelligence Establishment*, Cambridge, Mass., 1970.

Rapoport, Anatol, *Fights, Games and Debates*, Ann Arbor, Michigan, 1960.

Raymond, Jack, *Power at the Pentagon*, New York, 1964.

Reedy, George E., *The Twilight of the Presidency*, New York, 1970.

Reston, James, *The Artillery of the Press: Its Influence on American Foreign Policy*, New York, 1967.

Ries, John C., *The Management of Defence: Organization and Control of the U.S. Armed Services*, Baltimore, Md., 1964.

Roberts, Charles, *LBJ's Inner Circle*, New York, 1965.

Robinson, James A., *Congress and Foreign Policy-Making*, Homewood, Ill., 1962.

Rodberg, Leonard S., and Derek Shearer, eds., *The Pentagon Watchers: Student Report on the National Security State*, New York, 1970.

Roherty, James M., *Decisions of R.S. McNamara*, Coral Cables, Florida, 1970.

Rose, Arnold M., *The Power Structure: Political Process in American Society*, New York, 1967.

Rosenau, James, ed., *International Politics and Foreign Policy*, Glencoe, Ill., 1961.

———, *Domestic Sources of Foreign Policy*, New York, 1967.

Rosenau, James N., *The Scientific Study of Foreign Relations*, New York, 1971.

Rostow, W.W., *View from Seventh Floor*, New York, 1964.

Rourke, Francis E., *Bureacrancy and Foreign Policy*, Baltimore, 1972.

Russett, Bruce M., *What Price Vigilance ?* New Haven, Conn., 1970.

Sapin, Burton M., *The Making of United States Foreign Policy*, Washington, D.C., 1966.

Schelling, Thomas, *The Strategy of Conflict*, New York, 1960.

Schilling, Warner, *et al*, *Strategy, Politics, and Defence Budgets*, New York, 1962.

Shaplen, Robert, *The Lost Revolution*, New York, 1966.

Sidey, Hugh, *John F. Kennedy: Portrait of a President*, London, 1964.

Simon, Herbert, *Models of Man: Social and Rational*, New York, 1967.

Smith, R. Harris, *OSS: The Secret History of America's First Central Intelligence Agency*, London, 1972.

Snyder, Richard, *et al*, *Foreign Policy Decision-Making*, Glencoe, Ill., 1962.

Spanier, John W., *The Truman-MacArthur Controversy and the Korean War*, Cambridge, Mass., 1959.

Stein, H., ed., *American Civil-Military Decisions*, Birmingham, Alabama, 1963.

Taylor, Maxwell D., *Responsibility and Response*, New York, 1967.

Tucker, Robert W., *The Radical Left and American Foreign Policy*, Baltimore, 1971.

Waltz, Kenneth, *Foreign Policy and Democratic Politics*, Boston, 1967.

Whiting, Allen S., *China Crosses the Yalu*, New York, 1960.

Wicker, Tom, *JFK and LBJ: The Influence of Personality upon Politics*, New York, 1968.

Williams, William A., *The Tragedy of American Diplomacy*, New York, 1959.

Windchy, Eugene G., *Tonkin Gulf*, Garden City, N.Y., 1971.

Wise, David and Thomas B. Ross, *The Invisible Government*, New York, 1964.

Wohlstettar, Roberta, *Pearl Harbor: Warning and Decision*, Stanford, Calif., 1962.

Yarmolinsky, Adam, *The Military Establishment: Its Impacts on American Society*, New York, 1971.

Newspapers and Periodicals

Congressional Digest (Washington, D.C.).
Congressional Quarterly (Washington. D.C.).
Facts on File (New York).
New Republic (Washington, D.C.).
Newsweek (New York).
New York Herald Tribune.
New York Post.
New York Times.
The Nation (New York).
Time (Chicago).
Washington Post.

Articles

Ambrose, S.E., "The Military Impact on Foreign Policy," in S.E. Ambrose and J.A. Barber, Jr., eds., *The Military and American Society*, New York, 1972, pp. 121-36.

Baldwin, Hanson, "The McNamara Monarchy," *Saturday Evening Post* (New York) 9 March 1963, pp. 8-11.

Bingham, Jonathan B., "Can Military Spending be Controlled?" *Foreign Affairs*, October 1969, pp. 51-66.

Clark, Blair, "Westmoreland Appraised: Question and Answers," *Harper's* (New York) November 1970, pp. 96-103.

Cooper, Chester L., "The CIA and Decision-Making," *Foreign Affairs*, January 1972, pp. 223-36.

Dahl, Robert A., "A Critique of the Ruling Elite Model," *American Political Science Review* (Washington, D.C.) June 1958, pp. 463-9.

Davis, Vincent, "The Development of a Capability to Deliver Nuclear Weapons by Carrier-Based Aircraft," in Morton H. Halperin and Arnold Kanter, eds., *Readings in American Foreign Policy: A Breaucratic Perspective*, Boston, 1973, pp. 262-75.

———, "The Politics of Innovation: Patterns in Navy Cases,"

in Richard G. Head and Ervin J. Rokke, eds., *American Defence Policy*, Baltimore, Maryland, 1973, pp. 391-406.

Edinger, Lewis J., "Millitary Leaders and Foreign Policy-Making," *American Political Science Review*, June 1963, pp. 392-405.

Elowitz, Larry and John W. Spanier, "Korea and Vietnam: Limited War and the American Political System," *Orbis* (Philadelphia) Summer 1974, pp. 510-34.

Fleischman, Gordon K., "The Myth of the Military Mind," *Military Review* (Ft. Leavenworth, Ks.) November 1964.

Galbraith, John Kenneth, "Characteristics of Military-Industrial Complex," in Ambrose and Barber, eds., *The Military and American Society*, New York, 1972, pp. 64-71

Gelb, Leslie H., "The Essential Domino: American Politics and Vietnam," *Foreign Affairs*, April 1972, pp. 459-75.

———, "The Pentagon Papers and the Vantage Points," *Foreign Policy* (New York) Spring 1972, pp. 25-41.

George, Alexander L., "The Case for Multiple Advocacy in Making Foreign Policy," *American Political Science Review*, September 1972, pp. 751-85.

Gibson, George C., "Congressional Attitudes toward Defense," in Richard G. Head and E.J. Rokke, eds., *American Defence Policy*, Baltimore, Md., 1973, pp. 358-69.

Ginsburgh, Colonel Robert N., "The Challenge to Military Professionalism," *Foreign Affairs*, January 1964, pp. 255-68.

Graff, H.F., "Decision on Vietnam: How Johnson Makes Foreign Policy," *New York Times Magazine*, 4 July 1965, pp. 4-7.

Halberstam, David, "Return to Vietnam," *Harper's*, December 1967, pp. 47-58.

———, "The Very Expensive Education of McGeorge Bundy," *Harper's*, July 1969, pp. 21-41.

Halperin, Morton H., "The President and the Military," *Foreign Affairs*, January 1972, pp. 310-24.

Heurlin, Bertel, "Notes on Bureaucratic Politics in National Security Policy," *Cooperation and Conflict* (Oslo), No. 4, 1975, pp. 237-59.

Hilsman, Roger, "Congressional-Executive Relations and the Foreign Policy Consensus," *American Political Science*

Review, September 1958, pp. 725-44.

————, "The Foreign Policy Consensus : An Interim Research Report," *Journal of Conflict Resolution* (Ann Arbor, Michigan) December 1959, pp. 361-82.

Hitch, Charles J., "Evolution of Department of Defense," in Richard G. Head and Ervin J Rooke, eds., *American Defense Policy*, Baltimore, Md., 1973.

Kanter, Arnold, "Congress and the Defense Budget: 1960-1970," *American Political Science Review*, March 1972, pp. 129-43.

Kissinger, Henry, "Domestic Structure and Foreign Policy," *Daedalus* (Cambridge, Mass.) Spring 1966, pp. 503-29.

————, "The Viet Nam Negotiations," *Foreign Affairs*, January 1969, pp. 211-34.

Knoll, Erwin, "The Military Establishment Rides High," *The Progressive* (Madison, Wis.) February 1969, pp. 14-7.

Kolodziej, Edward A., "Rational Consent and Defense Budgets: The Role of Congress, 1945-1962," *Orbis*, Winter 1964, pp. 748-77.

Kraft, Joseph, "Washington Insight: The Enigma of Dean Rusk," *Harper's*, July 1965, pp. 100-3.

Krasner, Stephen Q., "Are Bureaucracies Important? (Or Allison's Wonderland)," in Richard G. Head and Ervin J. Rokke, eds., *American Defence Policy*, Baltimore, Md., 1973, pp. 311-20.

Lansdale, Edward, G., "Viet Nam: Do We Understand Revolution?", *Foreign Affairs*, October 1964, pp. 75-86.

————, "Vietnam: Still the Search for Goals," *Foreign Affairs*, October 1968, pp. 92-8.

Lasswell, Harold, "The Garrison State," *The American Journal of Sociology* (Chicago) 1971, pp. 455-68.

Legere, Laurence J., "A Presidential Perspective," *Foreign Policy*, Spring 1972, pp. 84-94.

Lyons, Gene M., "The New Civil-Military Relations," *American Political Science Review*, March 1961, pp. 53-63.

McCarthy, E.J., "Pentagon Papers : Games Presidents and Other People Play," *The New Republic*, 10 July 1971, pp. 14-7.

Modelski, George, "Comparative International System," *World*

Politics, July 1962, pp. 662-74.

Modelski, Herbert, "Perspectives on Personality and Foreign Policy," *World Politics*, October 1960, pp. 129-39.

Morgenthau, H. J., "We Are Deluding Ourselves in Vietnam," *New York Times Magazine*, 18 April 1965, pp. 24-5.

Olson, William C., "The Role of Congress in Making the Foreign Policy of the United States," *The Parliamentarian* (London) July 1975, pp. 151-8.

Paone, Rocco M., "Foreign Policy and the Military Power," *Military Review*, November 1964, pp. 9-13.

Powell, Craig, "Civilian/Military Rapport Reaches a New Maturity in the Defense Arena," *Armed Forces Management* (Washington, D.C.) December 1967, pp. 44-50.

Reston, James B., "The Press, the President and Foreign Policy," *Foreign Affairs*, July 1966, pp. 553-73.

Roberts, Chalmers M., "The Day We Didn't Go to War," *Reporter* (Madison) 14 September 1954, pp. 31-5.

Russett, Bruce M., "Testing Some Theories about American Foreign Policy," *Bulletin of Peace Proposals* (Oslo) 1975, pp. 85-93.

Salisbury, Harrison E., "Image and Reality in Indochina," *Foreign Affairs*, April 1971, pp. 381-94.

Schelling, Thomas, "The Strategy of Conflict: Prospects for a Reorientation of the Game Theory," *The Journal of Conflict Resolution*, September 1958, pp. 203-64.

———, "Experimental Games and Bargaining Theory," *World Politics*, October 1961, pp. 47-68.

Schlesinger, Jr., Arthur, "Congress and the Making of American Foreign Policy," *Foreign Affairs*, October 1972, pp. 78-113.

Severeid, Eric, "The Final Troubled Hours of Adlai Stevenson," *Look* (Des Moines, Iowa) 30 November 1965.

Shepley, James, "How Dulles Averted War," *Life* (Chicago) 16 January 1956, pp. 70-80.

Shoup, David M., and James A. Donovan, "The New American Militarism," *The Atlantic*, April 1969, pp. 51-6.

Singer, J. David, "The Level of Analysis Problem in International Relations," *World Politics*, October 1961, pp. 77-92.

Snyder, Richard C., "International Relations Theory—Continued," *World Politics*, January 1961, pp. 300-12.

Sprout, Harold and Margaret, "Environmental Factors in the Study of International Politics," in James N. Rosenau, ed., *International Politics and Foreign Policy*, New York, 1969, pp. 41-56.

Stockstill, Louis, "The Big DoD Buildup—Part II," *The Journal of Armed Forces* (Washington, D.C.) 5 August 1967, pp. 1, 8-9.

————, "The Approved List," *The Journal of Armed Forces*, 2 September 1967, p. 13.

Tatum, Lawrence B., "The Joint Chiefs of Staff and the Defense Policy Formulation: Part I", *Air University Review* (Washington, D.C.) May-June 1966, pp. 40-5.

Venkataramani, M.S., "The United States and Thailand: The Anatomy of Super Power Policy-Making, 1948-1963," *International Studies* (New Delhi) January-March 1973, pp. 57-110.

Verba, Sidney, "Assumptions of Rationality and Non-rationality in Models of the International System," *World Politics*, October 1961, pp. 93-117.

Warner, Geoffrey, "The United States and the Fall of Diem, Part II: The Death of Diem," *Australian Outlook* (Hobart, Tasmania) April 1975, pp. 3-17.

White, T.H., "What's Wrong with Civil-Military Relations," *Newsweek*, 7 October 1963, p. 28.

Wolf Jr., Charles, "Is United States Foreign Policy Militarized?", *Orbis*, Winter 1971, pp. 819-28.

INDEX